REVISED EDITION

HELPING CHILDREN LEARN TO READ

Patrick J. Finn

State University of New York at Buffalo

Longman

New York & London

**to Mary
I bless the day I found you.**

**Helping Children Learn to Read,
Revised Edition**

Copyright © 1990 by Longman.
All rights reserved.
No part of this publication may be reproduced,
stored in a retrieval system, or transmitted
in any form or by any means, electronic, mechanical,
photocopying, recording, or otherwise,
without the prior permission of the publisher.

Longman, 95 Church Street, White Plains, N.Y. 10601

Associated companies:
Longman Group Ltd., London
Longman Cheshire Pty., Melbourne
Longman Paul Pty., Auckland
Copp Clark Pitman, Toronto

Executive editor: Raymond T. O'Connell
Text design adaptation: Thomas W. Slomka
Cover design: Joseph Gillians
Text art: Vantage Art, Inc.

Library of Congress Cataloging-in-Publication Data
Finn, Patrick J.
    Helping children learn to read / Patrick J. Finn.—Rev. ed.
        p.   cm.
    Bibliography: p.
    Includes index.
    ISBN 0-8013-0321-4
    1. Reading (Elementary)   I. Title.
LB1573.F52   1990
372.4′1—dc20   89–34264
                                               CIP

ABCDEFGHIJ-AL-99 98 97 96 95 94 93 92 91 90

Contents

PART TWO: TEACHING WORD RECOGNITION

PART THREE: READING COMPREHENSION

PART FOUR: ASSESSMENT, DECISION MAKING,
AND TEACHING

Preface

In the 1985 edition of *Helping Children Learn to Read*, I set out to show that methods of teaching reading can be categorized on two dimensions. On one dimension teaching methods can be categorized in terms of two traditions or schools of thought that have a long history in the study of psychology. One school of thought concentrates on dividing learning into small steps to be presented to the learner one bit at a time, in a particular order. This school of thought has been characterized as "bottom-up" and atomistic. It concentrates on the "outer" aspects of reading (letter-sound correspondences and so on). Its adherents have a particular fascination with the relation between ease of learning and frequency. This is the time-honored empirical tradition.

The second tradition concentrates on whole tasks and large concepts that learners are expected to engage and apprehend, such as the idea that print represents meaning expressed in language or that words in print are related to words in speech. To move from such concepts to actual reading, the learner must take notice of details such as the sound usually associated with the letter *b* or the function of punctuation marks such as periods. But according to this school of thought, each learner will find different parts and details troublesome, so a teacher cannot predict which bits will need to be taught to individuals. This school of thought has been characterized as "top-down" and holistic. It concentrates on the "inner" aspects of reading (the reader's insights into whole tasks and concepts). Its adherents have a particular fascination with the relationship between the ease of learning and the individual learner's internal condition—his or her level of cognitive development, motivation, and so on. This is the time-honored rationalist tradition.

On the second dimension, teaching methods can be characterized in terms of the contrast between viewing learning as an individual process or as a social (group) process.

The first view is that learning can be conceptualized as a thing that takes place inside a learner's head—an individual thing. The implication of this point of view is that it is the teacher's job to structure each student's environment so as to maximize each individual's potential to learn.

A contrasting view is that learning can be conceptualized as a thing that takes place in society. This view concentrates on the social aspects of learning. The implication is that it is the teacher's job to create a community in the classroom where the thing to be learned is valued by the community and where members of the community who are lacking knowledge and skills have access to members of the community who possess knowledge and skills.

Viewing learning on these two dimensions leads to four possible combinations of perspectives:

Learning to read is a bottom-up, atomistic, individual process.	Learning to read is a bottom-up, atomistic, social process.
Learning to read is a top-down, holistic, individual process.	Learning to read is a top-down, holistic, social process.

In the 1985 edition I introduced topics related to teaching reading and attempted to analyze the teaching practices related to them in terms of assumptions that underlie them. I encouraged readers to examine their assumptions, to decide where their assumptions fit into this scheme of things, and to pursue teaching practices that were consistent with their beliefs. Although I have favored top-down, holistic assumptions for most of my professional career, I did not take a position on which assumptions were more valid.

When I was presented with the prospect of revising the book, I decided to follow the same general format, with one major change. I decided to express my point of view. I did this for two reasons: (1) Some readers of the 1985 edition who understood clearly what I had done and who appreciated the approach commented that it would have been helpful to have known what the author's position was. (2) Developments in the past several years have greatly influenced my commitment to the top-down, holistic, social point of view.

Research findings in three areas—early childhood language acquisition, emergent literacy, and the function of community in language and literacy learning—are confirming the assumption that language and literacy learning are holistic, top-down, social processes. At the same time, teaching practices that are consistent with these assumptions—literature-based reading programs, the language experience approach to beginning reading, and the process approach to teaching writing—are becoming more and more recognized as effective practices. Commitment to these assumptions and teaching practices that are consistent with them has developed into what is variously described as a movement, a method, or a philosophy. Of course, it is all three, and it is sometimes referred to as "whole language."

In this revised edition, I continue to urge readers to clarify their assumptions and to pursue practices that are consistent with their assumptions. Therefore, I have presented top-down, holistic, social assumptions and practices that arise from them and bottom-up, atomistic, individual assumptions and practices that are consistent with them. I do, however, present evidence and describe trends to show that the former assumptions are more valid, and I recommend teaching practices that are consistent with them.

However, there are certain problems inherent in a top-down, holistic, social approach to teaching reading. Teachers must command a thorough knowledge of the reading process; they must possess a high order of diagnostic skill—the ability to determine the sources of students' reading problems from observations; they must command a wide repertoire of methods and lessons to employ when they are needed; and, finally, they must have well-developed organizational and management skills.

My enthusiasm for this approach is somewhat tempered by my understanding of the demands it makes on teachers. Therefore, this book introduces teachers to a spectrum of methods that rest on the asumption that language and literacy learning are top-down, holistic, social processes. These methods include the judicious use of eclectic (as opposed to phonics- or skills-emphasis) basal reading programs.

There are those who will object that basal reading programs compromise certain ideals of the whole language approach, and I understand these objections. However, I am so committed to these ideals that I am determined to see the whole language approach prosper. I believe it will prosper if teachers

Understand the ideals of the whole language classroom.
Understand the assumptions about language and literacy learning upon which these ideals rest.
Work toward these ideals as they learn to teach reading and the language arts using familiar materials and methods, including eclectic basal reading programs.

As they become familiar with the curriculum, methods, and materials and as they develop leadership, organizational, and diagnostic skills, such teachers will move toward practices that are more and more consistent with these ideals and assumptions.

Acknowledgments

My thanks to the following people who helped get this revision completed. Amy Finn did all the original line drawings and lettering. I think they are perfect.

All the original photographs of classroom settings were done by Carolyn King. Rosemary Murray and other teachers and students at the College Learning Laboratory of the State University of New York College at Buffalo were most cooperative. The artwork portrayed in these photographs was done by Jeannie Martino.

Patti Milligan helped to assemble the bibliography. Suzanne D'Amato, Kristine Scrimshaw, and Anita Bollier helped to track down illustrations of children's work. Anita Bollier helped with obtaining permissions and getting figures in order.

Nancy Myers, Eileen McNamara, and Pat Glinski typed and retyped and retyped. I thank them for their good work and their goodwill—especially Nancy Myers who had the major responsibility for typing the manuscript.

The editors at Longman—Ray O'Connell, Naomi Silverman, Virginia Blanford, Richard Bretan, Linda Carbone, and Helen Ambrosio—have been very helpful and supportive.

My wife, Mary, and I have different interests, different fields of study, and different ways of thinking. We have talked a lot over a lot of years, and I don't know any longer which of my ideas were originally her ideas. I couldn't have written this book without her, and she was a great help in revising it. These are, however, among the less important reasons that I bless the day I found her.

Thanks also to my children, Amy and Molly, for their support.

PART ONE

Looking at Approaches to Reading Instruction

CHAPTER 1

Psychological Foundations
of Reading

For the past several decades teaching reading in the overwhelming majority of American schools has been based largely on basal reading programs. Basal readers can be classified in terms of two approaches, the *phonics- or skills-emphasis approach* and the *eclectic approach*. In recent years *the whole language approach* has appeared in relation to teaching reading in combination with the other "language arts"—writing, speaking, and listening.

As author of this book, I have attempted objectively to describe and discuss

The content, materials, and methods that are typical of the basal reader (both phonics emphasis and eclectic) and the whole language approaches,

The assumptions that underlie them.

The differences between them.

But I also play the role of advocate. Based on what is known about the nature of language and learning, what it means to acquire literacy (the ability to read and write), and the role of the teacher and learner in this process, I wish to present reasoned and convincing arguments to support the following position:

I least favor the phonics-, or skills-, emphasis approach.

I most favor the whole language approach, but I do *not* suggest that this be the sole approach, especially among inexperienced teachers.

I suggest starting with an eclectic approach basal reading program and working toward a whole language approach—perhaps never as a sole approach, but keeping it as an ideal toward which teachers should strive.

I will begin by describing lessons taught by two teachers whom I have created to introduce you to some of the practices that are typical of teachers who adopt the phonics or skills emphasis approach on the one hand, and those who adopt an eclectic approach while working toward a whole language approach on the other.

ASSUMPTIONS THAT UNDERLIE TEACHING PRACTICES

Observing Teachers Teaching: Charlotte's Beliefs

Reading Is Essentially Decoding Print into Language.   Charlotte Britain is an experienced second grade teacher. In teaching reading, she relies almost entirely on a phonics-emphasis basal reading series.* Her reading lessons typically begin with a review of letter-sound generalizations that she has taught recently—for instance, that the letters *ch* at the beginning of a word probably represent the first sound in the word *chip.* Then she frequently introduces a new generalization—for instance, that the letters *ou* may represent the vowel sound in *mouth,* but they may also represent the vowel sound in *pour.* Children then pronounce lists of words that represent these generalizations, and finally a story is presented in which these words appear. (A detailed description of such lessons appears in Figure 8.3, on page 167.)

During the remainder of the lesson the children might be asked to read portions of the story orally, to find answers to the teacher's questions in the story, to tell how they feel about the story, or to tell how people in the story might feel.

Charlotte is attentive to the students' performance at every stage, and she is alert to students who falter, particularly at the word recognition and comprehension stages of the lesson. When Charlotte observes a pattern of poor performance, she begins to look for the root of the problem. Newton, a serious red-headed boy, is a case in point. Through informal observations and some formal testing, Charlotte determines whether the child recognizes frequently appearing words such as *boy, red,* and *run.* She determines whether he recognizes the words *hat* and *hate* and what the letter *e* in *hate* tells

---

*Since basals are widely used in American schools, it is quite likely that you used them in elementary school. They are described in Chapter 15.

about the way the *a* is pronounced. She finds out whether Newton hears the same sound at the beginning of *nail* and *nap* but different sounds at the beginning of *dot* and *top*. If she is not satisfied with Newton's performance on these tasks, she may check to see whether he can name all the letters in the alphabet and whether he knows what sounds some letters like *b, d, f,* and *m* usually represent at the beginning of words.

Charlotte is acting out of certain assumptions she makes about reading—about what people do when they read and about how to teach people to read. She believes that language is encoded in print and that learning to read is learning to break the code. Once students break the code, they can turn print into language, and since they are language users, the meaning is revealed automatically. She believes that this process always proceeds from decoding print to language and from language to meaning or comprehension. She believes the difficult part is getting from print to language. That's what students have to learn.

Writing Is Essentially Encoding Language into Print.   Charlotte also teaches language arts, and her assumptions about language and learning have implications here too that are related to "whole language." Charlotte tries to have her students write two or three times a week. She works hard to find interesting and exciting writing assignments because she knows that students write better papers when they are interested in the assignment.

One technique her class seems to love is called "popcorn." The week before Mother's Day, for example, she gathers her class around the chalk board, and writes the word *Mother* in a circle on the board, and asks "What word does the word *Mother* make you think of?" The students, familiar with this activity, begin to volunteer words like *happy, nice, perfume,* and *love.* (See Figure 1.1.) Soon each student is drawing a picture and is

Figure 1.1. The "popcorn" technique.

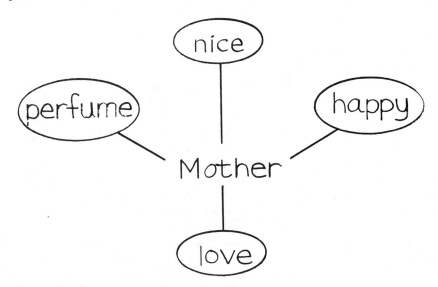

writing a Mother's Day message using the words that appear on the board. Charlotte reminds them to print neatly, to copy the correct spelling if they are using words from the board, to begin each sentence with a capital letter, and to end each sentence with a period.

Charlotte is acting out of certain assumptions about writing—what people do when they write and how to teach writing. She believes that writing is encoding spoken language into print. Learning to write is learning to form letters and words conventionally, neatly, and legibly; learning to spell correctly; and learning punctuation conventions. Charlotte would say the process always goes from ideas to language to encoding the language into print. She believes that the difficult part is getting the language encoded into print. That's what students have to learn.

Spelling and Handwriting: Separate Subjects.   Charlotte teaches spelling every day for 15 minutes following the lesson plans in the Teacher's Guide of the spelling series she uses. She teaches handwriting for 15 minutes each morning. She is concerned that students form their letters to look like the model she uses, that they stay on the line, and within the lines.

Observing Teachers Teaching: Matthew's Beliefs

Reading Is Essentially a Quest for Meaning.   Across the hall Matthew Nickelson teaches second grade. In contrast to Charlotte's phonics-emphasis basal readers, Matthew uses "eclectic" basal readers, ones that do not place as great an emphasis on phonics rules. He sometimes skips lessons on letter-sound correspondences, believing that if students can read the stories, they must be able to use these "rules" even if they may not be able to state them explicitly.

When a student seems not to recognize words while reading aloud or when a student's comprehension seems to suffer because of word recognition, Matthew includes them in a reading group where he is more scrupulous about covering phonics lessons as they appear in the basal reading series.

Matthew's reading lessons based on the basal readers nearly always start with a discussion of ideas and information related to the day's reading selection. For example, when the story is about a lonely fir tree that is chosen by a family to be their Christmas tree, he may start by asking which of the trees on the school lawn are fir trees, what is unusual about fir trees (needles instead of leaves, evergreen), and how they are used at Christmas time; finally, he might encourage children to share stories about decorating Christmas trees or about Christmas trees they have seen at shopping malls, on television, and so on.

The purpose of these discussions is to give the readers new knowledge or help them recall previous knowledge so that they approach the text with relevant prior knowledge and some expectations about the meaning of the story. This prepares the students to comprehend the story. In fact, Matthew believes, it aids in their word recognition.

Two days a week Matthew does not use the basal series at all. Instead, students read from books they choose from the classroom library or read "books" that classmates have written—four- to six-page stories, each page consisting of a picture and three or four lines of text that are printed by the teacher using conventional spelling, capitalization, and punctuation. (See Figure 1.2.)

Charlotte likes Wilbur very much because he is her friend.

I went to Como Park to go sledding with my brother, my sister and my dad.

Figure 1.2. Typical "published" books in a second grade writing process classroom. (*Source: We Went to Como Park,* by Kevin McMullen. Reproduced by permission of Patricia McMullen; *Me and Bonnie,* by Rebecca Onello. Reproduced by permission of Cynthia Onello; and *Our Charlotte's Web Book,* by Alyssa Hulse and Nichol Mroz. Reproduced by permission from Irene Hulse and Bernard Mroz.)

Matthew checks on students' progress in this reading by conducting brief conferences, where students talk about what they are reading, read short passages they have prepared to read orally, and plan ways to share their reading with the class. Matthew is alert to word recognition problems during these sessions, and at times he pursues the same diagnostic trail as Charlotte, checking out recognition of very common words, knowledge of spelling-sound correspondences, understanding of such concepts as "words that begin with the same sound," and letter recognition.

Matthew is always alert to opportunities to have students work together and learn from one another. Students take student-written "books" to their authors to ask help in recognizing words. Students read storybooks from the regular classroom library to each other, or they read them together. Students from upper grades come in and read their "books" to Matthew's class.

Writing Is Essentially Formulating Ideas and Expressing Them in Clear, Explicit Language. Matthew has writing class three afternoons a week for 25 minutes (at the beginning of the year) to 45 minutes (at the end of the year). In a somewhat untypical class the Monday after Thanksgiving vacation, Matthew asks students to tell what they

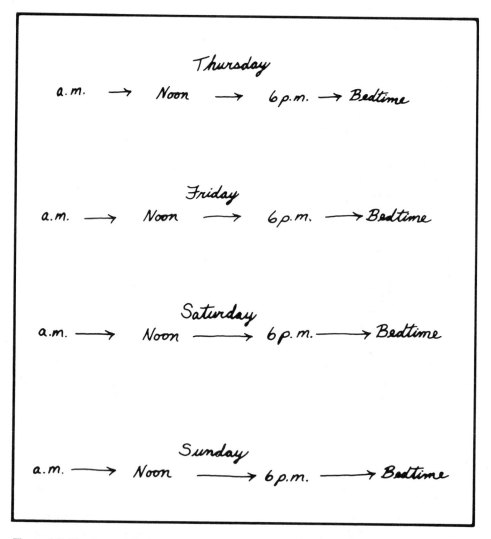

Figure 1.3. Teacher-supplied time line skeleton.

did on Thanksgiving Day, the preparations that led up to it, and their activities for the remaining three days of the weekend. He introduces the idea of a time line, hands out copies of the time line in Figure 1.3, and encourages students to work alone or in small groups recording holiday incidents using phrases, titles of possible stories, and pictures. The next day "finished" time lines begin to be displayed around the room (as in Figure 1.4) that become the basis for speaking and listening activities involving somewhat formal presentations by individuals to groups, small group discussions, and conversations.

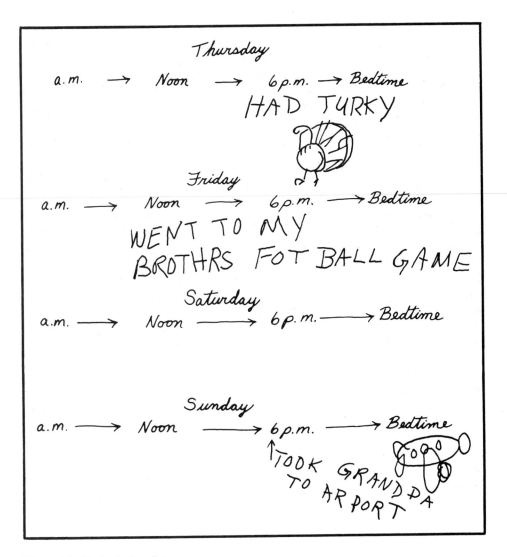

Figure 1.4. Student's time line.

In ensuing days topics developed in time lines become topics for writing for some students. Soon *publications* begin appearing in the classroom library, and students are reading each other's writing that developed out of the time line activity. Some students put their time lines into their writing folders and returned to them for topics later in the year. Some students such as Hannah, who was flower girl in her sister's wedding, created time lines around other events.

A few students did not pursue the time line idea beyond the original whole class activity. For example, the next day Jimmy returned to the story he had already begun about his brother who jumped off the top bunk bed and knocked down the plaster in the dining room ceiling below.

On a typical day Matthew announces that it is writing time, and a great variety of activities ensue. He keeps a sharp eye to see that everyone is working, but that might mean writing, drawing, talking to one another, or talking into a tape recorder. During each lesson, some students will be scheduled to talk briefly to Matthew on an individual basis. During these sessions Matthew looks at items in the student's writing folder, often items the student wants particular help with. There is a checklist stapled inside each folder so Matthew can record his observations about the quality of the student's writing and the writing skills he and the student have discussed and that the student has agreed to work on.

These skills might include spelling, punctuation, capitalization, and handwriting or such topics as "interesting opening sentences." But most of the time is spent talking about what the writer wants to say and how clearly and explicitly the ideas are stated.

Matthew also makes mental and sometimes oral and written observations during these sessions regarding evidence that the student has been working during writing class. He might have formed some opinion on this point from his day-to-day supervision of the class. When there are so many activities going on, students who are not "self-starters" can get lost in the shuffle if the teacher is not realistic about supervising the class and keeping everyone's nose to the grindstone—to use an old school marm's (master's) term!

Matthew's beliefs and procedures in teaching writing are modeled on the work of Donald Graves (1983). This is known as the *process approach to teaching writing.* It will be further described later in Chapter 11.

Handwriting and Spelling: Separate Subjects—but Only for Those Who Need Them. Matthew also has formal, nearly daily, handwriting lessons for students whose printing is unacceptable. These lessons are identical to Charlotte's, except they are not given to everyone in the class.

When Matthew teaches spelling, he uses the same books and about the same methods as Charlotte. He is inclined to think that students would learn most of the words taught in these lessons through massive experience with reading and writing, but he is not so sure this is true that he is willing to abandon his formal, textbook-based spelling program. He is aware that his principal and the pupil's parents expect a spelling program, and he is not ready to try to convince his principal and the pupils' parents that the formal spelling program is unnecessary.

Comparing Two Good Teachers

Charlotte focuses on word recognition in reading. She views meaning as something that happens automatically, once the reader breaks the code. When Charlotte teaches writing, she tries to motivate students and give them good ideas and concentrates her energy on matters of legible handwriting, spelling, sentence structure, and punctuation. She seems to believe that turning ideas into language or "inner speech" is automatic. The hard part is getting the language into conventional forms on the paper.

Matthew sees the reading process as one that begins with meaning and ends with meaning. He turns his attention to letter-sound relationships when students seem to be having trouble with them, but he presumes that students will discover ways to decode printed language through repeated experiences with reading and writing. Matthew believes that the teacher's job in teaching reading is to fuel the reader's aggressive search for meaning—if it needs fueling—and to help them work out the details—to discover the principles underlying the code that they do not discover for themselves.

In teaching writing Matthew also tries to motivate students and give them good ideas, but he practically never *tells* students what to write about. Matthew focuses his energy on helping students to turn *their* ideas to clear and explicit language. He attends to legibility of handwriting, spelling, sentence structure, and punctuation as well, but he presumes that students will discover many of the conventions governing these matters without his explicit instruction.

An important comparison between these two teachers is that Charlotte teaches the reading and writing skills that the curriculum (based on decades of carefully observing second graders learning to read and write) states are appropriate for second graders. Matthew teaches reading and writing skills when his individual students seem to need them to get the meaning (in reading) or express the meaning (in writing).

It is highly probable that Charlotte and Matthew will be teaching the same skills. We have every reason to believe that Matthew's second graders are reasonably like previous generations of second graders, so they will be using the same reading and writing skills as the curriculum guide recommends. The difference is that Charlotte teaches all these skills to every child in a fixed order. Matthew expects that some of his students will already know or will discover these skills without explicit instruction. He does not expect any child to acquire skills in a rigidly fixed order. So he doesn't teach all skills to every child, and he may teach skills in a different order to individual children.

Two Teaching Traditions

Charlotte's teaching methods reflect a psychological view of learning. Charlotte views herself as the source of her students' learning. She believes that knowledge, skills, and attitudes will develop in individual students, *if* she asks the right question, presents the right material, assigns the right task. Because she believes that the reading curriculum is learned in a fixed order and that each child needs to be taught each step, she would like to individualize instruction more so that she could present precisely the right question, material, or task to each child at precisely the right time.

Matthew's teaching methods reflect a sociological view of learning. Matthew views learning as something that happens in social interactions. Knowledge, skills, and attitudes that are important in a literate society (such as those involved in reading and writing) are sought by learners when, through social interaction, they become aware of them and of their usefulness. In this situation learners "try their hand" at what they see others doing around them. A teacher's job is to promote a classroom society where literacy skills will be valued and to recognize what the children are trying to do and collaborate with them in doing it.

Students are motivated by their peers as well as by the teacher to "try literacy" through reading each other's writing and sharing their reading. Accomplished students as well as teachers collaborate with learners in mastering tasks—recognizing words, writing a story, or fixing a J that is written backward. The accomplished student in one situation may be the learner in the next.

Charlotte and Matthew represent two traditions in teaching reading. Charlotte is comfortable calling herself a skills-emphasis, traditional teacher. Matthew is an eclectic, traditional teacher, but he is deliberately working to become a whole language teacher. Neither Matthew nor Charlotte represents an extreme or doctrinaire position, but they operate on clearly different sets of assumptions. These two traditions have a very long history in philosophy, linguistics, and psychology. Many controversies have developed as a result of the struggle between these two points of view. As a matter of fact, many of the controversies that arise in teaching reading originate in philosophy, linguistics and psychology. (See Activities 1.A and 1.B).

ACTIVITY 1.A DESCRIBING YOURSELF OR A TEACHER YOU KNOW

Write a one- or two-page description of yourself or a fellow teacher (if you are an in-service teacher) or of a teacher you have had in terms of the practices and beliefs ascribed to Charlotte and Matthew.

ACTIVITY 1.B DISCOVERING ASSUMPTIONS THAT UNDERLIE TEACHING PRACTICES

I. Many teaching strategies are described throughout this book. For example in Chapter 4, paired-associate learning (pages 92–93) and key vocabulary (pages 97–98) are described as methods of teaching word recognition.

Read about these two approaches/methods and decide

Would Charlotte or Matthew be more likely to employ this method?
What assumptions and beliefs of Charlotte or Matthew would make this approach/method a logical choice?

Divide the class into small groups. Have each group discuss one method or approach and report the results of their discussions to the class. Or have all the groups discuss both methods or approaches and compare the results of their discussion.

II. In Chapter 15, the individualized reading program (pages 332–335) and skills management systems (pages 341–346) are described as two extremely different approaches.

Read about these two approaches/methods and decide

Would Charlotte or Matthew be more likely to employ this method?
What assumptions and beliefs of Charlotte or Matthew would make this approach/method a logical choice?

Divide the class into four small groups. Have each group discuss one method or approach and report the results of their discussions to the class. Or have all the groups discuss both methods or approaches and compare the results of their discussion.

DIFFERENT PHILOSOPHIES OF LANGUAGE AND LEARNING

Reading programs that emphasize phonics and decoding—a bottom-up model by today's jargon—are descendents of a philosophical tradition, *empiricism*, that can be traced back to such worthies as John Locke (1632–1704) and David Hume (1711–1776). Reading programs that deemphasize phonics and decoding and emphasize "reading for meaning" are descendants of an equally respected tradition, *rationalism,* that can be traced back to such notables as Leibnitz (1646–1716) and Kant (1724–1804).

Of course, Locke, Hume, Leibnitz and Kant never addressed the question of how to teach reading, but the traditions they represent—empiricism and rationalism—have a direct bearing on what one thinks about the nature of the human mind, language, and learning. And these views, in turn, have a direct bearing on questions of how to teach reading.

The ideas associated with each of these traditions or schools of thought can be designated "spheres of influence." One of the major divisions between these spheres of influence rests on the question of whether or not it is profitable to study the human mind.

Counting, Measuring, Recording, Describing— the Empiricist Tradition

One group of social scientists believes it is not possible to study the human mind because the workings of the human mind are hidden from us. We can only know and study things we can perceive with our senses. For this group, explanations of human behavior do not refer to the mind. They rely on the relationship between observable behavior of humans and observable events in the environment.

This perspective leads to a particular kind of study, termed empiricism. Empiricists are preoccupied with describing the environment, with gathering data, with measurement. They are interested in measuring how often events occur (frequency), how perceptible they are (intensity), and what other events occur at the same—or nearly the same—time or place (contiguity).

In the last century, this kind of activity on the part of social scientists led them to become interested in and envious of the tremendous progress in the physical sciences. They believed that the social sciences were essentially the same as the physical sciences. The only difference was that the social sciences had not advanced their measurement devices to the point where they could describe their data in terms of mathematical formulas as the physical scientists had. This intensified their interest in measurement and also had an effect on the things they studied. For example, linguists of this school in the 19th century were preoccupied with the most physical, observable aspect of language—sound. The science of phonology is the study of language and sounds.

The Study of the Mind—the Rationalist Tradition

The other half of this division is represented by people who believe that the human mind can be studied and indeed must be studied if one is to make progress in the fields of psychology, language, and education. People in this camp do not believe that the human organism is simply assaulted by sensations or that the effect of sensations can be predicted in terms of their frequency or intensity and contiguity. They believe that the human mind is capable of and is prone to selecting sensations and organizing them.

These notions lead people in this camp to be less interested in describing the environment to which humans react and more interested in building theories of how the human mind acts and reacts. This means attempting to describe the workings of the mind, which of course cannot be seen. But rationalists do not deny the physical environment and events that take place in it. Therefore, rationalist theories of language tend to incorporate the mental and the physical aspects of language.

One of the earliest psychologists was Wilhelm Wundt (1832–1920). He believed that humans are able to focus attention—to select, structure, and direct experiences—from within. His study of human behavior included the study of cognitive or mental events. On the other hand, he believed it was also the legitimate concern of psychologists to study outer events—sensory motor events. And, therefore, he was interested in associations, frequency, intensity, and contiguity of events—the kinds of things that usually interest empiricists. Wundt took the same point of view in studying language: that language is an outer event (production and perception of sound), but that it is also an inner event (the train of thought).

Contrasts in the Two Traditions

When a person studies language as an inner *and* outer event, questions of how the two are related immediately emerge. Is thought simply inner language or are language and thought separate? In producing language, do people produce a series of sounds that add up to words and eventually to a sentence, or do they start with an undifferentiated thought (a sentence) and divide that thought into words and words into sounds and utter them one at a time? In receiving language, do we process sounds as they are heard, add the sounds into words, and add the words to sentences. Or do we assume that what is perceived is a sentence and organize what is heard and predict what will be heard in an aggressive search for meaning?

These questions reveal an important difference between the empiricist and rationalist tradition. Empiricists strive to break events down into their smallest parts and they strive to explain events by describing the way their parts add up to a whole. This is referred to as an atomistic or bottom-up approach. Rationalists tend to focus on wholes—large events—and to describe parts in terms of how they relate to the whole. This is referred to as a holistic or top-down approach.

Empiricists tend to study reading and teaching reading in terms of the outer aspects of the process—the relationship of print to sound, the perception of letters and words; they rely on frequency of words, letters, and so on, as a method of judging their ease of learning. Rationalists tend to study reading in terms of the inner aspects of language—the meaning—and in terms of the reader's interest, prior knowledge, and ability to direct attention and organize stimuli rather than passively accept them as they come.

The most fundamental difference between the empirical tradition and the rationalist tradition is evident in Charlotte's and Matthew's teaching practices. Charlotte starts with and focuses her energy on the "outer" aspects of reading, the things that can be observed, that are palpable to the senses—printed letters, printed words, and language sounds. Charlotte, a skills-emphasis, traditional teacher, is heir to the empiricist tradition.

Matthew starts with and focuses on the "inner" aspects of reading, the meaning—the relationships that exist in the mind and cannot be observed. Matthew, an eclectic,

BOX 1.1 SOME CHARACTERISTICS OF EMPIRICISM AND RATIONALISM

Empiricism	Rationalism
Focuses on outer aspects of language.	Focuses on inner aspects of language.
Focuses on how separate parts contribute to whole.	Focuses on whole and how parts relate within wholes.
Views language as perceived in parts that are added up to wholes (bottom-up).	Views language as perceived in wholes that are analyzed into parts (top-down).
Views the mind as a comparatively passive receiver of stimuli that attends to the most frequent or most intense stimuli.	Views the mind as an active seeker and organizer of stimuli that will attend to stimuli because it is meaningful or fits into a perceived organization.
In reading, focuses on perception of letters and words, relationship of print to sound, frequency of words as indicators of ease of learning; brings the atomistic and mechanical aspects of reading together finally to consider meaning.	In reading, focuses on meanings and on wholes; analyzes wholes to consider perception of words and letters and the relationship of print to sound finally to consider mechanical relationships of parts.
Atomistic.	Holistic.
Mechanistic.	Organic.

traditional teacher, is heir to the rationalist tradition. As he integrates more and more of the whole language approach, he moves more and more into the rationalist sphere.

It is very useful to refer to empiricism and rationalism as "spheres of influence" rather than as "philosophies" because the history of science, like the history of all human endeavors, is not orderly and compartmentalized (Blumenthal, 1980). There are characteristics associated with these spheres of influence, however, that enable us to see where a particular way of looking at language, learning, or teaching of reading fits into one sphere or the other. (See Box 1.1.)

In the next few pages I will show how trends in thinking and scholarship over the past half-century have tended to support rationalist assumptions about language and learning and, how over the same period, enthusiastic support among experts in teaching reading has shifted away from the skills emphasis to the whole language approach. (See Activities 1.C, 1.D, and 1.E.)

ACTIVITY 1.C CHOOSING WORDS TO TEACH BEGINNING READERS: THE INFLUENCE OF THE EMPIRICIST AND THE RATIONALIST TRADITIONS

What words would you choose to teach a beginning reader if you thought ease of learning was determined by the frequency of words in reading material (an empiricist assumption)?

What words would you choose to teach a beginning reader if you thought ease of learning was determined by the reader's interest, prior knowledge, and ability to direct attention and organize stimuli?

After you have thought about this, read "Selecting Words for the Whole Word Method" (pages 102–104). How do empiricist and rationalist ideas influence the selection of words taught to children in beginning reading programs?

ACTIVITY 1.D STRATEGIES FOR TEACHING WORD RECOGNITION: THE INFLUENCE OF THE EMPIRICIST AND THE RATIONALIST TRADITIONS

Suppose you wanted to teach a child to recognize the word *mother*. Would you begin by teaching the sound usually associated with the letter *m*, or by writing the word *mother* under a picture the child had drawn of his or her mother and calling the child's attention to it?

Which of these approaches is a skills-emphasis, bottom-up approach—heir to the empiricist tradition? Which of these approaches is a holistic, top-down approach—heir to the rationalist tradition?

ACTIVITY 1.E DISCOVERING THESE TRADITIONS IN RECENT TEACHING

Review Charlotte's and Matthew's teaching methods and classify them by

The characteristics of the empiricist sphere.
The characteristics of the rationalist sphere in Box 1.1.

Which approach do you think makes better sense?

THE HEYDAY OF EMPIRICISM

By the middle of this century the most prominent linguist in the United States was Leonard Bloomfield (1887–1949). Bloomfield was a follower of the Swiss linguist Ferdinand de Saussure (1857–1913), who is credited with being the founder of modern linguistics. De Saussure emphasized data collection and argued that language can and should be studied without reference to its history. Bloomfield shared these views and wanted the study of language to be as "scientific" as the study of physics. Development of these principles led to what became known as *structural linguistics*.

Structural Linguistics

Structural linguistics is an attempt to describe language as data without reference to meaning. One goes about doing this by collecting a great deal of data—transcriptions of language produced by people—and then looking at such things as frequency, intensity, and contiguity—all the classical concerns of the empiricists. This was taken to the limit by such linguists as Kenneth Pike, who attempted to write grammars of the languages of people who had had little contact with Western civilization. Theoretically, a linguist applying the principles of structural linguistics could write a grammar of a language he did not know.

That may seem like an impossible task. The following discussion will show how this was done. Suppose that an anthropologist who did not know English arrived on a street in New York City and wanted to write a grammar of the people. According to the methods of structural linguists, he would first collect a lot of data—or copy down in a phonetic notation a lot of speech that he heard around him. Suppose that he had a transcription system that was able to capture the sounds and the melody (pitch, rhythm, stress, and juncture) of the language, and that this system was good enough to enable him to divide the recorded speech into words, phrases, and sentences.

Imagine what rules (grammar) he would be able to formulate about the structure of English. He might make observations like the following: the word *the* is very frequent in this language; it never appears at the end of a sentence, and it frequently appears at the beginning of a phrase. He might observe that the syllables we represent in written English as "ing," "est," and "er" appear often at the end of words. He might surmise that *of, in,* and *on* belong to the same class of words because of their frequency and the position where they occur in phrases. When he had a great amount of data, he could compile many facts about the structure of English and write a description of this language in terms of these observations. Such a description of a language is a grammar of the language. Notice that there is no mention of the meaning of the language, only a description of the physical data.

Other linguists applied the principles of structural linguistics to describing English syntax. Subjects and predicates were defined in terms of their position in sentences. Nouns were described as words that follow "noun determiners"—that is, words that fit into the slots "a _____," "the _____," and "my _____." Adjectives were described as words that fit into the slots "more _____" and "most _____" or words to which you can add the suffix *-er* or *-est*. Words such as *because, if,* and *when* came to be called "clause markers" because they appear at the beginning of clauses. Linguists went to great lengths to describe the syntax of English without referring to meaning. (See Activity 1.F.)

ACTIVITY 1.F CLASSIFYING WORDS BY EMPIRICAL AND RATIONAL METHODS

The traditional definition of a noun is *A noun is a word that names a person, place, or thing.* This is a rationalist definition because it refers to meaning.

Look at these ways of classifying a noun that do not refer to meaning.

1. Nouns are words that end in the following derivational suffixes. (A definition and discussion of *derivational suffix* can be found in Chapter 6, pages 136–137. You may need to refer to these pages.)
   a. -ance *clearance, importance*
   b. -ity *vanity, scarcity*
   c. -ness *stillness, happiness*
   Can you think of other inflectional suffixes that identify nouns, verbs, adjectives, adverbs?
2. Nouns are words that end in the following inflectional suffixes. (A definition and discussion of *inflectional suffix* can be found in Chapter 6, pages 137–138. You may need to refer to these pages.)
   a. -s *boys, hats*
   b. -es *dishes, dresses*
   c. -'s *Tom's, girl's*
   Can you think of other inflectional suffixes that identify nouns, verbs, adjectives, adverbs?
3. Nouns will fit into the blanks in the following "sentence frames."
   One ____a____ had many ____b____.
   The can was in the ____c____.
Create sentence frames where the blanks must be filled by nouns, verbs, adjectives, prepositions, and conjunctions.

You will find many suggestions for structural linguistics word classifiers in *Language Arts* by Temple and Gillet (1989).

Do you find these classifiers easier to understand or apply than traditional definitions?

Which of these classifiers are the kind a linguist would be able to create for a language he or she did not understand?

Communication Theory

A second science of language appeared about the same time as structural linguistics and was connected particularly with World War II. This science was called *communication theory* (Miller, 1951; Cherry, 1957). The U.S. government was very interested in making telephone, radio, and radar communication as perfect as possible. This effort was motivated by wartime applications, and there was a great deal of money and talent—in the form of drafted psychologists and linguists—that went into this effort.

When a person receives messages (in Morse code, for example) on the radio receiver, there is sometimes noise in the channel. The essence of communication theory is that if the operators do not hear a particular letter code, they do not simply guess about the identity of the letter. If they have received "th___," for instance, they know that the likelihood that the missing letter is a vowel is rather high and that if the missing letter is a consonant, *r* is much more likely than any other consonant letter.

An interesting thing about communication theory is that predictions are based on recording thousands of words of messages and simply figuring out from observed messages the statistical probabilities of letters appearing after a particular letter. For example after the letter *h* within a word, the statistical probability of such letters as *a, e, i, o,* and *u* is quite high, while the statistical probability of such letters as *b, c,* and *z* is quite low. You could determine the exact probability of every letter by counting the number of times each letter follows *h* in a large sample, say, 10,000 words of English language messages.

Likewise, you can determine the probabilities of a letter occurring after two letters such as *ch, st,* and *lo;* after three letters such as *boa, str,* and *vac;* and so on.

In communication theory, predictions are *not* based on knowledge of English spelling or what we know about the order of words in sentences from our knowledge of English grammar. These latter approaches would rely on what the receiver *knows*—a mental phenomenon—and communication theory is an empirical science. In Figure 1.5 one of the people is relying on empiricist assumptions and the other is relying on rationalist assumptions—although they may not be conscious of their assumptions or of how their assumptions differ exactly. (See Activity 1.G.)

Figure 1.5. A scientist and a practitioner tackle a communications problem.

The Scientist

We fed 100,000 words of messages sent to and from ships at sea into a computer and calculated the number of times each letter is preceded and followed by every letter; the number of times each two-letter combination is preceded and followed by every letter, and so on, for three- and four-letter combinations.

When a ship's radio operator receives a message and certain letters are not received clearly, he simply types the surrounding letters into a computer and the computer tells him what letters could possibly have occurred and which letter most probably occurred. The operator can then make a judgment based on statistical probabilities about what the letter in doubt is.

The Practitioner

I've been a ship's radio operator for ten years. I speak English. I am a reasonably good speller, but I don't know many spelling "rules."

When I receive a message and certain letters are not received clearly, I almost always know what the letter is. I don't know how, exactly. I just know that it must be a certain letter because I recognize the word it is in. I usually recognize the word because I know the meaning of the sentence, or I get the gist of the whole message.

ACTIVITY 1.G A CLASSIC COMMUNICATION THEORY EXPERIMENT

One person (the Experimenter) looks at a printed passage and asks the Subject (another student in your class) to guess what the first letter in the passage is.

For example, if the passage begins with the sentence *Scientists believe that the first horses were small animals between 10 and 20 inches high,* the exchange might go as follows:

EXPERIMENTER: Guess the first letter in this passage.

SUBJECT: T.

EXPERIMENTER: No. The first letter is S. What's the next letter?

SUBJECT: U.

EXPERIMENTER: No. The letter is C. What's the next letter?

SUBJECT: L.

EXPERIMENTER: No. The letter is I. What's the next letter?

SUBJECT: E.

EXPERIMENTER: Yes. What's the next letter?

SUBJECT: N.

EXPERIMENTER: Yes. What's the next letter?

SUBJECT: C.

EXPERIMENTER: No. The letter is T. What's the next letter?

SUBJECT: I.

EXPERIMENTER: Yes. What's the next letter?

[And so on.]

A. Repeat this experiment using a newspaper story.

How predictable is the English language—if you define success in guessing letters as predictability? What percentage of the time is the subject correct?

At what point is the Subject

merely guessing?
using knowledge of English spelling?
using knowledge of English vocabulary?
using knowledge of the meaning of the passage?

An empiricist explanation of what you observe in this experiment is that previous experience has "taught" you to use the probabilities of what letters will occur based on the letters you have received. Each new bit of information is added to the information you have (the letters received), and the next prediction is made in a mechanical manner.

A rationalist explanation is that your knowledge of English syntax, spelling, and vocabulary and prior knowledge of the topic all operate in a holistic, organic fashion.

Which explanation do you find more convincing?

B. The cloze procedure is described in Chapter 10, pages 215–216.

You might want to read about the cloze procedure now and discuss it in relation to the questions asked about this communication theory experiment.

Behaviorism—Classical Stimulus-Response Theory

Empiricism had always dominated the study of psychology in America, and by the 1950s a particularly pure form of empiricism had emerged (Blumenthal, 1980.) The study of psychology was the study of observable behavior and the events in the environment that shaped behavior. Learning was defined as the association between some event in the environment (the stimulus) and an observable action on the part of the learner (the response). This branch of psychology is known as *behaviorism,* and the learning theory it explores is known as *stimulus-response-reinforcement theory.*

Behaviorism reflects the classic concerns of the empiricist tradition. Behaviorists are interested in observation, measurement, and the recording of observable events and behaviors, and they strive to analyze their data into its most elemental parts. They are interested in frequency, intensity, and contiguity of stimuli and responses. Much of the experimentation in behaviorist psychology has been done on animals—pigeons, cats, and rats. Applying learning theory derived from the study of animals to human learning reflects another aspect of the empiricist tradition: that one can describe human behavior as animal behavior without ascribing any special significance to the human mind.

Classical stimulus-response-reinforcement theory proposes that if an animal (a child in the case of reading) is rewarded for making a response to a stimulus, the animal is likely to make that response again in the presence of the stimulus. For example, one might present a monkey with a red lever; if the monkey presses the lever (the desired response), he is given food (the reinforcement). After a few trials the monkey will press the red lever every time he is presented with it. The monkey has *learned* through classic stimulus-response "conditioning." Teaching word recognition with flash cards is a typical application of classical stimulus-response learning theory in reading instruction.

The Impact of Empirical Assumptions on Education

Permissiveness.   Several aspects of structural linguistics have had a very real effect on education. Structural linguistics is purely descriptive; it is nonprescriptive and nonjudgmental. When transcribing data, a linguist does not ask whether it is considered correct to say such and such; he writes down what is said—it becomes part of the data. Going back to the earlier example, the linguist who is collecting data on a New York City street would copy down "ain't" and "you wasn't" and be interested only in identifying the frequency (how often it was uttered) and distribution (whether it appeared in certain parts of phrases and sentences and not others). The linguist might observe that "ain't" is frequently found in the language of some subjects and never in the language of others. He or she might guess that there is a dialect difference involved, but would not make a judgment about whether or not the word was "correct."

This had led to the notion that modern linguistics is permissive, that is, not concerned with standards. This was a misunderstanding. Linguists of the Bloomfield-Pike variety were simply not talking about English usage as it traditionally concerned the schools. They were not talking about dialect differences in terms of whether political and economic advantages are attached to particular dialects, let alone whether it is the business of the schools to teach some standard dialect. They were talking about studying language as a natural phenomenon—as a physicist or chemist studies matter.

Attitude Toward Dialect.   The notion of studying language from a nonjudgmental, nonprescriptive point of view had far-reaching effects. Books such as Hall's *Leave Your Language Alone!* (1950) were published expressing the point of view that one dialect is as good as another and that, therefore, one should not attempt to switch dialects or to switch anyone else's dialect (one's students, for example). Whether dialect differences play a part in learning to read became a central issue in this debate.

The matter of dialect differences became a politically charged issue in the decades that followed the heyday of structuralism. Attitudes of ''Middle America,'' and particularly of the schools, toward black English became a concern in the civil rights struggle.

Linguistic Readers.   Bloomfield was not only a leader in linguistics, he was directly interested in the teaching of reading. In keeping with his empiricist point of view, he saw teaching reading as teaching word recognition and letter-sound relationships—that is, the outer aspects of reading. He acknowledged that the goal of reading was comprehension of meaning but asserted that children comprehend language before they come to school; they do not know how to read. As an empiricist he was also interested in frequency and contiguity of events. His system (presented in *Let's Read*, Bloomfield & Barnhart, 1961), is based on the principle of teaching the most frequent and most consistent letter-sound relationships first. This direct attention to the reading process by a linguist resulted in a reading method, *the linguistic method*, and in textbooks based on this method, *linguistic readers*.

Psycholinguistics as an Empirical Science

It is perfectly natural that when the principles and methodologies of psychology (behaviorism) and linguistics (structural linguistics and communication theory) had so much in common, they should get together. Two conferences were held to explore the common interests of psychologists and linguists, the first at Cornell University in 1951 and the second at Indiana University in 1953. Out of these meetings grew great hope that through joint efforts, and by applying the empiricist principles of behavioral psychology, structural linguistics, and communication theory, there would soon be tremendous technological breakthroughs in such things as machine translation of language and speech-to-print typewriters.

The term *psycholinguistics* was popularized as a description of the joint study of language by psychologists and linguists. It was an unfortunate time to coin such a word because a revolution was about to take place in the study of linguistics and psychology. Ten years later the term *psycholinguistics* was still used to describe the study of language by psychologists and linguists, but both fields had come under the rival sphere of influence—rationalism. The suddenness of this turnabout and the fact that the same term, *psycholinguistics,* was used to refer to this field before and after the revolution has led to considerable confusion.

THE SHIFT TOWARD RATIONALISM

Chomsky

In the late 1950s, there was a revolution in linguistics and psychology that was caused by the work of a single individual, Noam Chomsky. Chomsky (1957) attacked the basic premise of structural linguistics. He showed that one cannot assign structure to a great many English sentences without reference to the meaning of the sentence. He further asserted that even in the many sentences where structures can be assigned in terms of frequency, position, stress, juncture, and so on (the physical characteristics of language attended to by the empiricist tradition), it is thoroughly wrongheaded to refuse to recognize an obvious fact: that sentences have meaning, and as speakers of a language, linguists know the meaning. Chomsky was asserting the time-honored rationalist position—that the mind exists and that it can and should be studied.

Chomsky proposed a *generative transformational grammar* that was a counter proposal to the grammars proposed by structural linguists. The main feature of this grammar is that every sentence has a deep structure—a structure in the mind of the speaker— as well as a surface structure—a physical manifestation of speech sounds. Transformational grammar is an attempt to describe the relationship between the two.

It is impossible to describe Chomsky's impact on the study of language without reference to B. F. Skinner's book *Verbal Behavior* (1957). Skinner is among the best known behavioral psychologists. Indeed, the word *Skinnerian* is synonymous with *behaviorist*. *Verbal Behavior* was the most thorough and literal application of behaviorism to language.

Chomsky's review in 1959 of Skinner's book is one of the few book reviews that has been more widely read, and is more influential, than the book it reviews. Chomsky very effectively criticized this purely behaviorist-empiricist approach to the study of language. One might say that Chomsky held this approach up to ridicule. The effectiveness of this review is indicated, perhaps, by the fact that Skinner never responded to it.

When one admits mind into the study of language, the question arises as to where the properties of the mind that account for language come from. The traditional answer of rationalists, and it is Chomsky's answer, is that human beings are born with the capacity to learn and to use language. We are genetically endowed with this capacity. It is a capacity that developed in our evolutionary history. This belief is referred to as "nativism."

The idea that language is "natural" rather than learned has a long history. Herodotus, a Greek historian of the fifth century B.C., wrote of an Egyptian king who is supposed to have isolated a child from birth to find out what language he would speak. The king wanted to know what the "natural" language of human beings was. At the end of the nineteenth century, according to Blumenthal (1980), language authorities commonly believed that a child raised in isolation would develop a language as rich as that of his or her parents.

Of course, the environment must have some effect or children would not learn French in a French-speaking community and English in an English-speaking community. Like Wundt, contemporary rationalists acknowledge that language is both an inner and an outer phenomenon. The inner aspects are thought to be genetically endowed and the outer aspects susceptible to influence from the environment. But perhaps as a reaction to behaviorism, and particularly because Skinner's behavioristic explanation of language in *Verbal Behavior* was so thoroughly discredited by Chomsky, psycholinguists tended to play down the effect of the environment on language. The term "language acquisition" was coined to avoid the word "learning."

Psycholinguists, following Chomsky, assumed the nativist position and studied how children acquired rules of language—how the genetically programmed mechanism for language develops. They acknowledged that the child must be exposed to language, but for the most part, they considered language in the environment as given. They tended not to study what effect language in the child's environment has on the child's language development. It was not their question.

The questions that have occupied psychologists and linguists since Chomsky are rationalist questions. The rationalist questions that are relevant to teaching reading and to choices reading teachers must make have to do with how language is related to other aspects of the mind—thinking, knowing, and perceiving. Scientists who study thinking, knowing, and perceiving are called *cognitive psychologists*.

Cognitive Psychology

Piaget on Mental Development. Among educators, probably the best known cognitive psychologist is Jean Piaget (1896–1980). The three prominent characteristics of Piaget's theory are (1) that cognitive growth proceeds in stages, (2) that there are radical shifts in children's cognitive capacity as they pass from one stage to another, and (3) that development depends primarily on the maturity of the child, but also on his or her interaction with the environment. For example, children at the early "preoperational stage" do not have the concept known as "conservation of volume." If water is poured from a short, wide vessel into a tall narrow vessel, children at this stage will assert that there is now more water (presumably because the water level is higher) in the narrow vessel even though they saw the water being poured and knew that no water had been added.

Piaget showed that with *maturation* and experience with the environment, the concept of conservation of volume emerges in a fairly sudden fashion. This is not a stimulus-response-reinforcement theory. It is a theory of the unfolding of a genetically preprogrammed cognitive development wherein children act on their environment, explore it, and manipulate it. The concepts children build from this interaction are dependent on their maturity level. They do not pass from one stage to another because they are rewarded for a new response to old experiences, but because, at their higher level of maturation, their old responses become inconsistent with the way they see the world; there has been a mental recognization.

Piaget on Language Development. Piaget views changes in language behavior as symptoms of changes in the child's mental development. His interest in language is always as an appendage to his main interest, the growth of cognition. According to Piaget, thought arises within the child as cognitive capacity matures; eventually thought becomes "inner speech," and eventually inner speech becomes audible speech. But when audible speech appears, the child is still egocentric. That is, the child has not come to understand fully that others know different things and have a different point of view; therefore, this audible speech is not directed at others as separate individuals. It is "egocentric speech."

By the end of the preoperational stage, the child's audible speech is almost entirely "socialized speech." It is directed at others whom he is finally aware of as being separate from himself, possessing, different knowledge and having a different point of view. This change from egocentric to socialized speech is seen as a natural outcome of a change in the child's view of the world, which in turn, depends in part on maturation and in part of interaction with others, particularly other children. The child's interactions with others help him to notice that others have a different perspective on the world.

This realization comes into conflict with the child's egocentric view of the world. Thus, maturation plus interaction leads to a change in mental organization, and this in turn, leads to an observable change in the use of language.

Since language plays an important part in interactions between people, one might ask what role language has in leading the child to notice that others have a different perspective from his own. This question is asked by others who are preoccupied with the role of social interaction in the development of both thought and language. But Piaget is a psychologist who is interested primarily in cognitive development and who has a strong belief in maturation as the essential factor in cognitive development. The question of the role of language in this process is simply not addressed. Put another way, Piaget was interested in how growth in cognition results in growth in language. He showed very little interest in how growth in language results in growth in cognition.

Educators who claim to be interpreters of Piaget have criticized some Piaget–inspired nursery school programs for attempting to accelerate children's cognitive development and for placing too much emphasis on language (Brainerd, 1978). For those not conversant with Piaget's writing, these may seem to be very startling criticisms of nursery school programs. Is it not the business of schools to accelerate cognitive development and to emphasize language development? But the fact is that Piaget's emphasis on maturation (a biological process), and his treating language as an outcome of development rather than as a cause of development, make these criticisms quite consistent with his views. (See Activities 1.H, 1.I, and 1.J.)

Shortcomings of Behaviorism, Psycholinguistics, and Cognitive Psychology from a Reading Teacher's Point of View

Piaget's theory of cognitive development and the psycholinguistic theories of language development are both strongly nativist theories. Certain capacities are genetically endowed and arise with maturation. The environment has a role in both cases, but the

ACTIVITY 1.H EGOCENTRISM AND COMMUNICATION: CONVEYING STRAIGHTFORWARD INFORMATION

Make two identical sets of cards (or blocks with similar shapes affixed to them) such as those in Figure 1.6.

I. Select two classmates. Designate one the Teller and the second one the Listener. Sit them at opposite sides of a table with a screen between them (or in some arrangement where they can hear each other, but cannot see each other's cards).

Place the Teller's cards in a pattern in front of him such as the one in Figure 1.6. Place the Listener's cards in random order in front of him or her.

Instruct the Teller to talk to the Listener so the Listener can make the same pattern with his cards as the Teller sees in front of him or her.

II. Try the same thing with two 5-year-olds and two 10-year-olds.

1. What communication difficulties do the 5- and 10-year-olds have as compared with those of classmates?
2. Can you explain the difficulties to the 5 year-olds in terms of the Teller's not being able to take the Listener's point of view—not being able to imagine what the Listener knows and what he or she needs to know to accomplish this task?

Figure 1.6. Cards for an egocentrism and communication experiment.

ACTIVITY 1.I EGOCENTRISM AND COMMUNICATION: PERSUASION

I. Select a classmate, and using a puppet, say the following:

Pretend the puppet is your mother. A friend has offered to give you a dog that you like a lot, but you know your mother doesn't want any pets. Talk to her and try to convince her to let you bring the dog home to keep.

II. Try the same thing with a 5-year-old and a 10-year-old.

Presumably, you will get more effective arguments from older participants. Can you explain the difficulties of the younger participants in terms of their being egocentric—that is, in terms of their not being able to take their listener's point of view or to tailor their arguments to respond to their mother's attitudes or objections?

ACTIVITY 1.J ARE YOU A PIAGETIAN?

A typical performance of a 5-year-old Teller in Activity 1.H is, "Put your cards the way mine are, James [the Listener]." This kind of response is thought to result from the Teller's inability to cope with the idea that the Listener can't see what the Teller can see.

A typical performance of a 5-year-old in Activity 1.I is, "Please let me have the dog because I want it." This may result from the child's inability to take the mother's perspective or to imagine her objections and argue "I'll take care of the dog. You won't have to" or to appeal to her self-interest and argue, "It would be a good watch dog, so we would be safer."

Many teachers are inclined to want to teach a child to perform a task well as soon as they discover the child has difficulty with the task. They believe that with the right stimulus-response-reward scheme, they could get a 5-year-old to perform the tasks in a more mature way than the typical responses suggested in the last two paragraphs.

Followers of Piaget are inclined to believe that the communication difficulties will be overcome with *maturation* and experience. There is a limit to how much you can improve performance, because part of the performance depends on biological maturity.

What do you think? Are you a Piagetian? Discuss this question with your classmates.

contribution of the environment to the growth of language and cognition are deemphasized. How differences in a child's environment affect cognitive and language development are not nativist's questions. However, these are important questions to educators, and so to some extent Piagetian psychology and psycholinguistics are not useful to education because they do not ask the questions to which educators seek answers.

We have seen in this discussion how behaviorists ask questions that are relevant to education: How is behavior explained in terms of the environment? How is learning affected by manipulating the environment? But psycholinguists and cognitive psychologists say behaviorists have the wrong slant on things. Language and learning are about the mind. The mind has genetically endowed properties, and if one does not recognize these properties, his or her explanations of learning are either wrong or incomplete. These cognitive psychologists and linguists, however, fail to explore the questions relevant to education: How do changes in the environment affect learning?

Fortunately there are psychologists and linguists who are both rationalists and nativists but whose emphasis is on the role of social interaction in both cognitive and language development. It is to this group that we will turn in the next chapter.

SUMMARY

I began this chapter with a description of two fictitious teachers whom I created to illustrate two different aproaches to teaching reading. Charlotte believes that reading is essentially decoding print into language and that writing is essentially encoding language into print. Charlotte treats reading, writing, spelling, and handwriting as separate subjects. Charlotte's teaching methods reflect a psychological view of learning.

Matthew believes that reading is essentially a quest for meaning, and that writing is essentially formulating ideas and expressing them in clear, explicit language. Matthew consciously introduces reading into his writing classes and writing into his reading classes. He treats handwriting as a separate subject—only for students who need it. Matthew treats spelling as a separate subject, but as an expediency. Matthew's teaching methods reflect a sociological view of learning.

Matthew and Charlotte represent teaching practices that grow out of two traditions that have their origins in philosophy. Charlotte is a traditional phonics or skills emphasis teacher—heir to the empirical tradition. Matthew is a traditional eclectic teacher who is working toward a whole language approach—heir to the rationalist tradition.

Scientists in the empirical tradition concentrate on the study of observable events and behaviors and attempt to explain language and learning in terms of observable events and behaviors. They tend to break down observations into their smallest parts and to explain whole processes in terms of their parts. Empiricism is a bottom-up, atomistic approach.

Scientists in the rationalist tradition study language and learning as functions of the mind that cannot be observed but that can be studied. They tend to create theories of how the mind operates and explain smaller behaviors and events in terms of theories of whole processes. Rationalism is a top-down, holistic approach.

In midcentury America, the empiricist tradition dominated the study of language. Structural linguistics, communication theory, and behaviorism are three manifestations of empiricism. An understanding of the principles governing these fields will help you to understand empiricism. Current attitudes toward nonstandard English and a method of teaching beginning reading that particularly emphasizes phonics—the linguistic approach—had their beginnings in this era.

However, by the 1960s a great shift had taken place in the study of psychology and linguistics. The rationalist tradition came to dominate the study of language and language development. The study of psychology became the study of cognitive psychology and the study of linguistics became dominated by the study of transformational grammar. The study of language acquisition and language performance from the point of view of psychology *and* linguistics became known as psycholinguistics (a term used in this book to refer to the period after 1965).

Psycholinguists believe that humans are *genetically* endowed with the capacity for language and that the human mind has a *genetically* determined capacity to organize input. Such theories are referred to as *nativistic*. Piaget, a well-known cognitive psychologist, is a nativist in that he believes that all cognitive development proceeds in stages and that these stages are determined by maturation in the individual. Piaget views language as part of cognitive development.

By the three-quarter-century mark (1975), rationalist assumptions dominated the study of language development, and the most influential thinkers in the field were nativists. Their explanation of linguistic and cognitive development emphasize the natural unfolding of genetically predetermined processes. Such explanations are not very useful to teachers.

Since the late 1970s, the study of language and cognitive development from a sociological point of view has come into prominence. Since schools and teachers are part of a child's social environment, such studies are very useful to teachers because they investigate social interactions and their effect on cognitive development and language learning. The sociological perspective on the study of language will be treated in the next chapter.

FOR FURTHER READING

Cleverly, J., & Phillips, D. C. (1986). *Visions of childhood.* New York: Teacher's College Press.

Menyuk, P. (1987). *Language development, knowledge and use.* Glenview, IL: Scott Foresman. Chapter 2: Theories of language development; Chapter 3: Cognition and language.

Phillips, D. C., & Soltes, J. F. (1985). *Perspectives on learning.* New York: Teacher's College Press.

Wells, G. (1986). *The meaning makers: Children learning language and using language to learn.* Portsmouth, NH: Heinemann. Chapter 3: Learning to talk: The construction of language; Chapter 4: Talking to learn.

Wells, G., & Nicholls, J. (1985). *Language and learning: An interactional perspective.* Philadelphia: Falmer Editor's introduction.

CHAPTER 2

Social Foundations of Language

LANGUAGE AND LEARNING: AN INTERACTIONAL PERSPECTIVE ON LINGUISTIC AND COGNITIVE DEVELOPMENT

Scholars and researchers in the 1980s accepted the nativist position on language and cognitive development, but they turned their attention to the question that interests educators: Given that language and cognitive development rely heavily on a genetic, biologically determined component, what part does the environment—particularly the social environment (other people)—play in language development? This line of inquiry has led to what is called the *interactional perspective*.

The term *interactional* refers to two interactions in this process. There is an interaction between the learner and others (parents, siblings, etc.), and there is an interaction between language development and cognitive development: learning new things facilitates a growth in language, and growth in language facilitates learning new things. The following narrative describes how language develops according to this perspective.

Infants begin life as part of society. At birth, children appear to act out of a special relationship to other humans as distinct from all other things in their new environment. Only hours after birth, children react differently to the human voice than they do to other sounds—even rhythmic sounds like music (Eimas et al., 1971). Infants show more interest in people than in inanimate objects (Snow, 1977). In the first several weeks of life, children show a preference for looking at human faces and respond differently to familiar and unfamiliar faces. Infants direct their earliest and most elaborate spontaneous behavior toward people (Trevarthen, 1979).

Emergence of Language

Emergence of "Conversation."   A conversation has three ingredients: two communicators and content. For most children a primitive form of conversation, called "protoconversation," begins during the first few weeks of life. From the start, the parent is attentive to the child's gestures, vocalizations, and changes of gaze and responds to them in various ways. This is the beginning of the initiation-response pattern that is essential to conversation.

Soon after initiation-response patterns are established, content is introduced when both parties to the protoconversation focus their attention on some aspect of the environment. The mother looks at the infant and—following the child's gaze—points at, touches, or picks up the object the child is looking at.

Parents use speech in their contributions to protoconversation. In repeated "conversations" revolving around the repeated routines of feeding, changing, and bathing, words are frequently matched with ongoing activities. These interactions of children with their parents are obviously important to the development of their communicative ability. During the same time, the child is making other discoveries about communication.

Meaningful but Unintentional Communication.   The cries, gurgles, coos, and vocalizations of newborn infants are undoubtedly instinctual. Although they may have no intentional meaning for the child, parents constantly attempt to assign meaning to the child's vocalizations. When Anthony cries, does he need a clean diaper? Does he want to be held? Does he need to be "burped"? When Sarah coos, is she happy to see mommy? Does she feel comfortable in her fresh diaper? Does she like being cuddled? Parents guess at the meaning of the child's behavior, and they act on their guesses. Mothers of very young infants often believe that they can distinguish between a cry of hunger, a cry of discomfort, and "just crying."

Child-initiated behaviors are followed by parental responses in regular and repeated patterns. Soon the child begins to act as if he or she has caught on to the cause-effect relationship between behaviors he or she initiates and the response of the adult.

Meaningful and Intentional Communication.   In time, a profound change occurs in these communication interactions between parent and child. The child cries *because* he wants his diaper changed; she coos and smiles *because* she feels warm and dry and safe in her mother's arms; he looks from his mother's eyes to the toy on the floor *because* he wants her to look there too. A great watershed in the development of language has occurred: the child *intends* to communicate. As early as six weeks, parents begin to interpret the child's facial expressions and changes of gaze as both *meaningful* and *intentional*.

Communication becomes intentional when the child has discovered she or he can do things to those around her or him. Michael A. K. Halliday (1975), in a careful study of his own son, determined that the boy learned to use communication to accomplish several purposes such as to get things done for himself (for example, to get food or a diaper change), to control the behavior of others (for example, to get his father to look at a book with him), to initiate and maintain contact with others (for example, to greet his mother when she entered a room), and to tell about himself and his feelings (for example, to express boredom, disgust, and anger). Halliday named these the instrumental, regulatory, interactional, and personal functions of language.

In discovering uses of communication and mastering them, children "learn how to mean." But they have not necessarily acquired language yet. Smiles, frowns, gestures, and vocalizations may communicate, but they are not language.

The Emergence of Unconventional Language.   Early communicative behavior relies heavily on vocalization. Language begins when a particular vocalization takes on a particular meaning (or meanings). When children consistently begin to say *uh, uh* when they want to be picked up or *ba* when they want milk, another monumental event has occurred. They are using an arbitrary symbol to communicate meaning. The vocal signal *uh, uh* has no connection with the act it elicits, except that the child and caretaker have come to an unspoken agreement that *uh, uh* means "pick me up." That is language, in a sense, but there is one more hurdle to cross.

Although the child's vocal communication is both *meaningful* and *intentional*, it is not *conventional*. Children are born into societies that have language. There are conventional symbols for expressing meanings such as "pick me up" or "give me milk."

The Emergence of Conventional Language.   Soon, however, children apparently notice that everyone around them has a different set of agreed-upon arbitrary vocal symbols for certain meanings. They abandon *uh, uh* in favor of *up* and *ba* in favor of *milk*. Their communicative behavior then possesses all the characteristics of human language. It is meaningful, intentional, and conventional. Another magnificent accomplishment—and the child is only 24 months old! (See Activity 2.A.)

ACTIVITY 2.A VERIFY THIS DISCUSSION THROUGH OBSERVATION

I. Observe a very young child (less than 18 months) interacting with a parent during bathing, feeding, and diaper changing, or while parent and child are playing. If possible, videotape the exchange to share with your classmates.

While observing, keep these questions in mind:

1. What is the role of vocalization in this episode?
2. What is the role of gestures, gazes, and references to context?
3. Do you see communication that is
   a. Meaningful but unintentional
   b. Meaningful and intentional, but unconventional
   c. Meaningful, intentional, and conventional as defined in this discussion?

II. If possible observe parents interacting with children of different ages—perhaps 4 months, 12 months, and 24 months—keeping the same questions in mind.

Lifelong Development of Language and Communication Resources

The preceding narrative of language and cognitive development is reenacted again and again throughout life. Children first learn what language can do, and then, with the cooperation of adults, they invent ways to accomplish these tasks. Next, children discover that there are *conventional* ways of accomplishing the tasks, and they adopt these conventions. The parent's job (and later the teacher's job) is

> To provide an atmosphere where new uses of spoken language are discovered (both as a speaker and as a listener) and where spoken language is encouraged.
> To cooperate with children's inventive attempts to use language.
> To provide a model for conventional spoken language.
> To help them adopt the conventions (of spoken language) when they are ready to adopt them.

In a literate society children soon learn to recognize writing. They learn what writing is used for—what a person can do with writing both as producers (writers) and consumers (readers). They simultaneously invent ways to accomplish these tasks. Next, children discover that there are *conventional* ways to do things with writing, and they adopt these conventions. It is the parent's job (and later the teacher's job)

> To provide an atmosphere where new uses of written language are discovered (both as a reader and a writer) and where written communication is encouraged.
> To cooperate with children's inventive attempts to use written language.
> To provide a model for conventional written communication.
> To help children adopt the conventions of written language when they are ready to adopt them.

PARENTS AS TEACHERS

Some years ago, John Holt wrote a description of how the schools would go about teaching infants language if infants learned language in schools.

> Suppose we decided that we had to "teach" children to speak. How would we go about it? First, some committee of experts would analyze speech and break it down into a number of separate "speech skills." We would probably say that, since speech is made up of sounds, a child must be taught to make all the sounds of his language before he can be taught to speak the language itself. Doubtless we would list these sounds, easiest and commonest ones first, harder and rarer ones next. Then we would begin to teach infants these sounds, working our way down the list. Perhaps, in order not to "confuse" the child—"confuse" is an evil word to many educators—we would not let the child hear much ordinary speech but would only expose him to the sounds we were trying to teach . . .
>
> Suppose we tried to do this; what would happen? What would happen, quite simply, is that most children, before they got very far, would become baffled, discouraged, humiliated, and fearful, and would quit trying to do what we asked them. . . . If our control of their lives was complete (the dream of too many educators), they would take refuge in deliberate failure and silence as so many of them do when the subject is reading. (Holt, 1967, pp. 56–57)

This is, of course, an ironic description. The more the reader is familiar with the way language evolves in children, the more obvious the irony becomes.

In contrast to this description, which you should recognize as a parody of an empiricist, bottom-up, behaviorist approach, in the next several pages I will present transcripts of children talking with their parents and ask you to think about three things:

1. What can the child do with language?
2. How is the parent helping the child
   a. to communicate the matter at hand?
   b. to *learn more about* effective communication?

I will then present responses of experts such as Wells (1986), and finally I will draw several principles out of this discussion that ought to inform our efforts in helping children to learn to read.

Observing Children Using Language I

Present: Mark, aged 23 months; Helen, aged 9 months; and Mother.

[Mark is in the kitchen with his mother and his sister Helen. He is holding a mirror in which he sees reflected now himself and now his mother.]

> MARK: Mummy, Mummy.
> MOTHER: What?
> MARK: There. There Mark.
> MOTHER: Is that Mark?
> MARK: Mark. [pointing to Mother] Mummy.
> MOTHER [exaggerated rising intonation]:   Mm.

MARK [pointing to Mother]:   Mummy.

MOTHER [exaggerated rising intonation]:   Yes, that's Mummy.

MARK: Mummy. Mummy. Mummy.

MOTHER: Mm.

MARK: There Mummy. Mummy, there—Mark there. [A minute later, looking out of the window at the birds in the garden] Look-at-that. Birds, Mummy.

MOTHER: Mm.

MARK: Jubs [birds].

MOTHER: What are they doing?

MARK: Jubs bread [Birds eating bread(?)].

MOTHER: Oh look! They're eating the berries, aren't they?

MARK: Yeh.

MOTHER: That's their food. They have berries for dinner.

MARK: Oh. (Wells, 1986, p. 22)

Ask yourself these questions about the example before reading on.

What can Mark do with language?

What is Mother's role in Mark's communication?

To what extent do you think mother is consciously teaching Mark about language? about the world around him?

Mark's Performance.   Mark initiates the conversation, introduces new topics, and responds to Mother's contributions. He has moved beyond the earliest stages of language use in that his language performs several functions at once. His whole conversation is interactional; it establishes and maintains contact. At times he is also informative. He has clearly begun to adopt the conventions of language. Most of his words are English words. He has begun to use more than one word per utterance, and therefore syntax (word order) is present.

Mother's Role in Mark's Communication.   Mark's mother's utterances are simple in form and restricted to topics rising from the immediate context. She particularly comments on topics introduced by Mark. Wells (1986) describes what Mother does in this conversation as "leading from behind." She follows the child's lead by asking questions, restating what Mark has said, and adding new information to support and extend the topics Mark has introduced.

Researchers (Garnica, 1977) have questioned mothers about their intention to teach their children in conversations like this. Mothers report that their aim is not to teach, but merely to communicate effectively. They speak in simple utterances so their children will understand. They question and rephrase to check on what the child means.

Although mothers do not consciously teach children, children undoubtedly learn from their parents' language. Parents' utterances are often conventional versions of what their children have just said or words matched to what their children have focused their attention on. Parents sometimes use words that may be new to their child (such as *berries*). The written transcripts do not show intonation, but, in fact, it is typical for mothers to exaggerate stress on words like *berries* in situations like this.

Observing Children Using Language II

Two months later Mark and his mother had the following conversation.
Present: Mark, aged 25 months, and Mother.
[Mark has seen a man working in his garden]

MARK: Where man gone? Where man gone?
MOTHER: I don't know. I expect he's gone inside because it's snowing.
MARK: Where man gone?
MOTHER: In the house.
MARK: Uh?
MOTHER: Into his house.
MARK: No. No. Gone to shop, Mummy. [The local shop is close to Mark's house.]
MOTHER: Gone where?
MARK: Gone shop.
MOTHER: To the shop?
MARK: Yeh.
MOTHER: What's he going to buy?
MARK: Er—biscuits.
MOTHER: Biscuits, mm.
MARK: Uh?
MOTHER: Mm. What else?
MARK: Er—meat.
MOTHER: Mm.
MARK: Meat. Er—sweeties. Buy a big bag sweets.
MOTHER: Buy sweets?
MARK: Yeh. M—er—man—buy, the man buy sweets.
MOTHER: Will he?
MARK: Yeh. Daddy buy sweets. Daddy buy sweets.
MOTHER: Why?
MARK: Oh er—shop.
MARK: Mark do buy some—sweet—sweeties. (Wells, 1981, p. 107)

Ask yourself these questions about the example before reading on:

What can Mark do with language?
What is Mother's role in Mark's communication?
To what extent do you think Mother is consciously teaching Mark about language? about the world around him?

Mark's Performance.   Mark's utterances have improved in terms of becoming more conventional. They are longer and have taken on the subject-verb-object form. However, the most remarkable progress he has made is revealed by the topic. This conversation is not about something going on in the immediate context. The man, the store, the purchases, and the action are not present. The topic is imaginative as well. The researcher who collected this example refers to it as the first "story" in the data.

Mother's Role in Mark's Communication.   Once again Mother's role is to lead from behind. She takes Mark's topic and, realizing he has invented a reason for the man's disappearance, helps him to develop an account of a shopping trip by asking what the man bought. Meaning is therefore "negotiated," and the story is a collaborative effort.

This conversation demonstrates the development of language and thinking (cognition) on dimensions that will continue throughout life and that have special relevance to school and success in reading and writing. Mark has begun to talk about events that are not going on in the immediate environment; he has begun to deal with literary forms—the story; and it may not be going too far to suggest that with his mother's help he has begun to think about and talk about abstract categories—things one buys at a shop.

Research does not tell us exactly how these monumental mental and linguistic accomplishments come about, but children seem to learn by matching what is being said to them in conversation with what they believe the language is about, using whatever clues are present in the context. By making sense of what they hear, they learn about the world and about language. But they also learn through speaking. They become clearer about their meaning and about the language used to express their meaning through conversation with a partner who is sensitive to their needs both as language learners and as learners about the world around them.

Observing Children Using Language III

Present: Mark, aged 28 months, and Mother.

MARK: All right. [Command.] You dry hands.
MOTHER: I've dried my hands now.
MARK: Put towel in there. [He wants her to put the towel in the basket.]
MOTHER: No, it's not dirty.
MARK: It is.
MOTHER: No, it isn't.
MARK: 'Tis. Mummy, play. Play, Mummy.
MOTHER: Well, I will play if you put the top on the basket.
MARK: All right. [He finally puts the lid on the basket.] There. There. Play, Mummy. Play. Play, Play, Mummy. Mummy, come on.
MOTHER: All right. (Wells, 1986, p. 26)

Ask yourself these questions about the example before reading on:

What can Mark do with language?
What is Mother's role in Mark's communication?
To what extent do you think Mother is consciously teaching Mark about language? about the world around him?

Mark's Performance.   In this short exchange Mark successfully attempts to regulate his mothers behavior—"you dry hands" (regulatory function) and to get her to do something for him—"Mummy play" (instrumental function). It is extremely important to look at Mark's successes and "failures" and to think about the truth of the commonly held belief that children learn easy things first and hard things later. Although conditional clauses are thought to be cognitively complex, Mark responds appropriately to his mother's conditional sentence (I'll play *if* you put the top down). But he does not supply articles (*the* towel), a task that seems so easy. Elsewhere in this conversation, Mark hands his mother a towel and makes an utterance that is a series of vowel sounds—not an English word. His mother interprets this to mean "Here you are." Yet he uses words like *dried* and *towel* and pronounces them correctly.

Mother's Role in Mark's Communication.   Mark's mother does not focus on his "mistakes" and failures. She ignores the unconventionality of his speech. She seems to assume that he will adopt the conventions that are now absent from his speech when he is ready. She focuses on the jobs Mark is attempting to accomplish with language and cooperates by responding in language and in action to his meaning.

Observing Children Using Language IV

Halliday's son Nigel, at 20 months, has been taken to the children's zoo. He has picked up a plastic lid that he is clutching in one hand while stroking a goat with the other. The goat, after the manner of its kind, starts to eat the lid. The keeper intervenes, and says kindly but firmly that the goat must not eat the lid—it would not be good for it. Here is Nigel reviewing the incident after returning home, some hours later:

> NIGEL: Try eat lid.
> FATHER: What tried to eat the lid?
> NIGEL: Try eat lid.
> FATHER: What tried to eat the lid?
> NIGEL: Goat . . . man said no . . . goat try eat lid . . . man said no.

Then, after a further interval, while being put to bed:

> NIGEL: Goat try eat lid . . . man said no.
> MOTHER: Why did the man say no?
> NIGEL: Goat shouldn't eat lid . . . (shaking head) good for it.
> MOTHER: The goat shouldn't eat the lid; it's not good for it.
> NIGEL: Goat try eat lid . . . man said no . . . goat shouldn't eat lid . . . (shaking head) good for it. (Halliday, 1975, pp. 111–112)

Ask yourself these questions about the example before reading on.

What can Nigel do with language?
What is Father's and Mother's role in Nigel's communication?
To what extent do you think the parents are consciously teaching Nigel about language? about the world around him?

Nigel's Performance.   Here again we have a child who is talking about an event that has occurred in the past in a different location. He is trying his hand as a raconteur—a person skilled in relating stories—and he includes several elements of the narrative form: character, action, and motivation.

Parents' Role in Nigel's Performance.   Applebee and Langer (1984) make the following observations about the role of Nigel's parents in his fledgling performance as a storyteller. This is an instance of ''scaffolding''—where the novice puts language to a use that is new to him or her in contexts where the more skilled language user provides support. The structure provided by the skilled language user is gradually internalized by the novice who eventually learns to engage in this new use of language conventionally and without outside support (or scaffolding). These authors make the following observations about Nigel's efforts at storytelling.

1. The parents' questions are embedded in the child's attempt to complete a task that he has undertaken but cannot complete successfully on his own; Nigel responds well to the questions because they serve his own intentions.
2. The questions are structured around an implicit model of appropriate structure for a narrative; they solicit information that will make the child's narrative more complete and better formed.
3. At times, the parents directly model appropriate forms that Nigel is in the process of mastering, recasting or expanding upon the child's efforts without ''correcting'' or rejecting what he has accomplished on his own.
4. Over time, the patterns provided by the parents' questions and models are internalized by the child and are used without external scaffolding in new contexts. In turn, the scaffolding the parents provide can be oriented toward the next steps in Nigel's growth as a language user. (Applebee & Langer, 1984, p. 184)

Some Generalizations: Parent-Child Interactions That Facilitate Development

Parent-child interactions that facilitate the child's language development have five characteristics:

Intentionality.   Children have an overall purpose that the parent recognizes, and parents' efforts are motivated by the desire to help the child to accomplish this purpose.

Proximal Development.   Children attempt to do things with language that they cannot quite accomplish on their own, but that can be accomplished with the help of an experienced language user. Facility with the use of language in question is not so much ''ripe'' as ''ripening.''

Collaboration.   The parent questions, expands, and recasts the child's efforts without rejecting what the child has accomplished on her or his own. The parent's responses are collaborative rather than evaluative.

Internalization.   As the child gains facility with the use of language in question, the ''leading from behind'' or ''scaffolding'' on the part of the parent becomes unnecessary.

Continuous Development.   As facility with a language use matures, new intentions to use language begin to ripen and the process continues.

These five characteristics of parent-child interactions that facilitate the child's language development are similar to Applebee and Langer's (1984, p. 185) five aspects of "natural language learning." For the purposes of this book, I chose to create a some-what different list, rather than adopting theirs.

Studies of parent-child interaction underscore the inappropriateness of the bottom-up, behaviorist style of teaching satirized by Holt in the passage just quoted. Parents try to gear their language to the child's language; they work with the child to establish whatever meaning the child is attempting to create. They do not set up a priori catego-ries of "easy" and "hard" and work on the easy things (whether linguistic or concep-tual) until they are mastered and only then proceed to the more difficult.

Children learn language and language use through interactions with experienced language users (parents and teachers, among others). In homes, these interactions are almost exclusively collaborative rather than directive. In schools, directive interactions appear more frequently due in large part to the necessity that arises when one teacher has many students; but the importance of collaborative interactions between teachers and students and between students as a group should never be underestimated.

Contrasting Home and School

Due in part to the fact that a single teacher usually has many students, the characteristics of parent-child interactions that facilitate development are absent to some degree from typical teacher-student interactions. In school it is more common for the teacher to decide the topic and to attempt to engage students, elicit responses from them, and cause learning to occur. That is, teachers tend to be more *directive* than parents.

However, teachers can choose to be more or less directive, or more or less collab-orative. Charlotte's style of teaching is based on the assumption that learning occurs best when teachers determine what a child should learn next, initiate lessons, and eval-uate the children's success. Charlotte is sensitive to student's proximal development and strives to have them internalize what she teaches them, but she is directive by design.

Matthew's style of teaching is based on the assumption that learning occurs best when his interactions with students are like parent-child interactions. If you review the description of Matthew's teaching practices, you will see much of what he does is motivated by the desire to incorporate intentionality, proximal development, collabora-tion, and internalization into his teaching. He is directive only insofar as is necessary to maintain a workable program. He will presumably become less directive as his teaching skills improve.

Scientists who have studied the relationship between language and cognitive devel-opment, on the one hand, and social interaction, on the other, have made other discov-eries that motivate Matthew's teaching strategies. In the next section I will turn to the work of scholars who have examined the way different societies and cultures effect the language and cognitive development of their members.

SOCIETY AND LANGUAGE

Once it has been recognized that development of cognition and language depends on social interaction, further questions arise: Do different communities provide different kinds of social interactions so that differences in cognitive and linguistic development occur between communities? Within communities, do different individuals have different social interactions such that differences in cognitive and linguistic development occur between individuals in a community?

These, of course, are educators' questions. If we can identify the kinds of community and/or the kinds of social interactions within communities that best develop the cognitive and language performance of individuals, we can apply this knowledge to our classrooms.

I will discuss these questions first. Then in the second part of this section I will discuss the implications these questions have for teaching reading.

Vygotsky's Account of the Development of Meaning

Vygotsky (1896–1934) was a Russian psychologist and educator who first became influential in America when his monograph *Thought and Language* was published in English in 1962 (see Vygotsky, 1986). More recently, in 1978, another collection of his essays has been published as a book entitled *Mind and Society*.

Vygotsky was a rationalist and a nativist like Chomsky and Piaget. Vygotsky believed that the *range* of possibilities for cognitive development are predetermined by the genetic endowment of human beings; however, he believed that the *actual* cognitive development of an individual is determined in part by his or her interaction with other human beings in society. Vygotsky's preoccupation with the role of social interaction can be seen in his discussion of how meaning develops for a child.

According to Vygotsky, meaning is always developed in society—in interaction with other persons—and later becomes internalized. The act of pointing is an example. Extending one's finger may be a random or meaningless act, but if one extends a finger *at* something and intends to direct the attention of others toward the object, the act has meaning. Such meaning can only arise in interaction with others.

Vygotsky suggests that this meaning arises when a child tries unsuccessfully to grasp an object and the act is *interpreted by others* as the child's directing their attention. Soon the child associates his or her gesture with the resulting behavior of others, and the gesture takes on meaning. The crucial elements of this example are that meaning is not created in a child's mind and then conveyed to others; meaning arises in social interaction and then becomes established in the child's mind. This is a central tenant of Vygotsky's cognitive theory: that interpersonal (social) processes become intrapersonal (mental) processes.

Vygotsky's Beliefs About Instruction

Vygotsky's theory of development and his theory of instruction stem from the idea that a child can solve more difficult problems and employ more difficult concepts in collaboration with others than he or she can alone. Vygotsky calls the difference between what children can do alone and what they can do in collaboration with others the "zone of proximal development." Within this zone, the new concepts are developing through social interactions. These concepts have not yet been internalized, and therefore the child cannot cope with them alone.

Vygotsky defines learning as interaction with others in solving problems or dealing with concepts that one is not capable of solving or dealing with alone. His notion of instruction is to identify the child's zone of proximal development and to present problems and tasks to the child that he or she can work through in collaboration with peers or teachers. When children are then capable of solving this set of problems by themselves, they have reached a new level of development, and the zone of proximal development will also have changed; they will have moved to a higher level. (See Activity 2.B.)

ACTIVITY 2.B VYGOTSKY AND THE INTERACTIONAL PERSPECTIVE

Compare Vygotsky's beliefs about instruction with the five characteristics of parent-child interactions that facilitate children's language development: intentionality, proximal development, collaboration, internalization, continuous development.

Can you see how influential Vygotsky's thought has been on the development of the interactional perspective?

CULTURAL DIFFERENCES AND DIFFERENCES IN COGNITION AND LANGUAGE

Culture and Cognition

Vygotsky believed that differences in society would produce differences in cognitive development. He suggested an investigation among the Soviet people of Central Asia at a time when there was a concentrated effort to eliminate the widespread illiteracy that existed there. What Vygotsky wanted to know was whether literacy would change the way the people thought. The investigation was carried out and published by Luria (Luria, 1976).

Luria asked questions and presented problems to groups of people in this remote area of the USSR. For example, he would ask, "How would you explain a car to someone who had never seen one?" Illiterate peasants from remote villages gave such answers as, "Everyone knows what a car is." Or, "If you get in a car and go for a drive, you'll find out." Or, "If a person hasn't seen a thing, he won't be able to understand it. And that's that." But a man who worked on a collective farm and had had a ten week school course responded, "A car is a thing that moves fast, uses electricity, water and air. It covers great distances, so it makes difficult work easier."

This investigation indicates that if society changes—in particular, if literacy is introduced into a culture—the way the people think will change. An interesting aspect of this study is that the people were asked to solve problems where the "given information" was contrary to known facts. For example, the fact may be that the journey from Center Town to North Town is six hours. The interviewer would pose a problem like, "From South Town to Center Town is three hours on foot and from Center Town to North Town is three hours. How long would it take to get from South Town to North Town?"

With illiterate peasants such exchanges as the following occurred:

Respondent: No, it's six hours from Center Town to North Town. You can't get there in three hours.

Interviewer: All right, but try to solve the problem. Even if it's wrong, try to figure it out.

Respondent: No. How can I solve a problem if it isn't so.

Peasants with schooling or experience on collective farms, on the other hand, solved such problems readily.

This is particularly interesting because the same kind of problems were presented to adolescents by Piaget to determine whether they had reached what he considered the highest stage of cognitive development. Piaget believed that a child does not reach this stage until he has matured sufficiently to reach it—but he also implied that everyone, in all societies *will* reach this stage. Luria showed that adults in a culture may not demonstrate certain cognitive capacities, but that if changes take place in society, these capacities may suddenly become manifest.

Other psychologists (Cole & Scribner, 1974, for example) have made observations similar to Luria's in cross-cultural research but have placed a different interpretation on it. They believe that all levels of cognitive development appear in all cultures, but that habitual ways of dealing with problems and habitual ways of expressing oneself in language are determined by aspects of society and culture. These psychologists would say that the peasant in the foregoing example was capable of solving the problem but would not do so because in his culture it doesn't make sense to deal with premises that are contrary to fact. It's a school teacher's game, and these people simply have not had any experience with it or use for it. (See Activity 2.C.)

ACTIVITY 2.C VERIFY THIS DISCUSSION THROUGH OBSERVATION

I. Find a young person and pose a simple problem, but make some of the "givens" obviously contrary to fact. For example, if, in fact, the skating rink is a block from the subject's home and school is three blocks in the opposite direction, pose the following problem.

If it were three blocks from your home to school and six blocks further from school to the skating rink, how far would you walk from your house to the skating rink?

1. Does the child answer forthwith, or does he argue?
2. Is he or she able ultimately to solve the problem?
3. If the child has difficulties, do you blame a lack of maturation or a lack of experience or both?

II. Try this with people of various ages (6 years, 10 years, 15 years, a classmate).

Culture and Language

Others have noted the relationship between the way people live and the way they habitually use language. Basil Bernstein (1971, 1973, and 1975) is one of the best known proponents of the idea that different characteristics of groups in Western society (his studies were done in England) result in differences in the way people habitually express themselves in language. Readers who are familiar with the extensive work of Bernstein and his colleagues will recognize the influence of this work on the following discussion.

In a now-classic study, Shatzman and Strauss (1955) went into a small town that had been hit by a tornado and asked citizens to describe what had happened. Responses like (1) were typical of business owners and professionals. Responses like (2) were typical of people who had menial jobs, little education, and little political power. These are not quotations from the study. I invented them to make the point by exaggerating the characteristics of the responses of the two groups.

1. It came from the southwest and destroyed the Methodist church on the edge of town. The whole church was leveled, but the education building next to it wasn't touched. It touched down again, hit the Jones's farm about two miles north of town where it demolished the house and killed all five of them—the parents and three teenaged children.
2. Well it came in over Miller's pond and touched down and wiped out the church. Then it lifted and didn't hurt anything till it hit the Jones's and killed the whole family.

One way of explaining the difference is that the first group appears to take into account the fact that they are talking to strangers—people who are not familiar with the town and its people. The second group describes the incident as if they were talking to other townspeople who knew where Miller's Pond is, what church is near there, where the Jones's lived, and how many people there were in the family.

This difference *cannot* be accounted for in terms of how these people think or what they know. The latter group could describe precisely where Miller's Pond is so that a stranger would understand it, identify the church explicitly, and so on, and they knew they were talking to strangers. They would not have been surprised at questions seeking this kind of information. Without such direct questions from a stranger, however, it would not occur to them to be explicit; they would not see the need.

The difference *can* be accounted for in terms of the life experiences of this group compared to the life experiences of the first group. They are not used to giving information to strangers. They are used to talking to other townspeople in situations where precise descriptions and explicit identification are not necessary—where indeed such explicitness would be superfluous and would be thought strange. They are in the habit of being *implicit* rather than *explicit*. They don't have much practice using explicit language.

The business owners and professional people of the town, members of the first group, are used to talking to strangers in situations where explicit language is required. They have plenty of practice is using explicit language and in recognizing occasions where it is appropriate. They are in the habit of being explicit. On the other hand, this group undoubtedly has a lot of experience in talking to family, friends, and neighbors and they undoubtedly also use implicit language when it is appropriate.

Failure to use explicit language appropriately is often observed when outsiders ask for directions from local people. I once asked a collector in a toll booth how to get to the Genesee County Museum, and she replied "Do you want to take Route 20 or River Road?" Of course, if I knew that I would not have asked the question. I can only presume she was new on the job and would gain experience with giving directions to strangers.

A linguist recounted a similar experience. She asked for directions at a gas station and was told to turn right at the puddle. After getting lost she learned that ''the puddle'' was dry during the summer (it was August), but all the local people knew where the puddle was. We can presume again that if this story got back to the gas station attendant, he would soon learn to give directions to strangers that did not rely on ''insider'' information. (See Activities 2.D and 2.E.)

ACTIVITY 2.D FINDING YOUR OWN EXAMPLES

Recount examples where people who are not used to dealing with ''outsiders'' gave directions that assumed the outsider had information he or she did not have.

Notice that your first reaction to such experiences might be that the person is not very bright. A more accurate explanation is probably that his or her experiences have not instilled the habit of using explicit language or in recognizing instances where it is appropriate.

Share your stories with classmates and discuss the source of the problem. Was it more probably cognitive limitations or lack of experience in using explicit language?

What questions on the part of the listener would have cleared up the difficulty?

ACTIVITY 2.E CHECK PEOPLE'S SENSITIVITY TO THE NEED FOR EXPLICIT LANGUAGE

I. Ask several people to write a grocery shopping list of nine items they might need. Ask them to write a list of the same items that they would give to a stranger who was going to shop for them.

You may notice that some people write very cryptic lists for themselves, such as List A, and very explicit lists for strangers, such as List B.

List A

1.	fruit	4.	yogurt	7.	beans
2.	tp	5.	turkey	8.	soap
3.	milk	6.	lettuce	9.	cat

List B

1. Six oranges, six apples, and three bananas—if bananas are under 25 cents a pound.
2. Toilet paper—cheapest.
3. Half-gallon skimmed milk
4. Low-fat yogurt with fruit. Not strawberry—cheapest. Four 5-oz containers.
5. Two 1-pound packages of Mr. Turkey frozen turkey.
6. Lettuce. Whatever is on sale but not iceberg.
7. One 40-oz can of dark red kidney beans.
8. One medium-sized Rinso. Not family size.
9. One 5-pound bag of dry cat food. Whatever is cheapest, but not No Name.

What would you make of people who write nearly the same list for themselves as for strangers?

II. Use this activity to teach about the need for explicit language and to give practice in using it.

Tell your subjects who write nearly the same list for themselves and for strangers what you would buy if you had their list. For example, for *milk,* you'd buy 2 gallons of whole milk.

Ask them if that is exactly what they wanted. If it isn't, ask what they would have to write on the list to get exactly what they wanted.

You will probably find that these subjects have the ability to be explicit but that they are not sensitive to the need for using explicit language and are not in the habit of using it.

Implicit Language. Implicit language arises where the experiences, knowledge, and attitudes of the participants are so closely shared that the need to rely on speech for communication is reduced. Such participants are steeped in their familiarity with each other and with the topic. Nonverbal means of communication gain importance, circumstances and manner of speech assume importance over content, and meanings tend to be descriptive and narrative rather than analytical or abstract.

Imagine the communication among three men who are old friends watching a Sunday afternoon football game. Chances are that a written transcript of their speech would not make sense to an outsider who did not know what they were doing. Such language is implicit and relies on context to convey meaning. Since each speaker knows the others share his information and attitudes on the topic, facts and attitudes are referred to implicitly or left unstated.

Explicit Language. Explicit language arises where participants are conscious of their lack of familiarity with one another, or where the speaker is conscious of the listener's lack of familiarity with the topic. Reliance on nonverbal means of communication is reduced; content is more important than circumstances or manner of speech; and analytical and abstract meanings are more likely.

Imagine a person discussing an automobile accident claim with an insurance investigator on the telephone. Outsiders reading a transcript of this exchange would probably understand it very well without detailed knowledge of the context of the discussion. (The speakers would not, in fact, share a physical context if they were on the telephone.) Such language is explicit and conveys meaning without relying on context. Since neither speaker can be sure of the other's information or attitudes on the topic, facts and attitudes are stated explicitly, and questions asking for further information and clarifications are frequent.

As described earlier, isolation is one factor that leads to the habitual use of explicit language. The following are three other characteristics of communities or families that are believed to encourage the use of implicit language and do not give youngsters much practice in using explicit language:

1. Authoritarian parents who will not discuss decisions with children
2. Parents who feel powerless in society and who do not articulate plans for the future or to deal with problems
3. Homes and neighborhoods that do not tolerate nonconformity and therefore impose uniform beliefs and attitudes.

Of course, the opposite characteristic of communities and families are believed to encourage the use of explicit language. Such characteristics are frequent contact with outsiders, parents whose style of authority encourages discussion of decisions, parents who feel powerful and frequently articulate plans for the future and ways to deal with problems, and homes and neighborhoods that are more tolerant of nonconformity and therefore encourage diverse beliefs, opinions, and attitudes.

Implications for Teaching Reading. Vygotsky's and Luria's views on the development of language and cognition, and Bernstein's views on the habitual use of implicit versus explicit language have all been influential in bringing about an interest in the sociological aspects of learning. All this intellectual activity has focused the attention of educators on the society of the classroom and its affects on learning, particularly on language development and learning language skills such as reading. (See Activity 2.F.)

ACTIVITY 2.F FINDING AND COMPARING EXAMPLES OF IMPLICIT AND EXPLICIT LANGUAGES

Audiotape-record 5 or 10 minutes of conversation at the dinner table in your home or comments between friends or family watching a sporting event on television.

Audiotape-record a few minutes of a lecture or a question-answer period in one of your classes.

Play these tapes in class and discuss the following.

How do the samples differ in terms of implicit and explicit language?

Are there examples of places where listeners fail to understand the tapes because they cannot see what the people on the tapes are looking at?

Are there examples of places where listeners fail to understand the tapes because the speakers rely on information and attitudes that they share but do not state in their communication?

Are there examples of places where speakers are particularly explicit? Do these examples seem to arise from presumed lack of shared knowledge and attitudes? Do these examples seem to arise sometimes simply from the speakers habit of using explicit language?

This activity should help you to become alert to the use of implicit and explicit language and the degree to which the speaker's habits determine whether they use implicit or explicit language.

School Success and Facility with Explicit Language

The child begins life by expressing meanings to a parent who is eager to establish the child's meaning. The child's meanings always arise out of the immediate physical or psychological context and are supported by these contexts. His or her language is implicit and context-dependent.

As children grow older, their audiences become more distant, less familiar, less intimately connected. Their language must become more explicit if they are to make themselves understood. Their meanings may remain context-related, but their communication partners become less willing to collaborate in establishing the children's meanings. Communication partners begin to insist on speaking about their own topics, at least part of the time.

In school these communication demands are intensified. Earlier in this chapter I discussed the fact that the communication style of classroom teachers is more directive than collaborative—in contrast to the communication style of parents dealing with preschoolers in the home. Children must learn to understand teachers, with whom they have no intimate connection, speaking about topics unrelated to the physical and psychological context. In turn, students must learn to make themselves understood by others with whom they have no intimate connection about topics that are unrelated to the physical and psychological context. The child, both as a listener and as a speaker, must learn to deal with explicit language.

The written language of the school intensifies these demands still further. Children must learn to read authors with whom they have no connection whatsoever; they must ultimately learn to read authors from distant locations, different cultures, and different times in history.

Written Language and Institutional Writing.   As the students' proficiency increases the written language they encounter takes on new characteristics that distinguish it from talk. These characteristics are associated with published, edited writing, and they become more pronounced as the child progresses through school and into adult life. Stubbs (1980) refers to the published, edited, written language of a literate society as "institutional writing."

Writing permits us to record language in a way that is accurate, permanent, and transportable. Writing overcomes the limitations of human memory. Its permanence permits us to check facts, correct errors, and revise after reflecting on what we have written. Because writing can be transported over great distances of time and space, it is often directed at a distant, unfamiliar audience rather than intimate acquaintances. As a result, institutional writing has the following characteristics:

> Institutional writing is public rather than private. It is not addressed to any individual, and the identity of the author is unimportant. The focus is on the content.
>
> Institutional writing is accurate. Writers can check facts and reformulate statements after reflecting on their accuracy, precision, and consistency.
>
> Institutional writing is explicit. It is intended for a large audience with whom the author is not intimately acquainted. Therefore the author cannot gauge the reader's knowledge, beliefs, and opinions with the same accuracy as is often possible in speech. Therefore, in institutional writing, facts are stated explicitly, descriptions and explanations are detailed, and arguments are spelled out precisely.
>
> Institutional writing is not redundant. Institutional writing is usually revised and edited both by the author and by an editor or editors. This process eliminates redundancy. Each sentence makes its unique contribution to the discourse, whereas in spoken language repetition is common. (See Activity 2.G.)

ACTIVITY 2.G CONTRASTING PERSONAL CORRESPONDENCE WITH INSTITUTIONAL WRITING

Stubbs (1980) distinguishes between institutional writing and personal correspondence. Personal correspondence retains many similarities to spoken language that result from the personal relationship between the writer and receiver, their familiarity with the topic, the shared experiences they have had regarding the topic, the informality of the language, and so on.

Share personal letters and notes with your classmates. Abridge them to retain confidentiality, if necessary. How often is clarification necessary for people who are barely acquainted with the receiver of the letter to understand it.

Rewrite these letters and notes so they can be clearly understood by classmates of the receiver, and observe how many characteristics of institutional writing appear in the rewritten version.

Spoken Language and Institutional Writing.   Implicit spoken language, the language spoken among people who are intimately acquainted with one another, tends to be quite the opposite of institutional writing. Such spoken language is private and inexact rather than public, detailed, explicit, and scrupulously accurate. It relies on reference to shared information, shared experience, and reference to things going on in the environment. Explicit spoken language, however, shares some characteristics of institutional writing. Such spoken language is public, detailed, and accurate.

For reasons discussed earlier in this chapter, some people have a great deal of experience with and a predisposition toward using explicit language, while others have little experience with using such language and are not accustomed to using it. Explicit language abounds in some homes and neighborhoods and is infrequently heard in others.

Since explicit language is typically the language of books used in school and the spoken language of the school, teachers should be alert to the possibility that reading difficulties as well as speaking, listening, and writing difficulties may result from a common source—lack of experience with explicit language. Just as in homes and in the larger community, facility with and the habitual use of explicit language is encouraged in a classroom community where there is frequent communication among individuals and *all* their classmates—not just self-selected few, a style of authority that encourages discussion of rules between teachers and students, empowerment of students, and tolerance of nonconformity.

On the other hand, teachers should be aware that gaining facility with explicit language in one language activity—speaking, listening, reading, or writing—can enhance facility with explicit language in the other three.

The Reading-Listening Connection.   As students become more exposed to the demands of institutional writing as readers, they are often also more exposed to the oral language in formal settings. Skills developed in comprehension of institutional writing will often improve a person's listening comprehension skills, and the comprehension skills gained in listening to formal oral language can bolster comprehension skills in reading institutional writing.

The Reading-Speaking Connection.   School offers numerous opportunities to speak in situations where explicit language is necessary for effective communication. Teacher-student conferences and small groups of students working together on a well-defined task offer excellent opportunities for this kind of language. By making effective communication the objective and giving the child feedback on his or her success in reaching this objective (in small groups by simply encouraging children to ask for clarification of others' remarks), all children gain facility with the use of explicit language—whether they are accustomed to hearing and using it outside school or not. Learning to use explicit language in speech will help children understand explicit language when they read.

The Reading-Writing Connection.   As students encounter more and more institutional writing in their role as readers, their own writing should be developing the characteristics of institutional writing. By the middle grades, typical questions and comments from teachers and fellow students regarding a student's writing might be

> Are you sure it was over one hundred and twenty degrees every day during your visit to Florida? (Be accurate. Check your facts.)
> The boy in your story [a fantasy] is only two inches tall, but you say he went upstairs. How did he get upstairs? (Be consistent.)
> You say it was a big house. How big was it? How many rooms? How many stories? (Be more explicit.)

> You said three times that the movie was boring. Why don't you tell us why it was boring. (Do not be redundant and be explicit.)

If things go well, students' reading comprehension is aided by what they learn as writers—that written language is accurate and explicit and not redundant. At the same time, they are encountering these characteristics more and more in their reading, which should help them to improve their writing.

Recently while teaching a writing workshop in an elementary school, I commented to the regular classroom teacher that one student was a particularly gifted writer. The teacher answered, "I know. She reads all the time." That may seem like a non sequitur, but there are few language arts teachers who would not understand and endorse the logic of the reply.

The Essence of Teaching Language Arts.   The essence of teaching language arts is not teaching such things as diction in speech, auditory discrimination in listening, the mechanics of forming letters in writing, or word recognition in reading. The essence of teaching language arts is teaching facility with explicit language—the language of institutional writing and public discourse. It is for this reason that language arts is a holistic, global affair. Facility gained with explicit language

> through reading makes students better speakers, listeners, and writers.
> through writing makes students better speakers, listeners, and readers.
> through speaking makes students better listeners, readers, and writers.
> through listening makes students better speakers, readers, and writers.

In language development, everything connects.

EXTENDING THE MEANING OF WHOLE LANGUAGE

Integrating the Language Arts

In discussing the meaning of the term "whole language" up to this point, I have been focusing on the idea that whole language describes teaching reading as a holistic process rather than an atomistic process. Having developed the idea that what children learn through listening, speaking, reading, and writing is closely connected, and that what they learn in one area facilitates growth in all others, I want to return to and emphasize another important aspect of the whole language approach. That is, in the whole language approach, the teaching of reading, writing, speaking and listening is integrated.

In describing Matthew's and Charlotte's programs in Chapter 1, I described the way they taught reading, writing, handwriting, and spelling. Charlotte views these as separate subjects and teaches them in different time periods during the day. Matthew's reading program incorporates "books" children have written during their writing class, and there is a great deal of oral language involved in both activities. Matthew's writing program includes a great deal of talking, listening, and reading. Conferences with the teacher are at the heart of reading and writing lessons, and the children are encouraged to share with one another.

This integration of the language arts is a consciously designed part of a whole language program. Although most whole language teachers maintain a reading time and a writing time and focus special attention of speaking and listening in particular lessons, they consciously attempt to integrate the language arts so as to capitalize on the fact that what children learn in one area promotes growth in the others.

Forerunners of the Whole Language Approach

Holistic approaches to teaching reading have been used for many years. The *language experience approach* is used in some primary-grade classrooms, and the *individualized reading program,* sometimes referred to as the *literature approach to teaching reading,* is used in some middle- and-upper grade classrooms.

Holistic approaches to teaching writing have been used in upper grades and high schools for many years, as well. *Writing without teachers* and *cultural journalism* are examples of such programs. More recently, *the process approach to teaching writing,* also referred to as *the writing process approach,* has been introduced into the elementary school, particularly at the primary-grade level.

Because of their holistic, top-down nature, a certain amount of integration of the language arts is characteristic of all these programs. However, many teachers who adopt a holistic writing program still teach reading in very traditional ways, and many teachers who adopt a holistic reading program still teach writing in very traditional ways. In recent years the similarity of the holistic reading and the holistic writing programs, and the recognition of the common assumptions upon which they rest, has led a number of teachers to integrate a holistic reading program with a holistic writing program. The result is what has come to be referred to as the whole language approach.

This approach is *whole* is two ways. It rests on holistic, rather than atomistic, assumptions about language and learning language, *and* it views the language arts as unified or whole, rather than separate.

In the description of Matthew's classroom, we have a thumbnail sketch of what such a program is like. I will further describe the language experience approach (Chapter 3), the individualized reading program (also referred to as the reading workshop or literature approach to teaching reading) (Chapter 15), and the writing process approach (Chapter 15) later in the book. Readers who want more particulars about these programs at this point are encouraged to look ahead.

A Summary of Assumptions that Underlie the Whole Language Approach

Box 2.1 presents a summary of trends in the study of language and language development. These fields of study have moved away from empiricist, bottom-up, atomistic assumptions and toward rationalist, top-down, holistic assumptions.

The whole language approach to teaching reading and language arts grows out of this trend. It is consistent with the interactional perspective on language and development. It results in student-teacher interactions that have the characteristics of parent-

**BOX 2.1 EMPHASIS IN THE STUDY OF LANGUAGE
IN THE LAST HALF-CENTURY**

1940   **Typical concerns of phonologists**

Position of speech organs during speech production
Order of appearance of speech sounds in language development
Melody and rhythm of language (stress, pitch, juncture, cadence)
Identification of speech sounds, meaningful combinations of sounds (morphemes and words)

1950   **Typical concerns of grammarians (syntax)**

Word categories (nouns, verbs, etc.)
Word structure (plural, past tense)
Relationships between words and phrases (nouns and modifiers, subject-verb-object, etc.)

1960   **Typical concerns of semanticists**

Meanings of words in an intellectual sense (denotative)
Meanings of words in an emotional sense (connotative)
Meanings expressed between words (In "Mary learns Latin," *learns* expresses an action and
    Mary is the learner—the agent. In "Mary knows Latin," *knows* expresses a state or con-
    dition and Mary is the person in that state or condition.)

1970   **Typical concerns of cognitive psychologists who study language**

In what way does language development depend on physical maturity and general intellectual
    development and learning?
In what way does language development and use affect general intellectual development and
    learning?

1980   **Typical concerns of a person who studies language *use* in society**

What jobs can be done with language (give orders, express affection, ask for information,
    etc.)?
How is language use related to the kind of job being done, the context, the relationship
    between speakers?
What is the relationship among culture, thought, language development, and the use of lan-
    guage?

---

child interactions that facilitate language and cognitive development. It is consistent
with the view that language and cognition develop in collaboration with other members
of society, particularly those who are more accomplished cognitively and linguistically
than the learner. It encourages in classroom communities, those characteristics that foster experience with and habitual use of the kind of language that abounds in schools—
explicit language. (See Activity 2.H.)

COMPARING APPROACHES

I will end this chapter by recalling Matthew and Charlotte, the two second grade teachers discussed in Chapter 1. Charlotte is a traditional teacher. She is intelligent, well-
prepared, hardworking, caring, and responsible. You will find her in millions of class-

ACTIVITY 2.H RELATING THE WHOLE LANGUAGE APPROACH TO UNDERLYING ASSUMPTIONS

Discuss the characteristics of the whole language approach as it is described in Matthew's classroom. Include the following:

1. The rationalist, holistic, top-down sphere of influence in the study of language and learning. (See Box 1.1.)
2. The interactional perspective, particularly the characteristics of parent-child interactions that facilitate language and cognitive development (intentionality, proximal development, collaboration, internalization, and continuous development) as described on page 37.
3. The Vygotskian notion that language and cognition develop in social interaction with other members of a community including those who have more facility with language and learning.
4. The characteristics of homes and communities that are believed to encourage the habitual use of explicit language: frequent contact with outsiders, parents whose style of authority encourages discussions about decisions, feelings of power, and acceptance of nonconformity.

Four small groups might take one item each and report summaries of their discussions to the class.

rooms. Matthew is at the cutting edge of reading and language arts education. He is working toward becoming a whole language teacher. He too is intelligent, well-prepared, hardworking, caring, and responsible. You will find him in comparatively few classrooms.

You may have been anticipating the news that Matthew's students read better, write better, and are happier. Sorry. There are no hard data to back up this claim. You may have been expecting to learn that Matthew's way is easier. Very sorry. Good teaching demands hard work. As you will see in the comparisons that follow, to be effective, Matthew will have to work as hard as Charlotte, perhaps harder.

Orderliness and Perception of Being in Control

There is a certain orderliness about Charlotte's method that you don't find in Matthew's. She can tell you in which reading and spelling group a child is, what skills those groups have had, and what skills they are working on. Since children are almost always working in groups on assigned lessons, she can spot a child who is not "on task" in an instant. Charlotte, her principal, and her school district curriculum coordinators can feel certain that every child has received instruction in every facet of the curriculum on schedule throughout the year. In short, at any given moment Charlotte usually believes she knows "where she's at."

Since portions of Matthew's reading program and most of his writing program rely on projects that individuals initiate, students are often engaged in many different activities at any given time. Under these circumstances, it is more difficult to specify the skills a particular individual is working on at any given moment.

Matthew can tell you in which reading and spelling group a child is and what skills those groups have had. He can also look at the children's individual reading folders and tell you what books they have read and what skills they have covered in their conferences. But since the curriculum is not covered with every child in a specific order, Matthew cannot be sure, nor can his principal and district language arts curriculum coordinator be so easily convinced that everyone is covering the curriculum on a pre-determined schedule.

Demand for "Diagnostic" Skills

When a teacher-student conference begins, Matthew is never sure what problems will arise. The following are just three examples. He may:

1. Detect a phonics problem, teach an impromptu lesson, and note it in the student's file.
2. Discover an oral reading problem and assign the child to a group of students who are practicing oral reading under the supervision of a teacher aide.
3. Discover comprehension problems traceable to a lack of prior knowledge and suggest an easier book on the same topic or recommend that the child join a discussion group made up of students who have read the same book.

Recognizing a reading problem and knowing what is probably causing it is called "diagnosis." A whole language teacher needs to be an extraordinary diagnostician. Charlotte might need to further develop her diagnostic skills if she were to attempt a whole language approach.

Demand for Flexibility and Knowledge of Methods and Materials

Having identified a skill the child needs help with, the whole language teachers need to have a repertoire of teaching strategies at the tip of their fingers (if not in their heads) to cover all skills. Charlotte might need to develop teaching strategies that would make her more independent of the basal reader Teacher's Guide if she were to attempt the whole language approach.

Demand for Leadership and Management Skills

The whole language approach succeeds when the classroom is a learning *community*. Building and maintaining a learning community takes leadership and management skills. If Charlotte were to attempt the whole language approach, she might need to develop a different style of leadership and management.

Why, then, Whole Language?

The whole language approach has cultural ancestors. Many of the classroom practices advocated by John Dewey (1859–1953) and the progressive education movement, and the ideas that lay behind them, are easily translatable into the whole language classroom. I believe that if the whole language approach is to survive in the present, educators must consider why it has appeared in the past—and why it has disappeared.

I believe this approach has failed to become the predominant mode of teaching in the past because the teaching profession did not acknowledge the added demands and skills needed by the teacher nor did it acknowledge the need for teachers to understand the reasons why this approach is superior. Parents, principals, and other teachers come into a classroom and see some fairly untraditional activities and ask "Why are you doing this?" If the teacher is not able to respond convincingly to this question, pressures from outside will soon put an end to the program.

I believe that this approach keeps reappearing because of its essential rightness.

1. Compared with traditional approaches, it is more consistent with the way children acquire language and literacy before school age and outside school.
2. Based on what we know about language and society, it empowers students, giving them something to use language for and giving them the language skills to get on with *their* agenda.
3. Despite the fact that there is no hard data showing that this method produces better readers, it has never been tried consistently and found wanting; it has simply never been tried consistently.

WORKING TOWARD A WHOLE LANGUAGE APPROACH

Purists may object to my referring to Matthew as a whole language teacher. He does use a basal reader three days out of five; he does teach spelling words from a commercial series, and he does teach handwriting to some students in a step-wise fashion following a handwriting program. Why doesn't he teach reading entirely out of library books chosen by students and teach spelling and handwriting incidentally as the need arises while students pursue their own literacy goals in their literate community (Matthew's classroom)?

First, Matthew is working toward the whole language ideal, but he is moving slowly. Teachers with the best understanding and highest ideals who do not test their leadership and management skills in a traditional setting and who do not give these skills a chance to develop and mature may soon find themselves overwhelmed by management and discipline problems in a whole language setting. Nothing puts an end to a program more quickly.

Second, there is nothing a traditional teacher knows that Matthew doesn't need to know, and there are no methods a traditional teacher uses that Matthew may not find useful with some child at some time. To cite just one example, Matthew is familiar with the lessons, activities, and teaching suggestions in his basal reader on the topic of "function words" such as *the, a, an, of, between,* and *and.* His experience gained through using a basal reader has taught him three things in connection with function words.

1. He is aware that failure to recognize such frequently occurring words instantly can become a real problem to some students.
2. Knowing this is a problem, he recognizes it when he sees it in a reading conference.
3. He has some ideas on how to overcome this problem and knows where he can find materials to use for creating lessons and activities to overcome this problem.

This example leads into a third reason why Matthew is working toward a whole language approach while using traditional methods and materials. There are no whole language materials. Basal readers and the workbooks, exercises, and Teachers Guides surrounding them may continue to be part of the materials used by the whole language teacher. Of course, Matthew's commitment to the whole language approach will influence the way he uses such materials. For example, he is likely to skip a lesson on the sound the digraphs that *sh, ch,* and *th* usually represent (explained in Chapter 5) if he doesn't think this is a problem for the children in the group, but if a child reading the caption on another child's drawing pronounces *push* as "puss," Matthew would recognize that the child has a problem with digraphs and might introduce a lesson on digraphs to that child at that time.

Books like *Classroom Experience* (Gordon, 1984) recount traditional classroom teacher's experiences with coming to understand the assumptions that underlie the whole language approach and experimenting with methods that grow out of these assumptions. Matthew Nickelson, the teacher I created to introduce the idea of whole language teaching in Chapter 1, is based on accounts in this book. These are accounts of gradual conversions of teachers who are thoroughly familiar with traditional teaching methods, materials, and assumptions. I believe this is an excellent model upon which to implement the whole language approach and thus assure it will continue to gain ground.

Sound teaching decisions must be based on (1) knowledge of the assumptions that underlie methods and approaches and (2) consideration of special problems that arise in the classroom setting. Without this understanding the whole language approach does not stand much chance of being widely accepted or of having a lasting influence on teaching reading and language arts. With this understanding, it will undoubtedly gain wide acceptance and have a lasting influence on teaching reading and language arts.

I advocate the whole language approach. I have been watching its development over 20 years. I recently taught writing in an eighth grade class using the whole language approach. (I have not been a regular elementary school teacher for some time.) It worked. The classroom teacher agreed it worked, and although she did not adopt it herself (she had much in common with Charlotte), she told me that she adopted some aspects of it and that the children did a lot of "peer conferencing" on their own after their experience with the whole language writing class.

SUMMARY

In the 1980s, a group of scholars who study the influence of society on the development of language and cognition in individuals have become influential. One manifestation of their studies is the interactional perspective on language and learning.

According to this perspective, socialization of the child begins with a kind of "conversation" between parent and child that consists of taking turns in looking at one another and looking away, or looking at one another and then looking at the same object. From birth, infants communicate with parents, but their communication is neither intentional nor conventional. Meaning is attributed to children's cries, coos, gurgles, smiles, and grimaces by the parents who respond to the meaning they impose on the children's behaviors.

Soon children begin to attach meanings to their own behaviors because of their parents' responses, and communication becomes intentional. Idiosyncratic vocalizations soon take on mutually agreed-upon meanings between parents and children, and "language" occurs—but it is not conventional. Later the child adopts conventional vocalizations (words), and true language emerges that is meaningful, intentional, and conventional (more or less).

Oral language (and in literate societies, written language) continues to develop throughout life as a reiteration of this process. It is an interactive process, where the learner discovers uses of language and invents ways to accomplish them. Through the cooperation and collaboration of more proficient language users, learners discover conventional ways to accomplish these uses and become better at accomplishing them. I believe this perspective is based on accurate insights into the process of language development and that it applies also to the acquisition of literacy—reading and writing.

In analyzing exchanges between Mark and Nigel and their parents, the following kinds of growth were noted in the children. Over time, new uses of language (informative, interactional, regulatory, instrumental, and imaginative) emerge. Syntax becomes more complex and language becomes more conventional. Children progress from speaking about topics supported by the environment and ongoing activity to imaginative happenings and events that occurred in the past and in different locations.

The following behaviors of parents were noted. Parents' utterances are simple in form. Parents rarely introduce topics. Instead they talk about child-introduced topics that are supported by the environment and ongoing activity. They follow the child's lead. They support and extend what the child has said by restating it and adding new information. When children begin to talk about imaginary events or events that have occurred in the past, parents help by asking questions and making suggestions. This collaboration and negotiation of meaning with the child is referred to as "leading from behind" or "scaffolding."

The following characteristics of parent-child interaction that are believed to facilitate children's language development were noted: intentionality, proximal development, collaboration, internalization, and continuous development. The whole language approach encourages this kind of interaction between teachers and students. The efficacy of these interactions for language development is a major motive for implementing the whole language approach.

The interactional perspective grew out of the work of scholars who study language from a cognitive and sociological point of view. Vygotsky's work is particularly useful since he takes issue with the nativist position that cognitive development depends primarily on biological maturation. Vygotsky believed that, in cooperation with others who are more proficient in language and thought, children can operate on a higher cognitive plane than they are capable of coping with on their own, and that such cooperation with others facilitates development. Luria has shown that changes in social experience, such as schooling of previously unschooled people, results in advanced levels of cognitive development. Others have argued that changes in society, such as the introduction of schooling, do not result in a change in the capacity to think. Instead, changes in society change the way people habitually think.

Characteristics of groups within society may lead to differences in the language habitually used by individuals within groups. *Implicit language* arises where the experiences, knowledge, and attitudes of the participants are so closely shared that the need to rely on speech for communication is reduced. Experience, knowledge, and attitudes are referred to rather than explicitly stated. Nonverbal means of communication gain importance, and meanings tend to be descriptive and narrative, rather than analytical and abstract.

Explicit language arises where participants are conscious of their lack of familiarity with one another's experiences, knowledge, and attitudes. Experiences, knowledge, and attitudes are clearly stated. Reliance on nonverbal means of communication is reduced, and analytical and abstract meanings are more likely to be expressed.

Characteristics of homes and communities that encourage the use of explicit language are (1) frequent communication with outsiders, (2) a style of exercising authority that encourages discussion of rules and the reasons for them, (3) feelings of power among members, and (4) tolerance of nonconformity. Opposite characteristics of homes and communities encourage the use of implicit language and present fewer situations where explicit language is necessary.

The typical language of the school, and particularly the written language encountered in the school, is explicit language. As children go through the grades, they encounter "institutional writing," which is not only explicit, it is public, highly accurate, and nonredundant. In school, spoken language tends to be formal and takes on many of the characteristics of institutional writing. Children who are accustomed to hearing and using explicit language have an advantage from the start over children who are not accustomed to hearing and using explicit language. Teachers should be alert to the possibility that lack of experience with explicit language is at the root of students' difficulties with in school demands of all the language arts—speaking, listening, reading, and writing.

The following characteristics of classrooms encourage facility with and habitual use of explicit language. There is (1) frequent communication between individuals and a variety of their classmates, not just close friends; (2) a style of authority that encourages discussion of rules and reasons for them between teachers and students; (3) empowerment of students; and (4) tolerance of nonconformity.

Teachers should take advantage of the commonality of the demands placed on students in school in reading, writing, speaking, and listening. Integrating the teaching of the language arts optimizes the carryover of skill gained in one mode of communication to all the others.

The whole language approach grows out of beliefs and principles that have been developed in Chapters 1 and 2. It is based on rationalist, top-down, holistic assumptions about language and language development. It is consistent with the interactional perspective on language and cognitive development. It is consistent with the view that language and cognition develop in collaboration with other members of society, particularly those who are more accomplished cognitively and linguistically than the learner. It encourages student-teacher interactions that are similar to the kind of parent-child interactions that facilitate language and cognitive development. It encourages classroom communities with those characteristics that foster experience with and habitual use of the kind of language that abounds in schools—explicit language.

However, the whole language approach is predicated on the assumption that teachers are thoroughly familiar with the reading curriculum and have methods and materials at their fingertips. It makes exceptional demands on teachers' organizational and leadership skills. It makes exceptional demands on teachers' diagnostic skills. For these reasons, I suggest that beginning teachers use an eclectic basal reading program, but emphasize the importance of understanding the ideals of the whole language classroom and the assumptions upon which these ideals rest. From the first day, *as* they become familiar with the curriculum, methods, and materials, develop organizational and leadership skills, and develop their diagnostic skills, teachers should begin to implement the whole language approach and continue to move in that direction as their knowledge and skills develop.

FOR FURTHER READING

Ashcroft, L. (1987). Defusing "empowering": The what and the why. *Language Arts, 64*(2), 142–156.

Bagford, J. (1985). What ever happened to individualized reading? *The Reading Teacher, 39*(2), 190–193.

Boomer, G. (1984). Literacy, Power, and the Community. *Language Arts, 61*(6), 575–584.

Bandermann, E. (1985). Expanding suitcases and perspectives. *Language Arts, 62*(5), 509–513.

Buckley, M. H. (1986). When teachers decide to integrate the language arts. *Language Arts, 63*(4), 369–377.

Clay, M. M. (1986). Constructive processes: Talking, reading, writing, art, and craft. *The Reading Teacher, 39*(8), 764–770.

Giroux, H. A. (1987). Critical literacy and student experience: Donald Graves' approach to literacy. *Language Arts, 64*(4), 175–181.

Gordon, N. (1984), *Classroom experiences.* Portsmouth, NH: Heinemann.

Graves, D. H. (1983). *Writings: Teachers and children at work.* Portsmouth, NH: Heinemann.

Green, F. (1986). Language arts instruction: Lessons from the British. *Language Arts, 63*(4), 378–383.

Hall, N. (1987). *The emergence of literacy.* Portsmouth, NH: Heinemann.

Hansen, J. (1987). *When writers read.* Portsmouth, NH: Heinemann.

Harms, J. M., & Lettow, L. J. (1986). Fostering ownership of the reading experience. *The Reading Teacher, 40*(3), 324–329.

Kushner, D. (1989). From the personal world of childhood to the public world of school. *Language Arts, 66*(1), 44–51.

Lindfors, J. W. (1984). How children learn and how teachers teach? A profound confusion. *Language Arts, 61*(6), 600–606.

Manning, J. C. (1985). What's needed now in reading education: The teacher as a scholar and romanticist. *The Reading Teacher, 39*(2), 132–139.

McCallum, R. D. (1988). Don't throw the basals out with the bath water. *The Reading Teacher, 42*(3), 204–208.

Rasinski, T. V., Nathenson-Mejia, S. (1988). Learning to read, learning community: Considerations of the social context for literacy instruction. *The Reading Teacher, 41*(3), 260–265.

Rich, S. J. (1985). On becoming teacher experts: Accountability, freedom, and negotiation. *Language Arts, 62*(5), 533–538.

Rich, S. J. (1985). Restoring power to teacher: The impact of "whole language." *Language Arts, 62*(7), 717–724.

Searle, D. (1984). Scaffolding: Who's building whose building? *Language Arts, 61*(5), 480–483.

Shannon, T. (1988). The reading-writing relationship: Seven instructional principles. *The Reading Teacher, 41*(7), 636–647.

Silvers, P. (1986). Process writing and the reading connection. *The Reading Teacher, 39*(7), 684–689.

Simon, R. I. (1987). Empowerment as a pedagogy of possibility. *Language Arts, 64*(4), 370–383.

Solsken, J. W. (1985). Authors of their own learning. *Language Arts, 62*(5), 491–499.

CHAPTER 3

Beginning Reading: The Reading Readiness and the Emergent Literacy Models

In this final chapter of Part One, I will discuss "emergent literacy," which is one view of the way the ability to read (and write) develops in very young children in a literate society. Later, I will show that this view is based on observations of very young children whose experiences with reading and writing are responded to and nurtured by attentive adults who are willing to support the children's earliest notions of what written language is and how people use it as readers and writers. This view and the observations that lead up to it parallels the interactional perspective on the development of spoken language in infancy.

The idea of emergent literacy is quite recent, and it is very different from the notion of "reading readiness." Reading readiness is a long-standing and enormously influential model of how the ability to read develops in young children. Therefore, before introducing the emergent literacy model. I will explain the reading readiness model. As you might suspect, the reading readiness and the emergent literacy models emerge from the two traditions represented by Charlotte and Matthew in Chapters 1 and 2.

Since Charlotte and Matthew are second grade teachers, the brief description of their beliefs and practices in Chapter 1 did not involve beginning reading. Therefore, I am going to describe the *beginning* lessons of two fictitious first grade teachers, Donald Vader and Mary Weiss. The programs they follow have been chosen to demonstrate contrasting assumptions about how the ability to read develops in young children and the teacher's role in the process. I will refer to these descriptions in explaining and discussing the reading readiness and emergent literacy models.

ASSUMPTIONS THAT UNDERLIE BEGINNING READING INSTRUCTION

Observing Teachers Teaching: Donald Vader

Donald Vader is a first grade teacher who uses a phonics emphasis basal reading series. Following the teacher's guide, Donald begins reading instruction by directing the children's attention to a page in their books that is something like Figure 3.1 and saying:

Figure 3.1. A typical first page in a phonics-emphasis basal reader.

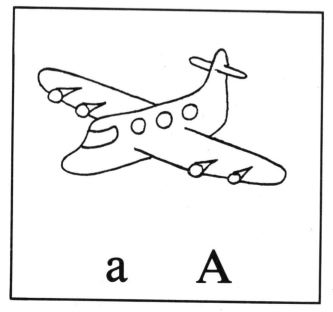

This is the letter "a." "A" stands for the first sound in *airplane*. "A" stands for the first sound in *an, ant, accident,* and *animal.*

He then introduces a variety of activities to give the children experience with identifying the form of the letter *a* and the sound /a/ and with associating the two. The following are some example activities the class might engage in over the next few days.

1. The children are each presented with a small card with the letter *a* printed on it, and they play a game. The children hold up their cards while Donald pronounces words such as *as, an, ant, be,* and *afternoon.* The object of the game is for the children to quickly put their cards down when they hear a word that does not begin with /a/.
2. They are directed to use their fingers like a pencil and draw over the letters *a* and *A* as the teacher says words beginning with /a/.
3. They write upper- and lowercase *A*'s on the chalkboard.
4. They underline words on the chalkboard that do not begin with *a,* as in the following set:

Alma	act	do
am	it	Alice
boy	on	art

5. They put circles around each *a,* as in the following set:

o	a	d	a	e
e	a	a	c	o

6. They print an *a* next to pictures as in Figure 3.2 whose names begin with /a/.
7. They put a circle around *a*'s as in the following set:

A	B	C	A	O
a	c	a	o	g

8. They cross out the letter that does not belong in each row as in the following set:

A	A	A	L
a	c	a	a

The next lessons take up the letters *e, i, o, u, m, n, r,* and so on. At the point that *m* is introduced, children are taught that by blending the sounds of the letters *a* and *m,* a word is formed and that words are made of several sounds together. Thereafter words are introduced made up of the letter-sound relationships that have been taught (*am, Nan, an, Ann, man, men, in, on, ran,* . . .)

After repeated experiences

Figure 3.2.

identifying sounds at the beginnings of words and ends of words,
identifying letters at the beginnings of words and ends off words, and
identifying words,

poems and stories are introduced containing words that give students practice using the skills and knowledge of spelling-sound relationships that they have been taught in these lessons. (See Activity 3.A.)

Observing Teachers Teaching: Mary Weiss

A typical beginning lesson using the language experience approach is as follows. Mary Weiss gathers her first graders around a table and uncovers a cage containing a white mouse. She opens the cage and soon the mouse ventures onto the table. She asks, "What do you think we should call her?" Billy suggests, "Whitey," and Mary prints WHITEY on the top of a large sheet of lined paper on an easel where all the children can see. She asks the children to tell something about Whitey and says she will print what they say on the paper. Soon the paper contains the following "story."

ACTIVITY 3.A EXAMINING PHONICS-EMPHASIS BASAL READERS

The following programs are frequently identified as phonics-emphasis basal reading series:

Economy Reading Series published by McGraw Hill, 1986.
Lippincott Basic Reading published by Scribner, 1981.
The Headway Program published by Open Court, 1985.

1. Examine copies of the Teacher's Editions for the beginning levels of each series.
2. "Teach" some of the beginning lessons to your classmates. Do you agree that I have fairly described the way these programs approach beginning reading?
3. The charge is sometimes made that these series lead beginning readers to believe that reading is associating meaningless letters with meaningless sounds. I have always thought that this is a somewhat unfair criticism. What evidence do you find in actually examining these programs that this is the case?

WHITEY

Patrick said, "Whitey sniffs on the table."
Molly said, "He looked at me."
Amy said, "Whitey has a long tail."
Ralph said, "I think she is a girl."

Mary then reads the story, pointing to each word as she says it. Next she asks the children to "read" with her as she points to the words and says them. Finally, she asks each child to draw a picture of Whitey, and she prints WHITEY at the top of each child's paper as they work.

The next day Mary reviews the story and asks the children to point to any words they know. Ralph points to his own name and the word WHITEY on the top line. Mickey recognizes Patrick's name and the word WHITEY at the top of the sheet. When asked if he sees the word Whitey anywhere else in the story, Mickey finds it in the third line. Lavonne appears to be able to read the entire story, relying somewhat on her memory of who said what, but relying also on her ability to recognize printed words.

Mary has engaged the students in an interesting and lively activity. She is not only teaching, she is observing what the children know. She is encouraging those who know things to share what they know with others.

As days and weeks pass, Mary continues to write stories with the children, to read the stories with the class, and to review them, encouraging individuals to identify words they recognize from day to day. Soon she begins to print the words each child recognizes by sight on small cards and to give these words to the child for his or her "word bank." After a couple of weeks of collecting words, Ada has 25 words in her word bank. Mary asks her to look at her words and to find two words that begin with the same sound as *bake* (one of Ada's words). Mary points out that the two words (*ball* and *best)* begin with the same letter. Ada is ready to begin to learn about sound-letter correspondences and about the names of letters if she does not know these things already.

In the language experience approach, children are encouraged to discover principles governing communication and language (including written language) through experience with language. Their discoveries are recognized, encouraged, and built upon. One of the great advantages of these programs is that children are given control over the language that will become their reading text. This retains some of the characteristics of the ideal home where parents follow the child's interest and "lead from behind."

Word recognition skills, the topic of Part Two, are an important part of the program. Skills are taught on an individual or small group basis as children appear to need them. They may not be taught explicitly to children who appear to catch on to them through experience with reading. They are not taught systematically since different children encounter difficulties with different skills, and even children who encounter difficulty with the same skills are likely to encounter them in a different order. But to repeat, since this is a point that is often misunderstood, word recognition skills are an important part of the language experience approach.

Dozens of experiences and activities with written language, such as the following, go on every day in Mary's classroom to reassure children that writing makes sense, that it means something, that it gets jobs done, that it communicates in the same way that spoken language does.

> Children dictate stories to teachers and older students who write them down.
> Teachers read storybooks to children.
> Children invent stories while turning pages of wordless picture books.
> Children write stories, journal entries, and news items.

Of course, you have recognized that Mary's language experience approach rests on whole language assumptions.

Some books that describe the language experience approach are *Language Experiences in Communication* by Roach Van Allen (1976), *The Language Experience Approach to the Teaching of Reading* by R. G. Stauffer (1980, rev. ed.), *Teaching Reading as a Language Experience* by MaryAnn Hall (1981), and *Key Words to Reading: The Language Experience Approach Begins* by Jeanette Veatch and others (1979). (See Activity 3.B.)

THE TRADITIONAL CONCEPT OF READING READINESS

In their excellent review of the history of the concept of reading readiness, Teale and Sulzby (1987) show that until the 1920s "The general belief was that literary development did not begin until the child encountered formal education in school" (p. viii). By the 1920s early childhood and kindergarten began to be viewed as a "period of preparation" and the concept of *reading readiness* took root.

From the start, reading readiness research was directed at identifying factors that "enabled children to be 'prepared mentally' for reading" (p. ix). The "factors" that researchers looked for were kinds of knowledge and skills that were presumed to be necessary *before* a child could learn to read.

A typical task designed to determine whether a child is ready to learn to read is shown in Figure 3.3. This task is designed to test a child's ability to make judgments about visual similarities and differences in familiar geometric shapes. This ability is referred to as *visual discrimination*.

ACTIVITY 3.B THE ASSUMPTIONS UNDERLYING DONALD'S AND MARY'S APPROACHES

Divide the class into three groups. Each group take one of the following discussion topics and report a summary of your discussion to the entire class.

I.   Bottom-Up or Top-Down?
     Has Donald adopted an atomistic, bottom-up approach or a top-down, whole language approach?
     Has Mary adopted an atomistic, bottom-up approach or a top-down, whole language approach?

II. A Psychological or Sociological View?
       The psychological view is based on the assumption that learning to read occurs when the individual is presented with the right stimulus at the right time and is rewarded for correct responses. The sociological view is based on the assumption that learning to read occurs when students' interactions within a literate community encourage them to initiate readinglike and writinglike behaviors that are supported by members of the community (including the teacher) who are more accomplished in literacy.
     Which view has Donald adopted?
     Which view has Mary adopted?

III. Assumptions about the Nature of the Reading Process
       The following two assumptions were discussed in Chapter 1.
       Reading is essentially decoding print into language.
       Reading is essentially a quest for meaning.
     Relate Donald's and Mary's teaching activities to these assumptions.

What would make anyone think that success on such a task is necessary before a child can learn to read? The reasoning goes something like this:

If a person is going to learn to read, he or she is going to have to be able to distinguish one letter from another and to distinguish one word from another. A child who does not recognize a difference between *bad* and *dad* is likely to have trouble learning to read. But, since the alphabet is probably a very strange set of symbols to prereaders and since the difference between *bad* and *dad* may be quite subtle for persons not familiar with the alphabet, it might be wise first to identify children who can see that (in Figure 3.3) the two triangles are alike, while the circle, square, and diamond are each unique in the set. People who are able to make these kinds of visual discriminations, it is assumed, are better prospects for learning to read than are people who cannot make these kinds of discriminations.

Figure 3.3. Task A

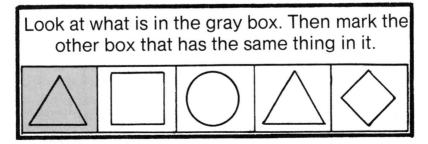

Concepts of Reading Readiness Incorporated into Published Tests

In this section a variety of items that are found on reading readiness tests will be presented, and the assumptions underlying them will be examined. Items will be presented in four broad categories according to the assumptions that appear to underlie them.

Visual and Auditory Discrimination.   One assumption underlying reading readiness test items is that to learn to read is to learn a set of specific skills that—when put together—make up the act of reading.

When one thinks of reading as putting together symbols and sounds so that individuals can say words when they see them, two kinds of skills appear to be necessary for learning to read: visual skills and auditory skills. To match sound to symbol one would expect that a person can tell one symbol from another and can distinguish one speech sound from another. Therefore tests of visual and auditory discrimination are frequently included in batteries of reading readiness.

In addition to Task A (Figure 3.3) other items designed to test visual discrimination are like Task B (Figure 3.4), where the task is to identify identical shapes among unfamiliar figures.

A typical item designed to test auditory discrimination would ask the student to match pictures of things that begin with the same sound. The correct response to Task C (Figure 3.5) would be to mark the picture of the rope as the teacher says the names of the pictures and asks which starts with the same sound as *road*.

Another test of auditory discrimination is to identify pictures of things whose names rhyme. The correct response to Task D (Figure 3.6) is to mark the picture of the jet as the teacher says the names of the pictures and asks which ends with the same sound as *net*.

Notice that the foregoing tasks do not involve print. The tasks involve oral language, pictures, shapes, and figures (but not letters).

Alphabet Knowledge.   A second set of reading readiness tasks *does* involve printed letters and words. The assumption underlying these tasks is that to find out whether a

Figure 3.4. Task B

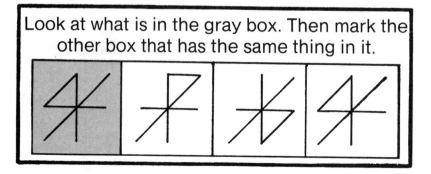

Figure 3.5. Task C

Figure 3.6. Task D

child is ready to learn to read, one should see if the child has the knowledge and skills that one teaches in the beginning stages of reading instruction.

Examples of such items are tasks where the student draws a line through the identical letters in Task E (Figure 3.7) or the identical words in Task F (Figure 3.8).

Although Tasks F and G use letters and words, the student would not necessarily need to know the names of the letters or recognize the words involved to perform satisfactorily. Task G (Figure 3.9) requires that the student know the names of the letters. The student's task is to put a mark on the letter in the row that the teacher names.

Tests of letter-name knowledge are also given individually. The teacher shows letters to the student, and the student tells the name of the letter.

Other items test letter-sound relationships in words. In Task H (Figure 3.10) students are asked to mark the picture whose name begins with the letter in the box, and in Task I (Figure 3.11) they are asked to mark the picture that ends with the sound of the letter in the box.

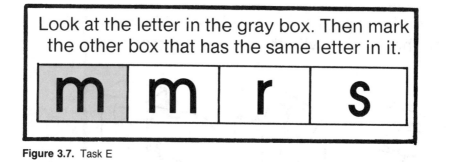

Look at the letter in the gray box. Then mark the other box that has the same letter in it.

m	m	r	s

Figure 3.7. Task E

Look at the word in the gray box. Then mark the other box that has the same word in it.

cat	mat	cut	cat

Figure 3.8. Task F

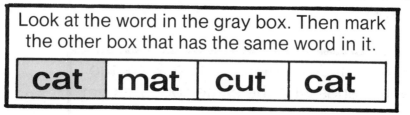

Mark the letter "C."

a   c   o   d   r

Figure 3.9. Task G

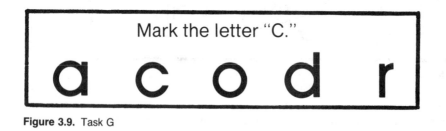

Look at the cup, pin, and fork. Mark the picture that begins with the sound of the letter in the box.

f

Figure 3.10. Task H

Look at the broom, banana, and mug. Mark the picture that ends with the sound of the letter in the box.

Figure 3.11. Task I

Word Learning Tasks. A third kind of task is called a word learning task. The assumption underlying such a task is that to find out whether children are ready to learn to read one should try to teach them to recognize words in print and discover whether they learn.

For example, children are taught words such as *walk, fly,* and *swim.* The children are shown the words printed on the board, and the children say the words as the teacher points to them. The words are presented on flash cards, and the children say them as the teacher presents each card and matches the word on the flash card to the word on the board. The words are used in several sentences by the teacher as the students look at the words: "Birds can fly. Airplanes can fly. You and I can't fly—except in an airplane." The teacher asks questions and holds up a card, and the students must know the word on the card to answer: "Can fish do this (holding up *swim*)? Yes, fish can swim."

Children are then tested on recognizing the words as in Task J (Figure 3.12). The test may be repeated an hour later.

Oral Language Comprehension. A fourth kind of task tests the students' understanding of oral language. The assumption underlying these tasks appears to be that reading is a language comprehension skill and that if children understand oral language, they will probably become good readers.

In an example of an item testing vocabulary knowledge, the child might be shown

Figure 3.12. Task J

Put a mark on the word
<u>swim</u>.

train   swim   build

Figure 3.13. Task K

a series of pictures as in Task K (Figure 3.13) and told to "put a mark on the picture of the baby."

In an example of an item testing oral sentence comprehension, the child might be shown a series of pictures as in Task L (Figure 3.14) and told to "put a mark on the boy who is following the girl."

Predicting Who Will Learn to Read

Most reading readiness research was done on a model that is very easy to understand. If you believe that a certain skill such as naming letters is a necessary prerequisite to learning to read, you can test children on letter names before reading instruction begins. If most of the children who know their letter names learn to read and most of the children who do not know their letter names do not learn to read, one would have strong evidence that learning letter names is an important prerequisite to learning to read. But studies are not usually that clear cut. What usually happens is that success in learning to read is far from infallibly predicted by scores on such tests as letter naming.

Using statistics, however, you can tell whether there is a relationship between children's scores on tests of letter naming that are administered before reading instruc-

Figure 3.14. Task L

tion begins and tests of reading that are administered after a year or so of reading instruction.

A frequent and consistent finding of research is that letter-name knowledge is among the best predictors of success in learning to read. Visual discrimination, performance on word learning tasks, and vocabulary knowledge have also been found to correlate with later reading achievement.

Two Applications of the Readiness Concept

If They're Not Ready, Wait. Two reasons were generally put forward when the question "Why test readiness?" was asked. One was that by testing readiness, the teacher could decide which children should begin to receive formal instruction in reading. That is, one tests readiness to *select* children for reading instruction. In the 1930s and 1940s educators talked about "neural ripeness" (Harris, 1940). The assumption was that children become ready to read or "ripen" at different rates or at different ages and that readiness tests identified children who were ripe. Teachers were advised to wait until children passed readiness tests before beginning to teach them to learn to read. Both this assumption and the advice that followed from it were challenged almost as soon as they were proposed. I will discuss the reasons for these challenges on the next several pages.

Predicting Individual Success on the Basis of Correlations. Success or failure on individual tasks like A through L (Figures 3.3 through 3.14) or on tests made up of combinations of these tasks do not infallibly predict success in learning to read. Although correlations between reading readiness tests and later reading scores are statistically significant, that simply means that low scorers on readiness tests *tend* to get low scores later on reading tests and high scorers on readiness tests *tend* to get high scores later on reading tests. But in a large group some students can get high scores on one test and low scores on the other and the correlations may still be significant.

A good analogy to keep in mind is that U.S. government studies have shown that there is a significant correlation between cigarette smoking and incidence of lung cancer. But it is not possible to say with any certainty whether a particular cigarette smoker will contact lung cancer. In the same way, studies have shown a significant correlation between failure on certain reading readiness tasks and low reading achievement test scores after instruction. It is not possible to say with any certainty whether a particular student who failed these reading readiness tasks will fail to learn to read. And, just as we cannot be certain that an individual who does not smoke will not contract cancer, we cannot be sure that an individual who can perform reading readiness tasks will learn to read.

Effects of Withholding Instruction. It has been shown that when schools identify children who are likely to fail, the children usually do fail. It has been suggested that at least some of these failures are due to the phenomenon of the "self-fulfilling prophecy." Subtle changes of teachers expectations and differential treatment of children increase the likelihood of failure. (Rosenthal & Jacobson, 1968). Lee and Rubin (1979) have argued that "the decision in advance that certain children are high risk candidates for learning to read, and subsequent treatment of them as such, cannot help but provide negative feedback" (p. 271).

The practice of segregating children who are not ready—by whatever criteria—from children who are ready to learn to read is thoroughly out of keeping with the Vygotsky, Piaget, and Interactional-interpersonal explanations of language development. As stated in Chapter 2, Vygotsky (1962, rev. 1986) believed that school learning should concentrate on areas of cognitive development that pupils cannot handle on their own, but that they can work through with others who are more advanced in the area. Piaget placed great emphasis on learning through interaction with peers (Brainerd, 1978). Observers who are influenced by the top-down, whole language school of thought would agree that a good way to keep a concept or skill from developing would be to keep children who do not have the concept or skill segregated from children who do.

The idea of using readiness tests to select children who are "ripe" for instruction has lost ground over the years, but you will still find many schools where primary-grade students are segregated for instruction on the basis of such tests.

If They're Not Ready, Get Them Ready!   The purpose of much of the research that was done in reading readiness was not to discover tasks that will enable teachers to select children for reading instruction but to discover the components of the reading task so that teachers know what to teach. Therefore, a second, frequently cited reason for administering reading readiness tests is to identify *necessary, prerequisite* skills that are lacking in a child with whom reading instruction is about to begin. This can be referred to as a "prerequisite subskills theory." Its followers believe that a child who is not ready must be taught these skills before reading instruction begins. The assumptions upon which this practice rests have also been challenged on the basis of research and classroom experience.

Research. It simply has not been shown that children must successfully perform all the tasks described Figures 3.3 through 3.14 before they will profit from reading instruction. There are two very consistent findings in reading readiness research. First, tasks that are the best predictors of success in learning to read are the tasks that most resemble reading (MacGinitie, 1969). For example, success on tasks involving geometric figures such as Tasks A and B (Figures 3.3 and 3.4) are not as reliable predictors of success in learning to read as are tasks involving letters and words such as Tasks E through J (Figures 3.7 through 3.12).

Second, training in skills that are quite clearly not reading, but are supposedly reading readiness (or skills prerequisite to reading), do not improve performance on skills that are clearly reading. For example, training on a task involving geometric shapes such as Tasks A and B (Figures 3.3 and 3.4) will not enhance performance on letter matching such as Task E (Figure 3.7) or word learning such as Task F (Figure 3.8)

Classroom Experience. Think about Donald's beginning lessons using the phonics-emphasis approach. It simply does not make sense to believe that success on a word learning task like the one described in connection with Figure 3.12 is a prerequisite to a student's success in these lessons. Whole word learning of this kind is not introduced into this approach until students are well into the program. Visual discrimination of letters, auditory discrimination of speech sounds, learning the names of letters, and matching letters to beginning and ending sounds in words *are* relevant to this approach, but they are *taught* at the initial stages. It is unreasonable to insist that students demonstrate these skills *before* instruction in the program begins.

In Mary Weiss's language experience approach, whole word learning does appear early, but the method is highly collaborative (the students select different words to learn, and the teacher helps them to remember them) in contrast to the teacher-directed word learning associated with Figure 3.12. Recognizing letters, learning the names of letters, and matching letters to beginning and ending sounds in words are not introduced until well into the program. As these skills become desirable, they are *taught* to those who have not acquired them from repeated experiences with written language and from each other. It is not reasonable to insist that students demonstrate these skills *before* instruction in the program begins.

Teale and Sulzby (1987) summarize their history of the "readiness movement" as follows:

1. The concept of reading readiness has been modified over the years, from "if they're not ready, wait" to "if they're not ready, get them ready."
2. By the 1980s reading readiness had become "firmly entrenched as the dominant approach" to beginning reading instruction.
3. The reading readiness approach leads one
   a. to view early childhood behaviors as precursors to "real" reading.
   b. to believe that only after the child has mastered the various subskills of reading readiness does the real part begin.
   c. to treat readiness skills as things that are taught in school in a fixed order and by direct instruction.

These authors conclude that "reading readiness was a good concept that got applied in a bad way." It was good in that it recognized that language development and certain kinds of knowledge probably facilitate learning to read and write. It was bad in that reading readiness programs are built on a bottom-up model developed by dividing early reading behavior into tiny skills, arranging them in a step-like fashion from easy to hard, or simple to complex—from an adult, accomplished reader's point of view. This view of learning to read might remind you of John Holt's satirical account of how an educator would teach a child to speak in Chapter 2.

For better or for worse, the beliefs, concepts, and vocabulary of the reading readiness model of beginning reading permeate the methods and materials used in beginning reading instruction in American schools. Programs to teach reading readiness skills appear in nursery schools and kindergartens, no longer as tests of readiness but as part of the teaching curriculum. Visual and auditory discrimination, alphabet knowledge, word learning tasks, and oral language comprehension are all incorporated into the initial stages of published reading programs at the point where they appear to be relevant to reading instruction. This was the state of affairs when emergent literacy, a contrasting view of how children go about learning to read, began to gain in influence.

EMERGENT LITERACY

In recent years educators have discovered that very young children learn many things about written language that cannot be attributed to formal instruction. The results are interesting and consistent. Just as children start with broad concepts about what they can do with speaking and listening, children also start with broad concepts about what reading is used for and what writing is used for. If permitted, they work out the details and learn the conventions *while using* reading and writing.

Observing Children Using Language V: Catching on to Writing

When "writing" their names and "signing" their papers and artwork, some 3-year-olds produced linear arrangements of marks, and they produced the *same linear arrangement of marks* when writing their names on different occasions. Examples can be found in Figure 3.15. These three-year-olds demonstrate that they know what writing is for and that they have discovered some of the characteristics of writing (Harste, Woodward, & Burke, 1984).

Observing Children Using Language VI: Catching on to Reading

When shown a Crest toothpaste box and asked to read what was written on the box, 3-year-olds responded with appropriate language such as "Brush your teeth," "Cavities," "It's called Aim." Some of them answered in fact "toothpaste" or "Crest." These 3-year-olds demonstrate that they recognize writing and know what it is used for (Harste, Woodward, & Burke, 1984).

Figure 3.15. "Signatures" of three-year-olds. (*Sources:* "Joshua" by Joshua Foels. Reproduced by permission of Beth Foels. "Curtis" by Curtis Woodward. Reproduced by permission of Gelia Woodward. "Allison" by Allison Glen. Reproduced by permission of Karen A. Glen. "Laura" by Laura Robinson. Reproduced by permission of Nancy Robinson.)

Joshua

Curtis

Allison

Laura

Observing Children Using Language VII:
Catching on to Story Form

Five-year-old Ashley wrote the ''story'' found in Figure 3.16. When Kris Scrimshaw, Ashley's kindergarten teacher, asked her to read the story, her intonation and delivery conveyed the idea that the letters at the top of the page are the title and the drawing is the story itself. Ashley read the story as follows:

The Runaway Elephant

The elephant squirted her and the girl couldn't find the elephant. But she finally found the elephant and they were friends again.

It can be assumed from her performance that Ashley's concept of ''story'' includes introducing characters and narrating some action. It can be argued that she has even introduced a problem and resolution. Her concept of ''writing a story'' is to make marks on paper that represent the story she has created. She has shown an understanding of conventions—the title comes first at the top of the page followed by the story itself. Ashley has a lot of details to get control of, but for a child who ''can't write,'' she shows a remarkable understanding of the imaginative use of language, of story form, of literary conventions, and of the function of writing. Similar examples can be found in Harste, Woodward, and Burke (1984).

Figure 3.16. Five-year-old Ashley's story. (*Source: The Runaway Elephant,* by Ashley Hatfield. Reproduced by permission of Joyce Hatfield.)

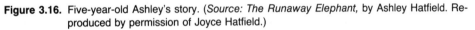

Observing Children Using Language VIII:
Catching on to Formal Aspects of Writing

The story in Figure 3.17 was written by a first grader (Cazden, Cordeiro, & Giacobbe, 1985). Roy has demonstrated in this story that he has certain broad concepts about written language. He has written a story with characters, conflict, a problem, and a solution. Although his printing is barely legible, and he does not employ standard spelling or standard punctuation, he has a concept of letter-sound relationships. He has a concept of what a period is used for—it comes at the end. He also has a strong sense of clauses and phrases. Each line ends at the end of a phrase or clause.

Commenting on Roy's apparent sense of where phrases and clauses end, Roy's teacher and her fellow researchers write of Roy and his classmates, "They have somehow learned more than we might have thought possible about . . . 'the structure of meaning' that punctuation indexes, and more than we could have explained even if we had tried" (p. 120).

In summary, here are some of the conclusions that can be drawn from the literature of what is currently called "emergent literacy." They are similar to the conclusions stated by Teale and Sulzby (1987, p. xvii):

1. Children exhibit reading and writing behaviors in the informal settings of home and community long before children start formal instruction.
2. Literacy develops in real-life settings and is used for real-life activities to "get things done."
3. Children learn written language through active engagement with their world. They interact socially with adults in writing and reading situations, they explore print on their own, and they profit from being presented with models of literate behavior by significant adults, particularly their parents. At a later stage children profit from similar social interactions with their peers.
4. The child develops as a writer/reader. The notion of reading preceding writing, or vice versa, is a misconception. Listening, speaking, reading, and writing abilities (as aspects of language—both oral and written) develop concurrently and interrelatedly rather than sequentially.
5. Although children's learning about literacy can be described in terms of generalized stages, children can pass through these stages in a variety of ways and at different ages. (See Activities 3.C and 3.D.)

ACTIVITY 3.C COMPARING THE READINESS MODEL TO THE EMERGENT LITERACY MODEL I

Compare the assumptions of emergent literacy with the assumptions on which the concept of reading readiness is built:

1. The reading readiness model views early childhood behaviors as precursors to "real" reading.
2. Only after the child has mastered the various subskills of reading does the real part begin.
3. Reading readiness skills should be taught in school, in a fixed order, and by direct instruction.

The cat climbed up the tree
because my dog scared the cat
My mom climbed up the tree
on the ladder to get the cat
The cat climbed
down the tree
A little of its skin came off.

Figure 3.17. Story written by a first grader. (*Source:* C. B. Cazden, P. Cordiero, and M. E. Giacobbe, "Spontaneous and scientific concepts; Young children's learning of punctuation," in G. Wells and J. Nicholls, eds., *Language learning: An interactional perspective* [Philadelphia: The Falmer Press, 1985], pp. 119–120.)

ACTIVITY 3.D COMPARING THE READINESS MODEL TO THE EMERGENT LITERACY MODEL II

Divide the class into four groups. Have each group take one of the following discussion topics and report a summary of your discussion to the entire class.

Relate the concepts of reading readiness and emergent literacy to

1. The teaching approaches of Matthew, Charlotte, Donald, and Mary.
2. The bottom-up, atomistic tradition and the top-down whole language approach.
3. The interactional perspective on language and learning.
4. The individual versus social concepts of learning.

PRESCHOOL AND KINDERGARTEN READING

Traditional Reading Readiness Skills

Tasks like Task A (Figure 3.3) are often used in preschool and kindergarten as a vehicle for achieving many legitimate objectives such as giving the children experience in using pencils, or in following directions. In such cases teaching visual discrimination would be a secondary objective, or perhaps not an objective at all. But many skills and concepts are taught in preschool and kindergarten on the assumption that they are relevant to the reading process or to reading instruction. Auditory discrimination and memory, visual discrimination and memory, and alphabet knowledge as exemplified by Tasks A through I (Figures 3.3 through 3.11) are often included in preschool and kindergarten programs.

There are additional skills and concepts that are taught in preschool and kindergarten explicitly because they are relevant to reading. They are often taught in combination with other objectives.

Concepts Related to Print and Reading

The following concepts are taught in many preschool and kindergarten programs:

1. Understanding that printing represents spoken language
2. Proceeding from left to right on a page
3. Proceeding from top to bottom on a page
4. Proceeding from page to page

Practice in proceeding from left to right and from top to bottom is worked into numerous activities in preschool programs. In reviewing the names of shapes, the teacher might hold up a triangle, and when the children name it, she will put it on the chalk board ledge or an easel and holds up a square. When the children name the square, she will put it to the right of the triangle. Soon several shapes are lined up, and the teacher reviews asking the children to name the shapes as she points to them proceeding from left to right.

On activity sheets as in Figure 3.18, children are directed to put a cross on the

Figure 3.18.

pictures that contain an animal starting at the top on the left side of the sheet and working across the sheet to the right, then to the next row, and so on. This might be a lesson in following directions, but practice with left-to-right and top-to-bottom processing is incorporated into the lesson as it is in other lessons having diverse objectives.

Children's artwork may be captioned and stapled into "books" that the children may go through, page by page, "reading" captions.

Teachers frequently read to children in preschool programs. Teachers may point to words as they read, holding the book up, and proceeding from page to page. Teachers sometimes create "big books" by copying illustrations and texts onto large chart paper so the children can see the text more clearly as the teacher reads and points (Slaughter, 1983). Commercial versions of such big books are also on the market.

Understanding the Vocabulary of Reading Instruction

Preschool and kindergarten programs include activities to teach children the meanings of terms that will be used early in nearly every reading program. A list of such terms is as follows.

above	letter	alphabet	in front of
after	line	beginning sound	looks like
before	next	begins with	next to
below	page	different from	rhymes with
beside	number	ends with	same as
end	under	first letter	sounds like
first	word		
last			

Preschool teachers take advantage of many opportunities to employ these terms in situations where the children will learn their meanings or get a wider understanding of their meanings. When the children are in line, the teacher may ask "Who is first in line?" "Who is last?" "Who is standing next to Ann?" In more formal lessons the teacher may ask the children to "find the one that's different from the others" in a row with three oranges and a banana.

However, all children have not had such experiences or have not benefited fully from such experiences. Some children may experience difficulty in reading lessons because they do not know the meaning of terms like those listed. When children are not performing as expected during reading instruction, the teacher must be alert to the possibility that it is a lack of understanding or a misunderstanding of the terms used in the instructions.

A formal procedure for discovering a child's knowledge of some of the concepts related to print and some of the vocabulary of reading instruction was developed by Clay (1972). Her "Concepts About Print Test" begins with the item "Show me the front of this book" and proceeds to test the child's knowledge of left to right progression, letters, words, punctuation marks, and so on. (See Activities 3.E and 3.F.)

Concepts Related to Storybooks

The following skills are taught in many preschool and kindergarten programs:

1. Following sequence of events in a story.
2. Recalling details to relate a story.
3. Interpreting pictures.
4. Making inferences.

Preschool and kindergarten curricula are replete with opportunities to learn, recite, recall, and listen to songs, poems, and stories. For example, teachers may teach songs like "There Was an Old Woman Who Swallowed a Fly" with the aid of cut-out "creatures." With each new verse the appropriate cut-out is added to the flannel board or easel. Children are then encouraged to recall what order the old woman swallowed the creatures after the cut-outs are scrambled. The same technique may be used with such poems as "The House That Jack Built" or stories like *Jenny's Hat* (Keats, 1966). In this picture storybook, Jenny thinks her hat is too plain, so on each page she adds a new decoration, including flowers, birds' nests, feathers, and so on. Some teachers bring in "props" to tell such stories and then leave them on a table where the children can come back to them and "play teacher," telling the story to others using the props.

ACTIVITY 3.E ADMINISTER THE "CONCEPTS ABOUT PRINT TEST"

The full details for administration of the Concepts About Print Test are given in *The Early Detection of Reading Difficulties: A Diagnostic Survey with Recovery Procedures*, 2nd edition by Marie Clay (1979).

Get a copy of this test and administer it to several kindergartners and first graders. It will heighten your awareness of the conventions and vocabulary connected with reading—conventions and vocabulary that accomplished readers respond to unconsciously, but that beginning readers must know or be taught.

ACTIVITY 3.F CREATING A SURVEY OF CONCEPTS RELATED
TO PRINT AND THE VOCABULARY
OF READING INSTRUCTION

It would be a useful exercise to create a survey of your own to explore beginning readers' knowledge of the conventions of print and the vocabulary of reading instruction.

1. Take a children's picture book and develop a list of questions about it to determine whether or not a child knows

—How to open a book.
—When a book is right-side up or up-side down.
—That when reading, people look at the print, and not at the picture.
—What words, letters, spaces, capitals, and punctuation marks are.
—That when reading, people go from left to right and top to bottom.
—What is meant by phrases such as
  —the words *under* the picture
  —the *beginning* of the line
  —the end of the line
  and so on.

Add to these phrases by consulting the "vocabulary of reading instruction" on page 79.

2. Administer your survey to several kindergartners and first graders. It will heighten your awareness of the conventions and vocabulary connected with reading—conventions and vocabulary that accomplished readers respond to unconsciously, but that beginning readers must know or be taught.

Children are also given experiences with interpreting pictures of happy faces, sad faces, and angry faces. Pictures such as Figure 3.19 are used to give students opportunities to make up stories, to retell stories presented by others, and to make inferences (Why is the girl sad?).

Such activities in preschool and kindergarten are universally approved of and are generally thought of as reading readiness activities since following sequence, recalling details, interpreting pictures, and making inferences are all skills that are demanded in reading and reading instruction. Although such experiences are obviously beneficial to children, reading instruction can begin with pupils who have not had these experiences in preschool. And, of course, because reading instruction begins is no reason why these experiences should stop. Such experiences should continue through the primary grades, and the skills used should be employed in relation to reading as the opportunities arise. (See Activity 3.G.)

ACTIVITY 3.G TESTING YOUR AWARENESS OF "READING"
ACTIVITIES IN THE PRESCHOOL CURRICULA

Visit a nursery school or kindergarten or view a televised educational show aimed at preschoolers. Record instances of attention to

1. Traditional reading readiness skills.
2. Concepts related to print and reading.
3. Understanding the vocabulary of reading instruction.
4. Concepts related to storybooks.

Figure 3.19. Telling stories and making inferences from pictures.

Handling the Concept of Readiness: A Phonics-Emphasis Teacher and a Whole Language Teacher

In the phonics-emphasis approach and the language experience approach, the teacher has many opportunities to observe pupil performance and to identify children who are not performing as expected. Both Mary Weiss and Donald Vader will ask traditional ''readiness'' questions:

Is the child making the auditory and visual discriminations that are necessary *for the lessons taught?*

Is each child's auditory and visual memory up to the tasks *that these lessons introduce?*

Does each child recognize the letters and know the corresponding sounds of the letters *involved in this task?*

Does each child understand the concepts related to print discussed on pages 78–79?

Does each child understand the vocabulary of reading instruction discussed on pages 79–80.

Does each child perform well on the concepts related to storybooks discussed on pages 80–81?

In employing either of these two widely divergent methods, a teacher may observe that a child needs explicit instruction in one of these areas. The difference, once again, in the two general approaches to reading discussed here is that all Donald's students will receive instruction in these skills in prescribed order. But in Mary's class, the order in which the need for these skills becomes apparent will vary from child to child, and questions about particular reading readiness skills will never arise with respect to some students.

SUMMARY

I began this chapter by describing Donald Vader's beginning reading lessons using a phonics-emphasis basal reading series and Mary Weiss's beginning reading lessons using the language experience approach.

Donald's phonics-emphasis approach is an atomistic, bottom-up approach that takes the psychological view that learning to read occurs when an individual is presented with the right stimulus and rewarded for correct responses; Donald sees reading as essentially decoding print into language.

Mary's language experience approach is a holistic, top-down approach that takes the sociological view that learning to read occurs when students interact within a literate community. These interactions encourage them to initiate readinglike behaviors that are supported by members of the community (including teachers) who are more accomplished in literacy. Mary sees reading as essentially a quest for meaning.

The traditional view of reading readiness is that certain knowledge and skills are *prerequisite* to learning to read. Visual and auditory discrimination, alphabet knowledge, success on word learning tasks, and a certain level of comprehension of oral language are traditional reading readiness tasks.

The concept of reading readiness was used originally to decide when individuals were ready for reading instruction. However, success or failure with these skills do not infallibly predict who will profit from instruction, and withholding reading instruction on a selective basis has proven to be problematic.

The concept was then used to identify prerequisite skills that should be taught as a regular prereading curriculum. However, different approaches (for example, the phonics-emphasis approach and the language experience approach) call on different skills in beginning lessons. Furthermore, experience and research have shown that these skills are best taught in connection with reading instruction when they are called for.

However, the beliefs, concepts, and vocabulary of the reading readiness approach permeate the beginning reading curriculum. This approach views early childhood behaviors related to written language as precursors to "real reading." It encourages teaching readiness subskills in a fixed order and by direct instruction *before* real reading instruction begins.

The concept of reading readiness is compatible with the phonics-emphasis approach to beginning reading. It is a bottom-up, atomistic model.

The concept of emergent literacy is a very different view of beginning reading. It parallels the international perspective on the development of spoken language and is based on observations of preliterate children who "read" and "write" in collaboration with nurturing adults who respond supportively to the children's earliest notions of what written language is and how people use it as readers and writers. Those who support this concept believe that

1. Children exhibit readinglike behaviors in real-life settings long before formal reading instruction begins in school.
2. They learn about print and its uses through social interactions.
3. Different children acquire literacy concepts and skills in different ways and in different sequences.

The concept of emergent literacy is compatible with the language experience approach. It is a holistic, top-down model.

The preschool and kindergarten curriculum is replete with concepts that relate to reading readiness. Visual discrimination tasks are often used to give children experience with using pencils and following directions. Concepts related to print are taught directly through picture activities where children are instructed to move from left to right and from top to bottom on the page. Such concepts are also taught through the teacher modeling reading behavior and guiding children's handling of books and sharing book experiences with them.

Both Donald, a phonics- or skills-emphasis traditional teacher, and Mary, a whole language teacher, need to understand the traditional readiness skills, the concepts related to print, and the concepts related to storybooks. They will both ask the same kinds of diagnostic questions about children who seem to be experiencing difficulty. The difference is that Donald will attempt to teach all the skills and concepts in his program in a fixed order to all his students. Mary will teach these skills and concepts as they appear to be necessary. Some children will learn some of them without direct instruction, and different children will need instruction on skills and concepts in a different order.

FOR FURTHER READING

Allen, R. V. (1976). *Language experiences in communication*. Boston: Houghton Mifflin.

Bissex, G. L. (1980). *Gnys At wrk: A child learns to read and write*. Cambridge, MA: Harvard University Press.

Clay, M. M. (1972). *Sand—Concepts About Print Test*. Auckland, NZ: Heinemann.

Clay, M. M. (1979). *Stones—Concepts About Print Test*. Auckland, NZ: Heinemann.

Clay, M. M. (1985). *The early detection of reader difficulty,* 3rd ed. Portsmouth, NH: Heinemann.

Clay, M. M. (1989). Concepts about print in English and other languages. *The Reading Teacher, 42*(4), 268–277.

Cochron-Smith, M. (1984). *The making of a reader*. Norwood, NJ: Ablex.

Collins, C. (1986). Is the cart before the horse? Effects of preschool reading instruction on 4 year olds. *The Reading Teacher, 40*(3), 332–339.

Combs, M. (1984). Developing concepts about print with patterned sentence stories. *The Reading Teacher, 38*(2), 178–181.

Crowell, D. C., Kawakami, A. J., & Wong, J. Emerging literacy: Reading-writing experiences in a kindergàrten classroom. *The Reading Teacher, 40*(2), 144–151.

Dreyer, L. G., Futtersak, K. R., & Boehm, A. E. Sight words for the computer age: An essential word list. *The Reading Teacher, 39*(1), 12–17.

Durkin, D. (1987). Testing in kindergarten. *The Reading Teacher, 40*(8), 766–771.

Dyson, A. H. (1984). "N spell my Grandma": Fostering early thinking about print. *The Reading Teacher, 38*(3), 262–271.

Goodman, Y. M. (1981). Test review: Concepts About Print Test. *The Reading Teacher, 34*(4), 144–149.

Hall, M. A. (1981). *Teaching reading as a language experience,* 3rd ed. Columbus, OH: Charles E. Merrill.

Harp, B. (1988). When the principal asks: When you do whole language instruction, how will you keep track of reading and writing skills?" *The Reading Teacher, 42*(2), 160–161.

Heller, M. F. (1988). Comprehending and composing through language experience. *The Reading Teacher, 42*(2), 130–135.

Jones, M. B., & Nessel, D. D. (1985). Enhancing the curriculum with experience stories. *The Reading Teacher, 39*(1), 18–23.

Lamme, L. L. (1987). Children's literature: The natural way to learn to read. In B. E. Cullinan, *Children's literature in the reading program*. Newark, DE: International Reading Association.

Mellon, B., & Berglund, R. (1984). The language experiences approach to reading: Recurring questions and their answers. *The Reading Teacher, 37*(9), 867–871.

Mavrogenes, N. A. (1986). What every reading teacher should know about emergent literacy. *The Reading Teacher, 40*(2), 174–179.

Snow, C. E., & Ninio, A. (1987). What children learn from learning to read books. In W. H. Teale and E. Sulzby (Eds.), *Emergent literacy: Writing and reading,* pp. 116–138. Norwood, NJ: Ablex.

Strickland, D. S., & Morrow, L. M. (1988a). Emerging readers and writers: Creating a print rich environment. *The Reading Teacher, 42*(2), 156–157.

Strickland, D. S., & Morrow, L. M. (1988b). Emerging readers and writers: Reading, writing and language. *The Reading Teacher, 42*(3), 240–241.

Strickland, D. S., & Morrow, L. M. (1988c). Emerging readers and writers: Interactive experiences with storybook reading. *The Reading Teacher, 42*(4), 302–309.

Sulzby, E. (1985). Children's emergent reading of favorite storybooks: A developmental study. *Reading Research Quarterly, 20*(4), 459–481.

Teale, W. H., Hiebert, E. H., & Chittenden, E. A. Assessing children's literacy development. *The Reading Teacher, 40*(8), 772–777.

Teale, W. H., & Sulzby, E. (1987). Emergent literacy as a perspective for examining how young children become writers and readers. In W. H. Teale and E. Sulzby (Eds.), *Emergent literacy: Writing and reading,* pp. vii–xxv, Norwood, NJ: Ablex.

Veatch, J., Sawicki, F., Elliot, G., Barnette, E., & Blakey, J. (1979). *Key words to reading: The language experience approach begins.* Columbus, OH: Charles E. Merrill.

Weiss, M. J., & Ranae, H. (1988). A key to literacy: Kindergartners' awareness of the functions of print. *The Reading Teacher, 41*(6), 574–579.

PART TWO

Teaching Word Recognition

Teaching Word Recognition:
Whole Word Method

SETTING THE STAGE

In Part One, I tried to show that reading teachers' assumptions about reading and how children become readers can be traced to two traditions in philosophy, psychology, and education: the empiricist tradition and the rationalist tradition.

The most clearly recognizable heir to the empiricist tradition is known as the phonics- or skills-emphasis approach. In current parlance this is known as a bottom-up approach, where individual skills are identified and taught in a specific order from what is believed to be easy or elemental to what is believed to be difficult or complex.

The most clearly recognizable heir to the rationalist tradition is known as the whole language approach. In current parlance this is known as a top-down approach, where it is assumed that children "catch on" to or apprehend the broad concepts of reading (and writing) propelled by an innate drive to make sense of the world. They attempt to function as readers and writers—to put reading and writing to use. When literate people cooperate and collaborate, lead from behind, or provide scaffolding, the neophytes work out the details and learn the individual skills that are necessary to become accomplished readers and writers.

Throughout Part One, I argued that the top-down, whole language approach is most consistent with trends in the study of language and with the beliefs based on the most recent research in the study of language acquisition and emergent literacy. On the other hand, I have argued that both the skills-emphasis and the whole language teacher need to be conversant with the many skills that come into play when a child reads.

The traditional teacher relies on "the program" to determine the scope and sequence of the curriculum and to dictate the methods. Whole language teachers attempt to teach the skills and behaviors that contribute to reading success *when they are needed.* And because the process of reading varies from child to child, from purpose to purpose, and from passage to passage, the skills and behaviors that contribute to success are somewhat unpredictable.

The reader's strengths and weaknesses can only be discerned by a person who is thoroughly familiar with the skills and behaviors taught in the traditional curriculum. Therefore, whole language teachers must be thoroughly familiar with the traditional curriculum. Since they strive not to teach the "next" lesson in the program but the "right" lesson for the particular child, they need to be thoroughly familiar with methods and have a wealth of ideas for lessons in their repertoire.

In Chapter 2 and elsewhere I have proposed that if the whole language approach is to succeed, whole language teachers must gain the experience, knowledge, and skills possessed by the best traditional reading teachers and work toward the whole language ideal. Matthew Nicholson and Mary Weiss need to know everything that Donald Vader and Charlotte Britain know.

In this part, I will introduce the traditional content and methodology of teaching word recognition with commentary on how the concepts and methods might be utilized in a traditional and in a whole language classroom.

DEFINING "WORD RECOGNITION"

The Beginning Reader's "Concept of Word"

Beginning readers do not necessarily know that spoken words are represented in printed texts as groups of letters bound by spaces. Morris and Henderson (1981) suggest a technique whereby children first memorize a nursery rhyme and then recite it with the teacher while the teacher points to the words of the rhyme printed on a card. After several trials, the child's "concept of word" is tested. For example, children may be asked to point to each word as they recite the poem and asked to say words as the teacher points to them. You will, of course, recognize the similarity of this "pointing while reading" technique to the language experience approach described in Chapter 3. Children who do not point accurately while reciting may need to learn the concept of what a printed word is. Without this concept, no word recognition strategies can succeed. (See Activities 4.A and 4.B.)

ACTIVITY 4.A OBSERVING THE TREATMENT OF THE "CONCEPT OF WORD" IN SKILLS-EMPHASIS AND WHOLE LANGUAGE APPROACHES

Compare the lessons taught by Mary Weiss and Donald Vader in Chapter 3. How do they treat the "concept of word" in their lessons? How do the concepts of "top-down" and "bottom-up" apply to the "concept of word" as it is incorporated into these lessons?

ACTIVITY 4.B TESTING YOUR AWARENESS OF "READING" IN THE PRESCHOOL CURRICULUM

Visit a nursery school or kindergarten or view an educational television show aimed at preschoolers. Record instances of attention to the "concept of word."

Learning the Meaning of a Word Versus Learning to Recognize a Word

There is a difference between *learning the meaning of a word* and *learning to recognize a word,* and it is an important difference to keep in mind. The word "recognize" is made up of a Latin prefix and root, *re* + *cognize,* meaning "to know again; to identify something as a thing one has known or seen previously." In teaching beginning reading, we are concerned with teaching children to recognize words in print that they already know in spoken form. Learning the meanings of new words is an important part of language development, but it is a different matter from learning to recognize words in print that one already knows in speech. Learning the meanings of new words will be treated in Chapter 11. Chapters 4 through 8 will deal exclusively with word recognition.

Recognizing Words Instantly Versus Learning Techniques for Recognizing Words

Children's skill in word recognition can be looked at in two ways:

1. How many words do children recognize instantly in print?
2. What skills or techniques are children able to use to recognize a word that they do not recognize instantly when they see it in print?

It is important for a teacher to recognize that these are two different questions, but that the questions are interrelated. A child who instantly recognizes many words is likely to be skillful at recognizing words he or she does not instantly recognize, and a child who has well-developed techniques for recognizing words is likely to recognize many words instantly. (See Activity 4.C.)

ACTIVITY 4.C TEACHING NEW SIGHT WORDS VERSUS TEACHING WORD RECOGNITION SKILLS

> Review lessons attributed to Charlotte, Matthew, Donald, and Mary. When is the lesson accurately described as helping children to recognize printed words through a whole word method? When is the lesson accurately described as teaching children techniques for recognizing words?

APPROACHES EMPLOYING THE WHOLE WORD METHOD

The objective of the whole word method is to have children see a printed word and identify it immediately without thinking about it, puzzling over it, or analyzing it. But instant recognition is the *ultimate* objective of all word-recognition skills; there is something more separating the whole word method from other methods. The whole word method can be classified by what the teacher does *not* do—he or she does not refer to letters, to sounds of letters, to syllables, to prefixes, to suffixes, or to roots.

Language Experience

There are many widely varying techniques that are whole word techniques. The initial stages of the language experience approach described in Chapter 3 is a whole word approach. Children tell the teacher which words they recognize from the previous day's story, and the teacher copies them down for each child's own word bank. Over several weeks, if things go well, each child has his or her own bank of many words that have been learned as whole words.

Key Vocabulary

Sylvia Ashton-Warner (1908–1984) was a New Zealand novelist and teacher who introduced an innovation in teaching beginning reading through a whole word approach that focuses on the interest of the individual child (Ashton-Warner, 1972, 1986a, 1986b). Her method is to elicit from each child words that are intimately connected with the child's life, words that have intense meaning. She starts with words one presumes are connected with any child's inner world such as *Mommy, kiss,* and *ghost.* Her aim is to elicit each child's individual words be they *house, jet, tiger,* or *bomb.* For example, she elicit each child's individual words be they *house, jet, tiger,* or *bomb.* For example, she recounts an incident where some of her students are discussing what they are frightened of. A violent Maori (New Zealand native) child shouted that he was frightened of nothing, that he would stick his knife into anything, even the tigers!

> So I give him "tigers" [that is, she prints *tigers* on a card and gives it to him] and I never have to repeat this word to him, and in the morning the little card shows the dirt and disrepair of violent usage. (Ashton-Warner, 1986b, p. 35)

Veatch and others (1979) recognize that the essence of Ashton-Warner's approach is that each child's key vocabulary is unique and largely unpredictable and that if one elicits the right words from a child, the words are learned instantly (what Ashton-Warner calls "one-look words"). Veatch and others suggest that every few days, the child go through his or her words and say them as fast as possible.

> Those he cannot recognize *instantly* must be thrown away without criticism. "Oh, that just wasn't a good enough word to remember. You will think of a better one today or tomorrow." (Veatch et al., 1979, p. 16)

Figure 4.1. Teacher-made labels for objects in the classroom.

Whole Words in the Environment

Teachers often put nicely lettered labels on objects around the room as in Figure 4.1.
They call the students' attention to these words and encourage the students to remember
them.

Primary-grade teachers often set aside an area for a "Calendar Board" as in Figure
4.2. They print the days of the week, months, and numerals on cards and encourage
children to remember them by having the children choose the correct cards to put up
the day's date each morning.

Another permanent bulletin board may be set aside for "Today's Weather," as in
Figure 4.3. Cards containing the words *sunny, rainy, cloudy, foggy, hot, cold, warm,*
and so on are displayed. The words are discussed, and students are encouraged to learn
to recognize them so they can add a weather dimension to the daily exercise of changing
the date.

A science lesson can be the occasion for teaching new words through the whole
word approach. The words *heat, cold, ice, melt,* and *water* might be part of a bulletin

Figure 4.2. Calendar board.

Figure 4.3. Weather board.

board display after they have been introduced during an experiment and added to a child's list of known words. (See Figure 4.4.)

Use of Picture Clues

Teachers frequently use pictures with words as clues to recognition. Teachers may make their own picture work cards as in Figure 4.5 or use the commercially available Dolch Basic Picture Words. Ninety-five frequently used nouns appear with a picture and the word on one side and the word only on the other side. Children can "learn" the picture and words together and then turn the cards over to see how many words they can remember without the pictures; then they can check their progress by turning the cards over again to see if they said the right word. They can work singly, in pairs, or in groups. The prudent teacher supervises such activities from time to time to make sure the child has assigned the right word to the picture.

This same idea has been used with the weather board (Figure 4.3). The "picture and word" side of the cards is shown at first and the "word only" side later, as in

Figure 4.4. Science bulletin board.

Figure 4.6. Children can then choose the weather card for the day and check to see if they are right.

The Challenge of Function Words

Words like *a, and, of,* and *in* are called function words because their chief purpose is to show syntactic relationships in sentences. Because they do not have much meaning on their own and because they are unstressed in normal speech, some children may not recognize function words in isolation (Huttenlocher, 1964; Ehri, 1975; Holden & MacGinitie, 1972). It is clear that many children do not perceive the word *to* in the spoken ''gonna go'' nor the word *have* in ''shoulda gone'' nor the word *of* in ''bag a' marbles.'' Written compositions show that even some college-age students fail to rec-

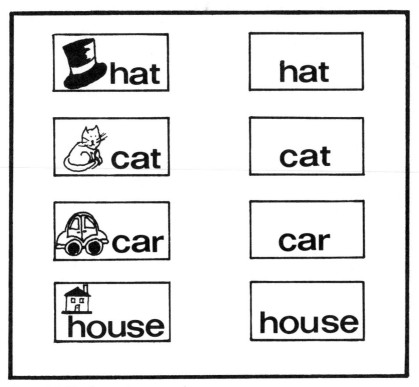

Figure 4.5. Teacher-made noun cards.

ognize function words as separate words in some contexts. Sloan (1979) found instances of such neologisms as *alot, noone, infact, nodoubt, intime,* and *fillup* in college writing. I recently saw a letter from a graduate student who wrote, "I spoke to both of them *intern.*" But because function words appear frequently, it makes sense to teach children to recognize them early in their word learning careers.

Flannel board activities can be created to encourage children to learn to recognize function words such as prepositions. An outline of a fish bowl and phrases printed on cards such as *in the bowl, on the bowl, under the bowl, near the bowl* can become the center of a group activity and put where individuals can work with them on their own or in small groups. (See Figure 4.7.)

Paired-Associate Learning

Because the immediate goal of the whole word method is recognition without analysis, this approach is also conducive to paired-associate, stimulus-response learning—the kinds of teaching and learning techniques associated with behaviorist psychology. Teachers can often be observed working with an individual, showing a word, saying it, asking the child to say it, and going on to the next word until several words are presented.

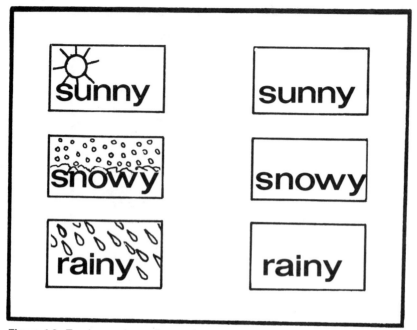

Figure 4.6. Teacher-made weather cards.

After this procedure is repeated several times, the teacher then shows a word, and the child says the word and is rewarded (''That's right! Good!''), or the child does not say the word and is not rewarded—or is ''punished'' (''No! We'll put that back in the pile of words you don't know''). Sometimes the rewards are more concrete—a token, a piece of candy, or a penny—and sometimes the punishments are more concrete—a token, a piece of candy, or a penny is withheld or taken away. Such procedures are used to introduce new words and to review words the child learned to recognize in previous lessons. This procedure was referred to in Chapter 1 as a classic behaviorist stimulus-response-reinforcement application to reading instruction.

Teachers sometimes take the special difficulty presented by function words into account by printing phrases or short sentences onto cards as in Figure 4.8 and using them in short paired-associate lessons.

Eclectic Basal Readers

Perhaps the most widespread use of the whole word approach is with eclectic basal readers. Many eclectic basal reading series begin by helping students learn words as whole words through activities such as those illustrated in Figures 4.9 and 4.10; students are helped to learn these words as whole words. These words are then repeated in new stories, and words are gradually added until longer stories with more complex sentences appear.

It is presumed that most readers of this book have themselves learned to read in American schools and will therefore know what basal readers are since basal readers

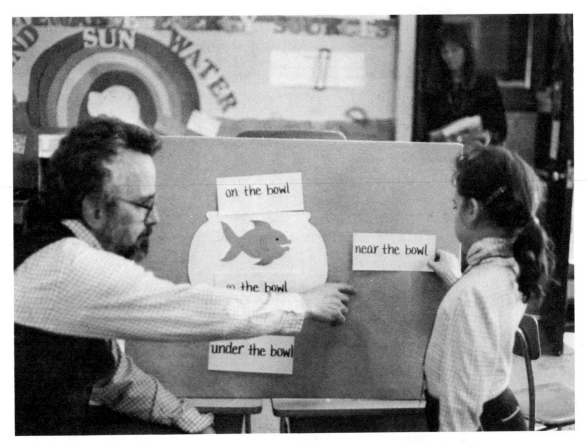

Figure 4.7. Flannel board activity encouraging children to recognize function words such as prepositions.

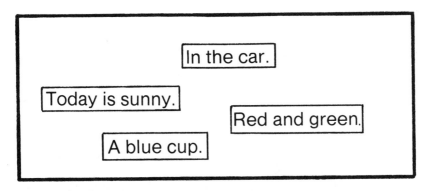

Figure 4.8. Incorporating function words into whole word recognition materials.

Make word cards for the text of **Look Inside.** Display pages 4–7 of the Big Storybook. Point to and read the first sentence. Remind children that sentences are made up of words that are read from left to right. On the chalkboard ledge, display in random order the word cards for the words in the first sentence. Ask a volunteer to find the word **This** and to place the word card at the left side of the top pocket of a pocket chart. Follow the same procedure for having children find the other words in the sentence. When the sentence is complete, have the children count the words in it, reminding them that words are separated by spaces. Then have children practice reading the entire sentence.

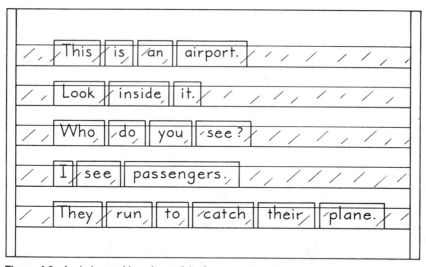

Figure 4.9. A whole word learning activity from an eclectic basal reader. (*Source: The Mouse in the House,* teacher's ed. [Lexington, MA: D.C. Heath, 1989], p. 118.)

have been used in the overwhelming majority of American schoolrooms for many decades. However, some readers may not have used basals or were not aware that the books used to teach them were basals.

Basal readers are textbooks published in a series for use in the elementary school grades beginning with first grade. Preschool and kindergarten materials are also frequently included. Each set of students' books is accompanied by a Teacher's Guide or Teacher's Manual with page-by-page suggestions and instructions for teaching reading using the materials in the students' books. Other materials such as workbooks, audiovisual teaching aids, and software for computerized lessons are published to accompany basal readers. The Teacher's Guide or Manual gives suggestions and directions for using these materials as well.

There are numerous basal reading series on the market. Greenlinger-Harless's (1987) index to "a number of popular basal reading series for the elementary school level" published between 1977 and 1987 lists 17 publishers and 40 different programs.

An important aspect of basal readers is that each book (ideally, each lesson) is created as part of a grand design. Decisions of what to teach, when to teach, and how to teach are guided by the authors' and editors' beliefs about the nature of reading, how one learns to read, in what order skills ought to be presented, and so on. Questions of

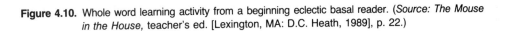

22   *Read and write* cat. *Name the animal and read the words* Cat *and* cat. *Then trace the word* Cat *or* cat *in each box.*
Then draw a line from the word to the picture of a cat.

Figure 4.10. Whole word learning activity from a beginning eclectic basal reader. (*Source: The Mouse in the House,* teacher's ed. [Lexington, MA: D.C. Heath, 1989], p. 22.)

content such as how minorities are portrayed, and whether once-taboo topics such as death, divorce, aging, or delinquency will be portrayed, are also answered in terms of a coherent policy.

Schools choose basal readers largely on the basis of the grand design or the policies that are reflected in the materials and teaching suggestions. The most fundamental distinction among reading series is whether they are categorized as ''phonics- or skills-emphasis'' or ''eclectic.'' Phonics-emphasis readers rely heavily on empiricist, atomistic, bottom-up assumptions about reading and learning to read. Although they pay attention to meaning and comprehending, they *begin* with attention to letter recognition and letter-sound relationships and continue to *emphasize* phonics and skills throughout the grades. The phonics-emphasis beginning reading lesson described in Chapter 3 is typical of such programs.

The word "eclectic" means "selecting, choosing from various sources." Eclectic reading programs usually teach a number of words as whole words as described earlier. They soon introduce phonics generalizations, and they continue to present phonics and skills lessons throughout the grades, but they focus less on phonics and skills. In comparison to phonics- or skills-emphasis programs, they rely much more on holistic, top-down assumptions about reading and learning to read. However, you can easily find lessons on phonics generalizations and isolated skills throughout these programs, which will remind you that they are indeed *eclectic*.

There is a detailed discussion of differences between phonics- or skills-emphasis reading programs and eclectic reading programs in Chapter 8.

The following programs are frequently identified as phonics-emphasis basal reading series:

Economy Reading Series published by McGraw-Hill, 1986.
Lippincott Basic Reading published by Scribner, 1981.
The Headway Program published by Open Court, 1985.

The following programs are frequently identified as eclectic basal reading series:

The Ginn Reading Program published by Silver Burdett and Ginn, 1985–1987.
HBJ Basic Reading published by Holt, Rinehart and Winston, 1980 and 1986.
Heath Reading published by D. C. Heath, 1989.
Houghton Mifflin Reading, 1986.
Series r: Macmillan Reading published by Macmillan, 1980, 1983, and 1986.
Scott, Foresman Reading: An American Tradition published by Scott, Foresman, 1987. (See Activity 4.D.)

ACTIVITY 4.D COMPARING PHONICS- OR SKILLS-EMPHASIS WITH ECLECTIC BASAL READERS

Go to a local school or to a university or college materials center and get materials from one or two of the phonics-emphasis basal reading series and one or two of the eclectic basal reading series identified.

Work through one or two lessons at the beginning first grade level from a series in each category. Choose two higher levels, say, fourth and seventh grades, and work through a couple of lessons from each category.

A. Demonstrate some of these lessons for your classmates.

B. Discuss whether these series and the differences between them have been described and compared accurately and fairly in this book.

C. Refer to this activity when evaluating statements made about basal readers and the two categories of basal readers in this book and elsewhere.

SELECTING WORDS FOR WHOLE WORD METHOD

Before instruction in other methods of word recognition is begun, two criteria determine the selection of words: interest of the children in the words and the frequency of the words.

Interest

From the start, particularly at the start, learning to read should be an exciting, stimulating, warm, human, useful, social, congenial, gregarious experience. Perhaps the aspect of the whole word approach that recommends it best is that children *read* from the first day. Children do not wait until they have learned some letter-sound relationships or the names of letters or how to print as they do in a phonics-first approach such as Donald Vader uses.

Key Vocabulary.   The key vocabulary approach reflects the view that learning originates within the children as they develop. Children will learn their own words. It has been suggested that eliciting the child's key vocabulary is analogous to discovering the child's stage of development in a Piagetian sense (Duckworth, 1967; Hartman, 1977). The main arena of learning is in the child's mind; the teacher's job is to discover where the child is by discovering the child's words and giving him or her as many and as broad experiences on that level as possible.

"Experience Story" and "Words in the Environment."   The "Experience Story" approach, and what has been termed here as "Words in the Environment" reflect the view that learning originates in society. In these examples, children are members of a learning community. They are engaged in a common enterprise. The teacher is talking and writing; the children are contributing. An interesting thing is happening. Some children know more than others. Some learn to recognize words faster than others. But they are all in it together, and they have the opportunity to learn from the teacher and from each other. The main arena of learning is the social group, and as a member of that group, the teacher can help children to extend their learning efforts into areas where they may encounter a little difficulty—into Vygotsky's zone of proximal development.

Basal Reading Programs.   Writers of eclectic basal reading programs take the interest of the children into account as well. Here, though, "interest" tends to be defined in terms of the "average" child. Primer stories are about Mommies and Daddies and puppies—things that presumably interest 6-year-olds. Words taught as sight words in these early stories are chosen because one can demonstrate that they are *frequent* words in most 6-year-olds' environments. Authors of basal reading series consult extensive word counts of young children's oral language (Murphy, 1957; Johnson, 1971; Moe et al., 1982). There is a belief that frequency of use in oral language is an indicator of children's interest in words.

The interest of the child is considered in all these methods, but different sources of interest are assumed in each method. This idea is summarized in Box 4.1.

BOX 4.1 HOW CHILD'S INTEREST IS TAKEN INTO ACCOUNT IN THREE WHOLE WORD TEACHING STRATEGIES

KEY VOCABULARY

The child learns *tiger* because it's his or her word. This approach concentrates on the inner life of the child, appeals to the child's emotions, and stresses the child's individuality.

EXPERIENCE STORY

The child learns *mouse* because of a social event of which he or she was part. Some children will learn more, and some will learn less, but community and learning together and from each other are stressed.

TYPICAL BASAL READER

Children learn words that are presumed to be interesting to them. This presumption is based on frequency counts and the principle that usefulness, interest, and frequency are related. Emphasis is on what all children have in common rather than on interests generated from a common experience or interests that are unique to individual children.

Frequency

One problem with choosing words on the basis of interest only is that children often choose words to learn (or words arise in an activity) that may be interesting but may not be very useful; that is, they may be words that will probably not appear again very soon in the child's reading. An enthusiastic child may want to learn to recognize *Bunsen burner* after a science demonstration. The teacher knows that the child will probably not see these words in print again for years.

On the other hand, *the, of, then, so,* and *like* are among the most frequently used words in print. Frequent words tend to be function words, and as has been pointed out before, such words tend not to have much meaning in isolation. As a result children are not likely to choose them out of interest. As a matter of fact, it has been demonstrated that such words tend to be harder for children to learn to recognize than "content words"—that is, nouns, verbs, adjectives, and adverbs (Ehri, 1976).

Word Frequency Counts and Basic Vocabulary Lists.   Many studies have been done to discover the relative frequency of words.

Thorndike. The first modern study in the field of education was done in 1921 by Thorndike (1921; Thorndike & Lorge, 1944) who counted word frequencies in a potpourri of English language publications. His study included American and British literature, literature intended for children and adults, and literature that had been published recently as well as literature from the distant past.

Dolch. Dolch (1936) counted word frequencies from school reading materials (preprimer to grade 6). Dolch developed the Dolch Basic Sight Vocabulary consisting of 220 words (excluding nouns) and a list of 95 nouns that are common in primary reading materials (published as *Dolch Picture-Word Cards,* Garrard Publishing Co., Champaign, Illinois).

Kucera-Francis. Since the advent of computers, three important word frequency counts have been done. Kucera and Francis (1967) counted a million running words of text published in the United States in the year 1961 in 15 categories of writing representing types of journalism, scientific writing, and fiction and nonfiction trade books. This had an advantage over the Thorndike lists in that it was contemporary, American, published writing, and was thought to give a better estimate of the probability of a word's being encountered by a contemporary American in his or her daily reading.

Carroll, Davies, and Richman. Carroll, Davies, and Richman (1971) published a frequency count of over 5 million words published in texts and other published materials used in American classrooms in 1969. This highly sophisticated study reports the frequency of words in the entire body of material, their frequency in each of 17 subject categories (reading, math, library fiction, magazines, and so on), and their frequency in each of grades 3 through 9 and ungraded. The study even reports the probability of one's encountering a word based on how often it was found plus *where* it was found. A word found fairly often in music books is not as likely to be encountered as a word found equally often in social studies books because more time is spent in school reading social studies than music.

Harris and Jacobson. Harris and Jacobson (1972) counted words in six basal reading series and eight content area textbook series for grades 1 through 6. Several word lists categorized by grade level are reported in this study, including "core" lists of 332 words categorized as preprimer, primer, and first reader level words.

Fry. Fry (1972) reviewed frequency counts done by others and devised six lists of 100 words each that he believes are necessary for successful reading in grades 1 through 4. Fry refers to words on these lists as "instant words," referring to his belief that these words should be known instantly by students at the grade level he has identified for each list.

A glance at any of these lists will convince the reader that many words chosen for teaching on the basis of frequency would not be found on a list of words chosen on the basis of interest.

Uses of Basic Vocabulary Lists.

Selecting Words. Basic vocabulary lists have come to be used for several purposes. One is to decide what words to teach at the early stages of reading. Writers of basal readers consult such lists, and editors and teachers refer to these lists in judging whether words in a particular book are too hard or too easy for the grade level.

Such lists are also useful to whole language teachers. Whether they employ language experience, key vocabulary, or language in the environment approaches, with each new experience children should gain more independence and be better prepared for the next experience. Therefore, teachers want to spend the time and effort of review on useful words and leave the others to each child's discretion. Although most teachers can trust their intuition on this question most of the time, familiarity with lists compiled by Dolch, Harris and Jacobson, and Fry helps teachers to identify high-frequency words. Whatever approach one is using, words are sometimes introduced that will not probably be encountered again for some time.

Assessment of Student Progress. Basic vocabulary lists are often used for assessment of reading skills. Primary-grade teachers often think of one aspect of a child's level of achievement in terms of how many of the Dolch Basic Sight Vocabulary Words or Dolch Picture Words a child knows, or whether he or she has mastered the first hundred, second hundred, and so on, of the Fry Instant Words or the Preprimer, Primer, or First Reader List of the Harris-Jacobson core words.

Confusing the assessment with the selection uses of these lists can lead to trouble, however. To insist upon teaching the first 25 words on a particular list before the second, to decide not to teach *ice* and *water* because they are not on the primer list, to decide not to teach the word *vote* on election day because it is not on any list is to violate the first principle of word selection—*interest*. Selection of words for whole word recognition is a matter of capitalizing on the interests of children at the moment and taking into consideration what their reading needs will be in the ongoing program. Teachers should not act on one criterion at the expense of the other; they should consider both. (See Activity 4.E.)

ACTIVITY 4.E WHAT YOU CAN LEARN FROM WORD COUNTS IN THE ORAL LANGUAGE OF PRESCHOOL AND PRIMARY-GRADE CHILDREN

Words children use have been the focus of attention of scholars who wish to understand children's language development and cognitive development. Writers of elementary school materials are interested in the words children use because they want to choose words for instructional material that will communicate with children. Teachers are interested in words children use because this knowledge helps them understand what they can expect children to know.

The following are lists of words children use:

Hopkins, C. J. (1979). The spontaneous oral vocabulary of children in grade one. *Elementary School Journal, 79,* 240–249.

Horn, E. (1925). Appropriate materials for instruction in reading. In G. M. Whipple (Ed.), *Report of the National Committee on Reading. Twenty-fourth Yearbook of the National Society for the Study of Education.* Bloomington, IL: Public School Publishing Company.

Johnson, D. D. (1971). A basic vocabulary for beginning reading. *Elementary School Journal, 72,* 29–34.

Moe, A. J., Hopkins, C. J., & Rush, R. T. (1982). *The vocabulary of first-grade children.* Springfield, IL: Charles C Thomas.

Murphy, H. (1957). The spontaneous speaking vocabulary of children in primary grades. *Journal of Education, 140,* 3–106.

Sherk, J. K. (1973). *A Word-Count of Spoken English of Culturally Disadvantaged Preschool and Elementary Pupils.* Kansas City: University of Missouri.

Obtain several of these lists and compare the methods by which the lists were compiled and the purpose the authors state for compiling the lists. How does the information contained in these lists differ from the word counts of published materials that are referred to in this chapter?

Criteria After Other Word Recognition Techniques Have Been Introduced

Consideration of Generalizations That Will Soon Be Taught.   As soon as the most rudimentary principles of phonics (Chapter 5) or structural analysis (Chapter 6) are introduced, a third criterion for choosing words by the whole word method arises. It is to choose words on the basis of skills that will be introduced in the near future. If, for instance, a teacher has determined to teach the letter-sound correspondence of the initial *p* as in *pan* and *put,* he or she wants to be sure that the child recognizes several words beginning with *p* as whole words. Much later, if some less obvious word analysis generalizations are going to be taught, such as where to divide two syllable words ending in *-le,* it is important to be sure that the child recognizes several words like *able, title, sample,* and *wrinkle* as whole words.

Irregular Spelling-Sound Relationships.   The whole word approach is sometimes a default option. For example, *colonel* and *isthmus* represent very uncommon spelling-sound relationships. Words borrowed from other languages (such as *frijole, pinochle,* and *spiel*) often fall into this class. Ruddell (1974) gives many more such examples. It is best simply to teach such words as whole words, perhaps with a comment on the unusual spelling.

Teachers should be aware of phonetic irregularity as a criterion for using the whole word approach at the very beginning stages of reading instruction as well. One of the most common words in English is *of;* it is the only word in English where the letter *f* represents the sound /v/. Many very frequent words are phonetically irregular such as *do, father,* and *women.*

The whole word method is perhaps the most commonly used method of teaching new words throughout all levels of reading instruction.

SOME PRINCIPLES FOR TEACHING WHOLE WORDS

The most commonly used, unadorned whole word method has been mentioned in several contexts earlier in this chapter. That method is to say a word while the students look at its printed form and encourage them to remember it so that they will recognize the printed form in the future. There are several principles involved in teaching words by this method and in follow-up techniques used to ensure future recognition.

Presenting Words in Context

One often-stated rule of reading instruction is that one should always teach words in context. This is based on three observations: (1) Context helps us to narrow down the possibilities of what an unrecognized word is and therefore helps us to recognize it. Children don't confuse *bed* with *bad* in the sentence *He sleeps in bed.* (2) Most words have more than one meaning. For example, *bear* can refer to the animal or mean "to carry." Out of context a word's meaning may be ambiguous. (3) Many words have more than one pronunciation (for example, *read* in *I do read* and *I have read*). Such words do not have one correct pronunciation out of context.

This should not be taken to mean that every word must appear in a printed context. Suppose the teacher says "Let's learn the words *clock* and *door.* I'll print the word *clock* on this card and tape it next to the clock and I'll print the word *door* and tape it to the door. What else should I print cards for?" The teacher is using the words in the context of his or her oral language and is presenting the printed word in that context. The teacher is also placing the printed word in a physical context. It *is* advisable to introduce function words in written phrases or short sentences for the reasons presented previously.

The influential reading expert William S. Gray, who is often cited as an advocate of teaching words in context, does not suggest that words always appear in *written context:*

> To make sure that every child will associate both sound and specific meaning with a sight word the first time he sees it, the teacher initiates an oral discussion in which the

word is used informally with the same meaning as it has in the story that pupils are about to read. During the discussion, as she uses the word in a sentence, the teacher shows its printed form (usually on a word card at early levels). (Gray, 1960, p. 17)

Deciding how much written context to supply in presenting a new word depends on what part the teacher expects the written context to play in the child's recognition of the word. These factors will be discussed again later in Chapter 7 when context is discussed as an aid to word recognition.

Pupils' Attention

The whole word method is often referred to as the look-and-say method for obvious reasons. Harris and Sipay (1985) have pointed out that *look while you say* would be a better term because it would remind both the teacher and learner that the child's attention must be focused on the visual form and the spoken form of the word at the same time and that the connection between the two must be understood by the child. Affixing a label to a door and a desk will not ensure that the child will learn these words, nor will the teacher's reading a story from a chart while pointing to each word accomplish much in the way of word recognition for a child who is gazing out the window.

Felt board activities displays, such as suggested in Figure 4.7, are not used or attended to by the children—unless the teacher has made their purpose clear and modeled for the children how they might be used.

Attention to Appropriate Stimulus

When using the whole word approach, it is difficult to say what aspect of a printed word enables an individual child to recognize it. One child may respond to length, another to shape, another to first letter, and so on. Teachers should be sure, however, that a child is not responding exclusively to some extraneous cue such as that there is an ink blot on the card that has the word *man* or that *Monday* is in the top slot of the "calendar words."

To ensure that children are responding to some aspects of the printed word itself, words should appear in different contexts in connection with different activities and as different physical entities (that is, printed in chalk on the board, in ink on a card, in the child's book, and so on). Some authorities discourage writing *red* in red ink and *green* in green ink and other such gimmicks because they encourage children to rely on memory aids that are not intrinsic to the printed words.

Calling Attention to the Shape of Words

It is often recommended that the first words taught should look as dissimilar as possible. If a class is asked to remember *an, for,* and *elephant* on a particular day, *elephant* may be learned first by most children because it's the most different from the others. Teachers capitalize on this reliance on differences and on peculiarity of shape by drawing outlines around the words as in Figure 4.11. Other memory aids are sometimes taught

Figure 4.11. Calling attention to the shape of words.

Figure 4.12. Memory aids for teaching sight words.

such as that *bed* looks like a bed, *looks* has two "eyes," and *monkey* has a "tail," as in Figure 4.12.

There is some objection to teaching aids of this sort because *bad* also looks like a bed, *took* also has two eyes, and *money* also has a tail. Bear in mind, however, that these suggestions are to aid memory only at the very earliest stages and that care would be taken not to introduce both *bad* and *bed, took* and *look,* and *money* and *monkey* at this stage anyway, on the principle that the first words should be as dissimilar as possible. Very early in the process letter names are learned and letter-sound correspondences begin to be discussed. Then differences between similar words can be discussed in terms that are relevant throughout one's reading career. For example, the teacher points out that *took* and *look* begin with different letters and correspondingly different sounds, but as soon as these clues are employed, the teacher is no longer using a purely whole word technique. Rudimentary phonics is involved.

Practice

Children need many exposures to some words before they recognize them, and they will forget many words if the words are not repeatedly seen and recognized. Both these facts indicate a need for practice. Repeating words that have already been introduced in new stories, felt board activities, flash cards, word banks, team games, and so on is essential. Word recognition drill need not be ruled out, but, like all activities, it should not be overused lest it become boring. One way to ensure that unadorned drill does not become boring is to keep the sessions short by concentrating only on words that have not been learned. Word cards like The Dolch Picture Words or The Dolch 220 (whether commercially prepared or teacher made) are particularly useful because each child's "hard words" will differ. An individual's hard words can be identified and separated out and can be used for drill.

WHY USE WHOLE WORD APPROACH?

There are several sound reasons for using a whole word approach in the beginning of reading instruction.

Purposeful Reading

With the whole word approach, purposeful reading begins on the first day of instruction or soon after. Reading pages of the preprimer, writing and reading experience stories, or doing calendar activities, weather activities, workbook pages, felt board activities, or team games can begin as soon as a child has learned to recognize a few words. One does not put off reading while children learn to recognize and name individual letters as in a phonics first approach such as Donald Vader uses, or until they have learned the most frequent sounds associated with letters.

Interest

The whole word approach capitalizes on interest. Just as a teacher-introduced experience like taking a white mouse out of a cage and letting it run around a table may motivate children to "write" a story and learn some words from that story, events of the day outside school may generate interest in words like *snow, parade,* or *vote.* From the start, written language is introduced as a thing that is relevant to the ordinary business of life.

Demonstrated Success

The whole word method is a time-honored approach to beginning reading. It was advocated by Horace Mann and began to be widely used in primers beginning around 1850 (Matthews, 1966). It has been advocated by the two most influential authorities on reading in this century—Edmund Huey (1908) and William S. Gray (1960)—and is still the most widely used method of teaching beginning reading. It is not nearly as important, but it is an interesting fact that Tolstoy, the Russian novelist, took a great interest in education and published a series of whole word method "primers" that sold over a million copies (Troyat, 1967).

In her study of children who learned to read before they entered school, Durkin (1966) discovered that many parents of such children claim that no one ever taught the children to read. Upon direct questioning, however, many parents reported that the children frequently asked "What's that word?" and were answered by attentive adults. This is, of course, a whole word method. Parents do not recognize it as a teaching method either because it is initiated by the child, or because there is no letter-sound element involved. It can be argued from this that the whole word approach is a "natural" approach if one defines *natural* as a method spontaneously initiated by many children who show an early interest in reading.

Directness

One great virtue of the whole word method is that it leads directly to the objective that all methods are ultimately designed to achieve: instant, automatic word recognition. For this reason the whole word approach is retained throughout reading instruction as one way to introduce new words.

A CONTRASTING VIEW: THE LINGUISTIC APPROACH

This chapter has presented the prevailing view of the usefulness of the whole word method in beginning reading instruction. The information and advice given in this chapter are consistent with the teaching practices recommended by the most widely used basal reading series.

However, much of the information given in this chapter is quite inconsistent with the so-called "linguistic approach." This approach was advocated by Bloomfield in his book *Let's Read* (Bloomfield & Barnhardt, 1961). I referred to Bloomfield and the linguistic approach in Chapter 1. Although the linguistic approach is heavily phonics laden, it does begin with whole words. Because its influence is still seen in some phonics-emphasis reading programs, the principles that determine which words are chosen at the early stages are worth mentioning here.

Minimal Differences Between Words Taught

Bloomfield believed that through learning words like *hen, pen,* and *men* as lists, students will learn to attend to the only clue in the word that can help them—the difference in a single letter. He also believed that from learning lists of highly similar words, students will discover that similar spellings represent similar sounds and that different spellings represent different sounds. Through learning lists of words with minimal spelling differences like those in Figure 4.13, students learn to attend to what Bloomfield believed is the only appropriate stimulus for word recognition—letter-sound relationships.

Consistent Spelling-Sound Relationships

A second important principle of the linguistic approach is derived from the belief that beginning readers would be harmed if forced to deal with the spelling-sound inconsistencies of written English. Words are chosen for beginning reading instruction on the basis of the regularity of the letter-sound relationships the words represent. Words like *can, man,* and *ran* are taught because they contain very regular spelling-sound relationships. If *can* is taught, *cent* is not taught until much later in the program because the initial *c* represents two different sounds in the words *can* and *cent.*

Although frequency and interest are taken into account, the overriding considerations for choosing words for the linguistic method are (1) the words employ letter-sound relationships that are regular, (2) words with inconsistent letter-sound relationships be avoided, and (3) words taught in the same lesson have minimal differences (single initial consonant letter contrasts in the beginning).

Certain function words such as *the* and *on* are introduced as sight words as they

Figure 4.13. A typical word list from a linguistic reader.

at	sat	fat
bat	mat	cat
hat	Pat	

The Hat on the Mat

Look at the hat.
The hat is on the mat.
Pat sat on the hat.

Figure 4.14. A typical story from a linguistic reader.

are needed to create sentences. Figure 4.14 shows a typical "story" from a linguistic reader.

SUMMARY

Both traditional teachers who rely heavily on published programs and teachers working toward a whole language approach need to understand word recognition strategies, the assumptions that underlie them, and methods employed in teaching them.

A few concepts need to be sorted out:

1. It is necessary for beginning readers to have the "concept of word" before they can begin to identify particular printed words.
2. Learning new word meanings is not the same as recognizing familiar words in print. Beginning reading instruction concentrates on the latter.
3. There is a difference between recognizing words instantly and learning techniques to recognize words.

This chapter deals with teaching children to recognize familiar words in print by the whole word method. The whole word method involves teaching children to recognize words without referring to letters, the sounds represented by letters, syllables, prefixes, suffixes, or roots.

The whole word method appears at some stage of many different approaches to reading instruction. The language experience approach, key vocabulary approach, whole words in the environment, eclectic basal readers, paired-associate learning, and Bloomfield's linguistic method are based on different assumptions and employ different methods, but they all teach whole words at some point.

Assumptions underlying the whole word method differ with the approach. Paired-associate learning rests on the assumption that when children are rewarded for the correct response to an external stimulus, they will make those responses in the future. The language experience and key vocabulary approach rest on the assumption that children are *interested* and will learn things they want to learn. The language experience approach attempts to engender interest in words through group language activities; the key vocabulary approach attempts to discover words that individuals are already interested in. Eclectic basal readers attempt to capitalize on the interests of the "average" child and rely on paired-associate assumptions as well.

Eclectic and phonics- or skills-emphasis basal readers were described and the major differences between them were stated. This discussion appears in this chapter because eclectic programs use the whole word method as the beginning approach. It was necessary that these widely used programs be described so that I could present a meaningful discussion. Basal readers will be referred to repeatedly in this book.

The criterion used to select words for teaching by the whole word method depends on the approach. The interest of the child in the words is paramount in the key vocabulary approach and the language experience approach. The frequency of words in the language is another consideration, however, because a child who does not learn to recognize *the, of,* and *and* will be severely handicapped in reading as these are very frequent words in written English.

Teachers and creators of materials for teaching reading use word frequency counts to guide their choices of words to include in word recognition lessons. Some lists identify words by the grade level where they are appropriately introduced.

These lists are sometimes used to get an estimate of a child's reading ability. Knowing that a child recognizes the first 100 of Fry's instant words tells an experienced teacher something about a child's reading ability. These lists guide teachers in choosing words that ought to be taught because they are likely to be encountered frequently at a particular level. They are not intended to limit the words that are taught at a particular level.

In most programs, phonics, word structure, and use of context are introduced at some point as methods of word recognition. Even then, words are sometimes taught as whole words because they represent phonics or structure generalizations that will soon be taught. Some words, such as *pinochle,* simply do not lend themselves to other methods of word recognition. The whole word approach is a frequently used method of teaching word recognition at all levels of teaching reading.

Success in using the whole word approach depends on several principles. Words should be taught in context (written or oral language or physical context) so that the meaning of the word is not ambiguous, the correct pronunciation is clear, and the learner can be helped to recognize the word through the context.

It is the teacher's responsibility to enlist the students' attention. The students should find it necessary to remember the word through appropriate visual clues (the first letter, the shape, the length, etc.). They should be kept from relying exclusively on irrelevant clues such as the one place the word is always found in their experience.

There are several sound reasons for using a whole word approach in the earliest stages of reading. Purposeful reading can begin soon after instruction begins. The whole word approach capitalizes on student interest. The whole word approach has a long history of success and has been advocated by many eminent scholars. Children who learn to read before coming to school and with no apparent instruction seem to learn to read through a whole word approach.

Bloomfield's linguistic approach begins by teaching whole words in a paired-associate fashion. Words are chosen because they represent regular letter-sound relationships, and groups of words having minimal differences are chosen. The assumption underlying this approach is that if words are carefully chosen, the student will discover for himself or herself the regular letter-sound relationships of English.

All the approaches discussed in this chapter introduce letter-sound relationships and other methods of word recognition at some point.

FOR FURTHER READING

Combs, M. (1984). Developing concepts about print with patterned sentence stories. *The Reading Teacher, 38*(2), 178–181.

Cunningham, P. M. (1980). Teaching were, with, what, and other "four-letter" words. *The Reading Teacher, 34*(2), 160–163.

Dickerson, D. P. (1982). A study of use of games to reinforce sight vocabulary. *The Reading Teacher, 36*(1), 46–49.

Dolch, E. W. (1936). A basic sight vocabulary. *Elementary School Journal, 36,* 456–460; *37,* 268–272.

Eeds, M. (1985). Bookwords: Using a beginning word list of high-frequency words from children's literature K–3. *The Reading Teacher, 38*(4), 418–423.

Ehri, L. C. (1975). Word consciousness in readers and prereaders. *Journal of Educational Psychology, 67,* 204–212.

Fry, E. B. (1987). Picture nouns for reading and vocabulary improvement. *The Reading Teacher, 41*(2), 185–193.

Goodall, M. (1984). Can four year olds "read" words in the environment? *The Reading Teacher, 37*(6), 478–482.

Gray, W. S. (1960). *On their own in reading* (rev. ed.). Chicago: Scott, Foresman.

Holden, M. H., & MacGinitie, W. H. (1972). Children's conceptions of word boundaries in speech and print. *Journal of Educational Psychology, 63,* 551–557.

Johnson, D. D. (1971). A basic vocabulary for beginning reading. *Elementary School Journal, 72,* 29–34.

Morris, D. (1981). Concept of word: A developmental phenomenon in the beginning reading and writing process. *Language Arts, 58,* 659–668.

Morris, D., & Henderson, E. H. (1981). Assessing the beginning reader's "concept of word." *Reading World,* 279–285.

Reimer, B. L. (1983). Recipes for language experience stories. *Reading Journal, 36*(4), 396–401.

Templeton, S. (1980). Young children invent words: Developing concepts of "wordness." *The Reading Teacher, 33*(4), 454–459.

CHAPTER 5

Teaching Word Recognition: Phonics

DEFINITIONS: PHONICS, PHONOLOGY, AND PHONETICS

There are relationships between ordinary English spelling and the pronunciation of words. For example, there is a generalization that can be drawn about the initial sound and the initial letter in the words *dad, dog, den,* and *dime.* The generalization is that printed words that begin with the letter *d* usually begin with the sound /d/. The study of the relationship between ordinary spelling and the pronunciation of words is called *phonics.* A collection of such generalizations into a body of knowledge is also called *phonics.* Teaching such generalizations to children as a method of word recognition is also called *phonics.*

Two other terms are sometimes confused with *phonics.* They are *phonology* and *phonetics.*

Phonology is the study of language sounds. A phonologist uses the same methods in studying the sounds of any language, for example, English, Russian, Greek, Arabic, or Chinese. The fact that these languages do not share a writing system is irrelevant to phonologists because they are studying the sounds of spoken language, not their writing systems.

Phonetics is a system of representing sounds in special symbols. For example, the International Phonetic Alphabet is a set of symbols that enables phonologists to represent the sounds of any language. (See *The Random House Dictionary of the English Language* (Flexner, 1987) under *International Phonetic Alphabet.*) A phonetic representation of a language might not even resemble the symbols or ordinary spelling of the written form of the language.

Phonics is concerned with the relationship between ordinary spelling and pronunciation.

MORE PHONICS OR LESS?

The question is often raised in shrill tones whether or not one should teach phonics. Critics of programs that do not emphasize phonics charge that children do not read as well today as children did in the past and claim that this is true because phonics—which was the proven method of the past—has recently been abandoned for a whole word, look-and-say method, where no phonics principles are ever taught. Critics of phonics-based programs charge that the aim of such programs is to teach word calling rather than understanding and that in such programs children do not learn that language has meaning.

Attacks from both sides contain false assumptions. First, although historical trends toward more phonics and less phonics have been observed in America, the level of literacy among children who attend school in America has remained fairly constant (Matthews, 1966). More recent studies (Farr et al., 1978) have shown that reading test scores have not declined over the recent decades but have improved slightly.

Second, although programs that teach phonics exclusively are available, they are intended to be used as supplements to regular reading programs. Among programs that are designed to be used as *the* major approach to reading instruction (for example, basal reading programs, individual reading programs, and so on; see Chapter 15), none teaches all phonics and no comprehension or all comprehension and no phonics. Programs do differ, however, in terms of when phonics generalizations are introduced, how many phonics generalizations are introduced, and the extent to which phonics generalizations are taught in isolation as distinct lessons.

In this chapter some phonics generalizations will be presented, and some principles will be suggested for deciding which phonics generalizations to teach and when to teach them.

DECIDING WHAT TO TEACH

A Compromise Between Simplicity and Truth

Phonics generalizations seem easy if a person knows them. They can seem hopelessly complicated if a person does not know them or if he or she is trying to teach them to someone who does not know them. One reason phonic generalizations may appear to be so complicated is that they are not immutable laws.

A discussion of the sound represented by the consonant letter *b* will help to demonstrate the problem. The letter *b* usually represents the sound /b/, but it does not represent the sound /b/ in *climb* or *lamb*. So what does one teach?

No Rule.   A person might decide that she will not teach any letter-sound correspondence for *b* since there is no hard and fast rule. This is clearly absurd since anyone who can read knows that *b* nearly always represents /b/. In a computerized study of letter-sound relationships (Hanna et al., 1966) in approximately 20,000 words, the letter *b* corresponds to the sound /b/ over 2,000 times and it is "silent" as in *climb* 27 times. Those 27 instances tend to occur in words that beginning readers are not likely to encounter in print such as *climb, dumb, limb, plumb,* and *womb.*

A Complicated Rule That Is Always True.   A person might decide that there is a generalization, but it is a bit more complicated: the letter *b* represents /b/ unless it is preceded by *m* at the end of a syllable. This may be too complicated for many students to understand. Imagine a child who has learned 50 words by sight. Does it seem wise to complicate a simple and widely applicable generalization by qualifying it so it will take into account a comparatively rare spelling?

A Simple Rule That Is Not Always True.   A person might decide that there is a generalization and that it is so widely applicable and the exceptions are so rare that she will teach it without qualifications, except to say *usually* instead of *always:* the letter *b* usually represents the sound /b/.

Later—perhaps a year later—a qualification of the generalization can be dealt with explicitly: the letters *mb* at the end of a syllable usually represent the sound /m/.

Teaching children that phonic generalizations are *usually* true is a major objective of phonics instruction. Children should learn that using phonics is something of a juggling act. When you encounter a word you do not recognize, you apply phonic generalizations on a trial and error basis. You are seeking a *probable* pronunciation that *approximates* or *suggests* a word you know and that makes sense in context. You realize that these generalizations may not apply in this particular case, and if one set of generalizations does not suggest a word you know and that makes sense, you are ready to try a different set of generalizations.

Some Phonics Generalizations Are Interesting, But Not Very Useful for Word Recognition

The question arises as to whether it ever makes sense to teach the generalization that *mb* at the end of a syllable usually represents /m/ *as a clue to word recognition.* It is not a very useful rule because it applies to so few words. Instead of teaching this generalization as a clue to word recognition, it might be taught as an observation about a group of words that one presumes the students already recognize.

Imagine the word *tomb* occurring in a fifth grade textbook. The teacher might take the opportunity to point out that this unusual spelling occurs in other words such as *bomb, climb, comb, crumb, dumb, lamb, limb, numb,* and *thumb.*

Teaching this kind of generalization at this stage will not result in students' using the generalization to recognize as yet unencountered words. Instead, it is just one of dozens of facts about written English that people who love the study of language find interesting. Classrooms should be places where knowledge about language is esteemed and where discovery and discussion of such facts are a source of pleasure—regardless of their immediate utility.

One point to be taken from this discussion is that teachers of reading should know a lot about phonics, but they must not think that they need to teach all they know at once, nor must they think that every phonics generalization they know will be useful to young readers for word recognition.

Principles for Deciding What to Teach

Regarding Content.   Some principles that will be developed in this chapter are these:

1. Teach generalizations that consistently apply to words that children will en-counter in beginning reading (such as that *b* usually represents /b/).
2. Avoid delving into qualifications until advanced stages of reading skill have been attained.
3. Realize that some qualifications of widely applied rules are legitimately taught as interesting facts about written language rather than as widely useful clues to word recognition.

Regarding Attitude.   Children should be taught the uses and limitations of phonics from the start. Children should develop attitudes based on the following facts:

1. Phonics clues lead to approximate pronunciations; while part of the student's attention should be on spelling-sound possibilities, another part of his or her attention should be devoted to guessing at known words that conform to the suggested pronunciation and that make sense.
2. The spelling of some words is tricky, and therefore some words are best learned as whole words or recognized primarily through context rather than phonics.

SOME PHONICS GENERALIZATIONS

Definition of Consonants and Vowels

Phonological Definitions.   Phonologists talk about two kinds of speech sounds—con-sonant sounds and vowel sounds. The difference is a technical one having to do with the physiology of language sound production. Speech sounds are made by the tongue, teeth, palate, and other organs. The one thing that all speech sounds in English have in common is that there is air moving out of the lungs during speech sound production. If the movement of air is stopped (as in /t/ or /g/, for example), diverted (as in /m/ or /n/, for example), or obstructed (as in /f/ or /s/, for example), the sound is considered a consonant sound. If the movement of air is not stopped, diverted, or obstructed, the sound is considered a vowel sound.

Phonics Definitions.   But one need not know the technical physiological definition of consonant and vowel sounds to learn phonics generalizations. Most reading pupils (and many reading teachers) learn simply that vowel letters are *a, e, i, o,* and *u* and that the vowel sounds are the sounds usually represented by these letters. Strictly speaking, *y* and *w* are sometimes involved in vowel spellings (as in *sky* and *how*). The consonant letters are all the rest. The consonant sounds are sounds usually represented by consonant letters.

Sounds Represented by Single Consonant Letters

The most consistent phonic generalizations are concerned with single consonant letters in one-syllable words. In phonics "a single consonant letter" is one that does not appear next to another consonant letter in a syllable. In *dog* the *d* and *g* are single consonant letters. In *save* the *s* and *v* are single consonant letters. In *spark* there are no single consonant letters. Each consonant letter, *s, p, r,* and *k,* appears next to another consonant letter in the same syllable.

One-to-One Correspondence.   There are 14 consonant letters that usually represent only one sound as long as they appear as single consonant letters. These letters are *b, d, f, h, j, k, l, m, n, p, r, t, v,* and *z.*

   Of course, these letters do not always conform to this rule. For example, single consonant letter *d* represents the sound /j/ in several longer words (words of several syllables) such as *educate, gradual* and *cordial.* (See Activity 5.A.)

ACTIVITY 5.A DECIDING WHAT TO TEACH, WHEN TO TEACH IT, AND WHY TO TEACH IT

> The question one must ask is whether the fact that the single consonant letter *d* sometimes represents /j/ is an important qualification of the generalization or a confusing quibble? Are words such as *educate* and *gradual* likely to appear in beginning reading?
>
> If a person is analyzing a word like *gradual* and he or she presumes the *d* represents /d/, will that person arrive at a pronunciation so close to the correct one that he or she will recognize the word? If you were writing a reading program for first grade, how would you handle the fact that *d* sometimes represents /j/? How would you handle this fact in a fifth grade program? Review the discussion of the sound represented by the letters *mb* in words like *bomb* and *climb* on page 117.

Single Consonant Letters That Represent More than One Sound.

Letters w and y. When *w* and *y* appear as single consonant letters at the beginning of syllables, they each represent only one sound as in *was* and *yet.*

   When *w* and *y* do not appear as single consonant letters at the beginning of a syllable they may represent other sounds. In *gym* and *cry, y* represents a vowel sound; in *how,* the *o* and *w* taken together represent a vowel sound.

The Letter s. When *s* appears as a single consonant letter at the beginning of a syllable, it usually represents only one sound, /s/ as in *sing.* When it appears at the end of a syllable it may represent /s/ as in *bus* or /z/ as in *has.*

The Letters c and g. When *c* appears as a single consonant, it may represent the sound /k/ as in *cut* or the sound /s/ as in *cent*. When *g* appears as a single consonant, it may represent the sound /g/ as in *gave* or /j/ as in *gem*.

The fact is that there are very reliable spelling clues to the sounds of the letters *c* and *g*. If *c* is followed by *e, i,* or *y,* it usually represents the /s/ sound as in *cent, city,* and *cycle*. If *c* is not followed by *e, i,* or *y,* it usually represents the /k/ sound as in *cat, cot, cut, crab,* and *picnic.*

If *g* is followed by *e, i,* or *y,* it usually represents the /j/ sound as in *gem, gin,* and *gym*. If *g* is not followed by *e, i,* or *y,* it usually represents the sound /g/ as in *gave, got, gum, grow,* and *bug.*

A more generalized rule that covers the sounds represented by the letters *c* and *g* is that if these letters are followed by *e, i,* or *y,* they usually represent their ''soft'' (sibilant) sounds, /s/ or /j/. If they are not followed by *e, i,* or *y,* they represent their ''hard'' (guttural) sounds, /k/ or /g/. (See Activity 5.B.)

ACTIVITY 5.B DECIDING WHAT TO TEACH, WHEN TO TEACH IT, AND WHY TO TEACH IT

Each of the paragraphs regarding the single consonant letters *c* and *g* states a generalization about these spellings and the sounds they usually represent.

1. If you were teaching first grade, which of the following attitudes would you adopt in regard to teaching each of these generalizations?

a. I would not teach it because I believe it is too confusing or abstract, and, therefore, it would not be helpful to children at this age and stage of reading skill.

b. I would teach it because I believe it would be a helpful aid to word recognition for children at this age and stage of reading skill.

c. I would teach it because it is an interesting observation about spelling-sound relationships in English.

2. If you were teaching third grade (fifth grade or eighth grade), what would your attitude be?

Make this activity the basis of a short written paper, a small group discussion, or a class discussion.

The Letter q. The consonant letter *q* is always followed by *u* and represents /kw/ as in *queen* or /k/ as in *bouquet.*

Although there are a half-dozen moderately common words where *qu* represents /kw/ (*quarter, queen, question, square,* for example), there are no common words where *qu* represents /k/. Furthermore, many words where *qu* represents /k/ do not conform to English spelling-sound principles in other ways (*bouquet* and *marquise,* for example). As these facts are presented, the option of teaching that *qu* usually represents /kw/ and letting it go at that may seem more and more reasonable.

The Letter x. The consonant letter *x* represents the sound /ks/ as in *box* or two consonant sounds /g/ plus /z/ as in *exist* or /z/ as in *xylophone.*

In the word frequency count of 5 million words in American schoolbooks (Carroll, Davies, & Richman, 1971), the most frequent word where *x* is pronounced /z/ is *xylophone.* According to this study the statistical probability of encountering the word *xylophone* in an American schoolbook is less than 1 in every million words. The probability of encountering this word outside a music book is even less than this. So if a class comes across *xylophone* in a story, does the teacher rush to teach that *x* sometimes represents /z/? Of course not. You teach the word as a sight word or students may even "sound it out" using the usual sound of *x* and arrive at something like /ksi lō fon/. If they know the word and it is in context, they have probably arrived at a pronunciation close enough to the correct pronunciation to recognize it.

In summary, this section on sounds represented by single consonant letters touched upon some important facts about phonics in general and about teaching phonics. Before proceeding, it will be useful to reflect upon some of these facts about the nature of spelling-sound relationships and to make some facts explicit that have only been implied.

1. The position of a letter in a syllable may be relevant to the sound the letter represents. (Review the sections on the letters *w*, *y*, and *s*.)
2. Letters following a letter in a syllable may be relevant to the sound the letter represents. (Review the section on the letters *c* and *g*.)

Suggestions About the Content and Timing of Phonics Instruction Regarding Single Consonant Letters.   Single consonant letters sometimes represent more than one sound. In deciding whether to teach only the most frequent correspondence or to teach alternative correspondences explicitly, one wants to consider whether or not

1. The alternative spelling-sound correspondences are likely to appear in many words the students will encounter *at their stage of progress*.
2. The alternative spelling-sound correspondences are similar enough to the most frequent one that students will arrive at pronunciations that will enable them to recognize words in context.
3. The alternative spelling-sound correspondences are likely to be useful in word recognition, or whether they are simply interesting observations about written language and should be taught as such as students progress in reading. (See Activity 5.C.)

ACTIVITY 5.C DECIDING WHAT TO TEACH, WHEN TO TEACH IT, AND WHY TO TEACH IT

Using Activity 5.B as a model, decide what you would teach in beginning reading about the sounds represented by the single consonant letters *d*, *w*, *y*, *s*, *q*, and *x*. What would you teach about the sounds usually represented by these single consonant letters in third grade, fifth grade, or eighth grade?

Sounds Represented by Consonant Letters Together in a Syllable

Consonant Digraphs.   Consonant digraphs are pairs of consonant letters that represent a single consonant sound that is different from the consonant sound either letter usually stands for. The letters *th* in *the* represent a sound different from /t/ or /h/. The most common digraphs are *ch* as in *church*, *sh* as in *ship*, *ph* as in *phone*, *ng* as in *ring*, and *th* as in *thaw* or *the*. Each of these digraphs represents a single sound except for *th*, which represents two subtly different sounds. The difference in the sounds represented by *th* is that one does not "voice" the initial sound of *thaw,* but one does voice the initial sound of *the.*

Consonant Blends.   Consonant blends are consonant letters that appear together and represent the usual sound of each letter "blended" one into the other. Consonant blends that frequently appear at the beginning of syllables are *bl* as in *black* and *str* as in *stripe.* See Box 5.1. Consonant blends that frequently appear at the ends of syllables are *ct* as in *act, nt* as in *rent,* and *st* as in *mist.* See Box 5.2.

In some dialects of American English, people pronounce and hear a difference between the words *witch* (pronounced /wich/) and *which* (pronounced /hwich/). In such dialects most words spelled with the beginning letters *wh* are pronounced with the initial consonant blend /hw/. This is peculiar because the order of the consonant letters is the reverse of the consonant sounds they represent in the word. In other equally standard dialects *witch* and *which* are pronounced the same—/wich/—and in these dialects words spelled with the beginning letters *wh* are pronounced with the initial consonant /w/.

This might leave one in something of a quandary as to what to teach. A couple of suggestions may relieve your anxiety. (1) Teach that the letters *wh* at the beginning of a syllable represent the beginning sound of *what* and *when.* You need not explicitly state what that beginning sound is. (2) Teach the usual sound represented by *w* and the usual sound represented by *wh* on different days. Do not comment on the similarity or difference.

In summary, it is important to distinguish between an interesting fact and a clue to word recognition. In a sixth or seventh grade class, a teacher might comment on the pronunciation of the words *which* and *witch* and the fact that some individuals pronounce *wh* in *which* as /hw/ and others pronounce it as /w/. But this is not a lesson in phonics as an aid to word recognition. It is a lesson in language study.

The objectives of the two lessons are very different and should not be confused. What might be hopelessly abstract and confusing to a 6-year-old trying to learn word recognition skills may be very interesting to a 12- or 15-year-old who recognizes all the words concerned but is learning something about phonology and the dialects of American English.

BOX 5.1 COMMON CONSONANT BLENDS AT THE BEGINNING OF SYLLABLES

bl *blue, blow, block*	**br** *brown, brave, brick*	**sp** *spell, space, spoon*
cl *clay, clock, clown*	**cr** *cross, crib, cry*	**st** *store, still, stop*
fl *flip, flag, flat*	**dr** *dress, drink, drum*	**sc** *scare, scream, school*
pl *plane, play, please*	**fr** *fright, frog, fry*	**sw** *swim, sweat, swan*
sl *sleep, slow, slip*	**tr** *tree, trick, tramp*	**tw** *twist, twelve, twig*

BOX 5.2 COMMON CONSONANT BLENDS AT THE END OF SYLLABLES

ct	st	sk	sp	nt	lk	ld	nd
fa*ct*	mo*st*	a*sk*	cri*sp*	we*nt*	mi*lk*	mo*ld*	hi*nd*
ta*ct*	be*st*	de*sk*	gra*sp*	hu*nt*	su*lk*	fo*ld*	mi*nd*
a*ct*	che*st*	ma*sk*	ra*sp*	li*nt*	e*lk*	we*ld*	wi*nd*

BOX 5.3 SILENT CONSONANT LETTERS

kn words	wr words	-ck ending	-mb ending	-lm ending
*kn*ee	*wr*ite	sa*ck*	co*mb*	a*l*m
*kn*ob	*wr*ing	blo*ck*	thu*mb*	ca*l*m
*kn*ife	*wr*ong	du*ck*	cli*mb*	pa*l*m

"Silent" Consonant Letters.   Sometimes two consonant letters appear together in a syllable, but they represent the usual sound of one letter. In *knee,* for example, the initial consonant sound is /n/; the *k* in the spelling is said to be silent. Other spellings that include silent letters are *ck, wr, lm,* and *mb* as in Box 5.3. "Double consonants" such as the two *l*'s in *tall* and two *g*'s in *egg* can be thought of as special cases of silent letters. One of the pair represents its usual sound and the other is silent.

Spelling Clues to Vowel Sounds in One-Syllable Words

Relationships between vowel sounds and ordinary spellings are less consistent than are the relationships between consonant sounds and ordinary spelling. The inconsistency of the relationship between vowel sounds and spelling has led some authors to advise students to try to recognize unfamiliar words by sounding out the consonants only and uttering a neutral vowel sound like the *a* in *alone* for the vowels. The idea is that if a word is in context, thinking of the correct consonant sounds and the (possibly distorted) vowel sounds in sequence will result in a pronunciation that will be close enough to the real one that the word will be recognized.

This is not a bad idea, particularly for advanced readers dealing with multisyllabic words, but spelling-sound relationships for vowels in one- and two-syllable words are reasonably dependable. Once again, however, the teacher must be prepared to deal with the tension between the desire to teach generalizations that are easy and generalizations that are always true. In this section, generalizations will be presented that are easy to understand and that apply often enough to be worth learning.

Single Vowel Letters.   In one-syllable words, a single vowel letter followed by one or more consonant letters usually represents the short sound of the vowel as in *pan, get, bin, mop,* and *fun.* See Box 5.4.

In one-syllable words, single vowel letters at the end of the word (not followed by consonant letter(s)) usually represent the long sound of the vowel as in *we, hi,* and *no.* See Box 5.5.

The fact is that there are very few one-syllable words that end with a single vowel letter. This generalization is useful, though, because it applies to syllables in longer words, as will be shown presently.

BOX 5.4 SINGLE VOWEL LETTERS IN ONE-SYLLABLE WORDS FOLLOWED BY ONE OR MORE CONSONANTS

bat	pep	bib	rod	hut
rap	den	fit	mom	bus
sand	bent	chimp	pond	just

BOX 5.5 SINGLE VOWEL LETTERS AT THE END OF ONE-SYLLABLE WORDS

me	hi	go	gnu	by
he		so	flu	my

BOX 5.6 LONG VOWELS REPRESENTED BY THE VOWEL-CONSONANT-SILENT *E* PATTERN

cake	kite	rode	flute	Pete
plate	bride	pole	tube	gene
spade	quite	hose	June	eve

BOX 5.7 SHORT VOWELS REPRESENTED BY THE VOWEL-CONSONANT-CONSONANT-SILENT *E* PATTERN

dance	else	since	bronze	dunce
prance	fence	bridge	lodge	judge
trance	twelve	ridge	dodge	fudge

BOX 5.8 TWO VOWELS TOGETHER REPRESENTING A LONG VOWEL SOUND

ai	ay	ea	ee	ie	oa	oe
bail	bay	beach	beef	die	bloat	doe
drain	gray	cheat	cheese	lie	foam	hoe
frail	pay	east	freeze	tie	goat	toe

BOX 5.9 TWO VOWEL LETTERS TOGETHER REPRESENTING DIPHTHONGS

oo	oo	au	aw	ou	ow	oi	oy
bloom	book	caught	awe	blouse	brow	broil	boy
boot	crook	fault	bawl	bounce	clown	choice	ploy
cool	good	cause	crawl	found	cow	foil	soy

Single Vowel Letters in One-Syllable Words Ending in -e. In a one-syllable word, a single vowel letter followed by a single consonant letter and final *e* usually represents the long sound of the vowel and the *e* is silent as in *take, bite, nose,* and *sure.* See Box 5.6.

In a one-syllable word a single vowel letter followed by two consonant letters and a final *e* usually represents the short sound of the vowel and the final *e* is silent as in *dance, else, since, bronze,* and *dunce.* See Box 5.7.

Two Vowel Letters Together in One-Syllable Words. In a one-syllable word, two vowel letters together may represent the long sound of the first vowel letter as in *mail, pay, weak, beef, die, boat, snow,* and *sue.* See Box 5.8.

In a one-syllable word two vowel letters together may represent one of the so-called ''glided vowel sounds'' or diphthongs as in *tool, took, haul, law, out, down, oil,* and *boy.* See Box 5.9.

Deciding whether two vowel letters together in a syllable represent a diphthong or the long sound of the first vowel letter is not as arbitrary as it may appear at first. Most of the common two-vowel letter combinations usually represent either one option or the other. Only the spellings *ow* (as in *how* contrasted with *row*) and *oo* (as in *tool* contrasted with *look*) frequently represent more than one sound. (See Activity 5.D.)

ACTIVITY 5.D LEARNING TO SPOT WORD RECOGNITION PROBLEMS THAT A PHONICS GENERALIZATION MIGHT HELP

We can presume that Charlotte will teach phonics generalizations when they appear in her phonics-emphasis basal reading program. Matthew will teach some generalizations when they appear in his eclectic basal reading program, but he might skip some, reasoning that they do not seem useful. He will teach some on occasions when he observes students having word recognition difficulties because they have not discovered a useful phonics generalization.

For example, in a reading conference with second grader Heather, the student might attempt to pronounce *law* something like this "lay-wa." That is, she attempts to pronounce the letter *a* with a long *a* sound and add a /w/ sound to it. Matthew might respond by saying "No, Heather. That word is 'law.' The letters *aw* are often pronounced /ô/ as in *law, straw,* and *draw*" (printing these words as he speaks).

He might let it go at that, or he might find a lesson on diphthongs and teach it to Heather and perhaps two or three other children who seem to have the same problem.

A. Work in pairs and role play a child mispronouncing a word because he or she fails to apply a spelling sound generalization presented in this chapter and the teacher's response, that is, the ensuing impromptu lesson.

The words used as examples in the discussion on pages 119–125 (begin with the letters *w* and *y* to present page) and the words in Boxes 5.1 to 5.9 will be good resources for this activity.

If time permits, the mispronounced words ought to be in sentences that might appear in children's books to make the activity more realistic.

B. Plan the "mistake" and the response with your partner at first and present your dialogue to the class.

C. After some practice have the "child" present "mistakes" to a "teacher" who was not in on the planning. See if the "teacher" can respond with an appropriate generalization in a way that the "child" might understand.

Spelling Clues to Vowel Sounds in Two-Syllable Words

Definition of Syllable.   A syllable is part of a word with one vowel sound that may be preceded and/or followed by consonant sounds. A syllable can be a single vowel sound like the word *I* or the first syllable in *acorn* (pronounced /a′ korn/); or a consonant and vowel sound like the first syllable in *paper* (pronounced /pā′ per/); or a vowel and consonant sound like the first syllable in *actor* (pronounced /ak′ tor/); or a consonant, vowel, and consonant sound like the first syllable in *lantern* (pronounced /lan′ tern/).

Once children begin to learn about vowel sounds, they can begin to identify spoken words with one, two, and three syllables by counting the number of separate vowel sounds they hear. This is a useful exercise for the purpose of learning the meaning of the word *syllable,* but for reading, the student must learn to divide printed words he or she does not recognize into syllables for the purpose of applying phonic generalizations to the syllables.

Vowel letter spellings (single vowel letters or two vowel letters together) usually represent a single vowel sound and are clues to the presence of a syllable. Even if the student did not recognize the following words, he or she would be fairly confident that they were two-syllable words because there are two vowel spellings separated by one or more consonant letters: *final, afraid; detour; heinous, matter, poignant.*

As in one-syllable words, a final *e* after a consonant letter usually does not represent a separate vowel sound and is, therefore, not a clue to the presence of a syllable. Even if the youngster did not recognize the following words, he or she would be fairly confident they were two-syllable words because there are two vowel spellings separated by one or more consonant letters and a final *e* that does not represent an additional vowel sound: *pleasure, senate, commerce, orange, knowledge.*

However, a final *e* preceded by a consonant and an *l* usually is a clue to the presence of a syllable. Even if the student did not recognize the following words, she or he would be fairly confident that they were two-syllable words because there is a vowel spelling followed by a final syllable ending in *-le: cable, eagle, crumble, little,* and *foible.*

The same generalizations apply to words having any number of syllables. One could determine that the following were three-syllable words because of the way they are spelled: *liberal, sufficient, tomorrow, camouflage, millionaire, orchestra, cuticle, boondoggle,* and *voluble.*

The clues to vowel sounds in words of more than one syllable are the same as clues to vowel sounds in one-syllable words, but there are two additional factors to consider:

1. A person cannot apply some spelling sound generalizations until he or she knows where syllables begin and end.
2. Syllables in English words having more than one syllable do not receive equal stress. Spelling sound generalizations apply regularly to stressed syllables, but vowels in unstressed syllables tend to sound like the vowel in the last syllable of *butter* or the first syllable in *alone,* regardless of how they are spelled.

Dividing Unrecognized Written Words into Syllables.   When students encounter a word they do not recognize, they do not know where one syllable ends and the next begins and they do not know which syllable is stressed. But, once again, there are fairly reliable generalizations for deciding where to divide words into syllables and for deciding which syllable to stress. Spelling clues to dividing written words into syllables are based on patterns of vowels and consonant letters.

Vowel-Consonant-Consonant-Vowel. When two consonant letters appear between two vowel letters, syllable division usually occurs between the two consonant letters as in Box 5.10.

Vowel-Consonant-Vowel. When one consonant letter appears between two vowel letters, syllable division often occurs between the first vowel and the consonant as in Box

BOX 5.10 SYLLABLE DIVISION FOR WORDS CONTAINING A VOWEL-CONSONANT-CONSONANT-VOWEL PATTERN.

af / ter	boun / ty	ac / count
sus / tain	al / ley	un / der
ar / gue	boul / der	bliz / zard

BOX 5.11 SYLLABLE DIVISION FOR WORDS CONTAINING A VOWEL-CONSONANT-VOWEL PATTERN

di / ner	fi / nal	ti / tle
ba / by	lo / go	fo / cus
re / tain	i / con	li / lac

5.11. This generalization is not easy to justify on the grounds that it usually applies. When researchers apply this generalization to lists of words in schoolbooks it has been found to work about half the time or slightly less than half the time (Clymer, 1963; Bailey, 1966–67; Emans, 1967).

Sometimes the rule is stated as follows:

When one consonant letter appears between two vowel letters, syllable division occurs before the consonant letter (as in *ba/by*) or after the consonant letter (as in *ov/en*).

This often leaves people scratching their heads. Which is it—before or after?

Most authorities choose to state the generalization as it is stated here (that syllable division often occurs between the consonant and vowel, as in *baby*) so the student will have a consistent first approach.

But you want to keep in mind that the purpose of teaching syllabication generalizations is that they give students a method for recognizing words that are unfamiliar to them at first sight. Visually breaking the word into syllables gives them manageable, pronounceable units to which spelling sound generalizations can be applied. Students should learn that if dividing the word one way does not suggest a word they know, they should try another way.

Consonant: -"le" at the End of a Word. When a word ends in *-le* preceded by one or more consonants, syllable division usually occurs before the consonant closest to *-le,* as in Box 5.12.

Consonant Digraphs. When a consonant digraph appears in a word, the consonant digraph is treated as a single consonant letter and the vowel-consonant-vowel rule or the vowel-consonant-consonant-vowel rule is followed as in Box 5.13.

BOX 5.12 SYLLABLE DIVISION FOR WORDS CONTAINING *-LE* AT THE END

ma / ple	strug / gle	i / dle
gam / ble	cy / cle	jin / gle
stee / ple	trem / ble	mum / ble

BOX 5.13 SYLLABLE DIVISION FOR WORDS CONTAINING CONSONANT DIGRAPHS

e / ther	mar / shal
pa / thos	en / chant
tro / phy	or / phan

Applying Clues to Vowel Sounds in Two-Syllable Words.   Look at the syllables resulting from applying the clues to syllable division in Boxes 5.10 to 5.13. Apply the clues to vowel sound in one-syllable words to these syllables. This procedure does not always result in exactly the same vowel sounds as one hears in the whole word, but it results in pronunciation close enough to the real one that it should lead to word recognition if the spoken word is familiar. This is particularly true if the word is in context.

This statement does not apply to the last syllable of words ending in a consonant plus *-le* as in Box 5.12. This spelling does not appear in one-syllable words.

You do not want to confuse dividing unrecognized words into syllables for the purpose of applying phonics with the task of the typist, printer, or editor in dividing words at the end of a printed line. Conventions for dividing words at the end of a printed line reflect knowledge of how the word is pronounced (which is precisely what the reader does not know) and knowledge of scholarly conventions (which is something the reader does not need to know).

Children who divide the word *writer—wri/ter—*and arrive at the correct pronunciation have accomplished their purpose. An editor who allows the word *writer* to be divided *wri/ter* at the end of a line is displaying his or her ignorance of printing conventions. As a reading teacher you are concerned with the performance of the child trying to identify an unfamiliar word. You are not concerned with the editor's knowledge of conventions for dividing words at the end of a line. (See Activity 5.E.)

ACTIVITY 5.E LEARNING TO SPOT A WORD RECOGNITION PROBLEM THAT KNOWLEDGE ABOUT SYLLABLES MIGHT HELP

Using Activity 5.D as a model, work in pairs and role play a child mispronouncing a word because he or she fails to divide a word correctly into syllables or fails to apply the rules to vowel sound after the word is divided correctly. For example,

CHILD [LOOKING AT *MARSHAL*]: Mars-hal
TEACHER: No. The letters *s* and *h* usually represent /sh/ as in *should,* so we keep them together. So where would you divide this word?
CHILD: I suppose *m-a-r* and *s-h-a-l.* Let's see. That's mar-shall. Oh! It's *marshal.*

The words used in Boxes 5.10 and 5.13 will be a good resource for this activity.
As in Activity 5.D, make this a two-part activity where the "teacher" is in on planning the "mistake" in the first part and where the teacher must respond appropriately without being in on the planning in the second part.

Generalizations for Applying Stress (Accent) to Unrecognized Words

In two-syllable words stress usually falls on the first syllable. In three-syllable words stress usually falls on the first or second syllable. If a word contains a prefix or a suffix (as longer words often do), special considerations apply that will be taken up in Chapter 6, on word structure.

In teaching about the application of stress in English words, it is most important to instill an attitude of flexibility and a willingness to experiment. There is some question as to whether the correct application of stress leads to recognition of words, or whether the recognition of words leads to the correct application of stress. For example, if children do not immediately recognize the word *cadet* in the sentence *Eisenhower was a cadet at West Point,* their knowledge of dividing words into syllables and of phonics would lead them to the pronunciation /kā det/ with equal stress on both syllables. If *cadet* is a familiar spoken word, they may recognize it and correctly pronounce it (/kə det'/) without further experimentation with stress. Likewise, if children encounter *potato* in the sentence *Put another potato in the soup* and do not immediately recognize it, they may arrive at the pronunciation /pō tā tō/ with equal stress on each syllable. If *potato* is a familiar spoken word, they would no doubt recognize it without any further experimentation with stress and arrive at the correct pronunciation, /pə tā' tō/. (See Activity 5.F.)

ACTIVITY 5.F CHECK YOUR KNOWLEDGE OF SYLLABLE DIVISION AND CLUES TO VOWEL SOUND IN TWO-SYLLABLE WORDS

Here is a scrambled list of words that appear in Boxes 5.10 through 5.13.

diner	logo	focus	after	alley	tremble
sustain	boulder	trophy	baby	account	lilac
orphan	struggle	idle	argue	maple	pathos
bounty	under	mumble	enchant	jingle	marshal
gamble	icon	steeple	retain	blizzard	final
cycle	ether	title			

To check your understanding of this entire section, divide the words into syllables and apply the clues to vowel sounds to the resulting syllables. If this process does not result in a pronunciation that is very close to the actual pronunciation of the word, you have not followed the generalizations for dividing the words into syllables, or you have not followed the generalizations concerning vowel spelling and sound. Reread the section or check with your classmates to see where you went wrong.

KNOWING PHONICS AND KNOWING WHAT TO TEACH

It will become apparent in Chapter 8 that in practice one teaches the generalizations presented here gradually, using words that appear in the reading program. As a result, learning and teaching phonics is not as abstract or as complicated as it may appear in this chapter where generalizations are presented one after the other. However, the danger of phonics instruction becoming overly abstract and overly complex is always present.

Several places in this chapter phonics generalizations have been discussed that are probably not very useful for word recognition, but one would expect a teacher of reading to know them. In this section, several more such generalizations will be discussed, and two examples of extraordinarily fine points regarding phonics will be introduced as further examples of the kind of information one would expect a teacher of reading to have regarding phonics, but one would not expect to see them become part of the word recognition curriculum.

Examples of Phonics Generalizations of Questionable Utility

A Consonant Letter-Sound Generalization.   It was stated earlier that the single consonant letter *t* usually represents the sound /t/, but there is a group of words where *t* represents /sh/. These are words ending in the spellings *-ation* and *-tion*, as in *action, adoption, installation,* and *accusation.* This spelling appears in a large number of English words, but these words tend not to be high-frequency words in primary-grade reading materials. Second, the spellings *-ation* and *-tion* result from adding suffixes to root words such as *act, adopt, install,* and *accuse.* For these two reasons the generalization that *t* sometimes represents /sh/ is frequently taught as part of the structure clues to word recognition (see Chapter 6) rather than as part of the phonics program.

A Vowel Spelling-Sound Generalization.   Single vowel letters followed by *r* and the letter *a* followed by *l* in the same syllable usually represent a sound unlike the short sound of the vowel letter. For example, compare the vowel sound of *cab* and *car, bed* and *her, cob* and *for, sit* and *sir, hat* and *halt.*

The question arises as to whether this additional set of vowel spelling-sound relationships will help or harm learners in reaching the primary objective of teaching phonics: enabling them to recognize words they do not recognize instantly. In context, would trying the short sounds of the vowel lead to a pronunciation close enough to the word so that they would recognize the word?

We are back to the tension between wanting to teach a few generalizations that will be easy to apply and wanting to teach generalizations that will cover every case. Teaching an "*r*-controlled vowel" generalization will certainly complicate matters. Is it worth it?

A Spelling Clue to Syllable Division.   In the discussion of spelling clues to vowel sound and in the discussion of determining the probable number of syllables in a word, it was stated that two vowel letters together in a word usually represent one vowel sound and, therefore, constitute one syllable (or part of one syllable). Burmeister (1968) found this to be true in frequent words. However, it is sometimes true that words divide into syllables between two vowel letters as in

cha/os	cre/ate	di/al
li/on	ne/on	bo/a

Think of all the words you can where two adjacent vowel letters represent vowel sounds in separate syllables, such as in *neon.* Are these words children are likely to encounter in beginning reading? Does it seem worthwhile to qualify the generalization that two adjacent vowel letters in a word probably represent one vowel sound to accommodate these words?

Examples of Fine Points Regarding Phonics

Are "Silent" Letters Silent?   Some reading specialists object to referring to the *e* in *safe* or the *i* in *mail* as "silent." They argue that referring to such letters as "silent" implies they are not related to the sound represented by the spelling of the word, but, in fact, these letters are part of the spelling code—they signal that the other vowel letter in the word represents its long sound.

There is some merit in this argument; however, most students are able to learn that the *e* signals the long sound of the other vowel letter in spellings of this kind and to understand what is meant when the *e*'s are referred to as silent. Introducing this fine point into word recognition instruction does not seem advisable. With older children a discussion of whether "silent letters" are silent may appeal to their interest in language, but it will probably not improve their word recognition skills.

How Many Syllables in Table?   Phonologists have observed that it is possible to form a syllable by pronouncing /l/ after certain consonants (for example, /b/) without inserting a vowel sound between them. Dictionaries record this fact by using what they refer to as a "syllabic *l*." In the *Webster's New World Dictionary of the American Language* (Guralnik, 1986), for example, the phonetic respelling of table is *tā b'l*. By the definition of syllable used in this chapter, therefore, *table* would be considered a one-syllable word, since only one vowel sound is heard in pronouncing the word.

The experience of most reading teachers would no doubt confirm that this is indeed a fine point. The untrained ear cannot distinguish between the last syllable in *bushel* (where phonologists agree that there is a vowel sound heard) and the last syllable in *cradle* (where phonologists hear a syllabic *l*). Attention to this difference would simply bewilder most readers.

Once again this is a fact that may interest older students simply because they are interested in language; it would not contribute to word recognition skill.

In this section several issues, some of them complex, have been introduced and discussed. In each case the conclusion was reached that it would not be useful to raise these issues in teaching word recognition skills to children. A fair and obvious question arises: Why bring these things up in this textbook?

Reading teachers and the profession of teaching reading have never lacked for critics. Most linguists know more about phonology than most reading teachers. Many linguists know more about phonics than many reading teachers. It is not uncommon, therefore, for a linguist to discover that some aspect of the reading curriculum is not wholly compatible with the current state of knowledge in linguistics. When linguists point out the error of reading teachers' ways, it often results in a rout rather than in a discussion, because the reading teacher is overwhelmed by what seems like superior knowledge. It is very important that reading teachers respond to such suggestions from a position that is secure enough to enable them to ask questions and to evaluate these suggestions in the context of what they know—how to teach reading.

SUMMARY

The meanings of the words *phonics, phonology,* and *phonetics* are sometimes confused. The word *phonics* has three meanings. (1) It is the study of the relationship between the ordinary spelling of words and the pronunciation of words. (2) It is the set of generalizations derived from this study, (3) It is the method of teaching word recognition through reference to these generalizations. *Phonology* is the study of spoken language sounds.

It is something linguists study. *Phonetics* is a system of representing speech sounds with written symbols. Phonetics ignores conventional spelling.

Whether or not to teach phonics is often the topic of emotional debate. Extremists who defend phonics as the *only* way to teach reading often claim that present-day students cannot read as well as students of former years because they are not taught phonics. In fact, reading ability among children who attend school in the United States has probably remained the same regardless of trends toward more phonics or less phonics. In the past quarter-century reading performance may have improved slightly in the elementary school grades where reading performance would seem to be most susceptible to methods of teaching word recognition—that is in the lower and middle grades.

Extremists who attack phonics claim that teaching phonics causes children to think that the purpose of reading is to decode words and that students, therefore, never learn to comprehend printed language. However, most published programs introduce both phonics and comprehension. Programs differ in terms of when phonics is introduced, how many generalizations are introduced, and whether phonics is taught separately as distinct lessons.

Phonics generalizations can become very complicated if one tries to state them in a way that covers nearly all words. Children should be taught simple rules that apply widely to words they will encounter at the early stages of learning to read. Some phonics rules may be taught to children at later stages of reading development, not to assist them in word recognition, but because they are interesting facts about written English, and learning to enjoy knowing about language is an important objective.

From the start children should be taught that phonics generalizations lead to *approximations* of the pronunciation of many words. Readers must learn to ask themselves whether the pronunciation they arrive at sounds similar to a word they know and if the word fits the context.

English speech sounds are classified as consonants or vowels. When the air is stopped, diverted, or obstructed by the organs of speech, it is considered a consonant sound; when the air is not stopped, diverted, or obstructed, it is considered a vowel sound. A less technical definition, and one that is preferable for teaching phonics, is that sounds usually represented by vowel letters (*a, e, i, o,* and *u*) are vowel sounds. Sounds usually represented by consonant letters (all letters except *a, e, i, o,* and *u)* are consonant sounds.

The most consistent phonic generalizations concern the sounds represented by single consonant letters. The single consonant letters *w, y, s, c, g, q,* and *x* represent two different sounds. The position in the syllable and letter following these letters often indicate which sound they represent.

Consonant digraphs are two consonant letters that appear together and represent a speech sound that is different from either letter (such as *ch* in *church*). When consonant letters appear adjacent to one another they often represent their usual sounds blended together (such as *str* in *stripe*). These spellings are called *consonant blends*. Sometimes consonant letters appear adjacent to one another, but the usual sound of only one of the letters is represented (such as *lm* in *calm*). In such spellings, the consonant letter whose usual sound is not represented is often referred to as a "silent letter."

The relationships between vowel sounds and spellings are far less consistent than the relationships between consonant sounds and spelling. The letter or letters following vowel letters in a syllable often indicate what sounds the vowel letter represents. The sound a vowel letter represents may depend on the following spelling patterns:

It is the last letter in the syllable.
It is followed by a consonant letter(s) in the syllable.
It is followed by one consonant letter and the letter *e*.
It is followed by two consonant letters and the letter *e*.
It is followed by another vowel letter.

A syllable is part of a spoken word that has one vowel sound. Learning how to divide unfamiliar printed words into parts that probably represent syllables is useful for two reasons. It gives the reader manageable units to attempt to pronounce, and letter-sound correspondences are often signaled by the position of the letter in the syllable.

Patterns formed by spelling sequences of vowel and consonant letters suggest to the knowledgeable reader how many syllables an unrecognized word contains, and which letters begin and end syllables within the word.

The stress with which a syllable is pronounced often has an effect on vowel sound. Two-syllable words are usually stressed on the first syllable. In attempting to recognize a longer word, a reader who takes phonic generalizations into account and pronounces each syllable with equal stress will probably recognize a word if it is a word he knows and if it is in context.

Although one would expect teachers of reading to know quite a lot about phonics, some phonics generalizations are probably not very useful for aiding recognition of words—especially in the early stages of learning to read. Linguists sometimes get into extraordinarily fine points of phonology that are not very useful for a person struggling to recognize a word. One must remember that the aim of phonics is to arrive at an approximate pronunciation. Teachers who do not know enough about phonics may be misled by suggestions from linguists who do not understand the teachers' purpose in teaching phonics. Therefore, reading teachers should know quite a lot about phonics so that they know what to teach—and what not to teach.

Teachers who rely on programs such as basal readers will teach phonics lessons when they appear in their programs. Teachers who are working toward whole language programs must be alert to word recognition problems that arise from failure to use phonics knowledge. Such teachers must understand phonics and be familiar with lessons and methods for teaching it when the need arises.

FOR FURTHER READING

Bailey, M. H. (1966–67). The utility of phonic generalizations in grades one through six. *The Reading Teacher, 20*, 413–418.

Clymer, T. (1963). The utility of phonic generalizations in the primary grades. *The Reading Teacher, 16*, 252–258.

Cunningham, P. M. (1978). Decoding polysyllabic words: An alternative strategy. *Journal of Reading, 21*, 608–614.

Emans, R. (1967). The usefulness of phonic generalizations above the primary grades. *The Reading Teacher, 20,* 419–425.

Groff, P. (1986). The maturing of phonics instruction. *The Reading Teacher, 39*(9), 919–923.

Harp, B. (1989). When the principal asks, "Why aren't you using the phonics workbooks?" *The Reading Teacher, 42*(4), 326–327.

Heilman, A. W. (1985). *Phonics in proper perspective.* Columbus, OH: Charles E. Merrill.

Maclean, R. (1988). Two paradoxes of phonics. *TRT, 41*(6), 514–519.

CHAPTER 6

Teaching Word Recognition: Analysis of Word Structure

Structural analysis, like syllabication, is a method that enables the reader to divide words that are not immediately familiar into smaller, manageable parts. Much of what is taught under the heading of structural analysis is derived from a branch of linguistics called *morphology*. Morphology is the study and description of word formation from meaningful parts called *morphemes*. In this section some facts regarding the structure of English words will be presented. In following sections some suggestions will be made for using these facts as the basis for word recognition.

DEFINITIONS

Morphemes

A morpheme is the smallest meaningful part of a word. There are two major categories of morphemes: free morphemes and bound morphemes.

Free Morphemes.   Free morphemes are English root words such as *apple* and *walk.* They can usually appear with prefixes and suffixes as in *coatless, reload,* and *walked,* and they sometimes appear together as one word as in *sometimes* or *carhop.* When a word is made up of two English root words it is referred to as a compound word.

English root words have approximately the same meaning when they appear alone, in combination with prefixes or suffixes, or with other English root words; thus they are morphemes. They may appear by themselves as words; thus they are free morphemes.

Bound Morphemes.   Bound morphemes are meaningful word parts that appear in many words but never appear alone as a word. The sound represented by *s* in *boys* and *trees* is a bound morpheme. *Un-* in *unkind* and *unhappy* and *-er* in *worker* and *talker* are bound morphemes. They are word parts that have approximately the same meaning in many words where they appear (thus they are *morphemes*), but they never appear on their own as words (thus they are *bound* morphemes). The bound morphemes in the example words are *affixes;* that is, they are added to base words to form new words. Affixes added to the beginning of base words are called *prefixes* as in *unkind* and *resale.* Affixes added to the end of base words are called suffixes as in *boys* and *worker.*

Another category of bound morphemes can be discovered by noticing the common element in such word lists as the following:

predict	spectacular
valedictorian	inspection
diction	spectator

The study of word history reveals that *dict* and *spect* are both derived from non-English words (Latin, in these two instances), and they survive with approximately the same meanings in several English words. Thus they are classified as morphemes— meaningful word parts. They do not appear alone as English words; they always appear with a prefix and/or a suffix, or they sometimes combine with other elements like themselves as in *dictaphone* and *spectragraph.*

Because they do not appear alone, they are bound morphemes, but since suffixes and prefixes can be added to them and because they can combine with each other, they are considered *roots* or *root words.* A list of non-English roots appears in Box 6.1.

This would all be very simple if one had to deal only with English root words and affixes. English roots are free morphemes. Affixes are bound morphemes.

What makes the discussion complicated is that non-English root words are like affixes in that they are bound morphemes, but they are like English root words because they combine together to make words and they combine with affixes to make words. It is easy to avoid this confusion by basing beginning lessons in word structure on words composed of familiar English root words and common affixes.

Two Kinds of Suffixes

Derivational Suffixes.   Suffixes serve two purposes in English. The difference between the two kinds of suffixes is determined by whether the suffix changes the function of the root word. For example, *predict* is usually used as a verb as in sentence 1. Through adding suffixes, new words with different functions can be derived from *predict* as in sentences 2, 3, and 4:

BOX 6.1 LIST OF NON-ENGLISH ROOT WORDS

Latin Root	Examples
audire	audience, audition, auditorium
cedere	precede, succeed, exceed
dicere	predict, dictaphone, dictionary
phobia	claustrophobia, hydrophobia, agoraphobia
portare	import, report, transport
scribere	postscript, transcript, scribble

Greek Root	Examples
cyclo	cycle, cyclone, cyclist
graph	phonograph, autograph, mimeograph
logos	monologue, logic, geology
meter	thermometer, perimeter, metrical
phonos	phonics, phonograph, telephone
scope	telescope, periscope, microscope

1. I *predict* rain. (verb)
2. The *prediction* came true. (noun)
3. His behavior was *predictable*. (adjective)
4. Harry behaved *predictably*. (adverb)

The suffixes added to *predict* to derive new parts of speech in sentences 2, 3, and 4 are called *derivational suffixes*. A list of derivational suffixes that appear frequently are listed in Box 6.2.

Inflectional Suffixes.   Other suffixes do not create words with different functions. Instead, they "modulate" (Brown, 1973) the meaning of the root word without changing its basic function. Nouns may take plural and possessive inflection as in sentences 5 and 6:

5. One *boy* chased two *boys*.
6. One *man* took another *man's* hat.

Verbs are inflected to show differences in tense. Examples of three English tenses appear in sentences 7, 8, and 9:

7. I *walk* to school. (indicative—often called "present" tense)
8. I *walked* to school. (past tense)
9. I *am walking* to school. (present progressive tense)

Verbs are also inflected to agree with the subject in certain cases as in sentence 10:

10. I *go* to school and she *goes* to work.

BOX 6.2 LIST OF DERIVATIONAL SUFFIXES

Suffix	Derivative
-y	rainy
	shiny
-ful	careful
	cheerful
	graceful
-ous	mountainous
	riotous
-er	farmer
	builder
-or	actor
	director
-ist	organist
	soloist
-tion	invention
	protection
-ness	sweetness
	greatness
-able	lovable
	movable
-ity	popularity
	polarity
-ive	excessive
	expressive

It is often asserted that when you want to change a singular noun to plural, you add -*s*, and if you want to change an uninflected verb to past tense you add -*ed*. That assertion is usually true when you are referring to written language, but if you stop to think about it, that assertion is not true in a large number of cases when you are referring to spoken language.

In spoken language, if you want to make *hat* or *cup* plural, you add /s/, but if you want to make *boy* or *pad* plural, you add /z/. Likewise, if you want to make *braid* or *defeat* past tense, you add /ed/, but if you want to make *play* or *hum* past tense, you add /d/, and if you want to make *laugh* or *pass* past tense, you add /t/.

These differences in the pronunciation of inflectional suffixes depend on the final sounds of the word to which they are added. Since the inflectional system is such an integral part of English, we learn to utter the proper inflection for nouns and verbs without being conscious of the "rules" we are following. That is why we can say that we add -*s* to nouns and -*ed* to verbs—even when we are referring to spoken language and people know what we mean.

Adjectives are inflected to show degrees of comparison as in sentences 11, 12, and 13:

11. Ann is tall.
12. Sue is *taller* than Ann. (comparative degree)
13. Mary is the *tallest* of the three girls. (superlative degree)

BOX 6.3 NOUNS THAT CONFORM TO IRREGULAR INFLECTIONAL SYSTEMS

mouse	mice	woman	women
goose	geese	child	children
ox	oxen		

BOX 6.4 VERBS THAT CONFORM TO IRREGULAR INFLECTIONAL SYSTEMS

bring	brought	tell	told
kneel	knelt	win	won
mean	meant		

Regular and Irregular Inflectional Systems.   Although the inflectional systems in English consist almost entirely of regular inflectional suffixes, there are small sets of words that conform to irregular inflectional systems. The plural of *mouse* is not *mouses* but *mice;* the past tense of *take* is not *taked* but *took*. Some other nouns and verbs that conform to irregular inflectional systems are listed in Boxes 6.3 and 6.4. Notice that most of the irregular inflected forms of nouns and verbs in Boxes 6.3 and 6.4 do not contain suffixes at all. Most of them result from a change in the pronunciation of the root word.

TEACHING STRUCTURAL ANALYSIS

The brief look in the last section into the study of English morphology revealed many facts about the structure of English words, and it led into the fairly complex concepts of bound and free morphemes, of root words and affixes, of English and non-English root words, of prefixes and suffixes, of derivational suffixes and inflectional suffixes. Dealing with these concepts led into the consideration of word functions (parts of speech), regularly and irregularly formed noun plurals and regularly and irregularly formed verb tenses.

In the course of a child's schooling, many of these facts and issues may become relevant to learning standard English usage in speaking and writing, to learning spelling, and to developing vocabulary, but many of the issues that have been raised here are not directly useful in learning to recognize words. What aspects of word structure are useful as aids to word recognition? What other purposes are served by teaching structural analysis in the reading curriculum?

As a Word Recognition Technique

For the purpose of word recognition, the study of word structure has much in common with the whole word technique of word recognition. The point is to help students recognize word parts—prefixes, suffixes, and roots—on sight to know how they are usually pronounced. Children who see *nonreturnable* may not recognize it immediately; if they recognize *non-* and *-able* as affixes, they are left with *return*. They may recognize *re-* as another affix and *turn* as an English root. If through this process they recognize a word they know and that makes sense in the context, they have used structural analysis for word recognition.

Notice nothing has been mentioned here about the *meanings* of *non-, re-,* and *-able*. It is presumed that the reader knows the meaning of the word *nonreturnable,* but did not recognize the word. In fact, consideration of the meanings of *re-* and *turn* would only cause confusion in this case, but recognizing *re-* and *turn* as familiar word parts, or morphemes, would be using word structure as a word recognition technique.

As Clues to Meaning of Unknown Words

Structural analysis may be useful in figuring out the meanings of words that are not in the readers' speaking or listening vocabulary. For example, knowledge of word structure may aid a reader in figuring out what *unquenchable* means in the following sentence:

The first sign of his illness was his unquenchable thirst.

Readers may recognize *un-* and *-able* as probable affixes and know how these affixes usually relate to the meanings of words. They may guess from this that *unquenchable* means that something could not be done to or changed about their thirst. Whether *quench* is a familiar word or not, the readers may guess the actual meaning of the word from this sentence or from the larger context, but if they did not know the word *unquenchable* before this encounter, this process would not lead to recognition. Readers must know a word before they can be said to recognize it. The use of structural analysis for clues to the meaning of unknown words will not be discussed further in this chapter. It will be taken up again in Chapter 11.

As an Aid to Word Learning

Many techniques for vocabulary development involve structural analysis. The biology teacher may refer to non-English roots in teaching the meaning of *hydrotropic* and *geotropic*. The reading teacher who is introducing the word *harmonious* before assigning a reading selection may discuss the fact that it is derived from *harmony* and is related to the words *philharmonic, harmonic,* and *harmonize*. In this case word structure is used as an aid to learning the meanings of several presumably new words and is not primarily taught as a word recognition technique. This use of knowledge of word structure will be taken up in Chapter 11.

As Interesting, Challenging Knowledge About Language

The study of morphology in English reveals many interesting facts that are of no apparent value as aids to word recognition, as clues to meanings of unknown words, or as aids to learning new words. For example, the reason for stressing *about* and *because* on the second syllable rather than the first (two-syllable words in English are usually stressed on the first syllable) is that the first syllables of these words were originally prefixes, and stress rarely falls on affixes in English words. A second example of an interesting idea related to word structure is that the suffix *-less* appears to have the same meaning in *hatless* and *helpless,* but the meaning is not exactly the same. A hatless person is a person without a hat, but a helpless person is not a person without help. A helpless person is a person who cannot help himself or herself.

To people who love the study of language, this kind of information is interesting, and it may increase their interest in language. Learning such facts may inspire interest in the study of language in those who are not particularly interested in such study to begin with.

If you do not see that these are four *different* ways that structural analysis may be useful, or if you confuse the four ways that word analysis is useful, you may make some unwise teaching decisions. For example, you may want students *to recognize* the prefixes *re-* and *dis-* in such words as *retreat* and *disfigure* as a strategy for recognizing words that students do not immediately recognize, but if you begin to discuss the meaning of *re-* and *dis-* in words such as *retreat* and *disfigure,* you are going to be in trouble.

It is interesting to talk about the stress pattern of *above* in terms of word structure. To introduce the possibility that unrecognized words beginning with *a* may be stressed on the second syllable because the *a* may have at one time been a prefix is madness. It could only confuse students struggling with word recognition.

Timing

As students progress from beginning reading through elementary school and beyond, the nature of words they encounter changes in terms of structure. In beginning reading material words are overwhelmingly one- or two-syllable English root words without prefixes or derivational suffixes. All the basic vocabulary lists confirm this statement. Inflectional suffixes (plural nouns and past tense verbs, for example) appear from the beginning; therefore, the first lessons in word structure usually treat inflectional suffixes.

Durkin (1987) suggests teaching both derivational and inflectional suffixes before prefixes on the grounds that English root words are more obvious when suffixes are added at the end than when prefixes are put at the beginning. That is, *play* is more apparent in *plays* and *player* than in *replay* (p. 402).

A reasonable principle to guide the introduction of later lessons on structural analysis for the purpose of word recognition is to teach suffixes, prefixes, and root words as they become frequent in reading materials as the level of reading skill increases. Some examples of lessons in structural analysis for the purpose of word recognition follow.

EXAMPLES OF SOME LESSONS
FOR BEGINNING READERS

Compound Words

The concept a student must learn to use word structure for word recognition is that words can sometimes be divided into parts based on the meaning of the parts (in contrast to dividing words into syllables that are based on pronunciation). This concept can be demonstrated by using compound words composed of English root words that the students already recognize. Suggestions for teaching recognition of compound words through structural analysis are found in Figures 6.1 through 6.5.

Figure 6.1. Flannel board activity.

Figure 6.2. Compound match.

Directions: The words in columns A and B can be placed together to form one new word. Write the two words together under column C. Say the new compound word you have formed.

A	B	C
some	day	someday
school	house	_____
any	one	_____
air	port	_____
drive	way	_____

Directions: Each word under column A can be added to a word in column B to form a new compound word. Find the two words that go together and write the new compound word in column C.

A	B	C
grand	port	grandmother_____
school	mother	_____
tooth	house	_____
air	ache	_____
drive	way	_____

Figure 6.3. Compound match.

Directions: Read each sentence. Underline the compound words you see. Draw a line between the two words in the compound word. The first one is done for you.

A. Grand/mother made us some cup/cakes.
B. The sailboat halfway overturned in the storm.
C. The schoolhouse was closed due to the snowstorm.
D. The basketball game that afternoon was exciting.

Figure 6.4. Find the compound.

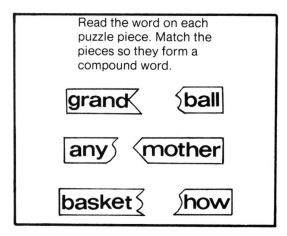

Figure 6.5. Game activity—jigsaw puzzle pieces.

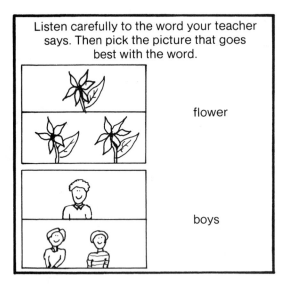

Figure 6.6. Exercise for hearing inflectional suffixes.

Figure 6.7. Exercise for hearing inflectional suffixes.

Figure 6.8. Exercise for hearing inflectional suffixes.

Words with Inflectional Suffixes

Hearing Inflectional Suffixes.   An early objective of lessons in word structure is to make the learner aware of the auditory distinction between the inflected and uninflected forms of words and how these forms relate to meaning. This may be accomplished through exercises such as those presented in Figures 6.6 through 6.8.

Recognizing Inflectional Suffixes in Printed Words.   Next, using previously taught words that are easily recognized, lessons can be devised to call attention to spelling differences between inflected and uninflected words by using exercises such as those presented in Figures 6.9 through 6.11.

The presence or absence of inflectional suffixes is one of the most striking differences between dialects spoken in America. Labov (1970) observed that the black youngsters he studied would tend to pronounce the verbs in the following three sentences identically. That is, the inflectional suffixes on the verb *jump* in sentences *b* and *c* tend not to appear in the speech of these youngsters.

- *a.*   They jump back quickly.
- *b.*   He jumps back quickly.
- *c.*   He jumped back quickly.

Figure 6.9. Exercises calling attention to spelling differences between inflected and uninflected words.

Mark the sentence that goes with the picture in the gray box.

"I see the smallest pig."

"I see the biggest pig."

Figure 6.10. Multiple-choice questions requiring the pupil to put proper endings on words.

Directions: Read the following sentences. Circle the word that has the correct ending for the sentence.

1. The girl was (look, looks, looking) out the door.

2. That is (funny, funnier, funniest) than the last joke you told.

3. The boys came (late, later, latest) than their scoutmaster.

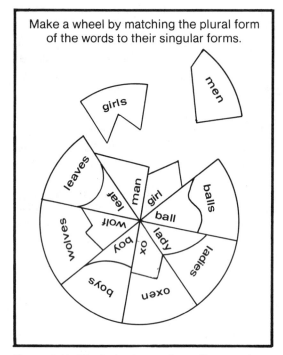

Make a wheel by matching the plural form of the words to their singular forms.

Figure 6.11. Word wheel—exercise calling attention to spelling differences between inflected and uninflected words.

In fact the past tense morpheme would tend not to appear in the speech of most Americans in sentence *c*. Whether inflectional suffixes appear in speech or not depends in part on the speech sounds before and after the suffixes—and that is true in all dialects, including standard English.

From a reading teacher's point of view, the important thing is that the student understands that there is a difference in the *meanings* of sentences *b* and *c*. Whether or not the student *pronounces* the inflection is not a reading problem—if it is a problem at all.

Words with Derivational Suffixes

As the need arises, students can be taught to recognize derivational suffixes by using exercises such as those presented in Figures 6.12 through 6.15.

Words with Prefixes

Recognition of prefixes can be taught by using exercises such as those presented in Figures 6.16 through 6.19.

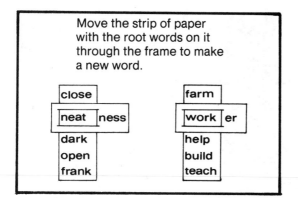

Figure 6.12. Suffix strips.

Figure 6.13. A bulletin board for working with derivational suffixes.

Directions: See how many sentences you can complete by using root words in the first slot and a root word with a suffix in the second slot.

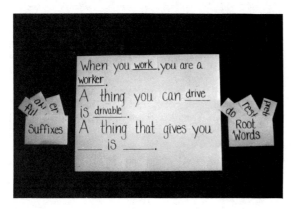

Figure 6.14. Sentence practice.

Directions: Write three sentences using the three different forms of the root word *joy.*

---

joyful   joyfully   joyous

Sample sentences:

1. Henry was a joyful child.
2. Mary laughed joyfully.
3. Christmas is a joyous occasion.

Similar exercises could be constructed using additional root words and adding suffixes to them.

Figure 6.15. Basketball match.

Directions: Match as many basketballs (suffixes) to basketball hoops (root words) as you can to form new words.

Figure 6.16. Exercise for teaching recognition of prefixes.

Directions: Match the root word in column A with a word containing that root in column B.

A	B
happy	dislike
use	disappear
like	unhappy
appear	repack
pack	disuse

Figure 6.17. Word match.

Figure 6.18. Building new words.

Directions: The prefix *un* means "not." Place the prefix *un* at the beginning of the following words and give their new meanings.

_____ known   _____ healthy

_____ able   _____ interesting

_____ important

Figure 6.19. Sentence sense.

Directions: Read the following sentences. Cross out the word that does not belong.

1. Ann (tied, untied) the string to see what was inside the box.
2. It is (safe, unsafe) to play with matches.
3. The poor boy had not eaten in weeks and was very (healthy, unhealthy).

TWO ADDITIONAL PROBLEMS WITH RECOGNIZING WORDS WITH INFLECTIONAL SUFFIXES

Spelling Changes

When suffixes are added to English root words, the resulting word is often spelled root plus suffix as in *cloudy, walks,* and *warmer*. But when root words have certain spellings there are slight spelling changes. The plural of *match* is *matches* (the plural morpheme is spelled *-es* rather than *-s*), and the plural of *half* is *halves*. In some words ending in *y* the *y* is changed to *i* before adding a suffix as in *happier, puppies,* and *married*. In root words ending in silent *e*, the *e* is usually dropped before adding a suffix as in *taking, baker,* and *operation*. In some words ending in a single consonant letter the final consonant is doubled before adding a suffix as in *winner, digging,* and *skipped*.

These spelling changes are not haphazard; the conditions under which they occur are presented in Boxes 6.5–6.9. Although it is useful to learn when these spelling changes occur to become a *good speller*, the task of the reader is to recognize roots and suffixes in words where these spelling changes appear. In other words, the job of readers is to realize that when they do not recognize a word like *digging*, they should suspect that *-ing* is a suffix and that the root is not *digg* but *dig*, or when they do not recognize

BOX 6.5 CONDITIONS FOR ADDING SUFFIXES AND SUBSEQUENT SPELLING CHANGES

If a word ends in *x, ss, sh,* or *ch* or *z*, we usually add *es* to make the plural form of the word.

church	churches	dish	dishes
glass	glasses	fizz	fizzes

BOX 6.6 CONDITIONS FOR ADDING SUFFIXES AND SUBSEQUENT SPELLING CHANGES

When a word ends in silent *e*, we drop the *e* before adding a suffix that begins with a vowel.

like	liked	love	loved
write	writer	skate	skater
trace	tracing	make	maker

BOX 6.7 ONDITIONS FOR ADDING SUFFIXES AND SUBSEQUENT SPELLING CHANGES

When a word ends in a single consonant preceded by a short vowel sound, we usually double the consonant before adding a suffix that begins with a vowel.

tag	tagged	hop	hopped
fat	fatter	swim	swimming
bat	batter	chop	chopping
rip	ripped	sip	sipped

BOX 6.8 CONDITIONS FOR ADDING SUFFIXES AND SUBSEQUENT SPELLING CHANGES

When a word ends in *y* after a consonant, change the *y* to *i* before adding the ending.

puppy	puppies	cherry	cherries
marry	marries	penny	pennies

BOX 6.9 CONDITIONS FOR ADDING SUFFIXES AND SUBSEQUENT SPELLING CHANGES

When a word ends in *f*, we sometimes change the *f* to *ve* and add *s*.

calf	calves	ourself	ourselves
hoof	hooves	thief	thieves
loaf	loaves		

a word like *crazier* they should suspect that *-er* is a suffix and that the root word is not *crazi* but *crazy*.

Changes in Pronunciation and Accent

When words are created by adding suffixes to root words, the root word is often pronounced the same in both its original form and its derived form such as in *delirious* and *deliriousness*. Frequently, however, the accent pattern and even the pronunciation of the root word changes in a derived form such as in *courage* and *courageous*.

Some examples of shifts in accent and resulting changes in pronunciation are presented in Box 6.10. But once again, it is well to remember that the principal task of the reader is to recognize printed forms of familiar spoken words. Suppose the readers do

BOX 6.10 SHIFTS IN STRESS PATTERNS RESULTING FROM ADDING SUFFIXES

symbol	symbolic	trivial	triviality
patriot	patriotic	conscience	conscientious
popular	popularity	pretense	pretentious

not recognize a word like *symbolic,* but suspect that *-ic* is a suffix and then recognize *symbol.* If they know the word *symbolic* they will undoubtedly recognize it and know how to pronounce it. For this reason, explicit lessons in shifts in stress patterns resulting from adding certain affixes are taught late in the reading program and are taught as interesting facts about language rather than as a word recognition skill. (See Activity 6.A.)

ACTIVITY 6.A CHECK YOUR KNOWLEDGE OF ANALYSIS OF WORD STRUCTURE

Here is a scrambled list of words that appear in the preceding boxes and figures.

audience	rainbow	joyful	autograph
mice	flowers	tracing	puppies
unhappy	tagged	sweetness	fearless
actor	monologue	spills	hooves
basketball	helper	swimming	smallest
airport	dislike	cyclist	excessive
perimeter	women	toothache	books
knelt	afternoon	reappear	looking
unable	thieves	brought	telephone

Decide whether each word is an example of

1. A word with a Latin or Greek root (Box 6.1).
2. A noun or verb that conforms to an irregular inflectional system (Boxes 6.3 and 6.4).
3. A compound word (Figures 6.1–6.5).
4. A word with an inflectional suffix (Figures 6.6–6.11).
5. A word with a derivational suffix (Box 6.2, Figures 6.12–6.14).
6. A word with a prefix (Figures 6.16–6.19).
7. A word whose spelling is changed when a suffix is added (Boxes 6.5 to 6.9).

WORD STRUCTURE AND WHOLE LANGUAGE

Teachers who rely on basal reading programs will teach word structure clues to word recognition as they appear in their basal reading programs. Teachers like Mary Weiss and Matthew Nicholson who engage in the language experience approach, and base some reading lessons on books children choose for themselves, may find children failing to recognize words because they do not respond to word structure clues.

For example, during a reading conference, George, a third grader, may come to the word *schoolhouse* and stop—apparently stymied by this "big word." The teacher might put his finger on the page, covering *-house* and ask "You know this word, don't you, George?" When George answers "school," the teacher asks, "How about this word?"

When George has recognized this big word the teacher might print *anyone, someday,* and *grandfather,* helping George to realize that big words are sometimes *compound words,* two words put together. A couple of experiences like this may prompt the teacher to find exercises on compound word awareness such as those in Figures 6.2 to 6.4. Basal reading programs have indexes of skills that would be useful in this search.

The teacher might decide that this kind of awareness would be useful to many children in the class and make flannel board activities like the one in Figure 6.1 and games like the one in Figure 6.5 available to groups or the whole class.

If the teacher regularly uses group lessons from the basal reading program, he or she might make the next group lesson on compound words more personal and immediate by observing "Last week George came to this word (printing *schoolhouse* onto the board), and he got it when he saw that it was two easy words. What are the two easy words in this compound word?" (See Activity 6.B.)

ACTIVITY 6.B LEARNING TO SPOT WORD RECOGNITION PROBLEMS THAT KNOWLEDGE OF WORD STRUCTURE MIGHT HELP

A. Work in pairs and role play a teacher-student reading conference where the child is struggling with a word because he or she is failing to use knowledge of word structure such as

added suffixes: musical, traveled, shortest.
added prefixes: disfigure, unknown, rebuild.
spelling changes involving affixes: whiter, families, cutting

B. Plan the students' "struggle" and the teacher's on-the-spot lesson with your partner and present your dialogue to the class.
C. Use the figures in this chapter to choose lessons that might be used with this child if the problem seems persistent.
D. Use the figures in this chapter to choose activities and games that might be used with groups of children who are experiencing the same problem.
E. If basal programs and other reading materials are available to you, find lessons, activities and games that might be useful in carrying out *C* and *D*.

SUMMARY

The branch of linguistics that studies word parts is called morphology. Morphology is the study of how words are formed from meaningful parts. A morpheme is the smallest meaningful word part. Free morphemes are English root words such as *window* and *walk*.

Bound morphemes are meaningful word parts that appear in many words but do not appear alone as words. One category of bound morphemes is made up of affixes; affixes are added to root words to form new words. *Un-* in *unkind* and *-er* in *worker* are affixes. Affixes that appear before root words are called prefixes. Affixes that are added after root words are called suffixes.

Non-English root words such as *dict* in *diction* and *predict* comprise another category of bound morphemes. Non-English root words combine with affixes (as in *diction*) or with each other (as in *phonograph*) to form words.

Derivational suffixes change the function of a word. For example, the noun *boy* is changed to an adjective through adding the derivational suffix *-ish* to form *boyish*. Inflectional suffixes "modulate" the meaning of words without changing their function. For example, inflectional suffixes signal plural and possessive on nouns, tense on verbs, and degrees of comparison on adjectives.

The inflectional system in English is made up almost entirely of regular inflectional suffixes, but there are some irregular inflected forms. For example, the regular plural suffix is *-s,* but the plural of *mouse* is *mice* and the plural of *man* is *men.*

There are four purposes served by teaching students about word structure.

1. Recognizing parts of words often enables a reader to recognize a word he did not recognize immediately.
2. Recognizing parts of a word and knowing what those parts frequently mean sometimes enables a reader to guess at the correct meaning of a word he does not recognize.
3. Teaching the meanings of word parts is often used as a technique for teaching new words to students.
4. Finally, there is a great deal that is interesting about language that comes under the heading of word structure. Helping children to develop an interest in the study of language is an ongoing goal of reading teachers.

Teaching word structure usually begins with teaching about compound words made of English root words the children recognize. Inflectional suffixes are taught next for two reasons: (1) It is believed that familiar root words are more recognizable when suffixes are added to them than when prefixes are placed before them. (2) Inflectional suffixes appear in the very earliest reading material.

Students are usually taught to recognize inflectional suffixes on spoken words and then to recognize them in print. Children are taught to recognize derivational suffixes and prefixes as they begin to appear in reading materials frequently enough to merit attention.

One complication that arises in teaching children to recognize suffixes is that the spelling of English root words sometimes changes when a suffix is added. A second problem is that the stress pattern and pronunciation of root words sometimes change when a suffix is added. These spelling, stress, and pronunciation changes are not haphazard. The spelling pattern may be taught as part of the spelling curriculum. Students should be made aware that when they recognize a root plus a suffix, it may be a word they know but that is not pronounced exactly like the root word.

Teachers who rely on programs such as basal readers will teach word structure lessons when they appear in their programs. Teachers who are working toward whole language programs must be alert to word recognition problems that arise from failure to use word structure knowledge. Such teachers must understand word structure and be familiar with lessons and methods for teaching it when the need arises.

FOR FURTHER READING

Stotsky, S. L. (1977). Teaching prefixes: Facts and falacies. *Language Arts, 54,* 887–890.

Thorndike, E. L. (1972). *The teaching of English suffixes.* New York: Bureau of Publications, Teachers College, Columbia University, 1941. Reprinted in New York: AMS Press, Inc.

White, T. G., Sowell, J., & Yanogiharu, A. (1989). Teaching elementary students to use word-part clues. *The Reading Teacher, 42*(4), 302–309.

CHAPTER 7

Context: The Necessary Unifying Medium for All Word Recognition Skills

DEFINING THE PHRASE "USE OF CONTEXT FOR WORD RECOGNITION"

A precise definition of what is meant by "use of context" in a discussion of word recognition is not easy to develop. It is like Supreme Court Justice Potter Stewart's observation regarding pornography: "I can't define it, but I know it when I see it." To arrive at an understanding of what is meant by the use of context for word recognition, it will be useful to think about how people are able to guess what words are missing from the following sentences.

1. Three cheers for the _____, white, and blue.
2. A daddy is big; a baby is _____.
3. Alexandra always _____ a red dress. (Choose *a* or *b*.)
   a. wore
   b. reviled
4. The ship sailed _____ into the sunset. (Choose *a* or *b*.)
   a. walnut
   b. slowly

How would you explain the following facts?

a. Most Americans would complete sentence 1 with the word "red."
b. Most people would complete sentence 2 with the word "little," "small," or perhaps "tiny."
c. Most people would choose "wore" to fill the blank in sentence 3 instead of "reviled."
d. Most people would choose "slowly" rather than "walnut" to fill the blank in sentence 4.
e. It would be more startling for a person to choose "walnut" for sentence 4 than for a person to choose "reviled" for sentence 3.

You might arrive at the following answers to these questions:

The phrase "red, white, and blue" embodies a concept in our culture. When we are given part of a familiar phrase, we recognize the concept and supply the missing part.

Sentence 2 is an analogy. We realize that the missing word relates to "baby" in the same way as "big" relates to "daddy."

In sentence 3 we realize that the missing word is a verb that states a relationship between a girl and a dress. "To wear" states a more typical relationship than "to revile."

In sentence 4 we realize that *walnut* cannot be the right word, because *walnut* is a noun and an adverb is needed.

These suggestions reflect the facts that we can guess missing words from context because (1) we have knowledge of the world, of our culture, and of our language, and (2) when dealing with language with a missing part, we recognize wholes and can guess what is missing.

USE OF CONTEXT CLUES BY EXPERIENCED READERS

In sentences 1 through 4 in the preceding discussion, a word has been replaced with a blank. When a person uses context to recognize words in a normal reading task, how-ever, the word is present. Examples of how experienced readers use context to recognize words are the following:

Readers encounter the word *victuals* in sentence 5.

5. The hungry cowboys crowded around the fire, tin plates in hand, as the aroma of hearty victuals filled the crisp night air.

They momentarily presume (through phonics clues) that the word is pronounced /vik′ tū els/, but that pronunciation does not suggest a word they know. They guess from context that it means "food," and they remember a term for food that they particularly associate with cowboys. That word is pronounced /vit′ els/. The spelling of *victuals* is close enough for them to conclude that they have identified the word.

Readers encounter the word *apropos* in sentence 6.

6. The jury could not help but notice that the witness's costume was not apropos to an appearance in court.

Through phonics they arrive at the pronunciation /ap′ ro pōs/, but that does not suggest a familiar word. From context they guess that the phrase *not apropos* means "not proper" or "not fitting," and they realize that the word is one they know; it is pronounced /ap ro pō′/.

These examples were chosen because *victuals* and *apropos* are words not frequently seen in print, and, therefore, they may be "new" to many readers. Second, the correspondence between their spelling and pronunciation is irregular, and therefore they may not be recognized immediately by many readers.

On the other hand, the use of context clues for word recognition is not necessarily secondary to the use of phonics or structure clues. Context may induce such high expectations of what a word will be that the reader attends to the word only to check to see if his or her expectations are correct. Avid readers of stories about the old West, for example, might recognize *victuals* in sentence 5 without an instant's hesitation because through context they might be certain of what the word is before they come to it. The use of context in identifying words correctly so permeates the reading process that it is usually taught explicitly, and all methods of word recognition should be taught in combination with the use of context from the beginning of reading instruction.

TEACHING THE USE OF CONTEXT CLUES

Physical Context

From their first encounter with print, children should be reminded as often as possible and in as many ways as possible that reading makes sense—that it fits in with what we know of the world and what we recognize as sensible language.

When looking at yesterday's language experience story, the children are reminded that the words centered at the top of the sheet are the title of yesterday's story.

"What are the words?"
"Snow White."
"Yes. Let's see who can find those words later on in the story."

The words on the attendance board are children's names.

"Who can find his or her own name?"
"Who can find Jim's name and put it in the 'Absent' column?"

The words on the calendar board are names of days and months. There are numbers here too.

"Today starts a new week. What day is it?" "Who can find *Monday* on the Calendar Board and put it in 'Today's Date'?"

These are all examples of using physical context to aid in word recognition. Further examples are calling attention to words labeling the clock, door, and desk and identifying words on the science table that were printed during a recent lesson. The point is that we expect certain words in certain places because of the meaning we have learned to attach to those places.

Picture Context

Children learn that sometimes words go with pictures. Teachers label children's drawings. Children learn sight words from picture word cards. Children write sentences to go with pictures. Children draw pictures to go with stories they have written. Many children's books have a fixed relationship between words and pictures.

Reminding children that the words they are trying to read "go with" pictures in some way that they have been taught or that they have discovered, gives them practice in using context for word recognition. The larger context (pictures) narrows the possibilities of what the words are and suggests what the words may be.

Linguistic Context

As children progress in reading, there are more and more occasions where physical context and pictures are not very useful, and readers have to rely on the language of the text to help identify words they do not immediately recognize. But the principle remains the same. The unrecognized word cannot be just any word because not just any word would make sense, and context may suggest only a few words that would make sense in this place.

Examples of the use of context for word recognition were presented with the words *apropos* and *victuals*. Teaching the use of this technique presents certain problems because you cannot be certain which word a reader will not recognize, and it is very difficult to tell precisely what aspect of the linguistic context restricts word possibilities or suggests probable words. Therefore, lessons are constructed where blanks are substituted for words and where the clues to the identity of the missing words appear to be obvious.

For example, nouns are deleted before appositives as in Figure 7.1, or words are deleted from similes as in Figure 7.2, or words are deleted from a series of words with the same features as in Figure 7.3.

In using context to identify a word that one does not immediately recognize, however, one must take the spelling into account in arriving at the word. One might have guessed *grub* in sentence 5, but the spelling of the word rules it out. In this example,

Figure 7.1. Nouns deleted before appositives.

_____, or men who travel in outer space, wear air-tight space suits.

The _____, a lizard that can change colors, makes an interesting pet.

The shoppers rode the _____, which is a moving staircase, to reach the second floor.

Mary had a little lamb whose fleece was white as _____ .

The beautiful maiden's lips were as red as a _____ .

She was as busy as a _____ .

Figure 7.2. Words deleted from similes.

1. The flowers were red, blue, and _____ .

2. They ran, jumped, and _____ in the park.

3. They ate apples, oranges, and _____ .

Figure 7.3. Words deleted from a series of words with the same feature.

the word was recognized partially by guessing the meaning through context and partly from arriving at a pronunciation through phonics.

To make lessons in using context for word recognition more like the task of the reader who does not immediately recognize a word, lessons sometimes supply part of a word (a letter, syllable, or affix) so that the student has two systems to benefit from— and two systems that must be taken into account in arriving at the word. Examples appear in Figure 7.4.

TEACHING THE USE OF CONTEXT WHEN THE NEED ARISES

Teachers should always be alert for opportunities to suggest the use of context for clues to word recognition. When a child does not know a word when reading orally, or when a child asks the teacher what a word is when reading silently, the teacher can often help the child through questioning or by modeling.

Figure 7.4. Lessons supplying part of a word (letter, syllable, affix).

Our basketball t____won the game.

We had br____d and butter.

He is the cap____of the ship.

She won a gold med____at the Olympics.

The baby drank from his bot____.

They had to re____the house after the fire.

When she returned she began to un____ her suitcase.

Automobiles played a large part in our family life. My father owned a drugstore in 1912, but he decided to become an Oldsmobile dealer on the side to make some easy money. To get the dealership he had to buy two cars, a blue sedan and a somewhat sportier red one. He had no showroom so he parked both vehicles in front of his store.

Figure 7.5. A passage where context may help with word recognition.

If, for example, the child does not recognize the word *vehicles* in Figure 7.5, the following scenarios may take place.

A Questioning Technique

TEACHER: Read the whole sentence and just say ''mmm'' for the word you don't know.

CHILD: He had no showroom so he parked both ''mmms'' in front of his store.

TEACHER: What did the father have that he parked in front of the store? What do you *park* on a street?

CHILD: Cars.

TEACHER: The word must mean . . .?

CHILD: Cars.

TEACHER: Divide the word into syllables. What do you think the first syllable is?

CHILD: Vee Hi Kuls. Oh! It's *vehicles!*

A Modeling Technique

TEACHER: Let's see. He parked both ''mmm'' in front of his store. The father has two cars in this story, so it probably says he parked both cars. Let's see. I would divide that word—v-e (long e), h-i (long i), c-l-e-s (probably a word ending in *le* and the *s* is plural). C-l-e at the end of a word is probably ''kel.'' That's ''vee-hi-kel-s.'' Oh! Of course! It's *vehicles!*

THE ULTIMATE GOAL: INTEGRATING CLUES TO WORD RECOGNITION

Although teaching sight words, phonics, structure, and context can be thought of as separate activities, the goal of teaching reading is for students to be able to recognize most words they encounter automatically and to use all the clues present (phonics, structure, and context) when they encounter a word they do not recognize immediately.

Some studies have shown that beginning readers' errors in oral reading demonstrate a heavy reliance on context and little reliance on graphic information (the spelling of the word) at first; however, successful readers soon begin to take graphic information into account and rely on both context and graphic information. Poor readers seem to continue to rely on context alone for a longer period of time. It follows that teachers should give attention to integrating the use of word recognition clues.

In the foregoing example, it was shown how a teacher might help a child who is reading to recognize *vehicles* in Figure 7.5. Similar scenarios might be constructed based on the recognition of the words *apropos* and *victuals* in the contexts described earlier in this chapter (sentences 5 and 6). In such examples the teacher would lead the student through the process of employing all the clues available through questioning or modeling. (See Activity 7.A.)

It takes both luck and considerable skill on the part of the teacher before lessons such as those proposed in Activity 7.A can take place spontaneously. Such lessons can be planned, however, by the teacher who reads a passage, judges which words may not be recognized by the pupil, and plans which clues to emphasize in leading the pupils to recognize them.

For example, if you were going to assign a fifth grade class to read the passage in Figure 7.5, you might expect the majority of the words to be recognized as sight words, but you might expect that *some* students would not immediately recognize *some* of the following words: *automobiles, drugstore, Oldsmobile, dealer, dealership, sedan, sportier,* and *vehicles.* You might stress clues for each word (in order of usefulness) as listed here:

> *automobiles*—structure, phonics, context. (Note that strong context clues come much later in the passage. One must read ahead to get to them.)
> *drugstore*—structure, phonics, context.
> *Oldsmobile*—structure, context, phonics.
> *dealer*—structure, phonics, context.
> *dealership*—structure, phonics, context.
> *sedan*—phonics, context.
> *sportier*—structure, phonics, context (very weak).
> *vehicles*—context, phonics, structure.

It would be a good exercise to stop and think out the scenario that might take place if you were the teacher and if a fifth grader in your class "got stuck" on one of the words

ACTIVITY 7.A LEARNING TO SPOT WORD RECOGNITION PROBLEMS WHERE THE USE OF CONTEXT CLUES MIGHT HELP

Find passages that are typical of elementary school reading material. Find words in these passages that are clearly supported by context. Since this is a demonstration, rewrite the passages to meet your needs, if necessary.

A. Work in pairs and role play a child failing to recognize a word and a teacher using a questioning technique to lead the child to use the word recognition skills that apply—particularly context.

B. Repeat this exercise having the teacher use a modeling technique.

C. Present your dialogues to the class.

D. After some practice, have the "child" act out his or her word recognition difficulty with a "teacher" who was not in on the planning. See if the "teacher" can respond appropriately utilizing the word recognition skills that apply—particularly context.

in this passage. You might try this exercise for several of the words suggested and discuss this exercise with classmates who have also tried it.

Teachers who create such lessons must keep in mind that they are based on predictions of which words will cause trouble and which clues will be most salient for the students reading the passage. A particular child may recognize *vehicles* immediately and get stopped by *somewhat*. Another child may arrive at the correct pronunciation of *sportier* through phonics and recognize the word without ever reflecting on the fact that this word is related to the words *sport* and *sporty*.

The purpose of lessons in integrating clues to word recognition is to teach the child to use everything handy rather than to dictate that structure will be referred to here and context will be referred to there.

SUMMARY

In general we think of using context for word recognition in terms of what experienced readers do when they encounter a word they do not recognize. Experienced readers rely on their knowledge of the world, of culture, and of language to arrive at an idea of what the word means and how it functions in the sentence. From their understanding of the whole, they make inferences about the missing part (the unrecognized word). They are aided in their inference making by the presence of the word. Through applying structural analysis, syllabication, and phonics, they are also able to make inferences about how the word is pronounced. All these sources interact to enable the experienced reader to recognize words that are not immediately recognized.

Teaching the use of context may proceed from the use of physical context (the child knows that the words in a certain place are names of days of the week, for example) to the use of picture clues and, finally, to the use of linguistic context alone. At every stage children are reminded that when they think they recognize a word, they should ask themselves whether the word makes sense in that context and whether the pronunciation of the word is suggested by the printed word in question.

Because one cannot predict which words any child will not immediately recognize, blanks are sometimes used to replace words, and children are taught how to arrive at the identity of the word that belongs in the blank through using context. Sometimes parts of the deleted words are supplied so that the students learn to use both spelling clues and context clues and so that they learn that the word they seek must be compatible with both the linguistic context and the spelling.

Teachers should always be alert to teach the use of context for word recognition as the need arises. Asking leading questions and modeling the process are suggested as ways of teaching the use of context for word recognition. However, incidental teaching of this kind cannot be relied upon exclusively. Many teachers preread passages and try to identify words students will not immediately identify. Through questioning or modeling, students are led to identify these words, and what the teacher believes to be the most useful source of word recognition is emphasized for each word. Although the use of context for word recognition is formally presented in this book after the use of the whole word approach, phonics, and structural analysis, the use of context has been referred to repeatedly in earlier chapters. The use of context pervades all word recognition activity. Able readers use whole word recognition, phonics, structure, and context simultaneously; they are able to emphasize one source of information after another until they are satisfied that they have recognized the word—or that they are dealing with a word that is not familiar to them. This facility and flexibility are the ultimate goal of all teaching of word recognition skills.

FOR FURTHER READING

Ames, W. S. (1966). The development of a classification scheme of contextual aids. *The Reading Research Quarterly, 2,* 57–62.

Artley, A. S. (1943). Teaching word meaning through context. *Elementary English Review, 20,* 68–74.

McCullough, C. M. (1943). Learning to use context clues. *Elementary English Review, 20,* 140–143.

Seibert, L. C. (1945). A study of the practice of guessing word meanings from context. *Modern Language Journal, 29,* 296–322.

CHAPTER 8

Teaching Word Recognition Skills: Practices, Issues, and Suggestions

WORKING TOWARD A WHOLE LANGUAGE CLASSROOM

Although there are a great variety of published materials designed for use with teaching reading, surveys consistently find that the basal reading series are the predominant tools of reading instruction. Some teachers, like Charlotte, rely on phonics-emphasis basal reading programs and are committed to a skills-emphasis, bottom-up approach, and they will probably remain committed to this approach. Others, like Matthew, currently use an eclectic basal reading program, but they are moving toward a whole language approach.

The latter group of teachers would agree with the conclusions that were developed at the end of Chapter 2. They find the assumptions underlying the whole language approach compelling, but they are aware of the added demands that this approach places on the teacher in terms of leadership, classroom management, diagnostic skill, and knowledge of methods and materials. Therefore, they are working toward the whole language ideal gradually—experimenting, learning, and mastering the skills they need as they go. They are well grounded in the use of eclectic basal readers and may never completely abandon their use.

This chapter will focus on issues inherent in teaching word recognition from basal readers. At the end of the chapter, the reader will be invited to examine some of the other widely used reading materials and to evaluate them in terms of the question raised in regard to basal readers.

HOW IS WORD RECOGNITION TAUGHT?

Following are two word recognition lessons from first grade basal readers. The first is typical of lessons from the widely used phonics-emphasis basal readers. The second is typical of lessons from the widely used eclectic basal reader.

Typical Word Recognition Lesson from a First Grade Phonics-Emphasis Basal Reader

The purpose of this lesson is (1) to present the spellings *ou* and *ow* and two sounds these letter pairs represent, and (2) to provide practice in analyzing words containing the spellings and sounds.

In preparation for the lesson, the teacher writes the sentences in Figure 8.1 on the board and prepares cards lettered *ou* and *ow* as in Figure 8.2. The lesson proceeds as in Figure 8.3.

Figure 8.1. Sentences written on the board in preparation for the lesson presented in Figure 8.3.

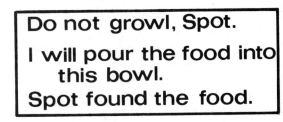

Do not growl, Spot.
I will pour the food into this bowl.
Spot found the food.

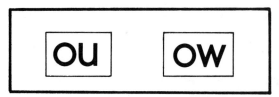

Figure 8.2. Letter cards made in preparation for the lesson presented in Figure 8.3.

Typical Word Recognition Lesson from a First Grade Eclectic Basal Reader

The purpose of this lesson is

1. To teach the children to recognize the words *cat, get, stop,* and *help.*
2. To teach the children to recognize an unfamiliar word by relying on spelling clues and context clues.

In preparation for the lesson, the teacher writes the sentences in Figure 8.4 on the board. The lesson proceeds as in Figure 8.5.

A person who is not an experienced reading teacher might have a difficult time seeing any differences in these two approaches—but very important differences do exist.

Perhaps you would like to think about and discuss the differences between the two lessons before reading on.

Differences Between the Two Example Lessons

In the Lesson from the Phonics-Emphasis Basal Reader.

1. The teacher presents letters in isolation (not as spellings of words). (step 1)
2. The teacher presents a letter-sound rule to the children before any written words are introduced. (steps 2, 3)
3. The children pronounce sounds in isolation. (step 4)
4. The children listen for sounds in words and identify words that contain target sounds in an auditory discrimination task. (steps 5, 6)
5. The children find words in the story on the board that contain the target spellings—a visual discrimination task. (step 7)
6. The children look at *growl* and try the /ou/ sound and are satisfied, because they recognize /groul/ as an English word. (steps 8, 9)
7. The children finally read the word *growl* in context and are asked again to reflect on the vowel sound of the word. (step 10)
8. Ten more words having the vowel spelling *ou* or *ow* are presented in isolation for the children to recognize and use in sentences. (step 11)

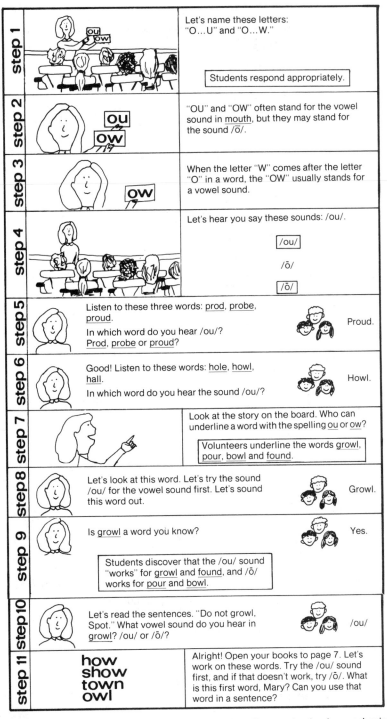

step 1
Let's name these letters: "O...U" and "O...W."

Students respond appropriately.

step 2
"OU" and "OW" often stand for the vowel sound in mouth, but they may stand for the sound /ō/.

ou
ow

step 3
When the letter "W" comes after the letter "O" in a word, the "OW" usually stands for a vowel sound.

ow

step 4
Let's hear you say these sounds: /ou/.

/ou/

/ō/

/ō/

step 5
Listen to these three words: prod, probe, proud.
In which word do you hear /ou/? Prod, probe or proud?

Proud.

step 6
Good! Listen to these words: hole, howl, hall.
In which word do you hear the sound /ou/?

Howl.

step 7
Look at the story on the board. Who can underline a word with the spelling ou or ow?

Volunteers underline the words growl, pour, bowl and found.

step 8
Let's look at this word. Let's try the sound /ou/ for the vowel sound first. Let's sound this word out.

Growl.

step 9
Is growl a word you know?

Yes.

Students discover that the /ou/ sound "works" for growl and found, and /ō/ works for pour and bowl.

step 10
Let's read the sentences. "Do not growl, Spot." What vowel sound do you hear in growl? /ou/ or /ō/?

/ou/

step 11
how
show
town
owl

Alright! Open your books to page 7. Let's work on these words. Try the /ou/ sound first, and if that doesn't work, try /ō/. What is this first word, Mary? Can you use that word in a sentence?

Figure 8.3. Typical word recognition lesson from a first grade phonics-emphasis basal reader.

It is a lion.
It is not a cat.

He will go.
He will get the cat.

He will go.
He will not stop.

Dan will go.
He will get help.

Figure 8.4. Sentences written on the board in preparation for the lesson presented in Figure 8.5.

In the Lesson from the Eclectic Basal Reader.

1. Words are presented, discussed, and recognized as parts of sentences, not in isolation. (steps 1, 3, 4, and 5)
2. Letters are discussed, named, and so on as parts of words, not in isolation. (steps 2, 5)
3. Children are encouraged to rely on what the word must mean in the given context. (step 4)
4. Children are encouraged to rely on spelling clues to recognize the word. (steps 2, 5)

Similarities Between the Two Lessons

On the other hand, there are similarities between the two lessons that should not be overlooked.

1. Both lessons teach the children to rely on the relationship between English spelling and the sounds that spellings generally represent. That is, sooner or later they both teach phonics.
2. Both lessons present words in written context, sooner or later.
3. Both lessons assume that the children have acquired a sight word vocabulary.

Differences in the Programs and Assumptions Underlying the Programs

Number of Words Introduced. In a phonics-emphasis lesson, new words are introduced at a rather fast pace. In the eclectic lesson new words are introduced at a slower pace.

step 1	It is not a lion. It is a cat.	Teacher: Let's look at the sentences on the board. You should know all the words except this one (pointing to <u>cat</u>).
step 2	**cat.**	Teacher: What letter does this word begin with? Students: "C" Teacher: What letter does the word end with? Students: "T" Teacher: Think of the sound that <u>c</u> usually stands for. Think of the sound that <u>t</u> usually stands for.
step 3	**cat.**	Teacher: George, will you read aloud except for the last word? George: It is not a lion. It is a . . . Teacher: What is the last word, George? George: <u>Cat.</u>
step 4		Teacher: How do you know it isn't <u>cut</u>? George: <u>Cut</u> would not make sense.
step 5	**cat.**	Teacher: How do you know it isn't <u>tiger</u>? George: <u>Tiger</u> begins with /t/. Teacher: Yes and we want a word that begins with /k/ and ends with /t/.

<u>Get</u>, <u>Stop</u>, and <u>help</u> are introduced in the same manner using the remaining sentences.

Figure 8.5. Typical word recognition lesson from a first grade eclectic basal reader.

Criteria for Choosing Words.   In the phonics-emphasis program, new words tend to be chosen because they demonstrate and give students practice with the rule that is being taught.

In eclectic programs, new words tend to be chosen because they are very frequent words and are therefore considered necessary sight words for even the "easiest" reading. They are not chosen because they demonstrate a particular phonics rule.

Complexity of Phonics Rules Introduced Early in the Program.   More difficult and more detailed phonic generalizations are taught at an earlier stage in phonics-emphasis readers than in eclectic readers.

The Phonics-Emphasis Approach Reflects the Bottom-Up Tradition.   The phonics-emphasis approach builds from parts to wholes. It concentrates on the outer aspect of the reading process (letter-sound relationships) and proceeds to the inner aspect of the reading process (meaning). The assumption is evident throughout the example lesson (Figure 8.3) that each step of the process must be taught to the child. There is an implication that the child is passive and does not actively search out stimulus and organize it for himself or herself in a meaningful way; instead, the lesson implies that the child performs each step as it is presented to him or her and waits for the next step to be presented.

The Eclectic Approach Reflects the Top-Down Tradition.   The eclectic approach focuses first on wholes (sentences and meaning) and proceeds to analyze the parts (the "new word" and finally the letter-sound relationships in the new word). Therefore, it focuses first on the inner aspect of reading (meaning) and proceeds to focus on the outer aspects (letters and sounds and their relationships). This lesson allows for the fact that the reader may make cognitive leaps. After the "new word" is recognized, "wrong words" are suggested so that the child will be forced to reflect on the role of phonics and context in recognizing the word. This happens because there is an assumption that the child may have recognized the word without conscious reference to phonics or context. (See Activity 8.A.)

ACTIVITY 8.A EXAMINE, TEACH, AND REFLECT ON WORD RECOGNITION LESSONS FROM BASAL READERS

> In Chapter 4, I listed several phonics-emphasis basal reading programs and several eclectic basal reading programs.
> **A.** Get a phonics-emphasis basal reading program and teach an early word recognition to your classmates.
> **B.** Get an eclectic basal reading program and teach an early word recognition lesson to your classmates.
> **C.** Discuss the similarities and differences in the lessons and the assumptions underlying the programs.

WHICH IS BETTER: A PHONICS-EMPHASIS APPROACH OR AN ECLECTIC APPROACH?

Straw Man Arguments

In discussing the relative merits of the phonics-emphasis approach and the eclectic approach, it is necessary to establish boundaries of what is being discussed. It is not difficult to find examples of either approach that are so extreme as to be indefensible and to attempt to discredit the entire approach by discrediting the extreme example.

Attack on the Phonics-Emphasis Approach.   Writers sometimes charge that the phonics-emphasis approach causes beginning readers to believe that reading is decoding one set of meaningless visual symbols (letters) into another set of meaningless sounds. It is questionable whether many children are actually taught beginning reading from materials that might lead to such a conclusion. It is certainly not true that the three widely used phonics-emphasis basal reading programs (Economy, Lippincott, and Open Court) would lead youngsters to believe this. It is programs such as these three that are referred to when the term "phonics-emphasis approach" is used in this book.

Attack on the Eclectic Approach.   On the other hand, to the mind of many critics, the chief difference between phonics-emphasis basal readers and eclectic readers is that phonics-emphasis readers teach word recognition through phonics and eclectic readers teach word recognition exclusively through whole word, look-and-say methods. For example, a well-known advocate of the phonics-emphasis approach once charged that many seventh and eighth graders who learned to read in a widely used eclectic basal reading program "don't know how to read" and "have never caught on to the fact that the letters stand for sound" (Flesch, 1979, pp. 2–3).

I urge you to examine one or two of the eclectic basal reading programs listed in Chapter 4. To imply that after six years of learning from these materials students would not know that letters stand for sounds is preposterous. (See Activity 8.B.)

ACTIVITY 8.B EVALUATING CHARGES LEVELED AT BASAL READING PROGRAMS

A. Examine the materials used at the very start of a phonics-emphasis basal reading program. (See Chapter 4.) Be sure to look at the Teacher's Manual, which gives directions for the use of the materials.

Is there any point where letter-sound relationships are taught and where there is no reference to the fact that these letter-sound relationships are useful in recognizing words?

When is the student first called upon to read a word in a meaningful context? When is the student first called upon to read a sentence in a meaningful context?

B. Examine the materials used at the very start of an eclectic basal reading program. (See Chapter 4.) Be sure to look at the Teacher's Manual, which gives directions for the use of these materials.

At what point are letter-sound relationships first introduced? At what point is it no longer fair to say that students are not taught that "letters stand for sounds"?

Research Findings

Numerous research projects have been conducted to discover whether the phonics-emphasis or eclectic approach is the one best method. The results of small-scale studies often favor one method or the other; because findings of such studies are inconsistent, they are of little help in answering the question.

Two major research efforts in the 1960s attempted to overcome the shortcomings of the small-scale studies. Chall (1967) attempted to reach a conclusion through a comprehensive review of the literature. Her conclusion was that "code emphasis" appeared to produce better results than the eclectic approaches current in the 1950s and 1960s. However, Chall's review of the literature has been criticized for not being exclusive enough—that is, she did not attempt to exclude poorly designed research from her survey.

The second research effort was a large-scale experimental research effort funded by the federal government in 1964 and 1965. It is usually referred to as the First Grade Studies (Stauffer, 1967). This research involved not only the phonics-emphasis and eclectic methods discussed here; it involved more extreme methods of teaching reading.

These studies were followed up in second grade (Dykstra, 1968) and third grade (Fry, 1967; Hayes & Wuest, 1967; Harris et al., 1968; Ruddell, 1968; Schneyer & Cowen, 1968; Stauffer & Hammond, 1969; Vilscek & Cleland, 1968).

A review of this extensive research reveals that

1. There are no consistent advantages for any method when followed through third grade.
2. Combinations of programs such as basal readers, supplemental phonics programs, and individualized reading programs, a forerunner of the whole language approach (see Chapter 15), are often superior to single programs.
3. Other factors, such as characteristics of the neighborhood, school environment, quality of teaching, and student ability, are more important in determining success in reading than is the method of instruction.
4. The number of children who fail to learn to read is about the same from method to method.

All methods result in a certain number of reading failures. The conventional wisdom is that if a child fails to learn to read using one method, a different method should be used to teach him or her. This is a further reason why it is desirable for reading teachers to remain open-minded about methods. When a child fails to learn by one's favorite method, it is sheer folly to refuse to try other methods that have been demonstrated to be effective with some children because of a dogmatic commitment to one method or a prejudice against another method.

The Role of the Teacher

A repeated finding in research that attempts to compare learning in different classrooms is that the most important variable, and one that often overshadows methods, is the teacher. This was one of the major conclusions of the First Grade Studies and related studies.

Weikart (1973) compared a Piagetian preschool program to two other kinds of programs and found that when teachers were motivated, conscientious, and hard working, the curriculum did not make a difference. Brainerd (1978), in reviewing preschool programs, concludes, "There is a suggestion that the teacher, not the curriculum being administered, is what makes the big difference" (p. 295).

Chomsky (1970), who is the foremost figure in the resurgence of rationalist assumptions in the study of language and language learning (see Chapter 1), turned his attention to teaching reading only once, when he wrote a chapter on how the study of phonology might contribute to research on problems of literacy. His remarks on teaching are as follows:

> [T]here is little reason to doubt that the dominant factor in successful teaching is and will always remain the teacher's skill in nourishing, and sometimes even arousing, the child's curiosity and interest and in providing a rich and challenging intellectual environment in which the child can find his own unique way toward understanding, knowledge, and skill. It is difficult to imagine that psychology or linguistics or any other

academic discipline will make much of a contribution to this end. (Chomsky, 1970, pp. 3–4)

TEACHING AND LEARNING BY DEDUCTIVE AND INDUCTIVE METHODS

Word recognition strategies are based on generalizations such as that the letter *b* usually represents the sound /b/ or that *un-* at the beginning of a word is often a prefix.

Such generalizations are usually taught in one of two ways:

1. You state the generalization and give students a number of words where it applies.
2. You call students' attention to a number of words where a generalization applies and help them to discover what the generalization is. That is, you help them to state the generalization.

Both methods are based on the assumption that in the future, students will remember the generalization and apply it on their own when it is appropriate.

Although both methods are used in all basal reading programs to some extent, the first method is highly associated with the phonics-emphasis approach and the second method is highly associated with the eclectic approach. These two methods and the reasons they are associated with the two types of basal reading programs are discussed in this section.

Figures 8.6 and 8.7 show two lessons in word structure that might be taught in fourth grade. In the first lesson (Figure 8.6), the deductive method is employed. In the second lesson (Figure 8.7), the inductive method is employed.

Differences Between the Deductive and Inductive Methods

Of course, the salient difference between these two lessons is that in the deductive method, the teacher presents the rule to the children and the rule is then applied to words. In the inductive method, words are presented that demonstrate the rule and children are led to discover the rule from the example words. The rule is then applied to new words.

The phrases "rule—egg" and "egg—rule" may help you remember this distinction. "Egg" stands for "example" ("egg" being a play on the pronunciation of the first syllable of *example*.) In deductive teaching one goes from the rule to examples; in inductive teaching one goes from examples to the rule.

Inductive teaching is often referred to as "the discovery method," because students are led to discover the generalization that you want them to learn.

In the inductive method, it is assumed that the students recognize the printed words used to teach the rule. The whole point is that students are led to discover generalizations about a set of words they have previously learned to recognize.

In the deductive method, it is assumed that students do not recognize the words where the rule applies until after the rule is taught.

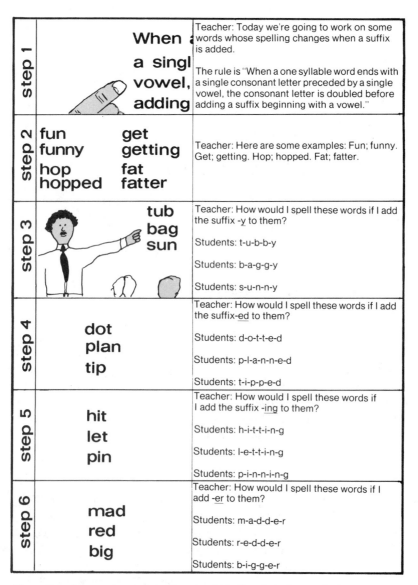

step 1	**When** a singl **vowel,** adding	Teacher: Today we're going to work on some words whose spelling changes when a suffix is added. The rule is "When a one syllable word ends with a single consonant letter preceded by a single vowel, the consonant letter is doubled before adding a suffix beginning with a vowel."
step 2	fun get funny getting hop hopped fat fatter	Teacher: Here are some examples: Fun; funny. Get; getting. Hop; hopped. Fat; fatter.
step 3	tub bag sun	Teacher: How would I spell these words if I add the suffix -y to them? Students: t-u-b-b-y Students: b-a-g-g-y Students: s-u-n-n-y
step 4	dot plan tip	Teacher: How would I spell these words if I add the suffix -ed to them? Students: d-o-t-t-e-d Students: p-l-a-n-n-e-d Students: t-i-p-p-e-d
step 5	hit let pin	Teacher: How would I spell these words if I add the suffix -ing to them? Students: h-i-t-t-i-n-g Students: l-e-t-t-i-n-g Students: p-i-n-n-i-n-g
step 6	mad red big	Teacher: How would I spell these words if I add -er to them? Students: m-a-d-d-e-r Students: r-e-d-d-e-r Students: b-i-g-g-e-r

Figure 8.6. A lesson in word structure taught by the deductive method.

Similarities Between the Inductive and Deductive Methods

In both lessons the teacher is quite clear on the rule to be taught. This is important to remember because the discovery (inductive) method is sometimes unjustly associated with haphazard goals and lesson planning. In both lessons the students are expected to apply the rule to words not used in the lesson when the lesson is over. (See Activity 8.C.)

step 1	I like fun. Pam is funny. Here is a bag. His shirt is baggy.	Teacher: Let's read these sentences and look at the underlined words. How is the word <u>fun</u> like <u>funny</u> and the word <u>bag</u> like <u>baggy</u>.
step 2	(fun**ny**) (bag**gy**)	Students: <u>Fun</u> is the root word <u>fun</u> plus the suffix <u>y</u>. Teacher: Let's circle the root words and suffixes. What is left over in each word? Where did the extra letter come from?
step 3		Students: You double the last letter when you add <u>y</u>. Teacher: Yes. Sometimes, when we add the suffix <u>y</u> to some words, we double the last letter. But not always. Let's look at these word pairs. Let's see what the difference is.
step 4	fun fruit funny fruity bag tear baggy teary sun rain sunny rainy	Teacher: <u>Fun</u>, <u>bag</u> and <u>sun</u> are one syllable words. <u>Fruit</u>, <u>tear</u> and <u>rain</u> are one syllable words. <u>Fun</u>, <u>bag</u> and <u>sun</u> end in single consonant letters. <u>Fruit</u>, <u>tear</u> and <u>rain</u> end in single consonant letters. What is the difference? Students: <u>Fun</u>, <u>bag</u> and <u>sun</u> are spelled with a single vowel letter but <u>fruit</u>, <u>tear</u> and <u>rain</u> are spelled with two vowel letters.
step 5	fun sand funny sandy bag string baggy stringy sun mess sunny messy	Teacher: Good! Let's look at the next list and see what the rule is. Students are led to discover that the root word must end in a single consonant letter.

In like manner the rule is derived for the suffixes -ed, -ing, and -er and finally the generalization is drawn that the rule works for suffixes beginning with a vowel letter.

Figure 8.7. A lesson in word structure taught by the inductive method.

Traditions Associated with the Methods

The Deductive Method Reflects the Empiricist Tradition. The deductive method is the usual method in reading programs that are based largely on empiricist assumptions, including phonics-emphasis programs. There are several reasons for this:

1. This method is compatible with the view of the learner as a receiver of stimulus to which an appropriate response is expected. Reading skills are analyzed, isolated, sequenced, and presented when they are needed for the next stage of progress. When learners are ready, they are trained to attend to the appropriate stimuli and to make the appropriate response. They are then given practice in making appropriate responses.

2. The method begins with parts. In Figure 8.6 the students are directed to consider roots and suffixes, consonant letters, vowel letters, and so on, and they are given

ACTIVITY 8.C CREATING, TEACHING, AND REFLECTING UPON WORD RECOGNITION LESSONS USING THE INDUCTIVE AND DEDUCTIVE METHODS

A. Work in three groups. Use Figures 8.6 and 8.7 as models.

Group 1. Choose a phonic generalization (Chapter 5) and create an inductive and a deductive lesson to teach it.

Group 2. Choose a syllabication generalization (Chapter 5) and create an inductive and deductive lesson to teach it.

Group 3. Choose a word structure generalization (Chapter 6) and create an inductive and deductive lesson to teach it.

B. Present your lessons to the class.

C. Discuss the similarities and differences in the lessons, the traditions and assumptions that underlie the lessons, and the advantages of each approach.

a rule for putting suffixes and roots together. The method focuses first on parts that are brought together (synthesized) into wholes.

Empiricists view the learner as comparatively passive, waiting to be presented with stimulus and rules for organizing the stimulus and rules for making the proper response; empiricists focus on the outer aspects of language; empiricists view learning as proceeding always from part to whole. It follows that empiricists teach rules before teaching words where such rules apply.

The Inductive Method Reflects the Rationalist Tradition.   The inductive method is the usual method in reading programs based on rationalist assumptions, including eclectic basal reading series. There are several reasons for this:

1. This method is compatible with the view that the learner is an active seeker and active organizer of stimuli, and an active discoverer of useful relationships.

2. The method introduces new words in context (calls attention to meaning) and encourages the learner to rely on context and phonics simultaneously.

3. This method focuses first on wholes (words) and proceeds to analysis of the wholes to discover parts (roots and suffixes) and to discover how the parts are related (the spelling rule).

Rationalists view the learner as active and aggressive, not merely responsive. Rationalists focus on the inner aspects of language (meaning); rationalists view learning as proceeding from wholes to parts. It follows that rationalists teach whole words in context before they focus on spelling rules that apply to the words.

The fact that phonics-emphasis basal readers are based on empiricist assumptions and that eclectic basal readers are based on rationalist assumptions explains their differences much more fully and satisfactorily than the difference in emphasis in phonics teaching. The differences in emphasis in phonics teaching follow from the basic assumptions (empiricist/rationalist) upon which the programs are built. The fact that phonics-emphasis readers typically use deductive methods and eclectic readers typically use inductive methods follows from the same source: one is compatible with empiricist assumptions and the other with rationalist assumptions. Box 8.1 shows this relationship graphically.

**BOX 8.1 HOW THE PHONICS-EMPHASIS APPROACH
AND THE DEDUCTIVE METHOD GROW OUT OF EMPIRICISM,
AND HOW THE ECLECTIC APPROACH AND THE INDUCTIVE
METHOD GROW OUT OF RATIONALISM**

Empiricism	Rationalism
Focuses on outer aspects of language	Focuses on inner aspects of language
Focuses on how separate parts contribute to whole	Focuses on whole and how parts relate within wholes
Views language as perceived in parts that are added up to wholes (bottom-up)	Views language as perceived in wholes that are analyzed into parts (top-down)
Views the mind as a comparatively passive receiver of stimuli that attends to the most frequent or most intense stimuli	Views the mind as an active seeker and organizer of stimuli that will attend to stimuli because they are meaningful or fit into a perceived organization
In reading, focuses on perception of letters and words, relationship of print to sound, frequency of words as indicators of ease of learning, brings the atomistic and mechanical aspects of reading together finally to consider meaning	In reading, focuses on meanings and on wholes, analyzes wholes to consider perception of words and letters and the relationship of print to sound finally to consider mechanical relationships of parts
From Which Follows ↓	*From Which Follows* ↓
The phonics-emphasis approach to teaching word recognition	The eclectic approach to teaching word recognition
↓	↓
The deductive method	The inductive method

Which Is Better: Inductive or Deductive Teaching?

Support for the Deductive Method. The deductive method is more efficient. The inductive method is very time consuming and can become laborious and boring. Notice that in the example deductive lesson (Figure 8.6), all the necessary conditions of the generalization were presented at once: (1) one-syllable words, (2) ending in a single consonant letter, (3) preceded by a single vowel letter, and (4) suffix beginning with a vowel letter. In the inductive lesson, more time and energy were needed to present the first three conditions, and only the suffix -y had been considered. The idea that this generalization applies to all suffixes beginning with a vowel had not yet been introduced.

You might question whether presenting more in a shorter space of time means that students learn more in a shorter space of time. It is because this kind of question arises that the debate over which method is better has not been decisively answered.

Support for the Inductive Method. There is considerable consensus among experts in the mainstream of educational thought favoring the inductive method of teaching particularly for teaching reading and language arts. For example, Farr and Roser (1979), commenting on a sample lesson, state

The concept was presented so that learning was inductive. That is, the children were given a number of examples, and discovered for themselves the idea that objects and words began alike. Having children discover such relationships, as opposed to telling them, encourages them to seek other such relationships on their own. (p. 215)

And Durkin (1976) states,

Inductive phonics instruction is often recommended for children with the hope that it will foster a better understanding of generalizations, and further, that it will enable children to make their own systematic observations about written words. It is viewed then as a way of helping them learn how to learn. (p. 78)

However, it is important to notice that these two statements are undocumented; that is, there is no reference to research findings. In fact, there is no published research that clearly supports or refutes these assertions. One reason the inductive method is in favor today is that the mainstream of thought in philosophy, psychology, and education is presently in the rationalist sphere of influence, and, of course, the whole language approach is the clearest present-day heir to that tradition.

Flexibility in Choosing Methods

On the other hand, the efficiency of the deductive method often leads teachers to choose this method, particularly in lessons growing out of unplanned problems that arise in a reading lesson. Recall the reading conference reported in Chapter 5 where the child unsuccessfully attempted to pronounce *law*.

The teacher simply states the generalization about the sound usually represented by the letters *aw* and shows the child several words other than *law* where the generalization applies.

However, a teacher could use the inductive method in such cases. The dialogue might go as follows:

TEACHER: I know you know this word (printing *paw*). What is it?
CHILD: Paw.
TEACHER: Yes. How about this one (printing *jaw*)?
CHILD: Jaw.
TEACHER: What's this (pointing to *law*)?
CHILD: Law.
TEACHER: Yes. When the letters *aw* come together they are often pronounced /aw/. (See Activities 8.D and 8.E.)

ADVICE TO THE BEGINNING TEACHER

Beginning reading teachers are sometimes not consulted about what materials will be available to them. Most beginning teachers will find two or more basal reading series available in the school system from which to choose. Of the mainstream basals dis-

ACTIVITY 8.D INTRODUCING FLEXIBILITY INTO IMPROMPTU WORD RECOGNITION LESSONS

> Look back at Activities 5.D, 5.E, and 6.A, where you role played a student having a word recognition problem and a teacher teaching an on-the-spot lesson in phonics, syllabication, or structure.
>
> Did you habitually use a deductive or an inductive approach? If you favored one, why do you think you favored it?
>
> Repeat two or three of these activities, but this time, make the lesson inductive, if it was deductive, and deductive, if it was inductive.
>
> Present your dialogues (using first one method and then the other) to the class.

ACTIVITY 8.E INTRODUCING FLEXIBILITY INTO LESSON PLANS SUGGESTED BY BASAL READERS

> A. Figure 8.3 shows a typical word recognition lesson in a phonics-emphasis basal reading program. The lesson uses the deductive method. Plan a lesson where you teach the two sounds usually represented by the spellings *ou* and *ow* by the inductive method.
>
> B. Find word recognition lessons in a basal reading program that are clearly inductive or deductive. Plan lessons where you teach the same word recognition generalizations by the *other* method.

cussed in this chapter, there is no clear evidence that eclectic readers are better than phonics-emphasis readers, or vice versa. However, for reasons put forward in Part One, I favor a rationalist, top-down, holistic approach to teaching reading and language arts. This approach has come to its fullest development in the whole language classroom.

The following themes have been stated repeatedly in this book:

> The whole language reading teacher must possess all the knowledge and skills that a teacher who relies on a basal reader as the mainstay of his or her reading program.
> The whole language approach demands more of teachers.

It follows that beginning teachers should depend on basal reading programs as they build their knowledge and teaching skills, but from the start, they should be aware of whole language ideals of teaching reading and writing and begin to work toward them.

Here, at the end of Part Two, a new theme can be stated explicitly—a theme that has been implied previously:

> The assumptions upon which phonics-emphasis basal readers are founded are inconsistent with rationalist, top-down, whole language assumptions.
> The assumptions upon which eclectic basal readers are founded are more consistent with rationalist, top-down, whole language assumptions.

It follows that I recommend teachers begin by using an eclectic basal reading program since their development toward a whole language approach will be a matter of cultivating skills and techniques that are consistent with their "basic training." Teachers who start with a phonics-emphasis basal reading program, and who wish to work toward a whole language approach, will have to revise their basic assumptions.

SUMMARY

Two lessons for teaching word recognition were discussed in this chapter. One is typical of a lesson found in phonics-emphasis basal reading series, and the other is typical of a lesson found in eclectic basal reading series. The two lessons differ in that in the phonics-emphasis approach, (1) letters are presented in isolation; (2) letter-sound correspondences are taught before words demonstrating the correspondences are presented; (3) letters are presented as a visual discrimination task, and speech sounds are presented in words as an auditory discrimination task; (4) the letter-sound correspondence that is taught is used to recognize new words; and (5) students are reminded that the word they "sound out" must be a word they recognize—if it is not, the generalization probably does not apply to the word.

In the eclectic reader lesson, (1) words are presented, discussed, and recognized as parts of sentences, not in isolation; (2) letters and the sounds they probably represent are presented and discussed as parts of words in sentences, not in isolation; and (3) children are encouraged to rely on phonics generalizations and context simultaneously to recognize words.

The lessons are similar in that both refer to phonics generalizations, sooner or later; both present words in context, sooner or later; and both presume that the children have acquired a sight word vocabulary.

The lesson that is typical of the phonics-emphasis basal reader reflects the empiricist tradition in that it proceeds from parts to wholes (bottom-up) in a stepwise progression. It concentrates on the outer aspects of reading and proceeds toward dealing with the inner aspects of reading. The lesson that is typical of the eclectic reader reflects the rationalist tradition in that it focuses on wholes first and proceeds to focus on parts. The lesson allows for the possibility that the student will make cognitive leaps rather than incremental steps leading to word recognition.

Two lessons (Figures 8.6 and 8.7) were presented showing how the deductive and inductive methods are used to teach a lesson related to structural analysis. In the deductive method, children are taught rules and are then taught to apply the rules to words. In the inductive method, the children are presented with a list of words and are led to discover the rule that applies to the words in the list. In both lessons, however, the teacher is quite clear on what rule is being taught, and in both lessons, the students are expected to apply the rule to words that are likely to be "new"—that is, not sight words.

The deductive method tends to appear regularly in phonics-emphasis programs because both the phonics-emphasis program and the deductive method rely on empiricist assumptions. Empiricism tends to view the learner as relatively passive and focuses on parts first. This is compatible with teaching small steps to the learner in a predetermined order.

The inductive method appears regularly in eclectic programs because both eclectic programs and the inductive method rely on rationalist assumptions. Rationalism tends to view the learner as aggressive and focuses on wholes first. This is compatible with presenting whole words and helping the learner to discover generalizations that apply to parts of the words.

There is considerable sentiment in favor of the inductive method of teaching reading because it is believed that this method teaches not only the lesson at hand, but helps children to learn a method of approaching problems. However, the deductive method has some characteristics that recommend it as well. It works. People do learn from being told. Second, it is usually more direct and, therefore, less time consuming. Finally, in regard to teaching word recognition, children can learn a rule before they recognize any word where the rule applies. Therefore, the deductive method permits one to introduce rules earlier, perhaps when they are useful as tools for word recognition. Since each method offers its own advantages, it is advisable to use both methods.

Basal programs tend to emphasize either the deductive or inductive teaching method. There are advantages to both methods. Teachers who understand the two methods can convert an inductive lesson to a deductive lesson, and vice versa. Whole language teachers should be able to use both methods and to be aware of when they are used.

Most reading teaching is done using basal readers. If a teacher is going to use a basal series, he or she ought to be aware of which series are phonics emphasis and which series are eclectic and choose a series that is compatible with his or her beliefs and intellectual commitment.

For reasons stated in Part One, I favor a holistics, top-down approach to teaching reading—and ultimately whole language teaching of language arts. I recommend that teachers use basals while working toward a whole language approach. I recommend eclectic basal reading programs because they are more consistent with the assumptions upon which the whole language approach rests.

PART THREE

Reading Comprehension

CHAPTER 9

Beliefs and Assumptions That Underlie the Teaching of Reading Comprehension

DEFINITIONS OF READING COMPREHENSION

Thorndike

In 1917, the renowned psychologist Edward L. Thorndike proposed the following description of the process of reading comprehension:

> Understanding a paragraph is like solving a problem in mathematics. It consists of selecting the right elements of the situation and putting them together in the right relations, and also with the right amount of weight or influence or force for each. The mind is assailed as it were by every word in the paragraph. It must repress, reflect, soften, emphasize, correlate and organize, all under the influence of the right mental set or purpose or demand. (as reprinted in *Reading Research Quarterly, 6,* 1971, 431)

Tierney and Pearson

A more recent description of the process of reading comprehension comes from Tierney and Pearson (1984) who view reading and creating written text as essentially similar processes of meaning construction.

> Both are acts of composing. From a reader's perspective, meaning is created as a reader uses his background of experience together with the author's cues to come to grips both with what the writer is getting him to do or think and what the reader decides and creates for himself. (p. 33)

You can probably agree with both descriptions, but notice the difference in the posture or stance of the reader in the two descriptions. Thorndike's reader is "assailed." Tierney and Pearson's reader "creates," "comes to grips."

These two descriptions are representative of the shift in the way reading comprehension was thought of in the past and the way it is thought of now. In the past, educators concentrated on what is in the text and considered the problems the text proposes for the prospective reader.

Currently, comprehension is seen as an interactive process. There *is* meaning and content in the text, the reader *does* bring certain knowledge and concepts to the text; comprehension occurs when the reader creates meaning through collaboration, negotiation, and coming to grips with the text and, by implication, the writer of the text.

In this chapter, I'll present a review of the ideas that have shaped the way comprehension is thought of and treated in today's reading curriculum.

INGREDIENTS OF READING COMPREHENSION

Comprehension of written text is a very-high-order cognitive process involving a great many ingredients. I will enumerate and discuss many of these ingredients under three headings: (1) the text, (2) the reader's prior knowledge, and (3) the composing-comprehending connection.

The Text

Sentence Comprehension.   Several important studies have shown that the ability to deal with syntactically complex sentences is related to success in reading comprehension. Simply determining the average number of words per sentence in a passage gives a fairly reliable idea of how difficult the passage is. The long history of research on what makes books readable (known as "readability" research) has shown that passages with shorter sentences (on average) are easier than are passages with longer sentences.

In Box 9.1 the simple sentence "a" is made more complex in each of the following sentences, and each of the following sentences becomes longer. Likewise, in each sentence triplet in Box 9.2, sentences "a" and "b" are combined to create sentence "c." In each case sentence "c" is longer and syntactically more complex than sentence "a" or "b." Since longer sentences tend to be syntactically more complex, it is presumed that it is syntactic complexity—not simply length—that accounts for the difficulty.

BOX 9.1 ADDED SYNTACTIC COMPLEXITY RESULTS IN LONGER SENTENCES

a. Mary ate the apple.
b. Mary didn't eat the apple.
c. The apple was not eaten by Mary.
d. The red apple was not eaten by Mary.
e. The red apple was not eaten by Mary this morning.
f. Mary's not eating the red apple this morning was a cause of concern.

Other researchers have shown that particular structures appear to be more difficult than others. In one study (Bormuth et al., 1970), for example, fourth graders understood the first sentence better than the second in each of the following pairs:

a. Finding him was easy.
b. For us to find him was easy.

a. Joe runs faster than Bill.
b. Joe runs as fast as Bill.

Another study showed that some young children interpret the question "Is the doll easy to see?" to mean "Is it easy for the doll to see?" and that they don't understand who is about to leave in a sentence like "Bozo promised Snoopy to leave" (C. Chomsky, 1969).

In reviewing the research, the relationship between knowledge of linguistic structures and facility with reading and writing, Flood and Lapp (1987) conclude

> These findings seem to indicate the following: (a) that children have great difficulty in reading sentences and passages which contain structures that they have not acquired (i.e., they cannot generate these sentences/passages in writing), (b) that they have some difficulty in reading/writing sentences and passages containing structures that they are in the process of acquiring, and (c) that they read/write automatically those structures that are well-learned (once they're able to recognize or write the words that make up those structures).

Although comprehension of sentences is undoubtedly a factor in comprehending a text, the experiment reported in Box 9.3 demonstrates that individual sentences lose

BOX 9.2 COMBINING SENTENCES RESULTS IN LONGER SENTENCES

1. a. The zebra ate the grass.
   b. The grass was green.
   c. The zebra ate the green grass.
2. a. The dog ran down the street.
   b. The dog had lost his master.
   c. The dog who had lost his master ran down the street.

BOX 9.3 AN EXPERIMENT ON REMEMBERING SENTENCES

Bransford and Franks (1971) tested the question of whether subjects remember individual sentences or "holistic, semantic ideas." They constructed "idea sets" composed of seven sentences. Four sentences (as sentences 1–4) each contained one idea. The fifth contained two of the ideas contained in the first four sentences (as sentence 5). The sixth and seventh sentences contained three and four of the ideas each (as in sentences 6 and 7).

One-Idea Sentences

1. The ants were in the kitchen.
2. The jelly was on the table.
3. The jelly was sweet.
4. The ants ate the jelly.

Two-Idea Sentence

5. The sweet jelly was on the table.

Three-Idea Sentence

6. The ants in the kitchen ate the sweet jelly.

Four-Idea Sentence

7. The ants in the kitchen ate the sweet jelly that was on the table.

In phase I *some* of these sentences were presented orally to subjects. In phase II, sentences were presented and subjects were asked whether they heard the sentence in the earlier phase or not. Subjects tended to report that they had *not* heard sentences that contained only one idea (like sentences 1–4) even when they had, and reported that they had heard sentences that contained more than one idea (like sentences 5–7) even when they had not. The authors concluded that "Individual sentences lost their unique status in memory in favor of more holistic representation of semantic events" (p. 348).

"their unique status in memory in favor of a more holistic representation of semantic events." That is, readers do not remember *sentences;* they remember *meaning* in a global fashion.

Quantity and Density of Information. Another characteristic of texts that affects comprehension is the amount of information. Sheer length of text in terms of number of words gives some indication of the amount of information in a text, but more exact measures have been proposed. Linguists have counted the number of propositions (subjects plus predicates) in texts. Comparing the number of predicates to the number of words in the text gives an estimate of the "density" of information. Redundancy, of course, affects this kind of measure. When propositions are repeated, they do not add new information.

Considerateness. It is presumed that speakers and writers are trying to be informative, and clear. It is the speaker's and writer's responsibility to estimate what the listener or reader knows and believes and to give enough information so that communication will be successful. Listeners can alert speakers to instances where attempts to communicate fail, but writers cannot get immediate feedback from their communication partners. Writers must, therefore, pay particular attention to their responsibility to be informative and clear. Writers who succeed particularly well at this task create texts that are more easily comprehended and remembered. This quality of text has been referred to as "considerateness" (Kantor, 1978).

Considerateness arises and succeeds when writers can imagine themselves to be readers of their own work. Writers who reflect on what they do when they read and the problems they face when they read are more likely to produce considerate texts.

Explicitness.   In all texts there is a certain amount of information that is implied or presupposed. In the sentence "George sold one of his sports cars," it is presupposed that George owned more than one sports car, and it is implied (or in the vocabulary of reading teachers, "a person could infer") that George is or was a wealthy man. There is reason to believe that, all things being equal, texts that state important information explicitly are easier to understand and remember than are texts that leave important information to be inferred. This variable may be more important to inexperienced readers whose inferential skills are less developed.

Organization.   Texts that have a clear organizational structure (cause-effect, chronological order, main idea supporting details, problem solution) are easier to comprehend and recall than are texts lacking such structure. The presence of topic sentences, headings, and words showing relationships like *but, however,* and *because* are generally thought to aid comprehension and recall.

Story Grammar.   In recent years, scientists interested in language have turned their attention to a particular kind of text organization that has come to be known as *story schema* or *story grammar.*

Certain story outlines are well known. For example, a man and woman appear in a story, they meet, they fall in love, they have a misunderstanding, they separate, they reconcile, they marry. Or a promising athlete appears in a story, she sets her heart on winning a competition, she suffers setbacks, she perseveres; she wins.

An outline or set of expectations that is even more general than the two described in the last paragraph is as follows: characters are introduced to the reader; a goal is set; they attempt to reach the goal; they encounter setbacks; they make further attempts; they reach the goal.

While all three outlines suggested are abstract, the third outline is considerably more abstract than the first two. A conceptual outline of stories at this high level of abstraction has come to be called a *story grammar.*

A simplified version of the Mandler and Johnson (1977) story grammar might be stated as follows: a story is a *setting* followed by one or more *episodes;* an *episode* is made up of a *beginning, reaction, attempt, outcome,* and *ending.* An example of a two-episode story that conforms to this grammar is presented as Figure 9.1.

A considerable amount of research has been devoted to the question of whether story grammar plays a part in comprehending and remembering spoken and written texts. The following conclusions have been reached:

Setting	Once there were twins, Tom and Jennifer, who had so much trouble their parents called them the unlucky twins.
Beginning 1	One day, Jennifer's parents gave her a dollar bill to buy the turtle she wanted, but on the way to the store she lost it.
Reaction 1	Jennifer was worried that her parents would be angry with her so she decided to search every bit of the sidewalk she had walked.
Attempt 1	She looked in all the cracks and in the grass along the way.
Outcome 1	She finally found the dollar bill in the grass.
Ending 1	But when Jennifer got to the store, the petstore man told her that someone else had just bought the last turtle, and he didn't have any more.
Beginning 2	The same day, Tom fell off a swing and broke his leg.
Reaction 2	He wanted to run and play with the other kids.
Attempt 2	So he got the kids to pull him around in his wagon.
Outcome 2	While they were playing, Tom fell out of the wagon and broke his arm.
Ending 2	Tom's parents said he was even unluckier than Jennifer and made him stay in bed until he got well.

Figure 9.1. A two-episode story conforming to the Mandler and Johnson (1977) story grammar. (*Source:* J. M. Mandler, "A Code in the Node: The Use of the Story Schema in Retrieval," *Discourse Processes*, vol. 1 [1978]. Reprinted by permission from Ablex Corporation.)

1. There is an underlying structure that can be detected and described for all or most stories. This underlying structure is described by story grammars.
2. The human mind is an avid organizer of past experience. After hearing and reading a number of stories, people formulate general outlines or sets of expectations or schemata for stories. These schemata are described by story grammars.
3. Once these schemata are internalized, people rely on them to organize the content of stories as they read or listen to them—that is, in the process of comprehension.
4. People also rely on schemata for remembering stories.

Several studies have shown that good readers expect stories to conform to story grammars (Stein & Glen, 1977; Whaley, 1981) and that stories that conform to story grammars are better understood and remembered than are stories that do not conform to story grammars (Mandler, 1978).

The Reader's Prior Knowledge

In a now-classic study, Bransford and Johnson (1973) read the passage in Figure 9.2 to subjects under two conditions: in the *no-context* condition, the passage was read to the subject with no preparation; in the *context* condition, the subjects looked at the picture in Figure 9.3 for 30 seconds before the passage was read.

If the balloons popped the sound wouldn't be able to carry since everything would be too far away from the correct floor. A closed window would also prevent the sound from carrying, since most buildings tend to be well insulated. Since the whole operation depends on a steady flow of electricity, a break in the middle of the wire would also cause problems. Of course, the fellow could shout, but the human voice is not loud enough to carry that far. An additional problem is that a string could break on the instrument. Then there could be no accompaniment to the message. It is clear that the best situation would involve less distance. Then there would be fewer potential problems. With face to face contact, the least number of things could go wrong.

Figure 9.2. The balloon passage, demonstrating how context can determine whether or not a reader can comprehend. (*Source: Visual Information Processing,* edited by W. G. Chase. Bransford and Johnson, 1973. Reprinted by permission of the Academic Press.)

Subjects were asked to rate the passage on a comprehension scale from 1 (very hard) to 7 (very easy). They were also asked to write down as many ideas from the passage as they could. Subjects in the *no-context* condition rated the passage as very difficult to comprehend and did not recall many ideas; subjects in the *context* condition rated the passage as easy to comprehend and recalled twice as many ideas as subjects in the *no-context* condition.

These researchers reached the following conclusions:

1. Context has a marked effect, but people can "learn" things they don't understand. (That is, subjects who did not see Figure 9.3 could not have understood the passage, but they could recall ideas from it.)
2. Subjects forget things they do not comprehend.
3. More research is needed to get at relationships between comprehension, retrieval, and memory, but absence of context can seriously affect acquisition. (Bransford & Johnson, 1973, p. 397)

Bransford and Johnson (1973) relate their findings to the "field theory" of the German-Austrian psychologist Karl Buhler (1879–1963). Field theory states that for communication to take place, the speaker and hearer must share the same field (knowledge, context, and language) to a certain degree. (See Activity 9.A.)

Schema in Its Broadest Sense.   In another well-known study, Anderson and others (1977) asked two groups of college students to read the passage in Figure 9.4. One group of students was made up of music majors and the other group of physical education majors.

There are two ways this passage could be interpreted: as a card game or as a rehearsal of a woodwind ensemble. The results of the experiment showed that physical education majors tended to interpret this as a passage describing a card game (as do most adult readers), but the music majors tended to interpret it as a rehearsal. Three further results emerged from this experiment.

1. When asked to recall the story, subjects from both groups stated ideas that were not in the story or that were only implied in the story. These *added ideas* revealed whether the subjects interpreted the story as a card game or music rehearsal.

2. These authors considered such *recall of information not in the story* as evidence of comprehension.

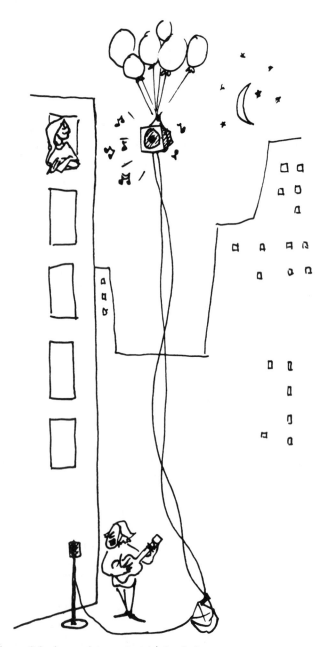

Figure 9.3. Appropriate context for the balloon passage. (*Source: Visual Information Processing*, edited by W. G. Chase. Bransford and Johnson, 1973. Reprinted by permission of the Academic Press.)

ACTIVITY 9.A TRY THESE EXPERIMENTS

Invite some fellow students who are not enrolled in your class to come in and act as subjects for the experiment described in Box 9.3 and for the experiment using the balloon passage (see Figures 9.2 and 9.3). You can probably re-create an experiment much like the original from the details supplied, but you may want to refer to the Bransford and Johnson (1973) article that describes the experiments in fuller detail.

A committee or individuals might do these experiments outside class and report the findings.

Discuss the findings and conclusions reported here in light of your observations in doing these two experiments.

3. When questioned after the experiment, more than 80 percent of the subjects reported that while reading the story, only one interpretation ever occurred to them. That is, subjects adopted an overview or a big picture of what the passage described, and their understanding of words, phrases, clauses, and ideas was governed by this overview.

Anderson and his colleagues (1977) propose that these results show that the "knowledge structures the reader brings to the text" are more important than the "structures which are in some sense 'in' the text" (p. 369). They refer to these knowledge structures the reader brings to the text as "high-level schemata" (p. 367).

It is important to notice that these authors are not referring to bringing particular knowledge to a text, such as knowledge that the subjects who saw the picture in Figure 9.3 brought to the text in Figure 9.2. If people have the "card game schema," for example, they know how to participate in a card game, they know what to expect from others in a card game, and they know how to organize information that they are told or that they read about a card game. A thousand details can change from card game to card game, but the schema or general outline remains the same.

The concept and the term *schema* (or its plural form *schemata*) are traced to Kant, the eighteenth-century rationalist philosopher mentioned in Chapter 1. Kant introduced the term in his discussion of human thinking (Kant, 1963; originally published in German in 1781). Bartlett (1932) is credited with directing the attention of modern scientists who are interested in the study of memory of spoken and written discourse to schema theory. (See Activity 9.B.)

This experiment demonstrates in a dramatic and unmistakable way that comprehension depends on the reader's prior knowledge. Reader's prior knowledge undoubtedly affects comprehension in less obvious ways. For example, I do not know much about hockey, and detailed accounts of hockey games are essentially unintelligible to me, although I recognize the vocabulary connected with the game, and I could probably

ACTIVITY 9.B TRY THIS EXPERIMENT

Invite some fellow students who are not enrolled in your class to come in and act as subjects for the experiment involving the card/music passage (see Figure 9.4). You can probably re-create an experiment much like the original from the details supplied here, but you may want to refer to the original study (Anderson et al., 1977) where the experiment is described in fuller detail.

A committee or individuals might do these experiments outside class and report the findings.

Discuss the findings and conclusions reported here in light of your observations in doing the experiment.

Every Saturday night, four good friends get together. When Jerry, Mike, and Pat arrived, Karen was sitting in her living room writing some notes. She quickly gathered the cards and stood up to greet her friends at the door. They followed her into the living room but as usual they couldn't agree on exactly what to play. Jerry eventually took a stand and set things up. Finally, they began to play. Karen's recorder filled the room with soft and pleasant music. Early in the evening, Mike noticed Pat's hand and the many diamonds. As the night progressed the tempo of play increased. Finally, a lull in the activities occurred. Taking advantage of this, Jerry pondered the arrangement in front of him. Mike interrupted Jerry's reverie and said, "Let's hear the score." They listened carefully and commented on their performance. When the comments were all heard, exhausted but happy, Karen's friends went home.

Figure 9.4. The card/music passage. A passage that could be given two distinct interpretations. (*Source:* Anderson et al., 1977, p. 372.)

answer a question about a sports page story I had read on the topic. Precisely how my comprehension fails in such a situation is more difficult to understand and describe, but it can be attributed to an easily identified lack of prior knowledge. This kind of knowledge has been referred to as "knowledge of the world," and it is closely related to vocabulary knowledge.

Vocabulary Knowledge.   There is one undisputed fact in the literature concerning comprehension. If vocabulary knowledge is included in a study in any way, it emerges as *the* major contributor to comprehension as a whole. This fact has been interpreted in three different ways: (1) an aptitude interpretation, (2) an instrumental interpretation, and (3) a knowledge of the world interpretation (Anderson & Freebody, 1981).

The Aptitude Interpretation.   The aptitude interpretation is the oldest and perhaps the most widely held. It is based on the well-known fact that word knowledge is an excellent indication of how well one will score on an intelligence test (Terman, 1918). The aptitude interpretation simply states that intelligent people know a lot of words and intelligent people are good at reading comprehension. Both large vocabulary and good reading comprehension spring from the same source—high intelligence.

The Instrumental Interpretation.   This view is something of a commonsense interpretation of the relationship. The instrumental interpretation is that people with large vocabularies are likely to know more words in any given passage than are people with small vocabularies; therefore, it is knowledge of word meanings that is the source of success on both measures—the vocabulary test and the comprehension test. This interpretation implies that if one knows all the words in a passage, he or she will automatically comprehend the passage, or, conversely, unknown words in a passage will cause failure to comprehend the passage.

The common sense of this interpretation is quite compelling, and it is appealing to teachers because it suggests possible solutions: to increase comprehension of a particular passage, teach the meanings of the words in the passage; to increase comprehension in general, teach the meanings of a lot of words in general.

But experiments designed to explore this interpretation do not always support it. For example, Tuinman and Brady (1974) reported that when they taught difficult vocabulary in a passage to fourth, fifth, and sixth graders, the subjects' scores on vocabulary tests of the words taught improved, but the subjects' scores on comprehension tests of the passages did not improve. Furthermore, it was demonstrated by Bransford and Johnson (1973) (see the earlier discussion) that knowledge of individual words does not ensure comprehension of a text.

Knowledge of the World Interpretation. This interpretation is based on the assumption that people who have wide exposure to culture learn two things: they learn a lot of words, because the concepts, categories, procedures, attributes, and relationships that are important to a culture are encoded in the vocabulary of the culture. Second, they learn a lot of knowledge structures or schemata—that is, they acquire overviews, "big pictures," of what to expect in a card game, or wedding, or ball game, or arithmetic lesson, or mystery story, or travelogue, or chapter in a physics book.

This interpretation of the relationship between word knowledge and comprehension states that people who have wide exposure to culture acquire a large number of words (and are therefore good at vocabulary tests) and a large number of schemata (and are therefore good at comprehension tests). Some similarities and contrasts among these three interpretations are diagrammed in Box 9.4.

BOX 9.4 CONTRASTS AND SIMILARITIES IN THREE INTERPRETATIONS OF THE RELATIONSHIP BETWEEN VOCABULARY AND COMPREHENSION

I. Aptitude Interpretation	II. Instrumental Interpretation	III. Knowledge of the World Interpretation
High IQ ↓ Good at everything ↓ ↓ Comprehension Vocabulary	Good Vocabulary ↓ Will know most words in most passages ↓ Will be good at comprehension	Wide Knowledge of the ↓ World ↓ Good Wide knowledge vocabulary of schema ↓ Good comprehension
Does not suggest any teaching strategy.	Suggests that direct teaching of vocabulary will increase comprehension.	Suggests that providing a rich cultural and intellectual environment will increase both vocabulary and comprehension.

I and III suggest that vocabulary and comprehension are independent, but are caused by a common antecedent.

II suggests that good vocabulary is a direct cause of good comprehension.

II and III suggest teaching strategies; I does not suggest any teaching strategy.

II suggests direct teaching of vocabulary; III suggests indirect teaching of both vocabulary and comprehension.

But note well: The first causes in the models—IQ in I, good vocabulary in II, and wide knowledge of the world in III—may be very highly related. For this reason, people tend to slip from one model to another without being aware of it.

The aptitude interpretation is no help to teachers. It seems to say that if you want better reading comprehension, produce more intelligent people. The instrumental interpretation proposes that if your students learn more word meanings, they will become better comprehenders. The knowledge of the world interpretation indicates that if your students are exposed to the concepts, procedures, events, and relationships that are important in their culture, particularly the literate culture to which they have access, they will not only learn the vocabulary but will also acquire the schemata that will facilitate comprehension of written texts.

"Qualitative" Reader Characteristics.   There are other somewhat less tangible characteristics of readers (as compared to prior knowledge or vocabulary knowledge) that affect comprehension. These characteristics are related to readers' strategies for acquiring and remembering information. For example, readers differ in terms of the strength of tendencies to do such things as

> Interpret language literally.
> Make inferences.
> Respond emotionally.
> Respond intellectually.
> Categorize, classify, and otherwise organize information.

Johnston (1983) suggests that in acquiring knowledge, middle-class people favor "main-pointedness" over "detail elaboration." It is a commonplace observation that some people's assimilation of knowledge is intuitive while others' is analytical. Followers of the psychoanalyst C. G. Jung (1875–1961) associate these styles with feminine and masculine tendencies that all people possess. More recently, these styles have been associated with left- and right-brain dominance. These characteristics also have been associated with cultural differences.

THE COMPOSING-COMPREHENDING CONNECTION

Kucer (1987) makes the following observations about the similarities between reading (comprehension) and writing (composition):

> Writers and readers both approach their task with prior knowledge of the topic and with a schema for the kind of text to be created or read.
> Writers and readers understand the function of the text, whether it is meant to inform, persuade, or transact business, for example.
> Writers and readers draw on the same knowledge of language and writing, such as sentence structure, vocabulary, spelling, and punctuation.
> Writers draft and revise to make their text true (consistent with their prior knowledge), internally consistent (not contradictory), and coherent (the relationships among ideas are clear). Readers also come to a series of understandings and revise. They revise their understanding to make it consistent with their prior knowledge, internally consistent, and coherent.

There is a good deal of evidence that composition and comprehension are related. Better writers tend to be better readers, and they tend to read more than poor writers (Stotsky, 1984). A review of the literature revealed that nearly all studies that used writing activities to improve reading comprehension were successful (Goodman & Goodman, 1984).

According to Graves and Hansen (1984), when first graders are given ample opportunity to both read and write, they begin to think of themselves as authors. They come to realize that the "books" they write could have been written differently. As authors, they exercise choices, and they become aware that the books they read are written by authors who exercise choices. Such children become more assertive in dealing with other authors. They ask questions like the following: "Why does the author make this statement?" "Is it true?" "How does the author know?" "Why should I believe it?" "Could it have been expressed more clearly, more pleasingly?" This is "critical reading"—the highest form of comprehension.

Earlier in this chapter, considerateness was suggested as a characteristic of texts that contributed to comprehension. Readers can in fact do something when faced with texts that are not considerate. Learning to write well is learning to be considerate of the reader. Assertive readers, readers who write, stand a better chance of detecting a writer's failure to be considerate and of compensating by figuring out the unstated connections, and working out the unclear structure of inconsiderate texts, rather than simply failing to comprehend and blaming themselves.

The belief that comprehension is closely related to composition has been expressed by many distinguished authorities in language arts and reading. Robert Tierney and P. David Pearson (1984) have proposed a "composing model of reading." Dorothy Grant Hennings (1984) proposes "a writing approach to reading comprehension." And James Squire (1984) refers to composing and comprehending as "two sides of the same basic process."

THE LISTENING-READING COMPREHENSION CONNECTION

There are three possible views regarding the relationship between language processing abilities used in listening comprehension (oral language) and language processing abilities used in reading (written language). They are

1. That they are unrelated. That children who understand oral language must learn to understand written language as an unrelated, independent skill. This position is patently untenable and receives no support from the literature.
2. That they are essentially identical—reading comprehension is nothing more than decoding plus oral language comprehension.
3. That there is a great deal of overlap between language processes employed in understanding spoken and written language, but there are some language processing abilities uniquely relevant to understanding written language. (See Figure 9.5.)

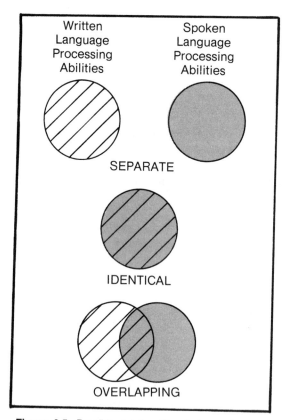

Figure 9.5. Possible relationships between language-processing abilities necessary to comprehend spoken language and to comprehend written language.

Essentially Identical

If reading comprehension is essentially identical to listening comprehension, it would seem that the only ceiling on reading comprehension is imposed by word recognition skills and listening comprehension. This would dictate a three-part strategy for teaching comprehension: (1) emphasize word recognition skills, (2) work on the *transfer* of listening comprehension to reading comprehension, and (3) work on oral language comprehension skills.

Emphasis on Decoding.   One problem with this analysis is that it sometimes leads to overemphasis on word recognition as a *prerequisite* to comprehension. This position implies a one-way relationship: decoding facilitates comprehension. However, it has been demonstrated by numerous writers (many of them cited earlier in this book) that *comprehension also facilitates decoding.*

The Transfer of Oral Language Comprehension Skills.   If you review Part One, Chapter 3, you will be reminded that in a literate society, the line between emergent literacy and early reading is unclear. Children begin to act upon the relationship between spoken language, written language, and meaning long before reading instruction begins. They recognize print on hamburger boxes and know with surprising accuracy what it "says." Children who are fortunate enough to be read to frequently, learn that the words spoken by the reader are the words they see on the page.

In the early stages of reading instruction the teacher's task is not so much to *teach* children that comprehending written language has much in common with comprehending spoken language; the teacher's task is to *continue to develop* this concept. It can be argued that a phonics emphasis at the initial stages of formal reading instruction may be counterproductive in this regard. On the other hand, one powerful argument in favor of the language experience approach to beginning reading is that the relationship between oral language and written language is apparent. The teacher writes what the children say, and the written text becomes reading material.

Emphasis on Oral Language Skills. Berger (1975) demonstrated that in early grades children who are superior in listening comprehension are also superior in reading comprehension. This relationship leads some experts to the conclusion that there is a ceiling imposed on reading comprehension by oral language comprehension and that, if oral language comprehension can be improved, reading comprehension will naturally follow.

In some circumstances these two conclusions may be valid; however, the conclusions are based on the premise that listening and reading comprehension demands are essentially identical. In the next section I will show that the premise is false. While increasing comprehension of oral language is a school objective in its own right, reading makes some comprehension demands for which experience with oral language does not prepare the reader.

Overlapping, but Not Identical

There is a great deal of evidence that comprehension skills gained through experience with oral language are necessary for comprehending written language, but they are not sufficient. That is, although there is overlap between listening and reading comprehension, written language presents certain unique challenges.

Formal Differences in Beginning Reading Materials. The language of the texts children are asked to read even at the very earliest stages of reading is different from oral language. In an effort to create a text using a limited number of words, sequences of sentences that would almost never appear in speech appear in beginning reading material.

> We will go to the zoo.
> We will go on a bus.
> Will you come?
> Will you come to the zoo?
> Will you come on the bus?

Also at the very earliest stages, the formality of written language intrudes, and children are asked to read sentences that are worded differently from what they are likely to hear in oral language. They read *We will go to the zoo* rather than *We're "gonna" go to the zoo,* as they would probably hear in speech.

Children in the first half of first grade are not expected to recognize very many words, and it is very difficult to write stories using only the words the children are expected to recognize. This leads to two peculiarities. Beck and her associates (1979) refer to these two problems as *alternative wording* and *omitted information.*

Alternative Wording. Among the stories presented very early in one basal reader (Clymer, 1976a) is an account of the fable of the tortoise and the hare. The story is entitled "Rabbit and Turtle." This is a story of a race, and one of the important events in the story is that the overly confident rabbit stops to rest and falls asleep. But because of the children's limited word recognition facility, the word *race* is not used in the text.

The authors attempt to overcome this problem by a combination of "round-about language" in the children's text and suggestions to the teacher in the Teacher's Manual. In the text Turtle says, "See the park. You and I will run. We'll run to the park." In the Teacher's Manual (Clymer, 1976a), the following suggestion is made to the teacher:

> Ask what Turtle meant by saying "We'll run to the park." If the idea of a race is not mentioned, suggest it. Help the children realize that Turtle was challenging Rabbit to a race. (p. 117)

Omitted Information. At times elements of stories are completely omitted in beginning reading materials. For example, in a story entitled "Who Said 'Hello'?" the children's text runs as follows:

> "Come with me, Ben.
> I want to see the zoo," said Bill.
> Ben said, "Stop, Bill.
> Who said 'Hello'?
> Who said 'Hello' to me?" (Clymer, 1976b, p. 7)

This text has a serious omission: there is no mention that anyone said "hello" to Ben. Beck et al. suggests that this omission could be remedied easily by supplying the missing information as part of the reading lesson. The teacher might say, "When Ben and Bill got to the zoo, Ben heard someone say something to him. Read this page and find out what someone said to Ben."

These are very typical examples of attempts to "teach" comprehension in the initial stages of reading instruction. Notice that it is not presumed that the children can simply apply what they know about understanding spoken language to the stories. On the contrary, the very legitimate concern for the comprehension of these stories has to do with the fact that the written texts are unlike spoken language.

The Unique Comprehension Demands of Institutional Writing. A frequently made observation is that when children's reading skills have progressed to where they can read materials written at around the fourth grade level, they begin to devote less energy to learning to read and more energy to reading to learn. What this means is that the materials children encounter in about the fourth grade and beyond are designed to convey information rather than to teach children to read. In other words, reading materials begin to display those characteristics that are typical of written language in general, or what Stubbs (1980) refers to as "institutional writing."

Facility with Explicit, Context-Independent Language in Speech and Writing.   In Chapter 2, I discussed implicit, context-dependent language, which is typical of (1) informal speech among people who are acquainted with each other and (2) personal correspondence between people who are well acquainted. I contrasted this with the explicit, context-independent language, which is typical of (1) more formal speech among people who are not acquainted and (2) formal writing, particularly institutional writing.

Reread this discussion in Chapter 2. You will be reminded that institutional writing has characteristics that make comprehension demands unlike spoken language and unlike personal correspondence. You will also be reminded that facility with spoken explicit language facilitates reading comprehension, that experience with reading institutional writing facilitates the ability to understand explicit speech in formal settings, and that experience with reading institutional writing facilitates effective spoken language in formal settings.

Some methods of teaching reading comprehension concentrate on comprehension strategies that apply to both listening and reading. Other methods concentrate on comprehension strategies that are demanded by the special characteristics of writing, particularly institutional writing. Some of these strategies appear early in reading programs because from the start, written language has characteristics that one does not find in oral language.

Lessons of this type continue throughout the reading program because, as the student progresses into the middle and upper grades, the characteristics of institutional written language become more pronounced in the texts children are expected to read. Lessons in study skills and reading in the content areas pay particular attention to comprehension of information conveyed through written texts and other print media such as graphs, maps, and charts.

PSYCHOLINGUISTIC PROCESSES

Kenneth and Yetta Goodman and their colleagues have devoted years of study to children's oral reading performance and their retelling of what they have read. This research has yielded valuable insights into the processes of comprehension, memory, and retrieval of information in written texts.

Miscues

For example, Figure 9.6 shows the first three sentences in a story and a transcript of a 9-year-old girl's oral reading of these sentences. The Goodmans point out that the things the child says that are not in the text (what might be called *oral reading errors,* but what the Goodmans prefer to call *miscues*) can be explained, but they cannot be explained in terms of any single process.

TEXT	TRANSCRIPT
1. Once upon a time there was a woodman who thought that no one worked as hard as he did.	1. *Once upon a time there was a woodman. He threw . . . who thought that no one worked as hard as he did.*
2. One evening when he came home from work, he said to his wife, "What do you do all day while I am away cutting wood?"	2. *One evening when he . . . when he came home from work, he said to his wife, "I want you do all day . . . what do you do all day when I am always cutting wood?"*
3. "I keep house," replied the wife, "and keeping house is hard work."	3. *"I keep . . . I keep house," replied the wife, "and keeping . . . and keeping . . . and keeping house is and work."*

Figure 9.6. The first three sentences of a written text and the transcript of a child's oral reading of the text. (*Source:* Goodman and Goodman, 1977, p. 318.)

For example, in sentence 1 the girl says "he threw" for the printed words *he thought*. She is probably paying some attention to letter-sound correspondences or *processing graphic information* since *threw* and *thought* begin with the same letters, but she is obviously not trying slavishly to "sound out" the words. She is undoubtedly relying on some knowledge of language (however unconsciously) since she produces a subject and verb where a subject and verb are called for. She is undoubtedly paying attention to the meaning of the language; she apparently cannot make sense of the next words when they follow *he threw,* and so she goes back, probably pays closer attention to the graphic information, and corrects herself.

A similar process seems to ensue in the second sentence when the same child renders *What do you do all day* as "I want you do all day," and then she corrects herself, but in the same sentence, she reads *while I am away cutting wood* as "when I am always cutting wood." Her knowledge of letter-sound relationships, her knowledge of syntax, and her knowledge of the world are not violated by this rendering; therefore, she does not check the clause again, although she has substituted *when* for *while* and *always* for *away.*

The Goodmans refer to this process as *miscue analysis. Miscue analysis* reveals that readers appear to draw on their knowledge of letter-sound correspondences, vocabulary, sentence structure, and prior knowledge in the process of comprehending.

Retelling

A second phase of miscue analysis calls for the child to retell what was in the text without prompting or leading questions. In analyzing the child's retelling, the observer is interested in how the child organizes (or reorganizes) what is learned from the text, and whether the child uses his or her own language or the author's language. Retelling also reveals a child's conceptions and misconceptions about the text. For example, the girl's retelling of the story in Figure 9.7 reveals that she knows that *woods* and *forest* are synonyms, but she also seems to know that the author used *forest* since she first says *woods* and corrects herself to say *forest*. For a further example, her retelling ap-

---

um . . . it was about this woodman and um . . . when he . . . he thought that he um . . . he had harder work to do than his wife. So he went home and he told his wife, "What have you been doing all day." And then his wife told him. And then, um . . . and then, he thought that it was easy work. And so . . . so . . . so his wife, so his wife, so she um . . . so the wife said, "well so you have to keep," no . . . the husband says that you have to go to the woods and cut . . . and have to go out in the forest and cut wood and I'll stay home. And the next day they did that.

Figure 9.7. The first segment of a child's retelling of a story after oral reading. (*Source:* Goodman and Goodman, 1977, p. 321.)

pears to confirm what her miscues suggest—that she is not familiar with the terms *keep house* and *keeping house*, although she apparently recognized the words *keep*, *keeping*, and *house*.

The Goodmans assert that the idea that every written text contains a precise meaning that readers passively receive is a misconception. They see the process of comprehending as one of constructing meaning, a process where the readers integrate their knowledge of reading, language, and the world and construct meaning while interacting with the printed page. This view of the reading process is known as the *psycholinguistic model of reading*.

You may want to look back at Chapter 1 where the meaning of the word *psycholinguistics* is discussed as a term applied to an empirical science in the 1950s and to a rationalist science by the end of the 1960s. The term psycholinguistics as it is used by the Goodmans refers to the *rationalist* science, as you can see from its top-down approach and its strong emphasis on the reader's assertive use of his or her knowledge of language and the world in constructing meaning. (See Activity 9.C.)

ACTIVITY 9.C UNDERSTANDING "READING COMPREHENSION"

The following observations were made in this section:

1. Readers do not remember accurately whether particular sentences were in a text.
2. Readers "learn" things they don't understand.
3. Readers sometimes forget things they comprehend.
4. "Recalling" information that is not in the text is sometimes evidence of comprehension.
5. Readers understand words, phrases and clauses in terms of an overview or schema—in the "knowledge about the world" sense.
6. Readers' ease in comprehension is related to their ability to predict what kind of information is coming next; that is, comprehension is related to the reader's schema in the "story grammar" sense.
7. Readers learn to be better readers by writing.
8. Composing and comprehending are two sides of the same basic process.
9. Oral reading miscues can be evidence of the reader's *mastery* of phonics, vocabulary sentence structure, and utilization of prior knowledge.

A. Form small groups of four to six students.

1. Discuss Thorndike's and Tierney and Pearson's description of the reading comprehension process in light of these observations.
2. How do these observations add to your understanding of the Tierney and Pearson description?

B. Compare summaries of the small groups' discussions and arrive at a class summary.

CONCEPTS OF READING COMPREHENSION DERIVED FROM EDUCATIONAL MEASUREMENT

Independent Subskills

In the previous discussion, I've referred to prior knowledge, knowledge of sentence structure, and vocabulary (to name a few) as elements that contribute to comprehension. The fact that several elements seem to be involved leads to an important question: Is comprehension a single skill, or is it several *independent* subskills?

From a teacher's point of view, the fact that several kinds of knowledge, skills, and abilities seem to be involved leads to the following important questions:

1. Can a person possess several of these skills and be missing just one or two, causing him or her to fail to comprehend?
2. Can we identify skills a person possesses and skills the person is missing so that we can teach only those skills that are lacking?
3. Can we isolate skills and teach them one at a time?
4. Are these skills only *logically* separable? Are they in fact always found together so that it is not possible to demonstrate that a person possesses some and is missing others? Are they in fact so intimately connected that it is impossible to isolate single skills and teach them in isolation?

You may recognize the two spheres of influence—empiricism and rationalism—lurking behind these questions. Questions 1, 2, and 3 reflect the atomistic, separate skills concept of comprehension, which is compatible with the bottom-up, skills-emphasis, empiricist tradition. Question 4 reflects the holistic, global concept of comprehension, which is compatible with the top-down rationalist traditions—found most recently in the whole language approach.

The question of whether comprehension can sensibly be thought of in terms of *independent* subskills led to a body of literature in the field of measurement that has had a profound effect on the teaching of reading. Some very complicated statistical procedures have been used to explore the question of whether or not it is useful to think of comprehension as a global skill or as a set of related subskills. One technique is called factor analysis. Factor analysis is used to analyze right and wrong answers on individual test items to see if the items are measuring the same or discrete kinds of knowledge or skill.

The Rationale Behind Factor Analysis. The rationale behind factor analysis is as follows. Suppose you gave the nine-item test in Figure 9.8 to 100 15-year-old students?

You would not be baffled by a student who answered the first three questions right and the remainder wrong; or who answered 4, 5, and 6 right and the remainder wrong; or who answered 7, 8, and 9 right and the remainder wrong. Or, conversely, you would not be baffled by a student who answered all right except 1, 2, and 3; or all right except 4, 5, and 6; or all right except 7, 8, and 9. The reason these patterns would not be

---

GRAMMAR

1. What is the subject of the following sentence? *Three boys were playing ball.*

2. Which noun in the following sentence is plural? *The women ran a race.*

3. Which noun is possessive in the following sentence? *You've got Mary's hat.*

HISTORY

4. Who discovered America?
   a. Drake   b. Balboa   c. Marco Polo   d. Columbus

5. Who was the first president of the United States?
   a. Franklin   b. Washington   c. Jefferson   d. Adams

6. When was the Declaration of Independence signed?
   a. 1492   b. 1609   c. 1776   d. 1789

SCIENCE

7. At what temperature does water freeze?
   a. 32°F   b. 0°F   c. 100°C   d. 32°C

8. What elements are in H_2O?
   a. Hydrogen and nitrogen
   b. Helium and oxygen
   c. Water and air
   d. Hydrogen and oxygen

9. Which statement is true?
   a. An ounce of sugar is heavier than an ounce of water.
   b. An ounce of sugar is heavier than a gram of water.
   c. An ounce of sugar weighs the same as a gram of water.
   d. You can't tell if an ounce of sugar is heavier than a gram of water.

Figure 9.8. An achievement test that presumably measures three separate kinds of knowledge.

surprising is that there are clearly three kinds of questions on this test—grammar, history, and science. Students who have one kind of knowledge may not have the other two kinds. Logically, the three kinds of knowledge are discrete and independent.

Of course, if you actually gave this test to 100 15-year-olds, you would get very confusing results. Some children would answer all the questions right, and some would answer all wrong. The performance of these children would not lend support to the assertion that three discrete kinds of knowledge were being tested by these nine items. Students also make mistakes. They give wrong answers when they know the correct answer. Students are also lucky at times and answer questions correctly when indeed they do not know the answer. And knowledge is not acquired in airtight categories. For example, many people who have never studied history know that Columbus discovered America.

But if these are discrete and independent categories of knowledge, the tendency to be right or wrong on all questions *within a group of questions* would be stronger than the tendency to answer randomly right and wrong across all questions. Factor analysis is a statistical procedure that reveals separate factors—that is, groups of questions that seem to be measuring the same kind of knowledge, and knowledge different from knowledge measured by other questions or groups of questions on a test.

As a matter of fact, certain demands of factor analysis procedure would make it necessary to write many more than 3 items for each category before using this procedure on test results. A 45-item test with 15 items in each category would be much more likely if this procedure were actually performed.

Presumably, then, if you were to administer a longer version of the test in Figure 9.8 and perform a factor analysis on the results, you would discover that there are three factors being tested by these items: one factor being addressed by such items as 1, 2, and 3; a second factor being addressed by such items as 4, 5, and 6; and a third factor being addressed by such items as 7, 8, and 9.

Several presumptions that follow from this discovery are probably consistent with your intuition.

1. Grammar, history, and science are separate kinds of knowledge, ability, or skill.
2. Students can possess one kind of knowledge, ability, or skill and not the other two, or two and not the other one.
3. These areas can be taught separately and independently.

Factor Analysis and Reading Comprehension Tests. Using the same kind of reasoning and the statistical procedure called factor analysis, Davis (1944) published a paper claiming to show that a particular test on reading comprehension measured nine separate factors:

1. Knowledge of word meanings.
2. Ability to select the appropriate meaning for a word or phrase in the light of its particular contextual setting.
3. Ability to follow the organization of a passage and to identify antecedents and references in it.
4. Ability to select the main thought of a passage.
5. Ability to answer questions that are specifically answered in a passage.
6. Ability to answer questions that are answered in a passage but not in words in which the question is asked.
7. Ability to draw inferences from a passage about its contents.
8. Ability to recognize the literary devices used in a passage and to determine its tone and mood.
9. Ability to determine a writer's purpose, intent, and point of view, that is, to draw inferences about a writer.

A short time later Thurston (1946) published a paper claiming to show that the test in question measured only one factor—reading ability. Davis (1946) reacted to the Thurston paper claiming that "Comprehension in reading involves at least five independent mental abilities, which appear to be

1. Word knowledge.
2. Ability to reason in reading.
3. Ability to follow the organization of a passage and to identify antecedents and references in it.
4. Ability to recognize the literary devices used in a passage and to determine its tone and mood.
5. Tendency to focus attention on a writer's explicit statements to the exclusion of their implications." (p. 254)

A long, interesting, and controversial literature emerged regarding the contention that one can identify "independent mental abilities" that contribute to reading comprehension. See Davis (1944, 1946, 1968, and 1972), R. L. Thorndike (1973), Thurston (1946), Spearritt (1972), and Lennon (1962).

Several lists of "factors" or "components" of reading comprehension have been proposed. The following list is from a well-known study by Lennon (1962):

1. A general verbal factor
   • breadth of vocabulary
   • depth of vocabulary
   • scope of vocabulary
   • extensive word mastery
   • fluency in handling words

2. Comprehension of explicitly stated material
   • locating specifically stated information
   • comprehension of literal meaning of what is written
   • ability to follow specific directions in what is read

3. Comprehension of implicit meanings
   • draw inferences from what is read
   • predict outcomes
   • derive the meaning of words from context
   • perceive the structure of what is read
   • perceive the main idea or central thought
   • perceive the hierarchical arrangement of ideas
   • interpret what is read
   • apply information to solution of a problem
   • derive some generalization or principles
   • all those abilities that demand active, productive, intellectual response and activity on the part of the reader

4. An element that might be termed "appreciation"
   • sensing the intent or purpose of the author
   • judging the mood or tone of the selection
   • perceiving literary devices

Although Lennon proposed this list, he hedged on the separateness of the factors. He conceded that the fourth factor, appreciation, had not been established to be *separate* from the first three and that factors 2 and 3 (comprehension of explicitly and implicitly stated material) cannot be differentiated. He observed that one would expect to find that comprehension of explicitly and implicitly stated material go together "because the ability to get at the implicit meaning of what is read presupposes the ability to understand the explicit or literal meaning" (p. 334). We're back to two factors, aren't we?

Hierarchically Related Subskills

The factor analytic and subskills approach seems to imply only two possibilities: that there are independent subskills or that reading comprehension is a single-factor, global affair. Lennon's explanation of why factors 2 and 3 cannot be differentiated (that one ability presupposes the other) offers a third possibility—that there are separate subskills, but they are not independent; namely, one presupposes the other. In other words, there are separate subskills, but they are hierarchically related.

Hierarchies Based on Research. Researchers have explored the possibility that reading comprehension can be usefully thought of as a group of subskills but that the subskills are related in a hierarchical fashion. For example, one would presume that any subject who could answer the second question in each of the following pairs could answer the first, but not all subjects who could answer the first question could answer the second.

1. a.   Which number is larger, 3 or 7?
    b.   What is 3 plus 2?
2. a.   How many points does a football team get for a field goal?
    b.   If team A had 6 points and team B had 12 points and team A made a field goal, which team would be winning?

Again, because of various sources of error, actual results of tests to determine hierarchies of knowledge or skills produce confusing results—even when the hierarchical relationship is as logically clear as it is in the two questions just posed. Confusion is much more pronounced when the logical relationship is less clear-cut, as it is among subskills presumed to exist in comprehension. As a result, various experimental techniques and statistical procedures have been used to test hierarchical theories.

For example, Wimmer (1979) demonstrated that (1) readers must understand individual sentences before they can understand connections between sentences and (2) recalling and retelling a story is dependent on understanding connections between sentences. Chapman (1971) showed that understanding sentences and understanding paragraphs are hierarchically related.

Logical Hierarchies in Comprehension. In 1948 a group of college examiners met informally at the American Psychological Association convention. It was proposed that there would be better communication between people engaged in test construction if they could agree upon the goals of education and classify these goals into educational objectives. A series of annual meetings was held that led to the publication of a little book with a long title: *Taxonomy of Educational Objectives—The Classification of Educational Goals—Handbook I: The Cognitive Domain* (Bloom et al., 1956). It is usually referred to as *Bloom's Taxonomy*. This book has had an important influence on the way reading comprehension is taught.

Bloom's Taxonomy. *Bloom's Taxonomy* classifies the intellectual objectives of education into two categories: (1) knowledge and (2) intellectual abilities and skills. *Knowledge* is further divided into:

1. Knowledge of specifics
2. Knowledge of ways and means of dealing with specifics
3. Knowledge of universals and abstractions

Intellectual abilities and skills are further divided into

1. Comprehension (the lowest level of understanding)
2. Application (use of abstraction in concrete situations)
3. Analysis (breakdown of communication into parts)
4. Synthesis (putting together elements to form a whole)
5. Evaluation (judgments about the value of material)

Each of these categories is further divided. In the condensed version of the taxonomy (pp. 201–207), there are 20 more categories arranged under *knowledge* or *intellectual abilities and skills*.

Hierarchical Taxonomies of Reading Comprehension. Several scholars have developed classification schemes for reading comprehension skills and abilities. Barrett (in Clymer, 1968) refers to his taxonomy as one of "cognitive and affective dimensions of reading comprehension." His major headings are

1. Literal comprehension
2. Reorganization
3. Inferential comprehension
4. Evaluation
5. Appreciation

Each of these categories is further divided so that in the entire taxonomy there are 35 categories arranged under these five major headings.

The Usefulness of a Subskills Approach to Reading Comprehension

The terms and concepts discussed in this literature have entered the materials used for teaching reading comprehension in the schools. Lists of kinds of knowledge, skills, outcomes, and abilities such as those just presented are frequently presented as comprehension objectives in reading programs.

In the methods that are presented in the next two chapters, you will see the influence of the subskills theory of comprehension, and you will see that the idea of a hierarchy of levels of comprehension underlies many of the methods.

SUMMARY

In the past educators viewed texts as containing information or knowledge and reading as the process of getting that information into the reader. Contemporary models of comprehension view comprehension as an interactive process. The text contains information; the reader brings prior knowledge to the text and actively pursues information in the text in an effort to assimilate text knowledge into his or her own store of knowledge. Therefore, in thinking about comprehension, it is necessary to consider the text, the reader, and the relation between the two.

Characteristics of texts that affect comprehension are quality and density of information, "considerateness," explicitness, and organization. Much recent research in comprehension has dealt with schema theory. Experience teaches more than simple isolated facts. The human mind perceives relationships between facts and imposes order on information. People use structures discovered through past experiences in perceiving and making sense of new experiences. These structures are called schemata. Comprehension depends to a certain extent on the schemata the reader possesses.

Forms of literature (stories, essays, editorials, etc.) follow general outlines. Stories, for example, often have the same structure: setting, beginning, reaction, attempt, outcome, and ending. This kind of outline is called a story grammar, and it describes a story schema. Research has shown that readers rely on story schema in their comprehension and recall of stories.

An important component of comprehension is the reader's prior knowledge. The same text can be easily understood or nearly incomprehensible based on the reader's knowledge of the situation to which the text refers. A reader's knowledge in a general sense can greatly affect his or her interpretation of texts.

Vocabulary or word knowledge is intimately related to comprehension. This fact has been interpreted in several ways:

1. It is proposed that people with a great capacity for learning acquire large vocabularies and are good at comprehension—thus comprehension and vocabulary are related because they both spring from intelligence. This is the *aptitude interpretation*.
2. It has been proposed that people who have good vocabularies are less likely to encounter words they don't know the meaning of than do people who have poor vocabularies—thus comprehension and vocabulary are related because comprehension depends on vocabulary. This is known as the *instrumental interpretation*.
3. It has been proposed that people who experience a rich cultural and intellectual environment acquire both good vocabularies and schemata that are relevant to the literature of the culture—thus comprehension and vocabulary are related because both depend on rich cultural and intellectual experiences. This is known as *the knowledge of the world interpretation*.

"Qualitative" reader characteristics such as the tendency to interpret language literally, to make inferences, to respond emotionally, to respond intellectually, and to categorize, classify, or otherwise organize information can also affect comprehension.

Reading, writing, speaking, and listening use language processes, and what is learned in one mode may enhance facility in the others. There is mounting evidence that experience as writers gives readers insights into what writers are trying to do. Because of the reciprocal nature of the reader's and the writer's tasks, insights into the writing process offer important insights into the reading comprehension process.

An important question for people who propose to improve students' reading comprehension is how reading comprehension is related to listening comprehension. The proposition that they are not related is patently false. The position that comprehension of written and spoken language are essentially the same thing has many adherents. On one side, this assumption leads to an emphasis on rapid, effortless decoding, since reading comprehension is viewed as listening comprehension (of which students are presumably already capable) plus decoding. However, this same position leads others to conclude that teachers should emphasize spoken language comprehension skill or transfer spoken language skills to reading.

The final position presented proposes that written language comprehension draws heavily on the same skills as oral language comprehension, but, because of the use to which written language is put, there are some characteristics of written language that are not present in oral language. This position leads to the conclusion that those characteristics that are unique to institutional written language need to be explained to students, and students need to be given practice in dealing with them. Strategies for teaching study skills and reading in the content areas tend to concentrate on these characteristics of institutional written language.

Observing the oral reading miscues of children reveals that comprehension is a complex process involving word recognition, knowledge of syntax and semantics, and previous knowledge of the world. The "psycholinguistic model" of reading is based on observations of this type. Proponents of this model stress the importance of the reader's knowledge of language and knowledge of the world; they deemphasize the "outer" aspects of reading, such as word recognition skills.

Practices of teaching comprehension have been greatly influenced by theories of testing comprehension. Tests have been developed that attempt to measure subskills thought to make up the comprehension process—such as perceiving the main idea, recalling details, and sensing the author's purpose. Attempts to demonstrate through factor analysis that these subskills are separate have not been successful.

One explanation for the failure of factor analysis to demonstrate the separateness of subskills is that subskills may be related hierarchically. It has been suggested, for example, that one can understand sentences and fail to understand relationships between sentences, but one cannot understand relationships between sentences without understanding the sentences. It would follow that there is a hierarchical relationship between sentence comprehension and paragraph comprehension—paragraph comprehension being the "higher" skill.

Hierarchical taxonomies that are based on logic rather than experimentation have had an enormous effect on the way reading comprehension is conceptualized and taught. The most influential of these taxonomies was developed by Bloom and his colleagues

(1956) for testing educational objectives in general. This taxonomy has been tailored to apply specifically to reading comprehension by several authors such as Barrett (in Clymer, 1968).

FOR FURTHER READING

Golden, J. M. (1984). Children's concept of story in reading and writing. *The Reading Teacher, 37*(7), 578–584.

Goodman, K. (1979). *Miscue analysis: Applications to reading instruction.* Urbana, IL: National Council of Teachers of English.

Gordon, C. J., & Braun, C. (1983). Using story schema as an aid to reading and writing. *The Reading Teacher, 37*(2), 116–121.

Lipson, M. Y. (1984). Some unexpected issues in prior knowledge and comprehension. *The Reading Teacher, 37*(8), 760–764.

McGea, L., & Richgels, D. (1985). Teaching expository text structure to elementary students. *The Reading Teacher, 38*(8), 739–749.

Moldofsky, P. B. (1983). Teaching students to determine the central story problem: A practical application of schema theory. *The Reading Teacher, 36*(8), 740–745.

Purcell-Gates, V. (1989). What oral/written language differences can tell us about beginning instruction. *The Reading Teacher, 42*(4), 290–295.

Rand, M. K. (1984). Story schema: Theory, research and practice. *The Reading Teacher, 37*(4), 377–383.

Roney, R. C. (1984). Background experience is the foundation of success in learning to read. *The Reading Teacher, 38*(2), 196–199.

Tatham, S. M. (1978). Comprehension taxonomies: Their uses and abuses. *The Reading Teacher, 32*(2), 190–194.

Wilson, C. R. (1983). Teaching reading comprehension by connecting the known to the new. *The Reading Teacher, 36*(4), 382–390.

CHAPTER 10

Teaching Reading Comprehension I

COMPREHENSION RESTS ON KNOWLEDGE OF LANGUAGE

Imagine a normal third grade child who recognizes each word in the following list but who reads the sentence that follows and reports that it says that George went to the movies or that Bob did the dishes.

Alphabetical List of Words in Sentence

Bob	do	go	the
dishes	George	if	to
		movies	will

George will go to the movies if Bob will do the dishes.

One can presume that word recognition is not the cause of difficulty, but that comprehension skills are to blame. What action would be indicated?

213

Teaching Explicitly—Directly About Language

This position would indicate that the child could be taught the meaning of this sentence directly through teaching the meanings of words such as *will* (indicating future) and *if* (indicating condition), or through teaching the child to recognize main clauses and subordinate clauses and the relationship between the clauses in sentences like the preceding sentence.

This is an extreme position, and it does not receive much support. Durkin (1979) adopted this position in defining *comprehension* for her classroom observation study. She found comprehension teaching by this definition to occur less than 1 percent of the time spent in reading instruction. One interpretation of this finding is that practically no teachers share Durkin's presumption about how comprehension is learned or how it should be taught.

This leads to a more often stated position that teaching comprehension is teaching how language works, but that children learn this indirectly rather than directly.

Teaching Indirectly About Language

There are many adherents to the point of view that children do not "learn" language by being taught directly, but that they acquire language through maturation and experience.

Children become involved in situations where one event is contingent upon another. There will be a shopping trip, *if* daddy gets home with the car. The child will cooperate, *if* he can have his favorite toy. When children attempt to express these conditional relationships, parents help by "leading from behind." Parents frequently express these relationships in their negotiations with young children. Recall that in Chapter 2, Mark's mother says to him "Well, I will play, if you put the top on the basket." Mark, aged 28 months, responds "All right. There. There. Mommy play."

Given enough cognitive development and enough such experience, the child will learn to understand such sentences. Adherents of this perspective tend to view providing any and all language experiences as *teaching comprehension.*

Promoting Metalinguistic Awareness

As children begin to read, a new kind of knowledge related to language emerges. This kind of knowledge can be demonstrated through the following example.

> **TEACHER:** I'm going to read this sentence (pointing to a page in a book). "The cups are on the counter. Now, tell me what are on the counter?"
> **STUDENT:** Cups.

The child has demonstrated that he or she understands the sentence. But now consider a second exchange:

> **TEACHER:** I'm going to read this sentence (pointing to a page in a book). "The cups are on the counter. Now, tell me how many words are in that sentence?"

STUDENT: Six.

TEACHER: Is one or more than one cup on the counter?

STUDENT: More than one.

TEACHER: How do you know?

STUDENT: *Cup* has an *-s* on it.

TEACHER: Good.

Here the child has demonstrated the ability to do something more than understand the sentence; he or she can talk about the language, reflect on it, and make statements about how it works. This kind of knowledge is referred to as metalinguistic awareness.

Metalinguistic awareness is an important component of learning to read. Students need to have the concept of word before they can recognize written words. Phonics generalizations, word structure generalizations, and the ability to reflect on context clues to word recognition are all forms of metalinguistic awareness. Much of our comprehension curriculum is composed of attempts to help children reflect on and state explicitly what they know about language.

Two methods for encouraging children to reflect on what they know about language have received considerable attention in recent years. One is the cloze technique and the other is sentence combining.

The Cloze Technique.   When using the cloze technique, the teacher deletes words from a printed passage and replaces the words with blank lines as in Figure 10.1. Students using the cloze technique write the words into the blank lines that they think are the words that were deleted. There are many ways to vary this technique. Teachers can delete every fifth word, tenth word, or whatever other numbered interval they wish. They can choose to delete only nouns, or nouns and verbs, or any words except function words. Another variation is to supply multiple-choice responses for the student to choose from in filling the blanks as in Figure 10.2. This is sometimes referred to as a maze.

You might want to look back at sentences 1 through 4 in Chapter 7 on the use of context for word recognition. These sentences are very similar to cloze and maze exercises, and the reasoning that goes into the use of context has as much to do with comprehension as it has to do with word recognition. The two are, of course, inextricably bound together, and it is important to remember that comprehension often precedes word recognition.

Figure 10.1. A passage made into a cloze exercise.

Directions: The following passage was taken from a book and some of the words were replaced by blanks. Write the word in each blank that you think was in the original passage.

Raccoons can live in cities too. They go into cities
_____ for food. They often take
treats _____ leave for birds. Tipping
_____ trash cans racoons find
_____ to eat. A chimney _____
hole in a tree _____ be their home.

Directions: Circle the word under each blank that you think makes the best sense for that sentence.

Raccoons can live in cities too. They go into cities

_____ for food. They often take
(searching, wanting, rest)

treats _____ leave for birds. Tipping
        (they, people, shall)

_____ trash cans racoons find
(on, hat, over)

_____ to eat. A chimney _____
(garbage, paper, small)   (the, or, wall)

hole in a tree _____ be their home.
                (stump, can, make)

Figure 10.2. A passage made into a multiple choice cloze exercise or maze.

Research suggests that using the cloze techniques *a basis for discussion* can be beneficial for students from primary grades through college. After students complete a cloze exercise the teacher asks

Why they chose the words they chose.
Whether the words they chose ''make sense.''
Which of the various words chosen by different students is best, and why.

Several attempts were made to show that simply having students complete cloze exercises would increase reading ability. These proved to be disappointing (Jongsma, 1971; Bortnick & Lopardo, 1973). It appears that the cloze technique can be valuable when it is used as a vehicle to promote discussion of language—to reflect upon and make explicit what students know about how language works, but simply performing cloze tasks without the additional discussion and reflection on the exercise has no benefit. (See Activity 10.A.)

Sentence Combining.   The example sentence-combining lesson in Figure 10.3 demonstrates the basic idea of sentence combining. At least two sentences and a relation between them are presented, and the student writes (or orally recites) the sentence that

ACTIVITY 10.A DO A CLOZE OR MAZE EXERCISE

I. Take three or four paragraphs from this book and make a cloze or maze passage from them.
   A. Do the cloze task as individuals.
   B. Discuss your ''answers.'' Are some better than others? Why?
   C. Compare your answers to the actual words deleted. Do some of the actual deleted words ''fit'' better than yours? Why?

II. Monitor your discussion. Tape record it and replay it, or have one student observe and make notes.
   1. What part did your knowledge of language play in your discussion?
   2. What part did your knowledge of the topic play in your discussion?
   This might be a good small group activity. Summaries of the activities can be shared with the class.

ACTIVITY 10.B DO SENTENCE-COMBINING EXERCISES

I. Following the model presented in Figures 10.3, 10.4, and 10.5 create several sentence-combining problems.

    A. Write solutions to the problems as individuals.
    B. Compare your solutions and discuss differences.

II. Monitor your discussion. Tape record it and replay it, or have one student observe and make notes.

    1. What part did your knowledge of language play in your discussion?
    2. Did people use words like *adjective, adverb, clause, conjunction?* These are words to describe the way language works.

This might be a good small group activity. Summaries of the activities can be shared with the class.

III. William Strong (1986) presents numerous sentence-combining activities in *Creative Approaches to Sentence Combining*. Get a copy of this booklet and report to the class on the various ways the idea of sentence combining can be used to promote metalinguistic awareness.

Figure 10.3. A lesson in sentence combining (1). (*Source:* Abridged from Lesson 1, Greenberg, Mc-Andrew, and Melerski, 1975, pp. 2–3.)

Lesson 1

This is the first type of problem in the workbook. It is also the simplest type. Once you understand how to do these, they will all be easy for you.

Every sentence-combining problem has a *matrix sentence* and one or more *insert sentences.* The way to solve the problem is to combine all the insert sentences with the matrix sentence.

The insert sentence will be indented underneath the matrix sentence, like this:

The zebra ate the grass.
    The zebra is *striped.*

The answer to this sample problem would be:

The striped zebra ate the grass.

There might be more than one insert sentence, like this:

The zebra ate the grass.
    The zebra is *striped*
    The grass is *green.*

The answer would be:

The striped zebra ate the green grass.

All you do is take the word *striped* from the first insert sentence and the word *green* from the second insert sentence. You put these words into the matrix sentence where they best fit. You don't have to change any of the words in the matrix sentence; all you do is add words to the *matrix sentence from the insert sentences.*

Look at this sample:

> The dog ran down the street.
>   The dog *had lost his master. (who)*

Here is the answer:

> The dog who had lost his master ran down the street.

Notice the word *who* in parentheses next to the insert sentence. This is a clue word that must also be added to the matrix sentence. From now on, whenever you see a word in parentheses next to an insert sentence, *you must use it in the answer.* The words *who had lost his master* form a clause that can be added to the matrix sentence.

Let's look at another example:

> My father can still hit the basket from half court.
>   My father *played varsity basketball in high school.* (who)

Here is the answer to this:

> My father who played varsity basketball in high school can still hit the basket from half court.

Figure 10.4. A lesson in sentence combining (2). (*Source:* Abridged from Lesson 5, Greenberg, McAndrew, and Melerski, 1975, pp. 9–12.)

Now let's combine all the different kinds of problems that you know how to do. Look at this one:

(a) The king wanted SOMETHING.
(b)   The king was lonely.
(c)   The king had never had a wife. *(who)*
(d)   He married the Princess Guinevere. *(to marry)*
(e)   Guinevere was beautiful.

The answer you should get is:

> The lonely king who never had a wife wanted to marry the beautiful Princess Guinevere.

We've lettered the lines to help discuss this one. By now you should be able to tell that line (a) is the matrix sentence. Line (b) is a simple word embedding problem. You simply have to add the word *lonely* to the matrix sentence. Line (c) requires that you add the clause *who never had a wife* to the matrix sentence. Line (d) you just learned how to do. You remove the word *something* from the matrix sentence and replace it with the words *to marry the Princess Guinevere.* Line (e) is an insert sentence. It requires you to put the word *beautiful* into the insert sentence above it, so that you end up with *to marry the beautiful Princess Guinevere* as the phrase that replaced the word *something.*

Figure 10.5. *A lesson in sentence combining (3).* (*Source:* Abridged from Lesson 12, Greenberg, McAndrew, and Melerski, 1975, pp. 29–32.)

results from combining the sentences. Examples of more complex sentence-combining exercises appear in Figures 10.4 and 10.5.

Doing sentence-combining exercises in groups or doing them individually and comparing and discussing the results are ways to facilitate discussion of how language works (Pearson & Camperell, 1981). William Strong (1986) presents numerous activities in *Creative Approaches to Sentence Combining* that will encourage students to reflect upon and state explicitly what they know about language. (See Activity 10.B.)

Metalinguistic Awareness of Particular Language Structures

Research and observation have determined that particular language structures may cause comprehension difficulties. Lessons to aid in the comprehension of such structures often appear in published reading programs. Figures 10.6 through 10.9 show teacher created activities to promote comprehension of sentence types that are believed to cause students difficulties.

Lessons like these are usually based on the observation that children behave as if they understand numerous sentences when they appear in a context that supports their meanings, but children do not reflect on their knowledge of how language works in such situations or pay particular attention to it. The presumption is that if children were to reflect on their knowledge of language and pay attention to it through exercises like those suggested here, their reading comprehension will improve.

Figure 10.6. Class activity to promote comprehension of sentence types known to cause comprehension problems.

Choose a partner. Choose a card on which one of the following sentences is printed. Act out the sentence on the card. Does the class agree that you have acted out the sentence correctly?

Bob put on his hat after Sue rang the bell.

Willie sat down before Bill turned on the water.

As Mary looked out the window, Jane clapped her hands.

Before Wanda stood up, Jane closed the door.

Make it so it is hard for the doll to see.

Make it so it is hard to see the doll.

Dwayne asked Susan what to give to Sandra.

Gus told Rita what to give the teacher.

Figure 10.7. Class activity to promote comprehension of comparisons stated in elliptical sentences.

Figure 10.8. Exercise to promote metalinguistic awareness of causal relationships in sentences.

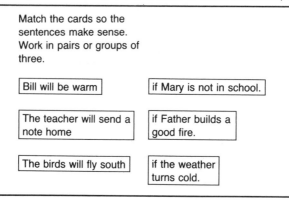

Match the cards so the
sentences make sense.
Work in pairs or groups of
three.

Bill will be warm	if Mary is not in school.
The teacher will send a note home	if Father builds a good fire.
The birds will fly south	if the weather turns cold.

Directions: Write a sentence that fits in the blank. Discuss your work with your classmates when you are finished. Do your sentences make good sense?

Bill will stop at Zeke's house if _____

Jane will buy ice cream if _____

We will not have school on Monday if _____

Figure 10.9. Exercise to promote metalinguistic awareness of causal relationships in sentences.

Comprehension Strategies Can Be Modeled

Promoting Metacomprehension.   Proficient readers display a kind of knowledge that poor readers seem to lack. Proficient readers can think about or talk about their own comprehension processes. This kind of knowledge can be demonstrated through the following example.

A teacher gives the following set of instructions for playing a card game to students and tells them that they will be asked about how to play the game after they have read the instructions.

> We each put our cards in a pile. We both turn over the top card in our pile. We look at the cards to see who has the special card. Then we turn over the next card in our pile to see who has the special card this time. In the end the person with the most cards wins the game. (Baker & Brown, 1980)

[After students have read the instructions.]

Teacher: Could you play the game?
Angelo: No.
Ernest: Yes.

Angelo shows an important characteristic of a person with metacomprehension awareness. He knows when he doesn't know something.

Teacher: How many cards does each player start with?
Angelo: I don't know.
Ernest: Twenty cards.
Teacher: How does a player win?
Angelo: He gets most cards.
Ernest: He wins most cards.
Teacher: What is a special card?
Angelo: I don't know.
Ernest: A joker.

Angelo shows a second characteristic of metacomprehension awareness. He knows what he *knows* as well as what he *doesn't know*. Ernest is not clear on this point.

TEACHER: What further information would you need to play the game?

ANGELO: How many cards are dealt to each player? What is a special card? Does the player with the special card keep his card and the other player's card?

ERNEST: I don't know.

Angelo shows the third characteristic of metacomprehension awareness: he knows what he *needs to know* to understand the text.

TEACHER: What did you do when you finished reading these instructions and you knew I was going to ask you about them?

ANGELO: I reread them to see if I missed something. I looked to see what a special card was because I thought I missed it.

ERNEST: I waited for the questions.

Angelo shows the fourth characteristic of metacomprehension awareness. He tries *repair strategies* that have worked in the past when comprehension has failed. He re-reads. He looks for specific information that he believes is crucial to understanding.

Alas, poor Ernest! His answers show that he does not monitor his own comprehension. (See Activity 10.C.)

Modeling Comprehension.   Fitzgerald (1983) suggests a variety of ways to foster metacomprehension. Modeling comprehension is one. Activities 10.D and 10.E are also suggested by Fitzgerald.

Teachers model comprehension by reading orally and "thinking aloud" the comprehension processes they engage in. For example, the teacher might take a text that begins with the words "He jumped out of the seat" and carry on the following monologue:

TEACHER: (reading from text) He jumped out of the seat.

(looking up . . . thinking aloud) I'm wondering who *he* is. Where is he?

(reading from text) He tried to get her to sit down so he could push her, but she refused.

(looking up . . . thinking aloud) Who is *she?* What does he want her to sit on "so he can push her"? Is it a wagon or a sled?

(reading from text) So the next time they were on the playground, he let her swing very high for a long time.

(looking up . . . thinking aloud) Oh! It's a boy and girl playing on swings. She probably wouldn't play because he hadn't given her a long enough turn on the swings.

ACTIVITY 10.C TEACHING METACOMPREHENSION AWARENESS

I. A. Using the card game instruction from Baker and Brown (1980), replicate the question and answer session reported with Angelo and Ernest. Act as the teacher and ask individuals not in your class to act as students.

B. In the course of your discussion, classify information referred to as "known" and "needs to be known."

C. Have students rewrite the instruction so that all the information is present.

II. Try this activity with younger students—fourth, eighth, and twelfth graders, for example.

ACTIVITY 10.D KEEPING TRACK OF WHAT'S KNOWN AND WHAT NEEDS TO BE KNOWN

Have one student act as teacher and several act as students. Engage in the following demonstration for the class.

Find a text, such as the example used in "Modeling Comprehension." Divide the chalkboard into two columns and label them *Known* and *Not Known*. Read the text sentence by sentence. Write facts in the *Known* column and questions in the *Not Known* column.

As each new sentence is read, facts may be added to the *Known* column, and questions may be removed from the *Not Know* column.

Experiences like this are designed to promote metacomprehension.

A monologue such as this is referred to as a "think-aloud protocol." (See Activity 10.E.)

Using longer texts, various kinds of comprehension strategies can be modeled. Brown and Lytle (1988) identified six "moves" readers make in attempting to comprehend a text. They are

1. *Monitoring*. I don't understand.
2. *Signaling*. What do I understand? (agrees, summarizes, paraphrases)
3. *Analyzing*. How does this text work? (comments on feature of the text such as words, text structure, and style)
4. *Elaborating*. What does this make me think of?
5. *Judging*. How good is this?
6. *Reasoning*. How can I figure this out? (asks questions, makes hypotheses and predictions)

Sensitivity to Text Structure.   Brown and Lytle's third move—"*Analyzing*. How does this text work?"—is an important comprehension skill. Good readers are sensitive to story grammar or schema (Chapter 9) and can predict what is coming in a text based on this concept. Subject matter textbooks often contain titles, headings, figures, tables, illustration, and introductory and summary paragraphs. "Surveying" or previewing such texts is a practice that can be taught to students. Surveying gives the reader a sense of the text structure, which in turn aids comprehension and recall. This topic is discussed in Chapter 11. (See Activity 10.E.)

TEACHING COMPREHENSION IN A DIRECTED READING LESSON

Reading lessons in eclectic basals and in many other materials used in teaching reading involve four steps:

ACTIVITY 10.E PREPARING A THINK-ALOUD PROTOCOL FOR MODELING COMPREHENSION STRATEGIES

Find a text that will enable you to make each of the six moves readers make in attempting to comprehend: monitoring, signaling, analyzing, elaborating, judging, and reasoning.

Do a think-aloud protocol for your classmates.

1. Preparation
2. Reading
3. Questions/discussion
4. Skills development

This four-part lesson scheme is known as a Directed Reading Lesson.

Selected practices for teaching comprehension in the framework of a Directed Reading Lesson will be presented in this section.

The Preparation Stage

There are three kinds of activities during the preparation phase that are designed to facilitate comprehension. They are supplying knowledge that the author of the text presumes the reader to have, presenting vocabulary, and setting a purpose for reading. The examples cited here are taken from Beck et al. (1979).

Supplying Background Knowledge.   A story in a third grade reader (Durr, 1976a) is about a village in China in 1913. The action of the story revolves around the fact that an airplane lands near the village and the people are very surprised. To mark this amazing event the village holds a kite-making contest. The story opens with the line, ''In the Year of the Water Ox, a long time ago. . .''

The program writers foresaw two possible impediments to a third grader's comprehension of the story. One is the reference to the Year of the Water Ox and the second is that a 9-year-old might not understand that an airplane would be unfamiliar in China in 1913.

In this case the Teacher's Guide simply suggests that the teacher tell the children that each year in the Old Chinese calendar is named for an animal and that 1913 was the Year of the Water Ox and that airplanes and automobiles were not commonly seen in China in 1913.

An innovative teacher might do more with these ideas; he or she might find out what the present year is on the Old Chinese calendar or find pictures of 1913 airplanes, cars, or American street scenes to help the children understand how different the world was in 1913. But the important point in terms of a Directed Reading Lesson is that reading selections are previewed to determine whether comprehension may be impeded because the students are unfamiliar with concepts that are necessary for understanding the story.

This is an example of an application of a very old idea: comprehension is relating information contained in a text to information already in the reader's possession. Some authorities believe that when students reach the point where they can read intermediate-level (grades 4–6) materials, the major cause of reading comprehension failure is limitation of knowledge on the part of the readers. That is, when students fail to comprehend texts, it is because they do not have the necessary prior knowledge to which to relate the information in the text.

Vocabulary.   In the primary grades, care is taken to introduce only those words that are already in the student's speaking-listening vocabularies. The objective is not to teach students new words in reading but to teach them to *recognize* printed words whose meanings are familiar. In intermediate grades, words begin to appear in texts whose meanings may not be known.

Teachers' Guides for basal readers supply lists of words whose meanings may be unknown to the students before each story. Teachers are urged to write the words on the chalk board and use them in a strong oral context. Some teacher's guides supply sentences such as the following for "target words."

After days of climbing, the party reached the *summit*, the highest point on the mountain.

Some basal readers identify words as either *general vocabulary* or *specialized vocabulary*. In a story about a weaver, for example, the words *woof* and *warp* and *shuttle* might be identified as specialized words. *Hardship* and *toil* and *efficient* might be identified as general words.

Attention to specialized vocabulary is more likely to be left up to individual teachers. The presumption seems to be that knowledge of specialized words is necessary for comprehension of the particular story so these words must be given some attention, but since they are not likely to appear again soon in a child's reading, they should not be given too much attention.

The practice of presenting words from a selection as an unrelated list of words whose meanings are to be learned before reading is based on the *instrumental interpretation* of the relationship between word knowledge and comprehension (Chapter 9)— that if one knows the words in a text he or she will probably understand the text. Another, slightly more complicated rationale for these kinds of lessons is that if a person does not recognize the meaning of a word in context automatically, some energy is directed toward trying to assign a meaning to the word, and comprehension suffers. When this happens frequently, comprehension may break down completely.

At times the line between filling in background knowledge and teaching vocabulary becomes indistinct. For example, in a story about the African American heroine Harriet Tubman, the following words might be identified for attention before reading: *Quaker*, *underground railroad*, *free states*, *slave states*, *overseer*, *traders*, *bloodhounds*, *runaways*, and *patrol*. A discussion of the list of words would supply a great deal of necessary background information for this story, and vice versa. When word lists like this appear, teaching them before reading is based on the *knowledge of the world interpretation* of the relationship between vocabulary knowledge and reading comprehension (see Chapter 9).

As students gain knowledge of the history and culture of their people, they learn concepts and words simultaneously. Their understanding of the concepts is so bound up with their knowledge of the vocabulary involved that it does not make sense to say simply that vocabulary knowledge causes comprehension. The fact is that comprehension facilitates vocabulary knowledge as much as vocabulary knowledge facilitates comprehension.

Vocabulary is also taught during the *skills development* phase of some Directed Reading Lessons, and it is also taught as a separate or supplemental program. Therefore, the topic of vocabulary development and comprehension will appear again in Chapter 11.

Purpose Setting. Purpose setting usually consists of remarks by the teacher intended to (1) get the students thinking along the lines of the story they are about to read and

(2) identify particular information that the students should be alert for or a question that the students should keep in mind as they read the selection.

In beginning reading, the story is often divided into short segments, and the preparation, reading, questioning cycle is repeated several times during the course of a story. At this stage, one is apt to find purpose-setting questions to be very concrete and designed to focus on one item of information that is explicitly stated in the text.

But beginning in the intermediate grades, purpose-setting questions that focus on one or two items of explicitly stated information are considered to be undesirable. Anderson and Biddle (1975) and Frase (1977) have pointed out that directing the readers' attention to small portions of the text may enhance their recollection of that portion of the text but may result in their failure to recall the selection in general.

Beyond primary grades, good purpose-setting activities ''should prepare children to construct the meaning of a text by evoking a network of relevant associations . . . direction-setting activities should provide a framework for the organization of events and concepts in the text so that many aspects of the text become interrelated and thus memorable'' (Beck et al., 1979, p. 87). Another way of stating this definition is to say that good purpose-setting activities supply the readers with a schema (Chapter 9) or framework into which they may fit the content of the selection they are about to read.

The following example of a *good* purpose-setting activity is found in the Teacher's Manual at the second grade level of a basal reading program (Durr, 1976b). The story is about a girl who attempts to convince a boy that she can pursue any profession she wishes regardless of her sex. In the Teacher's Manual it is suggested that the teachers say

> ''How many of you think that you know just what jobs you want to have someday? . . . Let's hear about some of these jobs . . .'' Following these responses, go around the group asking pupils the questions, ''How would you like to be a _____? Why or why not?'' Ask the girls about occupations that have often been associated with boys—pilot, firefighter, police officer, football coach, engineer, dentist, farmer, and so on. Ask the boys about occupations that have often been associated with girls—nurse, kindergarten teacher, nursery school teacher, baby sitter, secretary, dietitian, and so on. Through questioning and discussion, guide them to arrive at the conclusion—or to begin thinking in the direction—that there are really no valid reasons why a boy can't be a nurse or a girl can't be a pilot, provided that each is trained or prepared or educated for the job. ''In today's story, you're going to read about a boy and a girl who have some disagreements. You'll find out what those disagreements are and how they are settled.'' (Durr, 1976b, p. 127)

What recommends this purpose-setting activity is that it does not focus on some particular facts in the story the children are about to read, but it prompts the students to think along the lines of the story they are about to read, to identify the social issue this story relates to, to recall what they know about this issue and the attitudes they have heard expressed about it. This activity gives the readers an orientation or ideational framework (or schema) that will enable them to recognize important elements in the story and to relate them to each other under some larger design.

The Question-Discussion Stage

The most common classroom practice that is identified as teaching comprehension is asking questions. This is a curious fact since one would think that the reason a teacher asked questions would be to *test* comprehension rather than teach it. There is, however, good reason to believe that questioning, *if done properly,* does teach comprehension. Suggestions as to how questioning can be used as a legitimate and effective method of teaching comprehension can be found in many sources. Several of these sources are reviewed in the paragraphs that follow.

Dewey.   Dewey (1933) described the "art of questioning" as the art of showing pupils how to *"direct their own inquiries* and so to form in them the *independent habit of inquiry"* (p. 266). Dewey offered five suggestions to accomplish this goal.

1. Questions should require students to *use* information rather than to produce it literally and directly.
2. Emphasis should be on developing the subject and not on getting the one correct answer.
3. Questions should keep subject matter developing; each question should add to a continuous discussion. Questions should not be asked as if each one were complete in itself so that when the question is answered, the matter is disposed of, and another topic can be taken up.
4. There should be periodic reviews of what has gone before to extract the net meaning, to focus on what is significant in prior discussion, and to put old material into the new perspective that later material has supplied.
5. At the end of a question-discussion session there should be a sense of accomplishment and an expectation and desire that more is to come.

Vygotsky.   Vygotsky believed that the child's ability to think arises in society. Through speaking, the child collaborates with knowledgeable adults in solving problems. Soon the child uses egocentric speech to solve problems on his or her own. Eventually egocentric speech becomes inner speech. Thus, thinking evolves from interactions with others.

A second notion of Vygotsky supports the idea of using questions to teach comprehension. He believed that cognitive growth takes place in the "zone of proximal development." That is, the concepts that children are ready to learn are those that are beyond their grasp as individuals, but children can address these concepts in collaboration with others who have the concepts (Vygotsky, 1978).

From these two notions it follows that a child acting alone may be able to read a story about Andrew Jackson and see it as a collection of facts about an American patriot. Collaborating with a knowledgeable adult, she or he may come to understand that the story also tells how democratic ideas were especially useful for life on the frontier. A skillful teacher can bring such understanding out through questioning, and if done frequently enough, students will begin to ask themselves the kind of questions that the teacher asked and reach higher levels of comprehension when acting on their own. In this manner, comprehension is improved by collaborating with a skilled adult in dealing with concepts in the students' zone of proximal development. Social speech (questions and answers) becomes egocentric speech and finally inner speech or thought.

The Story Map Framework.   Beck and her associates (1979) propose that there are two reasons for asking questions after reading. The first is to *test* comprehension. This function of questioning is not pertinent to the present discussion. The second reason to ask questions is to *aid* comprehension. In this capacity,

> questions for a story should be generated with the aim of promoting the development of a unified conception of the story which we will call a *map* of the story. Any coherent story map must interweave the explicit and implicit story concepts. . . . To promote the development of a story map, the information elicited by each question should build on what has preceded. There are two notions here. First, questions should proceed in a sequence that matches the progression of ideas or of events in the story. Second, questions should be framed to highlight the interrelationship of story ideas.
>
> After a story map has been established through questioning and discussion, additional questions can then appropriately extend discussion to broader perspectives. (pp. 105–106)

For example, in a story in a second grade reader (Clymer, 1976) a family is harassed by a mischievous ghost to the point where they decide to move to another house. As the truck with the family and its belongings pulls away from the haunted house, the ghost perched on top of the load says, "We're off! Away we go!" Well-constructed questions would establish the problem (a troublesome ghost), the solution (the decision to move), the outcome (the ghost moves with them), and the ensuing problem (a troublesome ghost) in that order.

Final questions might lead the children to talk about what the family might do next or whether this is a typical ghost story or to relate this story to other stories where the antagonist outwits the protagonist. These kinds of questions will enhance story comprehension only if the story map has been well developed through earlier questions.

Practices That Violate the Story Map Framework. Some commonly seen questioning strategies violate the principle of constructing questions from a story map. For example, a series of factual questions such as the following questions 1, 2, and 3 do not relate to the main ideas of the story and do not promote a unified concept of the story.

1. How many children were in the family?
2. How long did the family live in the house?
3. What was the father's name?

Sometimes teachers begin with questions such as 4 and 5 that ask for speculations or emotional responses.

4. How would you feel if a mischievous ghost lived in your house?
5. When do you think this family will discover their problem has not been solved?

Such questions do not contribute to re-creating the progression of ideas or events in the story. In fact, such questions divert the students' attention away from the text; therefore, they should not be asked until the story map has been established.

Fact and inference questions are sometimes separated in story questions. This leads to taking the children through the story to recount the facts and then beginning over to discuss the inferences. Even if the teacher does an excellent job of selecting the facts and inferences relevant to the story map, the opportunity to create a unified concept of the story is lost.

How the Story Map Framework "Teaches" Comprehension. The story map concept of relating questioning to teaching comprehension echoes in some ways Dewey's (1933) suggestions for showing pupils how to use questions "to direct their own inquiries and so to form in them the independent habit of inquiry" (p. 266). Dewey's first point suggests that *facts* always be recalled in relation to a unified *concept* of the story; points two, three, and four suggest that questions should show a progression of interrelated ideas; and point five suggests that the final step should be to extend discussion to broader perspective.

This belief is wholly compatible with Vygotsky's ideas: (1) that much thought begins as social speech and travels inward to become egocentric speech and finally inner speech and (2) that learning takes place in the zone of proximal development. Through collaboration with a knowledgeable adult, a student can reach a level of comprehension that is beyond his or her grasp when working alone, and through such collaboration, the student will eventually attain that level of comprehension on his or her own.

Although Beck and her associates never say so explicitly, they clearly believe that when children repeatedly go through the process of answering questions derived from the story map, they internalize this procedure and begin to create maps of texts they read on their own. Through this process, therefore, children learn to comprehend written materials. (See Activity 10.F.)

The Skills by Level of Comprehension Framework.   Although the idea of using questioning as a device for teaching comprehension is widely recommended, the distressing fact is that classroom observations repeatedly reveal that generally teachers' questions require factual information stated explicitly in the text. Such questioning procedures are a far cry from those recommended by Dewey as long ago as 1933. Such questions fail to lead students to engage in higher levels of comprehension such as reorganization, inference, evaluation, or appreciation. They often fail, in fact, to lead students to basic understanding of sequences and plots.

The traditional response to such criticism is to encourage teachers and writers of reading programs to consider a "wider range of questions." Advocates of the idea that reading comprehension is composed of separate factors, skills, or abilities suggest that lists of abilities such as those proposed by Bloom and his associates or Lennon (see Chapter 9) be consulted and that questions tapping each ability (as far as possible) be derived from each passage in a Directed Reading Lesson.

Advocates of the notion that reading comprehension is composed of a hierarchy of

ACTIVITY 10.F USING THE STORY MAP FRAMEWORK

Form several small groups. Choose a story and write a list of questions using the story map framework. Compose and critique the results of each group's efforts and arrive at one list of questions that exemplifies the principles underlying the story map.

Repeat the exercise, if possible, using stories from various grade levels of materials (second, fifth, and eighth grade materials, for example).

ACTIVITY 10.G USING THE SKILLS BY LEVEL
OF COMMUNICATION FRAMEWORK

> Work in the small groups formed in Activity 10.F. Choose a story and write a list of questions using the skills by level of comprehension framework.
>
> Compose and critique the results of each group's efforts and arrive at one list of questions that exemplify the principles underlying the skills by level of comprehension framework.
>
> Repeat the exercise, if possible, using stories from various grade levels of materials (second, fifth, and eighth grade materials, for example).

subskills (see Chapter 9) suggest that questions tapping more elemental skills be asked first and questions tapping ''higher'' skills be asked later. The skills by level of comprehension framework (Ruddell, 1978) shown in Figure 10.10 combines the idea of independent subskills and of a hierarchy of skills. The questions that appear in Figure 10.11 are derived from a passage in *Charlotte's Web*. They are classified in terms of the comprehension framework in Figure 10.10. Ruddell suggests that teachers refer to the comprehension framework to be certain that their questions cover the seven skill competencies listed at the three comprehension levels. (See Activity 10.G.)

Comparing Question-Writing Frameworks. The skills by level of comprehension framework should generate questions that comply with Dewey's first and last suggestions cited earlier. The questions tap more than factual information stated explicitly in the passage, and they lead to activities like ''valuing'' (Ruddell's term) and applying knowledge gained in reading the passage.

However, this scheme does not ensure that questions will stress a sense of wholeness, development, and continuity in comprehending a passage such as Dewey's second, third, and fourth points suggest. Each of the three sample questions in Figure 10.11 could be considered complete in itself, so that, in Dewey's words ''when that question is answered that particular matter is disposed of and another topic can be taken up'' (p. 267).

Dewey's suggestions, and the ''story map'' strategy described in the last section, both urge the teacher to induce in the student a holistic, organic notion of comprehension. This is a top-down strategy, where parts are always seen in relation to and derived from the whole. Questioning strategies based on separate skills and taxonomies start by stressing parts and pull the parts together in the end through questions that evaluate the passage and apply information gained in reading to other situations. This is a bottom-up strategy. The classic division of empiricism and rationalism appears here once again. (See Activity 10.H.)

ACTIVITY 10.H COMPARING QUESTION-WRITING STRATEGIES

> Work in the small groups formed in Activities 10.F and 10.G. Compare the final questions arrived at by the entire class from Activities 10.F and 10.G. How are these lists similar? How are they different? Which set do you prefer? Why?
>
> Report summaries of your discussions to the class.

Questions may be generated from a passage to fit each cell in the framework where an X appears.

Skill Competencies	Comprehension Levels		
	Factual	Interpretive	Applicative
1. Details			
a. Identifying	X	X	
b. Comparing	X	X	X
c. Classifying		X	X
2. Sequence	X	X	X
3. Cause and effect	X	X	X
4. Main idea	X	X	X
5. Predicting outcome		X	X
6. Valuing			
a. Personal judgment	X	X	X
b. Character trait identification	X	X	X
c. Author's motive identification		X	X
7. Problem solving			X

Figure 10.10. Skills by level of comprehension framework based on separate skills and levels of comprehension. (*Source:* Ruddell, 1978, p. 112.)

1. What was written in Charlotte's web?
   Answer: SOME PIG!
   Comprehension level/skill competency: Factual—identifying details.

2. Why did Lurvy feel weak?
   Answer: Interpretation suggests that Lurvy believed it a rather unusual phenomenon to find the words SOME PIG! woven into a spider's web, and his actions express astonishment and surprise.
   Comprehension level/skill competency: Interpretive—cause and effect.

3. If you had been the first person to see Charlotte's web that morning, how would you have reacted?
   Answer: Responses will vary.
   Comprehension level/skill competency: Applicative—predicting outcomes.

Figure 10.11. Questions derived from a passage in *Charlotte's Web* and classified by the skills by level of comprehension framework (Figure 10.10). (*Source:* Ruddell, 1978, p. 113.)

A Word in Defense of Literal, Factual Questions.   It is an often-documented fact that teachers ask many literal, factual questions. This tendency has disturbed reading experts and others who are concerned with the intellectual atmosphere of the classroom. As a result, literal, factual questions have become almost taboo in some circles.

It has been suggested that this abhorrence of literal, factual questions and esteem for questions that call for inference, analysis, speculation, and critical reaction may in fact lead not to improving comprehension, but to teaching children to have little regard for what is on the printed page. One danger is that one may unwittingly teach students that it is not important to read for a precise understanding of a passage. The second danger is that one may unwittingly teach students that they do not have to read the passage *at all* to participate in a reading lesson or exercise.

Many teachers believe that habitually asking a few literal, factual questions encourages students to read the text, while habitually asking purely speculative questions causes the children to think they do not need to read the text to participate successfully in the reading lesson.

Comprehension Question Strategies and Metacognition.   As stated several times earlier in this book, Vygotsky believed that thinking processes originate as social speech, which becomes egocentric speech and finally inner speech and thought. Meichenbaum (1977) has adopted this belief and has suggested that this process can be enhanced by actually teaching the students to "talk to themselves," to teach them what to say to themselves when confronted with a problem. To do this, Meichenbaum believes that "from the onset one needs the pupil to be a collaborator in the generation of the cognitive strategies. It is important to insure that the purpose and rationale for the training is explained to the pupil as fully as possible" (1980, p. 17).

The Story Map Strategy.   Translated to the use of questions for teaching comprehension, this advice would seem to suggest that teachers who generated questions from a story map would make the connection between the questions and the story map as explicit as possible.

For example, in a story (Brand, 1969) in an upper-grade reading anthology, a villain's water canteen is filled with wine instead of water by his suspicious host. When the villain does great injury to the host and makes his escape across the desert, he is doomed to die because the wine will not satisfy his bodily need for water. Question 1 that follows is a factual question derived from a story map of this story; question 2 makes it clear to the students that this fact is crucial to understanding the climax of the story, thus making the connection between the fact and the story map explicit.

1.   What was kept in the jars by the door? (water in one jar and wine in the other)
2.   Why is that fact important later in the story?

In the middle and upper grades, lessons might also be devised where the class worked out a story map and derived questions from it. Students might evaluate suggested questions in terms of how the questions promote the development of a unified conception of the story. Question 1 would be judged to be good by this criterion. Question 3 would be judged to be poor because, although the information is in the story and it is interesting, it is an incidental fact rather than a fact that is necessary to the development of the story.

  3. Why were the jars made of porous stone? (The liquid evaporating through the pores kept the contents of the jars cool.)

This kind of lesson would enable the students to share in the intellectual exercise that is engaged in only by the teacher or writer under normal circumstances—despite the fact that it is this very process that teachers expect students to learn through answering comprehension questions. Lessons like this one would provide explicit instruction in the questioning strategy rather than relying on the students' abstracting and internalizing the strategy from repeated systematic experience with it.

The Skills by Level of Comprehension Framework Strategy. This same principle might be applied to teaching comprehension using the skills by level of comprehension framework. The teacher would not simply generate questions for different cells in Figure 10.10; he or she would explain the rationale for the questions as they are asked. For example, a teacher might say, "let's answer a few questions to see if everyone read the whole story." "Let's answer a few questions to see if we all understood the order in which things happened in the story." "Let's answer a few questions that will help us think about how we feel about the story." Such explicit statements of the "rationale for the training" might ensure that the process will become internalized and lead to habits of thinking.

Students who are learning (mistakenly) that the object of reading is to give the one right answer to factual questions will be set straight by teachers who discuss the rationale for their questions as a routine part of the question-discussion segment of Directed Reading Lessons.

Working with older children, teachers might divide the class into groups and ask one group to write three or four factual questions, another group to answer one or two inferential questions, and so on.

Teaching Question and Answer Relationships. Raphael (1982) proposed a questioning strategy to increase metacomprehension based on a somewhat different question classification scheme. She proposed that questions can be classified in terms of the source of the information required for the answer.

Raphael's three question classifications are illustrated and defined below using her example text and questions.

TEXT: Ralph sat on an old wooden rocking chair. He rocked harder and harder. Suddenly he found himself on the floor.

QUESTION: What kind of chair was Ralph sitting in?

TYPE: *Right there*

DEFINITION: "Right there" questions can be answered with words from one sentence.

QUESTION: What did Ralph do while sitting in the chair?

TYPE: *Think and search*

DEFINITION: "Think and search" questions require information from more than one sentence.

In this example, readers need only to find the antecedent of *he,* but since they must look across sentence boundaries, this is a think and search question.

QUESTION: Why did Ralph find himself sitting on the floor?
POSSIBLE ANSWERS: The chair broke. The chair tipped over.
TYPE: *On my own*
DEFINITION: "On my own" questions require prior knowledge on the part of the reader. The answer is not in the text. Readers need to reflect on their own experience and information to answer the question.

Raphael suggests that students learn these three categories of question-answer relationships (which she refers to as QARs) and that identifying question types should become a routine part of answering comprehension questions. This method has been shown to improve comprehension question answering performance in fourth grade (Raphael & Wannacott, 1985). An important aspect of the QAR strategy is that it calls attention to the importance of the reader's prior knowledge and experience in comprehension.

Working with middle- and upper-grade children teachers might ask students to write several questions of each variety (right there, think and search, and on my own) for selections they have read.

The Skills Development Stage

The reading selection is often used as a springboard for the skills development stage. For example, a lesson in Greek and Latin roots may start with several words from the reading selection that contain Greek and Latin roots and go on to consider the meanings of many other words that contain Greek and Latin roots but do not appear in the selection. This may, in turn, lead to a workbook exercise like the one in Figure 11.7 in Chapter 11.

Comprehension lessons that are not easily worked into the preparation or question-discussion stage of a Directed Reading Lesson are often treated in the skills development stage. They are also often taught in lessons separate from Directed Reading Lessons. Discussions based on cloze exercises and sentence-combining exercises and exercises like those shown in Figures 10.6 through 10.9 are the kinds of activities that are often considered "teaching comprehension" in the skills development stage of a Directed Reading Lesson.

The Directed Reading Lesson is a time-honored format for guiding students as they read selections usually from basal reading programs. Over the years variations on this procedure or elaborations on one phase of the procedure have been introduced. QARs is an example of such an elaboration of the question-discussion stage.

These later innovations usually differ from the Directed Reading Lesson in one of two ways: (1) They are *interactive* rather than directive. The students are more active in deciding what prior knowledge is relevant, what words they will need help with, what purpose to set for reading, and how to organize information for understanding and recall. (2) There is more attention to metacomprehension—making readers aware of their own comprehension processes, particularly the importance of the knowledge they bring to the text and their role as active seekers rather than passive receivers of information through reading.

OTHER INTERACTIVE STRATEGIES FOR TEACHING COMPREHENSION

Semantic Mapping

A group is about to read a selection entitled "The Raccoon." The teacher writes the word *Raccoon* on the chalkboard, draws a circle around it, and asks "What do you know about raccoons?"

The children respond, "They have striped tails." "They come out at night." "They knock over garbage cans to get food at the campground."

The teacher responds, "Well, we've got one fact, about what they look like. Let's call that *appearance* [writing the word 'appearance' on the board] and two things about what they do. Let's call that *behavior* [writing *behavior* on the board]."

As students volunteer more about the behavior and appearance of raccoons, the teacher adds words and phrases under these categories. As information that fits into new categories is suggested, the teacher creates new categories on the board. Soon a "semantic map" like the one in Figure 10.12 appears on the board.

This technique is referred to as semantic mapping. In this example it is used as a prereading activity to enable children to marshall their prior knowledge about a topic.

Teachers can work vocabulary development into semantic mapping by introducing words that will appear in the passage or supplying a word for a concept that students suggest. The teacher might write the word *nocturnal* after *comes out at night* and *habitat* after *where it lives*.

Figure 10.12. A semantic map of prior knowledge.

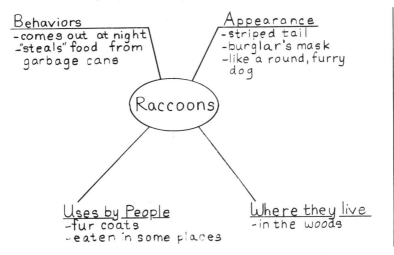

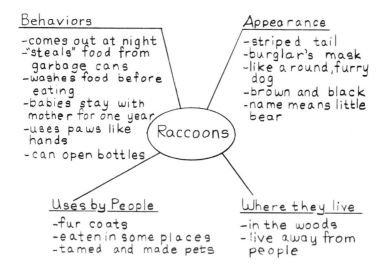

Figure 10.13. A semantic map as a postreading activity.

Semantic mapping can also be used as a postreading activity or during the question-discussion stage of a Directed Reading Lesson. In the case of ''The Raccoon,'' the story offers a great deal of information about raccoon behaviors, appearances, and a unique use by people—it is the story of a raccoon adopted as a pet. After reading the story, the class filled in more information on the semantic map (Figure 10.13) and made a new semantic map showing the main idea of the story—adopting wild animals as pets may create problems (Figure 10.14).

Figure 10.14. A semantic map for main ideas.

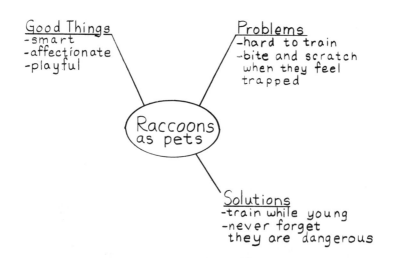

Semantic mapping is a useful strategy for activating prior knowledge, showing the relationships between prior knowledge and text information, and for organizing and integrating information. This strategy will be referred to again in the next chapter in relation to vocabulary building and study skills.

Directed Reading and Thinking Activity

A directed reading and thinking activity can be incorporated into a Directed Reading Lesson. It is an important variation on creating purpose setting questions. It differs from the purpose setting phase as described above in two important ways: (1) The students suggest the questions with teacher feedback and (2) purpose setting is reconsidered and repeated at predetermined intervals throughout the passage.

For example, the reading group is preparing to read a selection called "Show Business Was My Home," which is a short excerpt from a biography of Sammy Davis, Jr. The group looks at the title and two illustrations accompanying the text—a montage of photographs of Sammy Davis, Jr., appearing in night clubs and television shows and a picture of Sammy, aged 2, in a minstrel costume and black face makeup.

TEACHER: What will this story be about?

ANDREA: About Sammy Davis, Jr.

TEACHER: Right. What do you know about him? What will the story tell you about him?

ARTHUR: It will tell you how he got into show business.

REBECCA: It will tell you he got into show business when he was a little boy.

TEACHER: What makes you think that?

REBECCA: There is a picture of him as a little boy in a costume.

TEACHER: OK. Read page 143 and the top two lines on 144. When you've finished stop reading and look up at me.

[The introduction to the selection states that Sammy Davis, Jr.'s parents were both dancers on the vaudeville circuit, and his paternal grandmother took Sammy to raise him since his parents were always traveling.]

TEACHER: What do you think? Did our prediction come true?

PAUL: Yes. It's about how Sammy Davis, Jr., got into show business.

LILLIAN: It is about Sammy Davis, Jr., but it doesn't tell us how he got into show business, *yet.*

TEACHER: What do you think will happen in the next part?

PAUL: It will probably tell us where he went to school.

TEACHER: Why do you think that?

PAUL: It's the story of a little boy.

TEACHER: And little boys go to school. But do you think the next part will talk about school?

REBECCA: No. I think it will tell us about how he got into his first show. In the picture on page 146 he's in a show.

TEACHER: Yes. And he still looks like almost a baby. Any other ideas about what the rest of the story will tell us?

ARTHUR: It will tell how he went back to live with his parents and got into their act.

TEACHER: That's a pretty good prediction from what we know so far. Let's read the next two pages now. Stop and look up when you've read to the bottom of page 145.

An important point to underscore here is that the teacher does not tell any students that they are wrong. Predictions are evaluated and corrective feedback is given in terms of how reasonable the prediction is in terms of what has been revealed so far *in the text* and in terms of the reader's prior knowledge. A second important function of teacher feedback is to encourage students to reflect on the basis of their predictions, that is, to reflect on their thought processes.

Students who have had repeated practice with this procedure begin to make observations that are surprisingly insightful. Students begin to recognize stock characters and stock plots and base their predictions on them. They recognize genre such as mystery stories, adventure stories, expository passages in geography and history books, and so on and make predictions about what they will read based on these schemata.

A slight variation on this activity is to ask students to predict what a selection will contain before reading and to have follow-up after reading the entire selection. This is almost identical to the purpose-setting phase of a Directed Reading Lesson, except that the students rather than the teacher create the purpose setting questions.

Directed reading and thinking activities foster comprehension in these important ways:

1. They active prior knowledge activate.
2. They emphasize the importance of the relationship between *text knowledge* and prior knowledge.
3. They illustrate the concept that comprehension calls for *activity* rather than passivity on the part of the reader.
4. They encourage readers to reflect on their own comprehension processes. (See Activity 10.I.)

Directed Listening and Thinking Activity

A directed listening-thinking activity shares all the characteristics of a directed reading and thinking activity except that the teacher shows the book, pictures, title, and so on to the students and then the *teacher* reads a segment of the selection and stops and asks for predictions of what will come later in the text. This activity is frequently used in primary grades and preschools. It has all the advantages of a directed reading and think-

ACTIVITY 10.I DO A DIRECTED READING AND THINKING ACTIVITY

I. Have one student act as teacher and several act as students. Select a story or essay and conduct a directed reading and thinking activity as described in this chapter.

Use selections designed for primary, middle, and upper grades. How does the activity change as the nature of the material changes? For example, pictures may be useful for making predictions in primary materials but titles, subtitles, headings, diagrams, and so on may be useful in upper-grade materials.

II. Try this activity with younger students—second, fifth, and eighth graders, for example.

ACTIVITY 10.J DO A DIRECTED LISTENING AND THINKING ACTIVITY

Have one student act as teacher and several act as students. Select a story from a book intended for primary grades and conduct a directed listening and thinking activity as described in this chapter.

ing activity, but it permits the teacher to use books that the children are not yet ready to read for themselves. (See Activity 10.J.)

Reciprocal Teaching

Palincsar (1984) identified four activities that *foster* comprehension and at the same time enable students to *monitor* their comprehension, that is, think about the process, be conscious of it, and know when it is succeeding and when it is not. These four activities are self-questioning, summarizing, predicting, and clarifying. As in a directed reading and thinking lesson, children engage in these activities not only before and after reading but at intervals throughout the reading process.

Palincsar's teaching strategy is one of interactive dialogue. First, the teacher models a strategy. Second, students engage in the strategy while the teacher guides them through corrective feedback. This is called guided practice. Finally, students take over as "teachers." Palincsar refers to this final phase as *reciprocal teaching*.

The Modeling Phase.   For example, the teacher and students have books open to a story entitled "A Meeting with Stone Age Eskimos." In the modeling phase, the teacher suggests that they all read the first paragraph silently.

> TEACHER: (when everyone has finished) Let's see, how would I *summarize* this paragraph? "The exploring party sets out on a 250-mile trip across frozen, unoccupied territory."
>
> Now what *questions* will probably be answered in this story? How about "Why are they making this trip?" The author talks about his food supplies in this paragraph. I wonder "Will they run out of food?"
>
> What *predictions* might we make? Because of the title, I think they will meet a group of Eskimos. I'll bet they'll run out of food and meet Eskimos who will help them.
>
> Last, what is there in this paragraph that needs to be explained to me; what needs *clarifying?* Well, the author says they are heading east from Cape Parry. I wonder where that is exactly. We could look on a map, but maybe it won't be that important.

The teacher continues with this cycle—silent reading, *summarizing, questioning, predicting,* and *clarifying.* In each case, the teacher further defines these concepts by thinking aloud as he or she does the tasks. For example, after reading a particular paragraph, the teacher might say, "This section lists the hardships that the drop in temperature caused. I'll begin the *summary* with the words 'The sudden drop in temperature caused four problems. They were . . .'." After reading another group of paragraphs, the teacher might say, "This section talks about the author's Eskimo companions' fear of ghosts. I think they are going to meet an unfamiliar group of Eskimos and think they are ghosts. That's what I *predict*."

Teaching the *clarifying* concept presents a special problem. *Clarifying* may be called for when the meanings of words or phrases are unclear, but it is also called for when referents are unclear, when the text is disorganized, or when the reader lacks necessary prior knowledge or experience. In well-written texts that are appropriate for the reader's skill, the need to clarify should not occur in every paragraph. Encouraging children to find puzzles in every line is not constructive.

On the other hand, teachers should be alert to the need for clarification and bring examples to the attention of the class. Later in the passage about the Arctic journey, the sentence "we found footprints and sled tracks not more than three months old" occurs. It seems fair enough to wonder how three-month-old tracks would still be present. Citing such examples when they arise helps children to see that questions can arise because of problems in the text: the reader is not always at fault.

Guided Practice. *After* modeling the comprehension fostering/monitoring activities, the teacher asks students to summarize, question, predict, and clarify. If "A Meeting with Stone Age Eskimos" were a text used for the first time during the guided practice stage, the following dialogue might occur.

Summarizing

> STUDENT: They left Cape Parry for Cape Krusenstern with two weeks' supply of food. They had 250 miles to go, and they thought there were no animals to hunt and no people along the way and they went on dog sled.
> TEACHER: Yes. Well, that's quite a lot of detail for a summary. What are they doing—in one or two words?
> STUDENT: Taking a trip.
> TEACHER: Good. What's special about the trip?
> STUDENT: It's a long way.
> TEACHER: Where is it? What's special about where it is?
> STUDENT: It's in the Arctic.
> TEACHER: Good. Now put those three facts into a sentence.
> STUDENT: They started a long trip in the Arctic.
> TEACHER: Good.

Questioning

> STUDENT: How many people are on the trip? Will they make it?
> TEACHER: Those are both good questions. What does he say about hunting?
> STUDENT: There are no bears or seals to hunt on the way.
> TEACHER: Does that give you any ideas about what might happen?
> STUDENT: Yes. I think they'll meet a bear, and they won't be ready.
> TEACHER: Turn that into a question.
> STUDENT: Will they meet any bears on the way?
> TEACHER: Good.

Predicting. This phase of this technique is identical to the directed reading and thinking lesson.

Clarifying. As stated, teachers should not overdo this activity, because students might become *too* mistrustful of the text. In asking students for points that need clarification, teachers should imply that clarifying may not be necessary at every stopping point. For example, "Does anyone need anything cleared up at this point?"

Reciprocal Teaching. When students are familiar with the concepts of summarizing, questioning, predicting, and clarifying, and when they can perform these activities reasonably well, the teacher begins to turn the teaching job over to the students. For example, the adult teacher might introduce a text and act as teacher for the first silent reading segment and then say, "All right. Let's read the next three paragraphs—down to the bottom of page 221 and Donnell will be the teacher. Donnell will summarize, question, predict, and clarify—if any clarifying is necessary."

At this stage the adult teacher continues to give the "teacher" feedback through questioning, making suggestions and asking students for suggestions.

Palincsar and Brown (1986) suggest that each of the comprehension fostering/monitoring techniques be taught separately through explaining, modeling, and guided practice before the four techniques are put together.

Palincsar and Brown (1986) make the following observation about reciprocal or interactive teaching:

1. Reciprocal teaching promotes comprehension and comprehension monitoring.
2. The summarizing component teaches students to integrate information from the text.
3. The questioning and predicting components link prior knowledge to text information and encourage students to make use of text structure by reflecting on what usually comes next in a text of this type.
4. The clarifying component helps children to become aware of what they *don't* know. Making this explicit leads to discussions of what to do when clarification is necessary—reread, ask for help, look ahead.
5. Reciprocal teaching has been shown to have a good effect, especially on students whose comprehension lags behind their word recognition skill.
6. Reciprocal teaching has been used in peer tutoring. Students with better comprehension have been paired with students with poorer comprehension, and *both* tutor and tutoree have profited.

Reciprocal teaching is a superb application of the zone of proximal development concept. Students are introduced to a concept or set of concepts and are encouraged to use them in a collaboration with others who are more proficient in their use.

The interaction between teacher and student during guided practice and between the adult teacher and student-teacher in reciprocal teaching is similar to the scaffolding (Chapter 3) that parents supply for children in their fledgling attempts at language use. (See Activity 10.K.)

ACTIVITY 10.K COMPARE TWO APPROACHES

I. A. Form two small groups from volunteers.
    B. Find a selection from a basal or another source that would typically be used in the middle grades.
        Group 1: Prepare a Directed Reading Lesson for the selected passage.
        Group 2: Prepare a Reciprocal Teaching Lesson for the selected passage.
    C. Groups 1 and 2 present your lesson to other students in the class.
II. Class discussion: Referring to specific instances in the two lessons, discuss the following points:
    A. A Directed Reading Lesson is highly directive; a Reciprocal Teaching Lesson gives the students more initiative.
    B. In a Directed Reading Lesson, the teacher decides what knowledge is important; in a Reciprocal Teaching Lesson students have more opportunity to identify knowledge that they feel is important.
    C. In a Directed Reading Lesson, the teacher decides on correctness; in a Reciprocal Teaching Lesson there is greater opportunity for correctness to be negotiated.
    D. In a Directed Reading Lesson there is a great effort to foster comprehension, but practically no effort to teach metacomprehension; in a Reciprocal Teaching Lesson there is a great effort to foster comprehension and to teach metacomprehension.

SUMMARY

Five assumptions about teaching comprehension of language structure were examined in this chapter. To explore the first four of these assumptions, a child was introduced who recognized all the words but did not understand the sentence *George will go to the movies if Bob will do the dishes.* The first assumption is that comprehension of language structure can be taught directly. Teachers who believe this might try to teach the child the "meaning" of *if* and *will.* The second assumption is that comprehension of language structure can be taught indirectly through rich and varied language experiences. Teachers who believe this would invest in enriching the child's experiences and facilitate frequent interpretations of those experiences through language. The third assumption is that comprehension can be taught through general metalinguistic awareness. Teachers who believe this might have children engage in cloze exercises or sentence-combining activities and discuss their "answers" as vehicles for enabling students to reflect upon and make explicit the way language works. The fourth assumption is that comprehension can be taught through metalinguistic awareness of particular structures. Teachers who believe this might present sentences with the structure *If "A" then "B"* in situations where the context and the child's experience support his or her understanding as a first step in helping the child.

The fifth assumption is that the process of comprehension can be modeled. Good readers appear to be conscious of the state of their comprehension as they read. They know what they know, what they do not know, and what they need to know. Readers' consciousness about their own comprehension is called metacomprehension. A variety of ways of fostering metacomprehension were suggested. Six "moves" in comprehending were suggested: monitoring, signaling, analyzing, elaborating, judging, and reasoning.

Strategies for teaching the comprehension of stories were suggested for three of the four stages of a Directed Reading Lesson. At the preparation stage the children are supplied with information they must bring to the story for comprehension to take place, and vocabulary that may be new to the readers is introduced. Since knowledge of concepts and of word meanings are so intimately related, these two activities are often intermingled. A purpose for reading is also suggested to guide the reading and to aid in comprehension.

Questioning during the question-discussion stage of the Directed Reading Lesson can be a method of teaching comprehension. Dewey and Vygotsky were cited as authorities who endorse this belief. Comprehension is presumably enhanced through questioning if the questions are derived from a structure that is believed to occur repeatedly from story to story. Repeated experiences with answering questions that reflect a story map (or schema) or a skills by level of comprehension framework will result in the student internalizing that schema or framework and using it for comprehension and recall of future stories. The two structures suggested for generating questions for teaching comprehension reflect the often found contrast between the bottom-up concept of reading (reflected in the skills by level of comprehension framework) and the top-down concept of reading (reflected in the story map framework).

Both frameworks play down the value of literal factual questions. However, literal factual questions should not be taboo. They serve the very practical purpose of ensuring that students read the text. Students sometimes learn that they can participate fully in the lesson without having read the text.

There is merit in hoping to induce a comprehension framework in a reader's mind by repeatedly leading him through a particular framework. There is further merit in teachers' being more explicit in telling students what they hope to accomplish through their questioning strategy. With younger students, teachers can state the rationale for their questions as they proceed. Older students might be introduced to the concept of the story map or skills by level of comprehension frameworks and asked to create questions based on those frameworks or to evaluate questions in terms of how they fit those frameworks.

The question-answer relationships strategy (QAR) was described where students are taught explicitly that some questions require literal interpretation of sentences in the text (right there), others require putting together information from more than one sentence (think and search), and some require references to the reader's prior knowledge (on my own).

Comprehension skills that are only touched on in the selection are often singled out for attention during the skills development stage of the Directed Reading Lesson. Lessons found in the skills development stage tend to be the kind of lessons one finds in workbooks and other materials designed specifically to "teach comprehension." These lessons tend to focus on comprehension of language structures and on subskills described in the well-known taxonomies.

Other strategies for teaching comprehension were described. They are semantic mapping, the directed reading and thinking activity, the directed listening and thinking activity, and reciprocal teaching. Each of these is more interactive than directive in terms of the teachers' and the students' roles. Reciprocal teaching is similar to a teacher's "think-aloud" protocol except that a structure is suggested (summarize, question, predict, and clarify) and eventually the process is taken over by the students.

FOR FURTHER READING

Alvermann, D. E., Dillon, D. R., & O'Brien, D. G. (1987). *Using discussion to promote reading comprehension.* Newark, DE: International Reading Association.

Arnold, R. D., & Wilcox, E. (1982). Comparing types of comprehension questions found in fourth grade readers. *Reading Psychology, 3*(1), 43–49.

Babbs, P. J., & Moe, A. J. (1983). Metacognition: A key for independent learning from text. *The Reading Teacher, 36*(4), 422–426.

Baumann, J. F. (Ed.). (1986). *Teaching main idea comprehension.* Newark, DE: International Reading Association.

Carr, E., Dewitz, P., & Patberg, J. (1989). Using cloze for inference training with expository text. *The Reading Teacher, 42*(6), 380–385.

Cohen, R. (1983). Self-generated questions as an aid to reading comprehension. *The Reading Teacher, 36*(8), 770–775.

Duffy, G. G., Roehler, L. R., & Herrmann, B. A. (1988). Modeling mental processes helps poor readers become strategic readers. *The Reading Teacher, 41*(8), 762–767.

Farrar, M. T. (1984). Why do we ask comprehension questions? A new conception of comprehension instruction. *The Reading Teacher, 37*(6), 452–456.

Fitzgerald, J. (1983). Helping readers gain self-control over reading comprehension. *The Reading Teacher, 37*(3), 249–253.

Guthrie, J. T. (1984). Comprehension instruction. *The Reading Teacher, 38*(2), 236–238.

Haggard, M. R. (1988). Developing critical thinking with the directed reading-thinking activity. *The Reading Teacher, 41*(6), 526–535.

Heimlich, J. E., & Pittelman, S. D. (1986). *Semantic mapping: classroom applications.* Newark, DE: International Reading Association.

Koskinen, P. S., Gambrell, L. B., Kapinus, B. A., & Heathington, B. S. (1988). Retelling: A strategy for enhancing students' reading comprehension. *The Reading Teacher, 41*(9), 892–897.

Lindquist, D. B. (1988). Joining the literacy club. *The Reading Teacher, 41*(7), 676–681.

Nessel, D. (1987). The new face of comprehension instruction: A closer look at questions. *The Reading Teacher, 40*(7), 604–607.

Raphael, T. E. (1984). Teaching learners about sources of information for answering comprehension questions. *Journal of Reading, 27*(4), 303–311.

Raphael, T. E. (1986). Teaching question answer relationships, revisited. *The Reading Teacher, 39*(6), 516–523.

Riley, J. D. (1986). Progressive cloze as a remedial technique. *The Reading Teacher, 39*(6), 576–583.

Reutzel, D. R. (1986). Clozing in on comprehension: The cloze story map. *The Reading Teacher, 39*(6), 524–529.

Reutzel, D. R. (1986). The reading basal: A sentence combining composing book. *The Reading Teacher, 40*(2), 194–199.

Sanacore, J. (1984). Metacognition and the improvement of reading: Some important links. *Journal of Reading, 27*(8), 706–712.

Schmitt, M. C., & Baumann, J. F. (1986). How to incorporate comprehension monitoring strategies into basal reader instruction. *The Reading Teacher, 40*(1), 28–31.

Smith, M., & Bean, T. W. (1983). Four strategies that develop children's story comprehension and writing. *The Reading Teacher, 37*(3), 295–301.

Stauffer, R. G., & Harrel, M. M. (1975). Individualized reading-thinking activities. *The Reading Teacher, 28*(8), 765–769.

Uttero, D. A. (1988). Activating comprehension through cooperative learning. *The Reading Teacher, 41*(4), 390–395.

CHAPTER 11

Teaching Reading Comprehension II

WORKING TOWARD A WHOLE LANGUAGE APPROACH TO TEACHING READING COMPREHENSION

Reading Conferences

In her book *When Writers Read,* Hansen (1987) develops the concept of the *response* and the way in which responses operate in achieving reading comprehension. Children respond to texts (books, stories, essays, and so on). Teachers respond to students, affirming what students know, answering their questions, clarifying misunderstandings, and negotiating a shared meaning based on the text.

Teachers approach reading conferences with these principles in mind. Rather than explain these principles to students, teachers behave in accordance with them. After repeated experiences, the students understand how the reading conference works.

A conference between a teacher and child in the early stages of the process might go as follows:

> The teacher might stop beside Jeremy, for example, and say "Oh, you're reading 'Corduroy.' I've read it, too. What do you think of it?"
>
> Jeremy, when this response system is new to him, may say, "It's OK."
>
> The teacher has yet to find out what Jeremy knows, so she pursues, "Show me a part you think is OK."
>
> Jeremy shows the page where Corduroy emerges, shrunk, but doesn't say a word.
>
> The teacher still hasn't found out much about what he knows, so she continues, "Yes, he shrank. Tell me about that."
>
> Jeremy simply says, "The dryer was too hot."
>
> The teacher starts to get excited, "You know heat can cause things to shrink. That's important. Do you have anything else to tell me?"
>
> The child may or may not answer, but before the teacher leaves the child, she refocuses him, "Where were you when I came. . . . Please read just a bit to me."
>
> When Jeremy is on track, the teacher moves on.
>
> Over time, the student contributes more and more to the conference, usually starting to talk the moment the teacher pulls a chair up beside him. He knows she wants him to tell her about his book. Her goal is to find out one thing the student knows and restate it in specific terms. Often, when we respond to a student, he comes to understand his book better as he tells us about it.
>
> (Hansen, 1987, p. 184)

Students learn that the teacher wants to hear what they know from reading the text. Students learn that they are to re-create the meaning, to compose what they have comprehended. In such conferences, misunderstandings are revealed that questioning by the teacher might never have uncovered.

> One day when researcher Tom Romano met with Matt and Randy, they talked about *Soup* by Robert Peck. The boys thought Rob had hit a nurse with a ball because they thought that "throwing the ball" back to the other person in conversation meant throwing a real ball. Romano didn't come to this session with a list of questions to ask the boys. He came to find out what they knew. They talked and he listened. When he realized that they misunderstood the words, he explained. He taught. (Hansen, pp. 41–42)

Teachers Ask "Real" Questions.   In such conferences teachers ask real questions, that is, questions to which they do not know the answers. A teacher who has not read a story a child is reading might say, "You said the boy didn't like his father. Why didn't he like him?" This is not a "comprehension question" that can be classified as "factual" or "inference" and that has a "right" answer. The teacher really wants to know why the student thinks the boy in the story didn't like his father.

The child may explain, "Well, when he didn't want to play football his father made fun of him in front of his friends, and things like that." The teacher might respond "I see. That's a pretty good reason not to like someone."

Or the student may reformulate his or her understanding. "Well, he always was in trouble with his father. His father was always mad at him. I guess he liked him but he was kind of afraid of him."

Students Ask "Real" Questions.   When students become accustomed to answering real questions and having their answers listened to, responded to, and validated, they stop trying to hide what they don't know and ask real questions themselves. When teachers know the answers to real questions, they simply answer them. When they do not, they must find out the answer or encourage students to seek answers elsewhere. For example,

> One day first-grader Amanda came to me with a question: "I know the horse is friendly and the goat isn't but I don't understand why they become friends." I hadn't read the book, so I asked some questions. Amanda couldn't explain the story well enough for me to figure out why the two animals became friends. Amanda sat. I suggested that she read the book to someone. Amanda continued to sit. Finally she said, "I'll read the whole book to Stephanie. Then me and her can talk about it." (Hansen, p. 42)

Students Are Encouraged to Tell What They Know.   In Chapter 3, under the topic of emergent literacy, I discussed the astonishing discoveries that preschool children make about reading, writing, story form, and such aspects of writing as punctuation. Such emergent knowledge becomes apparent when we permit children to display what they know. When children are empowered to express their opinions about such high levels of comprehension as imputing motives to story characters, similar discoveries have been made. For example,

> In October, Barry, a child in Pat McLure's first grade, shared *Tales of Oliver Pig,* by Jean VanLeeuwen, in which Grandmother Pig comes to visit, and little Oliver Pig gets his monster books and toy elephant to put in Grandmother's room . . . Barry requested comments and questions about his book, and Chris asked, "Why do you suppose he got monster books and a toy elephant for an adult?"
>
> "Maybe he was being sneaky," Barry suggested. "She wouldn't really care about that stuff, but Oliver could sneak right in with her and cuddle up and she'd read him the book."
>
> "I don't think so," Roger stated. "Oliver's a nice pig. I think he gave her his favorite monster books to read; then he thought if she was scared, she could hug his elephant." . . .
>
> The children attributed deeper motives to Oliver's actions than their teacher had considered. (See Activity 11.A.)

ACTIVITY 11.A ROLE PLAYING A READING CONFERENCE

I. Choose a reading selection and work with a partner. Plan a dialogue between a teacher and student engaging in a conference like those described in this section.

Decide on the following conditions before starting:

1. The teacher has (or has not) read the story.
2. The child is (or is not) used to these conferences and is (or is not) forthcoming.

II. Present a variety of these skits to the class where different conditions are evident. Comment on the teacher's performance and his or her fidelity to the principles of the whole language approach as you understand them.

III. Do this exercise using the same texts as you used in Activities 10.F and 10.G. Compare the evidence of comprehension that emerges from these skits with the evidence of comprehension you might see in asking the questions derived in Activities 10.F and 10.G.

Students Help Each Other.   In a whole language classroom students are encouraged to seek help from one another. When students read "books" written by fellow students, they go to the author for help with reading. When students read books that have been read by other students, they can seek out these others and ask for help in understanding what they are reading.

When students' interests become known to their classmates, individuals may be identified as knowledgeable on certain topics. Jenny is a good person to talk to about sports books because she loves sports and reads such books herself. Mark can probably answer questions about dogs because his mother is a veterinarian and he likes to read about dogs.

The Process Approach to Teaching Writing

One important assumption underlying the whole language approach is that children learn to read by writing. I am going to describe the process approach to teaching writing in this section to show how children learn to read as they learn to write.

The following narratives illustrate how the process approach to teaching writing incorporates two important ideals that whole language teachers strive to achieve: it helps to turn a classroom into a literate community where students learn from one another as well as from the teacher, and it integrates the teaching and learning of the language arts—reading, writing, speaking, and listening.

Observing Teachers Teaching: Marla McCurdy.   Marla McCurdy (1984) began using the process approach one day by gathering her first graders around her and asking them how they would spell some words. Soon she had the sentence "The dog chased the cat" written on the board in the following way:

a dg sd a ct

After writing a few such sentences as a class project, Marla suggested to the children that in the future, when they were writing, they should try to write their own words without asking her how to spell them. She reminded them to put a space or dash between words and to write from left to right.

At first she was a little discouraged, but soon she found that, if she got to the children as soon as they had finished, many of them could read back what they had written. For example, a nonreader wrote what you see in Figure 11.1 and read back to her, "This is my imaginary friend, Bgooga." The writing of other children was more easily understood. (See Figure 11.2.)

Figure 11.1.

AND I SAW A LION HE ASK ME
ME NAM WS ABBY

Figure 11.2.

Encouraged by these results, Marla continued her experiment. By the end of the year, her writing program incorporated the following features:

A Storybook Corner. Blank "books" made from lined paper and construction paper covers are always available in the storybook corner. Children's work-in-progress is kept here also. Children are expected to write every day.

Conferencing. Marla talks individually with the children on a regular basis. She helps them decide what to write about. She listens as they read their books to her. She reads their books as they listen. She asks them questions. For example, for the following "story"

> *When I go home, I play with my dog*

she might ask, "What kind of dog is it? What color? What games do you play? How old is the dog? How is the dog special?" Sometimes, as a result of these conferences, the children add to their stories.

Publishing. When children are satisfied that their stories are finished, Marla or an aide types them, using conventional spelling, punctuation, and capitalization. Covers are made and books are created that are added to the classroom library of children's works.

A Literate Community. Children often read works-in-progress and borrow ideas from one another. They read one another's published books from the library and show a great deal of interest in stories that are published.

Teaching and Learning Language Arts Is Integrated. Learning to read and write occurs simultaneously. It is often impossible to say whether children are engaged in reading or writing, and the whole process is buoyed up on a sea of talk—speaking and listening.

Marla sums up her experience with the process approach to teaching writing as follows.

> In thinking about the process I have gone through in learning about this writing method, I am most impressed with its naturalness for small children. It builds on what children do themselves when left with crayons, pencils, paper, and felt pens. Instead of holding children back from producing valuable materials until they learn to read and spell, it encourages, approves of, and helps to implement children's interest in expressing their own creative and imaginative thoughts and ideas. The acceptance and praise teachers give to children at this early age for their actual writing leads them to self-acceptance.

This self-acceptance paves the way for their growth in being able to revise, rethink, and improve their writing skills and abilities in future years. (McCurdy, 1984, p. 22)

Observing Teachers Teaching: Irene Silo-Miller.   In recounting her experience with teaching the process approach to writing, Irene Silo-Miller (1984), a fourth grade teacher, tells a similar story, but her concerns are somewhat different since she is dealing with more mature writers—writers with a more mature zone of proximal development.

Irene encourages her students to write true stories since she believes they can write more freely and accurately about information that is real to them. Since she does not assign topics, she uses a number of techniques to help children find topics and get started writing. She visits children individually as they begin to write and expresses interest in their topics. She asks children who have begun to write to read aloud what they have written so far. This often gives ideas to those who have not started. She encourages children to draw, and she has brief conferences with the artists, asking questions about the picture and developing a topic for a story. She encourages children to speak their stories into tape recorders and insists that a written product follow. She points out good examples of story openers in books the children read and in books she reads to the children.

Irene teaches the children how to participate in a conference. She first holds a writing conference with an individual child in front of the class. The child reads his or her story slowly and clearly. She asks questions to help the author expand and clarify the story. This process is then incorporated into individual student-teacher conferences, group student-teacher conferences, conferences between two students, and group conferences among students. Irene teaches the students how to function in conferences both as authors and as audiences and supplies guidelines for responding to writing such as the following:

1. Say something positive about the story.
2. If the story does not have a title, ask what a good title might be.
3. Comment on the lead. Is it interesting?
4. Ask what the author's favorite part of the story is. Is it explained clearly so you can picture what is happening? Ask what more you would like to know to make that part clear.

An important part of the writing process approach is to remember who *owns* the writing. Irene could tell students what to write about and how to revise it to make their writing acceptable to her, but she feels the children need to feel a sense of responsibility for their writing and to retain decision-making power in revising their own writing.

> One of my most gratifying moments as a teacher was when I said to an eighth grade student during a conference—"Do you mind if I write on your paper?" At first she didn't understand that I considered the page we were discussing to be her paper and that I, the teacher, should ask permission before putting pencil marks on it. In a moment she understood, said "sure," and squared her shoulders and sat up straighter. I've had similar experiences since.

After two conferences on the story itself, the author and teacher have a proofreading session. In discussion with each child, Irene identifies three or four problems that the child agrees to work on, such as capitalizing first words in sentences or indenting paragraphs.

After proofreading, the student can decide to publish, which means binding the neatly and correctly recopied story into a decorated cover, putting the copyright date inside, making a card for the classroom library card catalog, and placing the book on the library shelf.

Children often sit with each other during free time reading one another's books. They also share their books with children from different grade levels. Authors from different classes sometimes come in and read their stories to Irene's class, and authors from Irene's class go to other classes and read their stories.

Once again reading and writing are occurring simultaneously. Children are speaking and listening in conferences, and formal oral presentations to groups become part of the writing program.

Teachers who are committed to a whole language approach might work from using basal readers, Directed Reading Lessons, and other more interactive approaches to teaching reading comprehension and work toward a reading conference—writing process approach. Teachers who are particularly skillful and committed to the whole language approach might finally abandon their basal reading programs entirely. In Chapter 15 I will describe the individualized reading program and the writing workshop, two approaches that offer guidance to teachers who wish to move in this direction.

However, many teachers will probably never completely abandon their basal reading programs, and teachers who do should be familiar with the numerous methods covered in these chapters and the assumptions upon which these methods rest. Such familiarity will give all teachers insights into students' comprehension problems and suggest methods for addressing them.

TEACHING VOCABULARY

The Complexities of Word Meaning

The question of why vocabulary knowledge is so closely related to reading comprehension ability was raised in the last chapter. Three possible answers were suggested, but no one answer has been agreed upon. The relationship between word knowledge and thought is an age-old topic of study. Psychologists have shown that word knowledge is a good measure of intelligence. Vygotsky (1986) has noted that the relationship between thought and word is an "immense and complex problem" (p. 153). It is no wonder then that there is no clear, easy definition of what it means to "know a word."

What Does It Mean to Know a Word?

Ways of Defining Words. Johnson and Pearson (1978) list seven "ways of defining words" (p. 45):

1. Using words in a sentence.
2. Giving a synonym.
3. Giving an antonym.

4. Classifying (e.g., A *woman* is an adult female human being.).
5. Giving an example (e.g., Lassie is an example of a *canine*.).
6. Giving a comparison (e.g., An *ocean* is like a lake, but larger.).
7. Describing a physical relationship (e.g., An *arm* is connected to the shoulder and to the hand).

Denotative and Connotative Meanings. It is a commonplace observation that words have both denotative and connotative meanings; that is, to say that a man is *rugged* and to say that he is *uncouth* may refer to the same characteristics of the man (*rugged* and *uncouth* have similar denotations), but *rugged* implies that the speaker approves of the characteristics and *uncouth* implies the speaker does not approve (*rugged* and *uncouth* have different connotations). It is impossible to say whether the denotative or connotative meanings of words are more important without a thorough knowledge of the context where they appear.

Nuances. Words can take on nuances that are too subtle and too specific for any dictionary to record. When Quakers say in a Quaker meeting that they are "concerned," they mean what the average American means but they also mean something more because of the long tradition connected with the word *concern* among Quakers.

"Insider's" Meaning. Slang is deliberately invented so that "outsiders" will not know what is being said among members of in-groups such as musicians and teenagers. To "be cool" has nothing to do with one's temperature or the temperature of the room. A built-in problem with dictionaries of slang is they are outdated almost as soon as they are published. When the meaning of slang terms becomes widely known they are often abandoned by "insiders" and new terms are invented.

Historical Change. Meanings of words change over time. A glance at a glossed edition of any Shakespeare play will reveal dozens of examples. For example, in *Julius Caesar* the word *emulation* means *jealousy* and the word *napkins* means *handkerchiefs*.

Sarcasm, Irony, and Humor. Sarcasm, irony, and humor prompt people to use words to mean the opposite of what they usually mean. A person may ask why someone is "all dressed-up" when the person is actually in particularly sloppy attire, or a person may comment on another's stinginess by asking why he or she is so generous.

"Narrowing" Meaning. People use words in particular contexts to denote only part of the usual meaning of the word. A married man whose wife is away for a weekend may refer to himself as a bachelor. A person may remark on a man's general attractiveness by saying "He's no Robert Redford." (See Activity 11.B.)

Opportunities Arising from the Complexity of Word Meaning

Given the profound implications of the relationships among word knowledge, reading comprehension, and thought, and given the rich variabilities in connotation, denotation, historical change, local variation, and creative use of language, it is no wonder that

ACTIVITY 11.B CREATING VOCABULARY LESSONS

Create lessons utilizing the following concepts:

1. Seven ways of defining words.
2. Denotative and connotative meanings.
3. Nuances.
4. "Insider's" meaning.
5. Historical change.
6. Sarcasm, irony, and humor.
7. "Narrowing" meaning.

You might form small groups. Each group could create lessons using two concepts and present them to the class.

there is no pat curriculum for teaching vocabulary. On the other hand, it is no wonder that there are so many interesting things that can be done with vocabulary in connection with nearly every reading selection or as separate exercises. A brief look at one of the many activities books for reading and language arts will reveal dozens of activities for increasing children's vocabulary knowledge. Here are three suggestions from *Language Arts Activities* (Tiedt & Tiedt, 1978):

1. Have students work in small groups to develop word lists centered on specific topics such as the following:

Animals: cats, dogs, tigers, chickens
Recreations: games, fishing, swimming
Games: Monopoly, checkers

Small group discussion should stimulate knowledge of categories and encourage students to share word knowledge.

2. Have students write alliterative phrases or sentences:

Ten timid tomcats
Big brown boisterous bears
Tiny Tim talked tendentiously to Ted.
Stolid Stephen stopped stalling.

Students will soon be poring over dictionaries to find words starting with the right letter, and they will encounter new vocabulary and discuss its appropriateness.

3. While teaching, use words in contexts where the meaning is clear. Make such introduction of new vocabulary part of your daily routine:

Our class didn't know that there was a dog in the hallway. We were **oblivious** to the whole event.

All right, class, there's too much **chaos.** Let's all be quiet for a minute, and then return to *work,* not play, *work.*

After a selection about a famous performer's childhood career in vaudeville.

WORDS IN ACTION

Words often have a special meaning among people in a particular trade or profession. What do the following expressions mean to people in the occupations named?

1. **line:** dancer, telephone operator, printer, salesman, railroad engineer
2. **mugger:** actor, policeman
3. **wings:** actor, airplane pilot, house builder, politician
4. **get booked:** actor, policeman

Figure 11.3. Example of a Vocabulary Activity Following a Story in a Reading Anthology. (*Source:* Dunning et al., 1969, p. 187.)

Lessons Suggested by Words in Reading Selections

Figure 11.3 presents a lesson that follows a selection in an upper-grade literature anthology (Dunning et al., 1969) under the heading, ''Words in Action.'' It is an example of the way a reading selection can be used as an entree into word study. Similar examples can be found in other anthologies, basals, and materials designed for teaching reading.

Teaching Words Related Through the ''Semantic Network''

Johnson and Pearson (1978) have used the scheme referred to as a *semantic network* (Collins & Quillian, 1969) as a basis for creating vocabulary lessons. A semantic network portrays relationships among words in terms of *class, example,* and *property.*

A few examples will demonstrate the meaning of the terms *class, example,* and *property.* The word *animal* represents a class; fish, birds, and mammals are examples of this class. The examples of a class have *common properties* (all animals are living; all animals do not manufacture food) and *particular properties* (fish have scales, fins, and gills and live in water; birds have feathers and wings; mammals have hair and mammary glands and give birth to living offspring).

Vehicles are a class of things; bicycles, rowboats, and cars are examples of this class. The examples share some properties and not others. They are all used to transport people and goods. Bicycles have wheels and are powered by the rider's energy; a rowboat has no wheels, goes on water, and is powered by the rider's energy; a car has wheels and is powered by an engine.

Johnson and Pearson (1978) suggest exercises that will help children to see the class, example, and property relationships among words. One such exercise is called semantic feature analysis. In this scheme, properties of a word such as ''living,'' ''feathered,'' and ''flies'' are referred to as *semantic features.*

In one exercise the teacher suggests a class such as ''Vehicles.'' Examples of the class are listed down the left side of the board and students are asked to name properties (or features) that at least one of the examples possesses. These properties are listed across the top of the board. Then the students are asked whether each example has the

	Fur	Feathers	Can Fly	Two Legs	Four Legs	Horns
Elephant	−	−	−	−	+	−
Eagle	−	+	+	+	−	−
Tiger	+	−	−	−	+	−
Goat	+	−	−	−	+	+

Figure 11.4. Early stages of a semantic feature analysis for the class "animals."

property named in the column, and a plus or minus sign is put beside each example under each property as shown in Figure 11.4.

Once this technique is learned, students are encouraged to add new words belonging to the class, introduce new semantic features, and continue to expand the chart with plus and minus signs. Students are encouraged to discover and discuss the similarities and differences between words in terms of features that are shared and not shared.

The technique can be used with new classes of words beginning with familiar, concrete classes such as foods, tools, and pets and proceeding to less familiar, more abstract categories such as moods, shapes, and entertainments.

The advantage of this kind of exercise is that it enables children

1. To learn new words within a class.
2. To learn new properties or properties they had not thought of.
3. To view the meanings of words in a more complete and precise way.
4. To see that word meanings are related but that no two words' meanings are identical. (See Activity 11.C.)

Teaching Words Having the Same Morphemes

Identifying prefixes, suffixes, and roots was discussed in Chapter 6 as a method of word recognition. Students familiar with the word *graceful* in spoken form might not recognize it in print, but if they realized that *-ful* is a common suffix, they might analyze the word as *grace/ful* and recognize *grace* either as a sight word or through phonics.

Vocabulary lessons are frequently based on words having the same prefix, suffix, or root. These lessons differ from word recognition lessons in that the point is not to teach recognition of familiar words through structural analysis; the point is to teach the students the meaning of words that may not be familiar to them and to recognize those words in print.

Lists of non-English root words (Box 6.1) and derivational suffixes (Box 6.2) are found in Chapter 6. A list of the most commonly used prefixes appears in Box 11.1. Three examples of lessons that concentrate on word structure as a vehicle for teaching new vocabulary appear in Figures 11.5, 11.6, and 11.7.

ACTIVITY 11.C DO A SEMANTIC FEATURE ANALYSIS

I. Following the discussion of semantic feature analysis and the example in Figure 11.4, do a semantic feature analysis of a familiar, concrete category such as foods, tools, or pets.

II. Do a semantic feature analysis of an abstract category such as nations, moods, or occupations.

BOX 11.1 COMMONLY USED PREFIXES

Prefix	Meaning
anti	against
auto	self
de	from, down
dis	not, away
in, im	into, not
inter	between
il, ir	not
mis	wrong
multi	many
non	not
out	over, surpass
para	beside
post	after
pre	before
re	back
semi	half
sub	under
super	above
trans	across
ultra	above
un	not

Figure 11.5. Workbook exercise: using prefixes to build word meaning. (*Source:* Reprinted with permission of Macmillan Publishing Company from *Catch the Wind,* Skills Practice Book [Series r: Macmillan Reading Program, Grade 6], Carl B. Smith and Ronald Wardhaugh, senior editors. Copyright 1980 Macmillan Publishing Company.)

Name _____   **Date** _____

A. Read the meaning of each prefix. Then circle the letter next to the correct meaning of each word.

> sub— under; below   semi— half
> pro— for, supporting   trans— across
> super— beyond, better than others of its kind

1. prowar   **a.** across a war   **(b.)** supporting war

2. superhuman   **a.** half human   **b.** better than other humans

3. semicircle   **a.** half a circle   **b.** under a circle

4. transoceanic **a.** across the ocean   **b.** below the ocean

5. subsoil   **a.** top layer of soil   **b.** soil beneath the surface

Name _____ Date _____

When the suffix -ic is added to a word, the new word is
an adjective (angel: angelic). When the suffix -ure
is added to a word, the new word is a noun (create:
creature).

A. Add the suffix -ic to the underlined word to
complete each sentence.

1. A person who is a hero is a heroic person.

2. Sounds with the quality of rhythm are _____ sounds.

3. One with the quality of an acrobat is called _____.

4. A word that describes one who is an artist is _____.

5. A person who is a democrat is a _____ person.

B. Drop the final -e or -y from the underlined word.
Then add the suffix -ic to the word to complete each
sentence.

1. An event for an athlete is an athletic event.

2. A thing with the shape of a cube is called _____.

3. Maps showing the geography of an area are _____ maps.

4. A song with a nice melody is a _____ song.

C. Add the suffix -ure to the underlined word to complete
each sentence. If the underlined word ends in e, drop the
e before adding -ure.

1. If a thing happens to fail, it is called a failure.

2. When you press against something, you apply _____.

3. If things please you, they give you _____.

4. When you sculpt clay, you make a _____.

Macmillan Publishing Co. Inc.

Figure 11.6. Workbook exercise: using suffixes to build word meaning. (*Source:* Reprinted with permission of Macmillan
Publishing Company from *Catch the Wind*, Skills Practice Book [Series r: Macmillan Reading Program, Grade
6], Carl B. Smith and Ronald Wardhaugh, senior editors. Copyright 1980 Macmillan Publishing Company.)

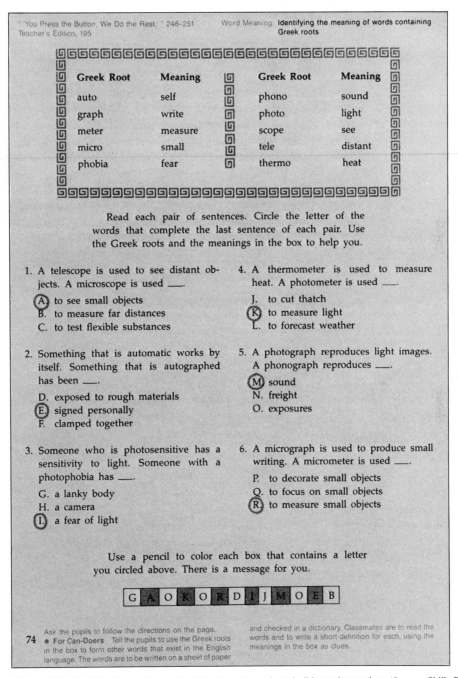

" 'You Press the Button, We Do the Rest,' " 246–251
Teacher's Edition, 195

Word Meaning: Identifying the meaning of words containing Greek roots

Greek Root	Meaning	Greek Root	Meaning
auto	self	phono	sound
graph	write	photo	light
meter	measure	scope	see
micro	small	tele	distant
phobia	fear	thermo	heat

Read each pair of sentences. Circle the letter of the words that complete the last sentence of each pair. Use the Greek roots and the meanings in the box to help you.

1. A telescope is used to see distant objects. A microscope is used ___.

   A. to see small objects
   B. to measure far distances
   C. to test flexible substances

2. Something that is automatic works by itself. Something that is autographed has been ___.

   D. exposed to rough materials
   E. signed personally
   F. clamped together

3. Someone who is photosensitive has a sensitivity to light. Someone with a photophobia has ___.

   G. a lanky body
   H. a camera
   I. a fear of light

4. A thermometer is used to measure heat. A photometer is used ___.

   J. to cut thatch
   K. to measure light
   L. to forecast weather

5. A photograph reproduces light images. A phonograph reproduces ___.

   M. sound
   N. freight
   O. exposures

6. A micrograph is used to produce small writing. A micrometer is used ___.

   P. to decorate small objects
   Q. to focus on small objects
   R. to measure small objects

Use a pencil to color each box that contains a letter you circled above. There is a message for you.

G A O K O R D I J M O E B

74   Ask the pupils to follow the directions on the page.
• For Can-Doers   Tell the pupils to use the Greek roots in the box to form other words that exist in the English language. The words are to be written on a sheet of paper

and checked in a dictionary. Classmates are to read the words and to write a short definition for each, using the meanings in the box as clues.

Figure 11.7. Workbook exercise: using Greek root words to build word meaning. (*Source:* Skills Book to accompany *Voyages* [from The Laidlaw Reading Program], by Eller, Hester, Farr, et al. Macmillan Publishing Company, 1982.)

COMPREHENSION, FLUENCY, RATE OF READING, AND FLEXIBILITY

Fluency

It has been pointed out in several places in this book that the demands on readers change as they master the skills of beginning reading, proceed to read more difficult materials, and use reading as a tool for learning. In the early stages the energy of the children engaged in reading is devoted almost entirely to *learning to read*. For accomplished readers, reading becomes a tool that they use with little conscious effort; nearly all their energy while reading is devoted to *reading to learn*. At this last stage, the reader is said to be *fluent*.

Before students become fluent in reading, the rate at which they read is determined largely by the degree to which the text challenges their skills. Attention to increasing rate at this point is inappropriate. The question of speed of reading should not arise until the reader is fluent.

Fluency is usually achieved through practice. If students are encouraged to read material that is interesting, that has very few words that present recognition problems, and that can be read with a high level of comprehension, both fluency and a reasonable rate of reading will usually develop. However, when some students attain fluency but their rate lags seriously behind their classmates, steps should be taken to help them increase their rate of reading.

Rate of Reading

Measuring Rate of Reading.   Reading rate is usually reported in words per minute. A simple procedure to measure rate is to give the students a passage of several hundred words and tell the students to copy the last number on the board onto their papers as soon as they have finished reading. After about one minute, the teacher begins to write the time elapses in ten-second intervals: 1:00, 1:10, . . . , 2:00, 2:10, 2:20, ... Each student's rate is calculated by dividing the number of words in the passage by the time expressed in minutes and *fractions of minutes*. (One minute and fifteen seconds is *not* 1.15 minutes; it is one and one-fourth minute or 1.25 minutes.)

An alternative method is to tell everyone to stop reading at precisely the same time (at the end of three minutes, for example) and to circle the word they are reading at the moment they are told to stop. Each student's rate is calculated by dividing the number of words read by the number of minutes elapsed before time was called.

How Slow Is Too Slow?   Norms for standardized tests of rate of silent reading vary widely. Harris and Sipay (1985) report that the average speed of reading on several standardized tests varies from 171 to 230 words per minute at grade 6 and from 216 to 295 words per minute at grade 12 (p. 556).

The question of how slow is too slow cannot be answered in terms of numbers alone. If a student reads slowly because of a lack of fluency, efforts to increase the student's rate are inappropriate. One study (Shores & Husband, 1950) showed that among bright students, faster readers appear to comprehend better, while among less bright students slower readers comprehend better.

The one category of student where rate of reading should unquestionably be addressed is composed of those students who are fluent readers of average or better intelligence but who read very slowly from habit. Timing these students on easy materials and giving them comprehension tests may convince them that they *can* read faster without loss of comprehension and this may be all they need. Encouraging them to read widely in easy and interesting materials and to remind themselves to read as fast as they can may also help.

Mechanical Reading Pacers.   There are about ten mechanical devices on the market that expose reading material to a student at a controlled rate, either by a shutter that descends over a page of print from top to bottom or by projecting words, phrases, or lines of print onto a screen. The Controlled Reader (Educational Development Laboratories, New York) and the Reading Accelerator (Science Research Associates, Chicago) are two such devices. Enthusiasts for these kinds of devices claim that they engender a great deal of interest and motivate students to improve their reading rate.

Those who are less enthusiastic point out that these devices present reading material in a highly artificial format, that there may be little carryover to normal reading situations, and that students can be motivated through less expensive and less cumbersome means.

Flexibility

Speeding Up and Slowing Down a Single Process.   A second category of reading behavior that should unquestionably be corrected is exhibited by students who read everything in exactly the same way; they start at the beginning, read every line at the same speed, and progress to the end of the passage—no matter what they are reading or what their purpose is for reading. McDonald (1965) found that most students exhibit this behavior even when they are instructed to read for different purposes and they are given materials that differ in content, difficulty, and style.

There is general agreement among experts that when a reader is fluent, this kind of inflexibility is a definite handicap. There is a little less agreement as to what one is teaching students to do when he or she teaches them to vary the rate.

Switching from One Process to Another.   Some experimental evidence indicates that people vary the rate at which they read difficult sections and easy sections of texts (Rankin, 1970), and several investigators suggest that students can be taught to vary their rate in response to purposes set for reading (Samuels & Dahl, 1975). Others (Sticht et al., 1974), however, argue that fluent adult readers read at a fairly constant rate of speed. What *appears* to be very fast reading and very slow reading is accounted for by the fact that the accomplished reader engages in different processes; the process the reader chooses depends on the content, difficulty, and style of the reading material and his or her purpose for reading it.

Scanning. Scanning is the process by which one seeks to find specific words or kinds of information. Readers wishing to know Tolstoy's wife's name might scan an encyclopedia entry on Tolstoy looking only for names, stop when they find one, go ahead if it is a male name, stop and read if it is a female name, go ahead as soon as they discover whose name it is, or stop finally if they discover it is Tolstoy's wife's name. In this process the readers are looking at words but they are making no attempt to make sense of them unless they meet the criterion—"a name." An accomplished reader scans to answer such questions as "In what year did Elizabeth II ascend the throne?" and "Where is Harvard University located?"

Skimming. Skimming is a process whereby a person goes quickly through a text looking for titles, subtitles, headings, key words, topic sentences, summary statements, and so on, to get the gist of what information the passage contains.

Striving for Understanding. Striving for understanding is a process whereby a reader attempts to read a very difficult passage by hypothesizing the meanings of words, phrases, and sentences and checking to see if the hypothesized meaning is consistent with what he or she does understand about the passage or knows about the topic.

Memorizing. Memorizing is a process whereby one attempts to increase the probability of verbatim recall by rereading, reciting, recalling, and reviewing.

Accomplished readers know when to skim or scan material; they appear to read very fast when they do this because they can answer questions about material on which they have spent very little time. (This, incidentally, is what speed reading courses teach people to do.) At the other end of the continuum, accomplished readers know when to stop to strive to understand a very difficult passage or to attempt to memorize material. When they do this, they appear to read very slowly because of the great amount of time they spend on the material.

It follows from this point of view, that to teach flexibility, one ought not encourage students to slow down or speed up their normal reading process. Instead, one ought to teach students to engage in processes that are considerably different from normal reading, and to teach them to know when these processes are appropriate.

Specific suggestions for teaching these processes will not be addressed in this chapter, but the reader will find several citations in the "For Further Reading" section for books on study skills. Further discussion of these processes and suggestions for teaching them can be found in these sources.

TEACHING COMPREHENSION AS "READING TO LEARN"

Reading enters into the teaching of school subjects such as history, science, and mathematics in two ways. First, teachers must help students to learn to read materials that are appropriate to the different school subject matter areas. This activity is usually referred to as *teaching reading in the content areas.* Second, teachers must help students to use reading as a tool in the effort to learn subject matter in a particular subject or class. This activity is usually referred to as *teaching study skills*.

Teaching Reading in the Content Areas

Each subject area presents unique demands on the readers' reading comprehension skills. Each subject presents specialized and technical vocabularies and unique text formats such as equations, maps, charts, graphs, and tables. When a person engages in teaching students to cope with these special demands of content areas, he or she is teaching *reading*. It is in this sense that all teachers are teachers of reading, and it is for this reason that reading specialists are often called upon by content area teachers to help in the teaching of reading.

To the extent that the characteristics of all texts written in English overlap (and that is to a great extent), the techniques for teaching comprehension presented in this chapter apply to all subjects. For example, a Directed Reading Lesson for a chapter in a science or social studies textbook written in straight prose follows the same steps and relies on the same principles as the Directed Reading Lesson described in Chapter 10. But since each different subject area presents unique challenges, special considerations for teaching comprehension are necessary.

Vocabulary.   A heavy load of new vocabulary is one of the greatest challenges in content area reading. An elementary school science teacher expressed her belief that

> Although we do a lot of "action learning"—experiments, demonstrations, model build-ing, field trips, and the like—I often think of my job as teaching vocabulary almost exclusively. You go to the zoo to teach the meanings of the words *vertebrate, fish, reptile, bird,* and *mammal*. You time kids as they run up a flight of stairs to teach the meaning of *weight, velocity,* and *horsepower*. When it comes down to it, there is a word for each concept, and my job is to teach the meanings of those words.

Teaching vocabulary in the content areas often means teaching the content area plus word recognition. All the word recognition skills—whole word, phonics, structure, and context—come into play. Structure is often particularly useful in teaching vocabulary in content areas because a large part of scientific vocabulary consists of consciously invented words. The meanings of affixes and roots are often aids to learning to recognize and remember the meanings of such words.

Teacher's Guides to content area textbooks often designate subject matter vocabulary for each chapter or lesson. Lists of technical words and terms are often useful aids in preparing lessons in reading in the content areas. One such list is the *EDL Core Vocabularies in Reading, Mathematics, Science, and Social Studies* (Taylor et al., 1979).

Graphs, Diagrams, and Pictures.   There are many ways to present information in graphic, diagrammatic, and pictorial form in print media. With the addition of audio-visual media and particularly with the combination of interactive computers and tele-vision displays, the possibilities seem endless.

In print media one finds bar graphs, line graphs, tables, time lines, flowcharts, diagrams of hierarchical relationships, pictorial step-by-step directions, political cartoons, time tables, and maps; of course, this list does not exhaust the possibilities. Furthermore, each of these categories has many variations. For example, different maps may show political boundaries, roads, air routes, distribution of crops, rainfall, minerals, and so on.

In preparing to teach any text, the teacher should be sensitive to the format in which information is presented and be aware that information that is easily, almost unconsciously, obtained from "graphics" by an experienced reader may be inaccessible to some students. Teaching students to interpret such material may occur during the preparation, question and discussion, or skills development stages of a Directed Reading Lesson. Teacher's Guides that accompany content area textbooks often offer suggestions as to when and how to teach students to interpret graphic materials in the text.

Teaching Study Skills

Students are faced with numerous tasks that require them to read, comprehend, remember, and express what they have read. Requiring students to answer questions, or to discuss the content, or to express their feelings about a text immediately after reading is usually considered teaching or testing comprehension. Many such activities are discussed in this chapter and in Chapter 10.

However, many tasks require the student to remember and express ideas from texts that were read on the previous day or within the past week or semester. Furthermore, tasks often require students to solve problems or answer questions that were not directly addressed in the material that was read, they are asked to analyze ideas and discuss the ways these ideas are related, they are asked to read several sources and synthesize what they have read in answering a question or presenting an argument, and they are asked to compare and evaluate materials they have read.

These tasks have two ingredients that the typical comprehension lesson does not have: the students' performances demonstrate that they have remembered over a period of time what they read, and their performance demonstrates that they have the ability to select and organize what they have read for a coherent presentation.

Commonplace tasks that make these demands are preparing oral and written reports and writing essay examinations. The skills demonstrated are referred to as *study skills.*

Although teaching study skills is often presented as something that comes after teaching comprehension, you must not get the idea that the processes of reading, comprehending, remembering, and organizing are separate processes performed in that order. Organizing materials is often suggested as a first step to remembering. In fact, the discussions of schema in Chapter 9 and of story maps in Chapter 10 indicate that sensing the organization of written material is a first step in comprehension.

Study skills include techniques for (1) locating information, (2) interpreting information, (3) recording information in useful ways, and (4) recalling information.

Locating Information

Library Skills. Using the card catalog is an important library skill. This skill encompasses alphabetizing; using guide words and letters; understanding the concepts of title, author, and topic; as well as understanding how to locate books shelved by the Dewey Decimal System or the Library of Congress Classification System.

A second library skill is using standard indexes to information such as the *Reader's Guide to Periodical Literature* and *The Short Story Index*. Using such guides requires all the skills needed in using the card catalog plus knowledge of which index to use to find the particular information that one seeks.

A third library skill is using standard reference works such as encyclopedias, atlases, dictionaries, and almanacs. Using these sources makes particular demands on a student's knowledge of using key words to find information, knowledge of which source to use, and ability to scan texts to find particular information.

Book Use Skills. Book use skills for locating information include knowledge of how to use the table of contents, index, chapter titles, and subheadings within a text. Book use skills also include knowledge of what one can expect to find in a preface, an appendix, or a bibliography. Teaching students to properly cite the source of information includes finding the title, author (or editor), publisher, and the place and date of publication.

Interpreting Information. Study skills depend on comprehension of what is read; therefore, if one embarks on a program of "teaching study skills," a component of that program will naturally include techniques for "teaching comprehension" and "teaching reading in the content areas." These topics have been discussed previously.

Recording Information in Useful Ways. Underlining, outlining, taking notes, recording the relationship of ideas in flowcharts or diagrams, and summarizing are all ways of organizing information so that it can be put to use by the readers. Students need to learn when each technique is appropriate as well as how to accomplish each technique.

Semantic Mapping. Semantic mapping (Heimlich & Pittelman, 1986) can be utilized as early as first grade to organize information in a text in a way that has characteristics of both outlining and summarizing. For example, a first grade class has read a story about "Kate's trip to the zoo." In a circle on the board they label five "spokes" extending from the center: "Things Kate sees at the zoo," "Things Kate does at the zoo," "Things Kate likes at the zoo," "How Kate looks," and "How Kate feels." Taking categories one at a time, the teacher elicits information from the students and produces the semantic map in Figure 11.8.

A fifth grade teacher using a similar technique has students use the titles and section headings in a text to identify main ideas and "secondary categories" and "supporting details" to create postreading "study maps" such as the one in Figure 11.9. Such maps can easily be turned into outlines and are a good first step to summarizing.

Summarizing. Summarizing is an important comprehension and study skill (Brown & Day, 1983). According to one model of comprehension (Kintsch & Van Dijk, 1978), the following strategies (listed in order from easiest to most difficult) are employed in creating a summary:

1. Delete trivial information.
2. Delete redundant information.
3. Write category names for lists of items.
4. Write category names for lists of actions.

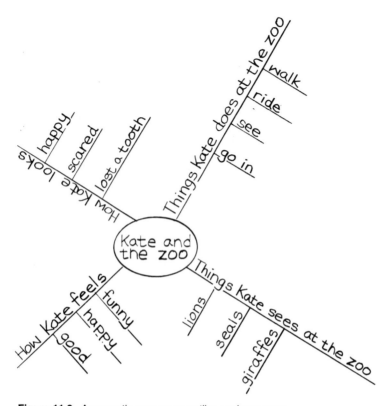

Figure 11.8. A semantic map as an outline and summary.

5. Select a topic sentence.
6. Invent a topic sentence.

Hare and Borchardt (1984) collapsed these six rules into three and added a fourth rule of their own to teach summarizing.

1. *Collapse lists.* If you see a list of things, try to think of a word or phrase name for the whole list. For example, if you saw a list like eyes, ears, neck, arms, and legs, you could say "body parts." Or if you saw a list like ice skating, skiing, or sledding, you could say "winter sports."

2. *Use topic sentences.* Often authors write a sentence that summarizes a whole paragraph. It is called a topic sentence. If the author gives you one, you can use it in your summary. Unfortunately, not all paragraphs contain topic sentences. That means you may have to make up one for yourself.

3. *Get rid of unnecessary detail.* Some text information can be repeated in a passage. In other words, the same thing can be said in a number of different ways, all in one passage. Other text information can be unimportant, or trivial. Since summaries are meant to be short, get rid of repetitive or trivial information.

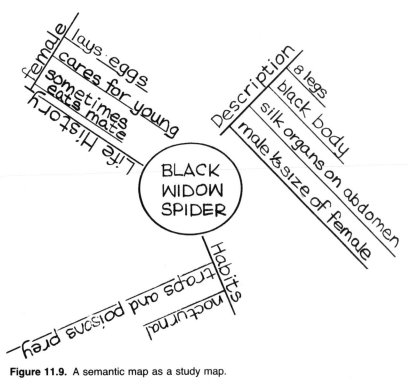

Figure 11.9. A semantic map as a study map.

4. *Collapse paragraphs.* Paragraphs are often related to one another. Some paragraphs explain one or more other paragraphs. Some paragraphs just expand on the information presented in other paragraphs. Some paragraphs are more necessary than other paragraphs. Decide which paragraphs should be kept or gotten rid of, and which might be joined together. (p. 66)

Based on a review of numerous studies, Hare and Borchardt (1984) conclude that summarizing is a high-level skill that not even some able college students have mastered. For this reason, it is a skill that should not be addressed before middle grades, and teachers should not expect all elementary school students to master it. Through a combination of activities based on semantic mapping, Kintsch and Van Dijk's six strategies, and Hare and Borchardt's four strategies, elementary school students can learn the concept of summarizing, and some might become reasonably good at doing it.

Recalling Information.   Study is frequently associated with test taking. Test taking always demands that the students remember what they have learned and it often demands that they have reorganized what they have learned. Verbatim memorization is practically never desirable for several reasons. One reason is that well-constructed tests demand that students demonstrate their *understanding* of the subject matter, and it is possible for a person to memorize language verbatim that he or she does not understand.

To demonstrate understanding of a topic, students should be able to distinguish main ideas and important facts from details. They should also be able to organize the information in a text to answer a question or to solve a problem that was not precisely addressed in the text. Techniques such as note taking, outlining, and so on mentioned in the previous section are often suggested as first steps in aiding recall.

A Formula for Effective Study: SQ3R.   After a great deal of experience in guiding college students in formulating successful study habits, Robinson (1970, originally published in 1961) presented what he found to be a sound systematic approach to study. The approach involves five steps:

1. *Survey*. Read chapter title, subtitles, and headings; read topic and summary sentences and introductory and summary paragraphs.
2. *Question*. Formulate questions based on chapter titles, subtitles, paragraph headings, and main ideas discovered in step 1.
3. *Read*. Seek answers to the questions developed in step 2.
4. *Recite*. Answer questions orally or silently to check on recall of the content and one's ability to express the content.
5. *Review*. Go over material that presented difficulties in step 4.

Robinson (1961) originally referred to this process by the formula "Survey QRRR." It is currently referred to by the more abbreviated formula "SQ3R."

The Guided Reading Procedure.   The Guided Reading Procedure (Manzo, 1975; Ankney & McClurg, 1981) is a seven-step group comprehension/study activity.

1. Preparation for Reading and Reading. Students survey the text, predict its content, and create several purpose-setting questions.

This is of course similar to the *survey, question,* and *read* phases of SQ3R. It is at the *recite* and *review* stages that the guided reading procedure differs.

2. Unaided Recall. When they are finished reading, students close their books and volunteers give as much information as they can recall from the text. The teacher jots down all the information in the order it is volunteered without evaluation or comment. When completed, this list often contains inconsistencies, and students will become aware of information in the text that cannot be recalled.

3. Aided Recall. Students open their books and read to clarify inconsistencies and to look for unrecalled information. The teacher corrects the items and adds items of information as the students find the relevant text.

4. Organization. Teachers and students work together to organize the information on the board in the form of an outline, diagram, or semantic map.

5. Comprehension Questioning. Teachers ask "higher-level" comprehension questions calling for synthesis, interpretation, inference, judgment, or application.

6. Comprehension Testing. Teachers administer a quiz testing factual recall (steps 2 and 3), organization (step 4), and higher-level comprehension (step 5).

7. Application. An optional last step calls for applying the information in the text to a new problem or situation.

This procedure works best with texts containing a heavy load of factual material. It is suggested that the texts be divided into sections of about 500 words and that the procedure be repeated to cover longer texts.

The Reading Teacher's Responsibility in Teaching "Reading to Learn"

The skills a student must master in reading in the content areas and in study skills have been enumerated in this section. Many of these skills appear in social studies, science, written and oral language arts, and other school subjects. Familiarity with content area reading and study skills will make elementary school teachers aware of the many opportunities to address reading skills while they are teaching other subjects and to address content area skills while they are teaching reading.

Teachers who specialize in teaching reading will be expected to teach reading in the content areas and study skills as part of the reading curriculum beyond the primary grades, and they will be called upon by subject matter teachers for help in teaching these skills. These topics may be pursued in greater depth by following the suggestions in Activity 11.D.

ACTIVITY 11.D INVESTIGATE STUDY SKILLS

Form small groups to investigate

Fluency, rate of reading, and flexibility.
Teaching vocabulary in the content areas.
The use of graphics, diagrams, and charts.
Locating information.
Recording information.
Recalling information.

The following books might be helpful:

Askov, E. N., & Kamm, K. (1982). *Study skills in the content areas.* Boston: Allyn & Bacon.
Dupuis, M. M. (1983). *Reading in the content areas: Research for teachers.* Newark, DE: International Reading Association.
Graham, K. G. (1984). *Study skills handbook: A guide for all teachers.* Newark, DE: International Reading Association.
Moore, D. W., Moore, S. A., Cunningham, P. M., & Cunningham, J. W. (1986). *Developing readers and writers in the content areas.* New York: Longman.
Rubin, D. (1985). *Reading and learning power,* 2nd ed. New York: Macmillan.

SUMMARY

In a whole language classroom, comprehension is taught in reading conferences through teachers' responses to students. Students learn that in conferences, they are to re-create meaning or compose what they have comprehended. When teachers detect misunderstanding, they teach. They ask "real" questions about texts. They encourage students to learn from each other. They encourage students to tell what they know rather than control what students tell them through teacher-determined questions.

The process approach to teaching writing results in a storybook corner, conferencing, publishing, the creation of a literate community, and the integration of reading and writing. These things underscore the complementary nature of reading and writing so that facility with comprehension is enhanced in both reading and writing experiences.

It is a well-established fact that word knowledge, or vocabulary, is intimately related to comprehension. It is also a well-established fact that learning the meaning of a word is a many-faceted process. According to Vygotsky, the study of word knowledge involves not only the development of thought in an individual but also the historical growth of consciousness in the human race.

Words are defined through their correct use in sentences, by use of synonyms, antonyms, classification, examples, comparisons, and descriptions. Word definition and usage are complicated by the presence of connotations, denotations, nuances, invented "insider's" meanings, historical changes, sarcasm, irony, humor, and narrowing of meanings.

Because of the profound relationship between the development of word meaning and thought and because of the great complexity of defining words and the many processes that affect word meanings, there is a nearly endless variety of lessons and activities designed for teaching vocabulary. Words in a selection are often introduced during the preparation stage of a Directed Reading Lesson. Words appearing in selections are often used as the basis for lessons in word histories, word structure, the use of figurative language, jargon, and so on. Through these lessons, new words that are not in the selection are often introduced.

Lessons designed to increase word knowledge often appear as activities separate from Directed Reading Lessons. Semantic feature analysis is a vehicle for students to learn relationships among words in terms of class, examples of a class, common properties of a class, and particular properties of examples. Lessons built on words having the same morphemes help students to use word structure as a word learning tool.

When students become fluent readers, rate or speed of reading should be given some attention. There is no established "average rate" for readers at any level of reading proficiency. Furthermore, the relationship between speed and comprehension is not straightforward. It is simply not true that in all groups, faster readers comprehend better than slower readers. However, there are undoubtedly students who would profit from speeding up their reading. Bright students who read remarkably more slowly than their classmates make up one group of such students.

Mechanical pacers are suggested by some experts for their motivational value. However, mechanical pacers are expensive and cumbersome. Timed reading of easy material followed by comprehension tests may demonstrate to students who read unnecessarily slowly that they *can* read faster and still comprehend.

Good readers do not engage in the same reading process for every text and for every purpose. It has been proposed that proficient readers speed up and slow down the rate at which they read, depending on the difficulty of the text and their purpose for reading the text. A more current and probably more correct notion is that good readers do not engage in the same process with every text and for every purpose. Depending on their purpose and the difficulty of the text, readers skim, scan, read, strive for understanding, and memorize. Rather than teaching students to read faster and slower, students should be taught how and when to engage in these different processes.

All the strategies for teaching comprehension can and should be used in teaching reading in the content areas. However, reading in each of the content areas presents its own unique challenges to the reader. Content areas have specialized vocabularies. Information is often presented in graphic, diagrammatic, and pictorial forms. Students must learn to "read" these graphic displays, just as they must learn to read printed texts.

The content areas place special demands on the student's study skills. Study skills include (1) learning how to locate information through using the card catalog, standard indexes, and standard reference works and books; (2) learning how to record information in useful ways such as underlining, outlining, note taking, semantic mapping, and summarizing; and (3) techniques for committing information to memory or recalling information. Since so much of a student's time is spent in studying textbooks in preparation for examinations, the study skills curriculum gives special attention to this process. The SQ3R formula (survey, question, read, recite, review) is often recommended as a guide to effective study.

The Guided Reading Procedure, consisting of preparation and reading, unaided recall, aided recall, organization, comprehension questioning, comprehension testing, and application, is recommended as a way of understanding, organizing, and remembering texts with a great deal of factual information.

Many elementary school teachers teach content areas as well as reading; they will find themselves teaching reading during content area classes and teaching content area skills and study skills during the reading period. Teachers who specialize in teaching reading will often be called upon by content area teachers for help in teaching reading and study skills.

FOR FURTHER READING

Alvermann, D. E. (Guest Ed.). (1987). *Journal of reading: Making readers independent.* Newark, DE: International Reading Association.

Barrow, L. H., Kristo, J. V., & Andrew, B. (1984). Building bridges between science and reading. *The Reading Teacher, 38*(2), 188–192.

Beck, I. L., & McKeown, M. G. (1983). Learning words well—a program to enhance vocabulary and comprehension. *The Reading Teacher, 36*(7), 622–625.

Blachowicz, C. L. Z. (1987). Vocabulary instruction: What goes on in the classroom? *The Reading Teacher, 41*(2), 132–137.

Brozo, W. G., & Tomlinson, C. M. (1986). Literature: The key to lively content courses. *The Reading Teacher, 40*(3), 288–293.

Cudd, E. T., & Roberts, L. (1989). Using writing to enhance content area learning in the primary grades. *The Reading Teacher, 42*(6), 392–405.

Cunningham, P. M., & Cunningham, J. W. (1987). Content area reading-writing lessons. *The Reading Teacher, 40*(6), 506–513.

Dionisio, M. (1983). Write? Isn't this reading class? *The Reading Teacher, 36*(8), 746–750.

Dupuis, M. M. (Ed.). (1983). *Reading in the content areas: Research for teachers.* Newark, DE: International Reading Association.

Gambrell, L. B. (1985). Dialogue journals: Reading-writing interaction. *The Reading Teacher, 38*(6), 512–515.

Gaskins, I. W. (1982). A writing program for poor readers and writers and the rest of the class, too. *Language Arts, 59*(8), 854–863.

Gerhard, C. (1975). *Making sense: Reading comprehension improved through categorizing.* Newark, DE: International Reading Association.

Graham, K. G., & Robinson, H. A. (1984). *Study skills handbook: A guide for all teachers.* Newark, DE: International Reading Association.

Guthrie, J. T. (1984). Writing connections. *The Reading Teacher, 37*(6), 540–542.

Howell, H. (1987). Language, literature, and vocabulary development for gifted students. *The Reading Teacher, 40*(6), 500–505.

Johnson, D. D. (Guest Ed.). (1986). *Journal of reading: Vocabulary.* Newark, DE: International Reading Association.

Lunstrum, J., & Taylor, B. (1978). *Teaching reading in the social studies.* Newark, DE: International Reading Association.

Manolakes, G. (1988). Comprehension: A personal experience in content area reading. *The Reading Teacher, 42*(3), 200–203.

Marzano, R. J., & Marzano, J. S. (1988). *A cluster approach to elementary vocabulary instruction.* Newark, DE: International Reading Association.

Piccolo, J. A. (1987). Expository text structure: Teaching and learning strategies. *The Reading Teacher, 40*(9), 838–847.

Poostay, E. J. (1984). Show me your underlines: A strategy to teach comprehension. *The Reading Teacher, 37*(9), 828–830.

Santa, C. M., Isaacson, L., & Manning, G. (1987). Changing content instruction through action research. *The Reading Teacher, 40*(4), 434–438.

Schwartz, R., & Raphael, T. (in press). Concept of definition: A key to improving students' vocabulary. *The Reading Teacher.*

Taylor, B. M. (1982). A summarizing strategy to improve middle grade students' reading and writing skills. *The Reading Teacher, 36*(2), 202–205.

Thelen, J. N. (1984). *Improving reading in science* (2nd ed.). Newark, DE: International Reading Association.

Wong, J. A., & Hu-pei Au, K. (1985). The concept-text-application approach: Helping elementary students comprehend expository text. *The Reading Teacher, 38*(7), 612–618.

Wrights, J. P., & Andreasen, N. L. (1980). Practice in using location skills in a content area. *The Reading Teacher, 34*(2), 184–186.

PART FOUR

Assessment, Decision Making, and Teaching

CHAPTER 12

Assessment Using Standardized Tests

THE RELATIONSHIP OF ASSESSMENT, DECISION MAKING, AND TEACHING

Teachers must continuously assess what a child can do. A teacher like Charlotte might explain this as follows: I know the knowledge, skills, and attitudes (curriculum) that add up to skilled reading, and I have a pretty good idea of the order in which to teach this curriculum. My job is to find out what the children already know and what skills they already have so I can decide what to teach next. If I do not continuously do this assessment, I will probably be wrong a lot of the time and I will be teaching things individuals already know or I will be teaching things too hard for them to learn—things they are not ready to learn.

A teacher like Matthew might explain the need to assess children's skill knowledge and attitudes continuously as follows: I observe the children while they engage in reading and other language activities and watch for strengths and weaknesses. I concentrate on reading particularly during individual reading conferences. When I observe strengths and successes, I ask myself, "How can I encourage this child to build on this strength—to parlay this success?" When I observe a child encountering difficulty, I ask myself, "What is it that this child does not know, that he or she is not doing, or what attitude has he or she failed to cultivate that is causing this difficulty?" When I've answered these questions, I know what to teach. If I did not do this assessment, I would not know what to teach.

If we had not met Charlotte and Matthew before, we might think that they are saying the same thing—but they are not. Charlotte assumes that through assessment she can tell where a child has been and where to lead him or her next. She is familiar with the curriculum as it is typically laid out in a basal reading series, and she believes that every child must be taught each step of the curriculum in nearly the same order. Matthew assumes that through assessment he can tell what a child is trying to do so that he can decide how to help him or her. He is familiar with the reading curriculum as it is typically laid out in a basal reading series, but he does not assume that every child will need to be taught every step; he does not believe that every child will encounter difficulties in the same order.

How do teachers make these assessments?

I have been describing assessment procedures throughout this book, and I will continue to describe them in the remaining chapters. When Mary Weiss looks at Victor's "word bank" in the language experience approach, she is making an assessment. If Victor has only three words, she may decide to pay closer attention to him during lessons to ensure that his word bank increases.

When she looks at Sonja's word bank and discovers that Sonja has 20 words, she may ask Sonja to put all her words that begin with the letter *b* in one pile and begin to discuss letter-sound relationships with her. In both cases assessment is intrinsic to the approach.

As Donald Vader conducts visual discrimination lessons using the letter *a*, he observes the children's responses. He notices that Boris did not cross out all the letters that are not *a*'s in an exercise. Is it possible that Boris cannot see the difference between an *a* and a *t*? Is it possible that he does not understand the directions? Is it possible that he does not see the point of all this and he is simply not paying attention?

These are all questions Donald will pursue in decision making. Observation shows that Boris is not making good progress. Donald must decide what to do about that fact.

Of course the same kind of observation and decision making occurs with every lesson and activity described in this book. At the end of Chapter 13 I will suggest ways for you to reflect on the assessment component of lessons, activities, and teacher-student conferences, but I will first discuss instruments and techniques that have been developed to focus on assessment.

METHODS OF ASSESSMENT DETERMINED BY PURPOSE

There are many purposes for evaluation of students, and there are many ways of conducting assessments. The method of assessment should be chosen to fit the purpose. There are three kinds of questions that lead to assessment: there are teacher's questions, parent's questions, and questions asked by school officials and public policymakers. One way of determining the purpose of assessment is to determine what question is being asked and who is asking the question.

Teacher's Questions

When teachers are engaged in assessment as part of their teaching strategy, one question they ask is: "What does this child know and what can he or she do?" The reason teachers want the answer to this question is so they can answer a second question: "What does the child need to learn next?" A third teachers' question is: "What can I learn by observing the child engaged in reading that will help determine my teaching strategy?"

The kind of assessment that follows from teacher's questions has often been called diagnostic assessment or formative evaluation (Bloom, Hastings, & Madaus, 1971).

Parent's Questions

Although parents are often interested in formative evaluation and the questions that lead to it, they are usually interested in a further question: "What does the child know or how does he perform *in comparison with what the teacher expects of him?*"

The teacher's expectations of the child depend on (1) the child's intellectual and perceptual characteristics, (2) the child's general achievement in reading as compared with others in his or her grade, and (3) the child's progress in achieving the learning objectives that grow out of diagnostic assessment. Assessment of children's intellectual and perceptual characteristics will be taken up in Chapter 14.

Public Policymaker's and School Administrator's Questions

Members of school boards, education departments, legislative bodies, and so on are responsible to the general public for money spent on education, and they are responsible to constituents for the education of their children. Such individuals ask the question, "How well are the students in my charge (or the students among my constituents) learning to read?"

This question does not seek information on what children know in an absolute sense. The question seeks an evaluation in a comparative sense: "What do these children know compared to others the same age or in the same grade in other schools or school districts?" These questions are best answered by standardized tests of reading achievement.

School administrators and supervisors are also interested in individual students' reading achievement for purposes of placing them in classes. But the question once again is not what individuals know in an absolute sense, but what individuals know in comparison to what other children know. This kind of question is best addressed by standardized tests of reading achievement.

In a sense, assessment yielded by standardized tests of reading achievement is the least interesting and the least useful to teachers. It does not determine what children know, nor does it give teachers any insights about how to help children learn. However, many concepts and issues that are essential to proper assessment are most easily introduced in connection with standardized tests of reading achievement. Therefore, standardized tests of reading achievement will be discussed first.

CHARACTERISTICS OF STANDARDIZED READING ACHIEVEMENT TESTS

Interest in educational measurement in the last half-century has given rise to an enormous technology of test construction and test interpretation. This technology has produced reading achievement tests that possess the following characteristics: they are published, standardized, norm-referenced, group-administered, survey tests of reading.

Published

Standardized group survey tests are published—that is, they are not teacher-made tests. Several of the characteristics of these tests demand technical and financial resources that prohibit their construction by individual teachers.

Standardized Administration Procedures

Directions are explicit, clear, and workable. Typically, the administration procedures are field tested in an effort to ensure that, as nearly as possible, every child taking the test will take it under the same conditions as every other child. Answer sheets are supplied so that every child will record his or her answers in the same way. The directions are *read* by the teacher from the Teacher's Manual, and limitations on the amount and kind of help the teacher can offer are delineated. The amount of time permitted in taking the test is explicitly stated. Suggestions are offered to ensure that the test will be administered in a well-lighted, comfortable, distraction-free setting.

Norm Referenced

In the course of preparing these tests for publication they are given to large numbers of students who represent the kind of students for whom the test is designed. That is, if the test is designed to be used throughout the nation for pupils in grades 4, 5, and 6, it is administered to large numbers of students throughout the nation in grades 4, 5, and 6 before the test is published. These students are chosen to represent all children in this category—rich and poor; boys and girls; urban, suburban, and rural; high, medium, and low ability; white, black, Hispanic, and others; and so on. This group is referred to as the *normative group*.

Statistics are gathered to describe the test performance of the normative group. Based on these statistics, tables are provided with the tests that enable a person to interpret a child's score on the test in terms of how it compares with scores of children in the normative group. For example, you may discover that a score of 46 correct on the test compares with the average score of the children in the normative sample who are in the fifth month of fourth grade. One would interpret the child's score as a *grade-equivalent score* of 4.5 (fourth grade, fifth month). All scores possible on the test can be converted to a grade-equivalent score using the tables in the User's Manual accompanying the test.

Using the same procedure, tables are often devised and published that enable one to convert scores to *age-equivalent scores*. If a child's age-equivalent score is 9.1, for example, it means that the score he or she made on the test compares with the average score of children in the normative sample who were nine years, one month old.

Using statistical descriptions of the test performance of the normative sample, tables of *percentile* equivalents are often provided also. If a child is in sixth grade, for example, and has a score in the 86th percentile, it means that of all sixth graders represented by the normative group one would expect 85 percent of them to score below and 14 percent to score above him or her.

Grade-equivalent scores, age-equivalent scores, and percentile rankings are all called *derived scores;* that is, the number correct (called the *observed score* or the *raw score*) is converted to a score that compares an individual's test performance with the performance of the normative group. Such tests are called *norm-referenced tests.*

When a test is said to be *standardized,* one presumes that it is both norm referenced and the administration procedures are explicit, clear, and workable. The rules and conditions under which the test is administered must match the rules and conditions under which the normative group took the test; otherwise, comparisons between a child's score and the scores of the normative group are meaningless.

Group Administered

These tests are designed to be administered in groups. They are sometimes referred to as ''pencil-and-paper tests'' because responses are recorded by the child, individually, with a pencil (as opposed to an oral response or gesture that would require individual attention by the person administering the test).

Survey Tests

These tests usually yield a single derived score (grade-equivalent, age-equivalent percentile, for example). This score is interpreted as an estimate of the child's global reading ability; for this reason, the tests are referred to as *survey* tests. (See Activity 12.A.)

ACTIVITY 12.A EXAMINING STANDARDIZED READING TESTS

Several widely used standardized group survey tests of reading achievement are the Gates-MacGinitie Reading Tests, the Metropolitan Reading Tests, and the reading sections from the California Achievement Tests and the Iowa Test of Basic Skills.

Obtain copies of one or more of these tests together with the manuals for administering and interpreting the scores, and examine them in terms of characteristics described in this discussion: published, standardized administration procedures, norm-referenced (look for discussions of the normative group and derived scores—grade-equivalent scores, age-equivalent scores, percentiles, and standard scores), group-administered, and survey tests.

VALIDITY AND RELIABILITY: CHARACTERISTICS THAT ALL TESTS MUST POSSESS

Validity

Just because a test is *named* a reading test, it is no guarantee that it is a test of reading. For example, many people are not convinced that the ability to look at a *list* of words and say them is a test of reading, although that is precisely what some "tests of reading" consist of (the reading test of the Wide Range Achievement Test, for example). When informed people generally agree that a test measures what its authors claim it measures, the test is said to be *valid*.

Face Validity.   A reasonable way for teachers to determine a test's validity is to obtain a copy of the test, look at it (perhaps administer it to a child or "take it" themselves), and decide whether they believe the test is a valid measure of what it is alleged to measure. To argue that reasonable and informed people would be convinced of a test's validity by this procedure is to argue that the test has *face validity*. However, face validity is a subjective concept. Reasonable and informed people are liable to disagree on whether a test is valid.

Content Validity.   Test publishers often attempt to establish the validity of a test with reasoned arguments. For example, authors may describe how the items on a test were derived from objectives stated in reading curriculum guides published by state departments of education and local school districts. Or authors may attempt to show that items on their test are related to objectives stated in basal reading series and other published reading programs. Such arguments attempt to establish *content validity*.

Concurrent Validity.   Authors sometimes show that students who score high (or low) on their test also score high (or low) on other tests that are widely acknowledged to be valid measures of reading ability. Or they ask teachers to rate students as good readers or poor readers. If the students identified as good readers obtain high scores and the students identified as poor readers obtain poor scores on a test, the test author may use this fact to convince users that the test is a *valid* measure of reading achievement. This kind of argument is referred to as evidence of *concurrent validity*.

Reliability

If a fifth grade student took a 50-item test in the morning and scored 40 correct, what would one guess the student's score would be if the same test was taken in the afternoon of the same day? It seems reasonable that the score would be 40 correct. The student might, however, have made some mistakes (i.e., made an incorrect response when he or she knew the correct response) on one or both tests, and the student may have made some lucky guesses on one or both tests. Therefore, one might guess that the student would score *around* 40. This guess is based on the assumption that the test is a *reliable* measure of a skill that the student possesses to some degree and that the degree to which he or she possesses the skill will not change significantly over a short time. In the language of testing, one would say the test is *reliable*.

On the other hand, one would be very surprised if the student scored 40 on one performance and 20 on the other. If one could presume that the student made a serious effort on both attempts and that the conditions under which the test was taken were the same he or she would conclude that there was something very wrong. The test does not appear to be a reliable measure of what it is thought to measure. In the language of testing one would say the test is *unreliable*.

There is no point in giving such a test because one cannot trust the score of an unreliable test. Administering an unreliable test is worse than pointless because people tend to put great faith (or *reliance*) in test scores.

Test-Retest Reliability.   Of course, one cannot assume that a test is reliable or unreliable on the basis of the performance of one child. Tests are administered to many students on two separate occasions, not too distant in time, and the results are examined for evidence that each student's score remains approximately the same. Because other influences (mistakes, luck, effort) enter into test scores, one cannot expect a perfect match. A statistical procedure known as *correlation* is done on the results of the two tests.

If students' scores remain approximately the same, the *correlation coefficient* will be high. (Positive correlations can vary from .00 to .99.) If students' scores on the second administration of the test bear little resemblance to their scores on the first administration, the correlation coefficient will be very low. This procedure is known as *test-retest reliability,* and it is expressed in terms of a correlation coefficient. Experts agree that test-retest reliability of less than .80 is cause for serious concern (Diederich, 1974, for example).

There are other aspects of testing where reliability is an important factor. Three kinds of reliability that are usually established for standardized tests are as follows:

Internal-Consistency Reliability.   If a test has many items, one presumes that every item is about as valid and about as reliable as every other; that is, one presumes the test is internally consistent as a measuring instrument. This is referred to as *internal-consistency reliability* or *split-half reliability*. "Split-half" refers to the statistical technique used to establish internal-consistency reliability.

Alternate-Form Reliability.   Standardized tests are often published in two or more equivalent forms. For example, Gates-MacGinitie Reading Test, Level A, appears in two forms, Form 1 and Form 2. A student should earn the same derived scores (grade-equivalent score, percentile, etc.) on one form of a standardized test as he or she would earn on an equivalent form. This is referred to as *alternate-form reliability*.

Interrater Reliability. Two or more persons grading the same test should arrive at the same score. This is referred to as *interrater reliability*. Interrater reliability is rarely an issue in standardized testing because standardized tests are typically multiple-choice, machine-scorable tests. Interrater reliability becomes an issue in assessment procedures that rely on observation of behaviors that are less rigidly controlled than are responses on multiple-choice, paper-and-pencil tests.

Evaluating Publishers' Claims

One expects that the authors of published tests will attempt to establish the validity and reliability of the test and report the data in the User's Manual. The data are often missing. When they are missing, one suspects that the data, if reported, would not establish the test's validity and reliability. These data are sometimes supplied but, if properly interpreted, they fail to establish the test's validity and reliability. Since this is a very technical and specialized field, it is advisable to look at reviews of tests by experts in the field to determine whether the test is satisfactory in terms of validity and reliability. A standard reference for reviews of tests is Buros's *Mental Measurements Yearbook* (1978). Salvia and Ysseldyke (1985) is another valuable source for reviews of standardized tests of reading achievement. (See Activity 12.B.)

ACTIVITY 12.B EXAMINING CLAIMS OF VALIDITY AND RELIABILITY

> Several widely used standardized group survey tests of reading achievement are the Gates-MacGinitie Reading Tests, the Metropolitan Reading Tests, and the reading sections from the California Achievement Tests and the Iowa Test of Basic Skills.
>
> Obtain copies of one or more of these tests together with the manuals for administering and interpreting the scores and examine their claims of validity and reliability.
>
> 1. Look for evidence of face validity, content validity, and concurrent validity.
>
> 2. Look for evidence of test-retest reliability, internal-consistency or split-half reliability, and alternate-form reliability.

MISUSES OF STANDARDIZED TESTS OF READING ACHIEVEMENT

The most pervasive misuse of standardized tests of reading ability results from making naive assumptions about their validity; that is, to assume that if Sidney obtains a poor score on a comprehension test, we know exactly what comprehension means and that Sidney is not very good at it.

Standardized tests of reading comprehension consist of short passages followed by questions. If you examine such a test, you will find that the questions usually cover various "levels of comprehension"—literal comprehension, reorganization, inference, evaluation, and application. (See Chapter 9.)

There are two problems with accepting students' scores on such a test as a measure of their "comprehension." First, such test scores may reflect factors that most people would agree are *not* comprehension, such as the following factors:

Memory and Retrieval.   Students might comprehend text information but not remember it, or they might remember it but not be able to retrieve it to answer a question. For example, a person may state a fact if asked to retell a story, but may not be able to answer an isolated question soliciting the fact.

Reasoning.   In answering multiple-choice questions, students can sometimes figure out answers they did not remember from the text. On the other hand, students sometimes choose wrong answers because they read too much into the question or the text.

Motivation.   Motivation begets effort, which accounts for part of test-taking success. Interest in the text, the general desire to do well, and anxiety are all factors that can affect test performance.

Purpose.   Reading strategies that lead to success in answering multiple-choice questions might be quite inappropriate to many real-world reading situations. Because of their artificial purpose, success on a test may not reflect general comprehension ability.

These are some of the more straightforward factors that may influence performance on a standardized comprehension test. These and other more subtle factors are more fully discussed by Johnston (1983). Teachers who realize that these factors may influence a score on a standardized test of reading comprehension are very cautious about interpreting the meaning of such test scores.

Further, such tests do not measure many factors that are believed to play an important role in the process of comprehension. They do not measure students' prior knowledge or their ability to relate prior knowledge to text information. They do not measure the students' ability to pose questions or make predictions about texts before and during reading. They do not measure students' sensitivity to text organization, use of schema, headings, illustrations, outlines, and so on. They do not measure the students' ability to sort out what they know, what they don't know, and what they need to know.

FORMATIVE OR DIAGNOSTIC EVALUATION

When the purpose of assessment is to answer teachers' question: What does the child know? What can he or she do? What does the child need to learn? What can I learn by observing the child engaged in reading that will help determine my teaching strategy?—diagnostic or formative evaluation is in order.

In the remainder of this chapter, and in Chapter 13, I will describe three categories of diagnostic assessment: (1) standardized diagnostic tests, (2) the informal reading inventory, and (3) ongoing, informal assessment in everyday teaching-learning interactions with students.

Standardized diagnostic tests reflect a bottom-up, atomistic view of the reading process. Ongoing, informal assessment reflects a top-down, holistic view of the reading process. The informal reading inventory falls somewhere between the two.

Individual Standardized Diagnostic Tests

Durrell Analysis of Reading Difficulties.   The Durrell Analysis of Reading Difficulties (Durrell and Catterson, 1980) is an individually administered test of oral reading, silent reading, listening comprehension, word recognition, and word analysis. It is designed for use with children whose reading ability falls within the range of nonreader through sixth grade. Optional subtests include tests of letter knowledge, hearing sounds in words, visual memory of words, phonic spelling of words, spelling, and handwriting.

Although grade-equivalent norms are provided, the authors state that the test is "designed primarily for observing faulty habits and weaknesses in reading which are pertinent to planning a 'remedial program.'" In keeping with their aims, the authors have included numerous checklists designed to alert the examiner to behaviors that may be important in making instructional decisions. The authors believe that observing the behaviors included on these checklists is more important than grade-equivalent scores. This is undoubtedly true. Salvia and Ysseldyke (1985) assert that because there are no data in the manual about the normative sample, reliability, or validity, the grade-equivalent scores should not be used.

The Durrell Analysis enables the examiner to observe the reader in a wide variety of reading and reading-related activities, and the checklists guide the examiner's observations. For these reasons, this test is useful for learning to use diagnostic techniques. It is desirable to learn and practice administering the test under the guidance of a reading specialist and to compare notes with other examiners observing the same student's performance.

Experienced users of the Durrell Analysis of Reading Difficulties rarely use all the subtests. Some experts (Pikulski, 1978) claim that the considerable time necessary to administer the Durrell Analysis of Reading Difficulties would be better spent using informal techniques. What is suggested here is that gaining proficiency on the Durrell will enhance teachers' informal diagnostic skills, whether or not they continue to use the Durrell after learning these skills. (See Activity 12.C.)

Other Standardized Individual Diagnostic Tests.   Persons specializing in diagnosis of reading disabilities will want to become familiar with other standardized individual diagnostic tests such as the Gray Oral Reading Test, the Gilmore Oral Reading Test, the Spache Diagnostic Reading Scales, and the Gates-McKillop Reading Diagnostic Tests.

Standardized Group Diagnostic Tests

Standardized group diagnostic tests are paper-and-pencil tests administered to groups of students, but the tests attempt to measure progress in individual skill areas in reading rather than to measure reading achievement in a general sense as survey tests of reading achievement do. The Stanford Diagnostic Reading Test, for example, has subtests in auditory vocabulary, auditory discrimination, phonetic analysis, structural analysis, word

ACTIVITY 12.C ADMINISTERING THE DURRELL ANALYSIS
OF READING DIFFICULTIES

Divide the class into groups of at least three persons each. Designate one person in each group as the "student." Designate the remaining two (or more) persons the "examiners."

Choose a subtest of the Durrell Analysis of Reading Difficulties.

1. After studying the subtest, the student's method of responding to it, and the recorder's method of recording the student's performance, the student will prepare to take the subtest, planning a variety of errors.

2. Meanwhile the examiners will study the subtest and prepare to administer it.

3. One examiner will administer the subtest to the student. All examiners will record the student's responses individually.

4. Examiners will compare their observations and discuss their differences until they arrive at a consensus.

5. Repeat this process, identifying a new subtest and a new student.

reading, reading comprehension, and reading rate. (Note: Not all subtests appear on all four levels of the test, which cover grades 1 through 12.)

Another battery of tests, the Silent Reading Diagnostic Tests, are designed for pupils whose reading skills range from grades 2 through 6. It has subtests in recognizing words in isolation, recognizing words in context, identifying root words, separating words into syllables, applying syllabication rules, blending sounds, distinguishing beginning sounds, distinguishing ending sounds, and distinguishing vowel and consonant sounds.

The advantage of group diagnostic tests is that many tests can be administered at once. However, although the results of these tests may help the teacher to pinpoint *areas* of weakness in students' reading skill, a teacher cannot plan a program for a child without knowing which items the student failed to answer correctly. These tests also fail to give the teacher the opportunity to observe the child while taking the test. For these reasons, simply knowing the score a child received on a subtest of a group diagnostic test is practically useless by itself—but it can be a starting point in making teaching decisions.

Finding Reasons for Incorrect Responses.   If, for example, the directions on a diagnostic test are to mark the word that has the same sound as the "sound" underlined in the example word, and Ellen, a fifth grader, marks the test item as in Figure 12.1, would you assume that Ellen does not hear the difference between /s/ (as in *sit*) and /z/ (as in *hose*)?

Which word ends with the same sound as hou<u>se</u>?

a. rise
(b.) hose
c. lease
d. tease

Figure 12.1. Diagnostic test item marked with an incorrect response.

To discover the real reason why a child makes an incorrect response one needs to sit down with the child individually and go over the items she answered incorrectly. She may give the correct response when given individual attention, or she may respond incorrectly or appear to be guessing.

You may discover that Ellen simply had a lapse of attention and chose *hose* because it had a letter *s* in it.

You may discover that she doesn't discriminate between /s/ and /z/ at the ends of words. In that case a short lesson like the following may be in order.

TEACHER: Listen to these words: *tease, hose, rise*. They all end in the sound of the letter *z*.
Listen to these words: *lease, house, rice*. They all end with the sound of the letter *s*.
Now listen to these two words: *tease, lease*. Which ends with the sound of the letter *z*—*tease* or *lease?*
ELLEN: Tease.
TEACHER: Good. Now listen to these two words: *house, hose*. Which ends with the sound of the letter *z*—*house* or *hose?*
ELLEN: Hose.

[And so on.]

In time you should discover what caused the child to make the wrong response. The problem may not be that she fails to discriminate between sounds, but the problem may be something that is quite crucial to reading instruction. For example, the child may not know what the phrase *has the same sound* means in this context. To find out that this is the problem and to go to work on correcting the problem is sound diagnostic teaching.

Or one may find that the child can do the task with a little coaching, but is unable to do it alone. The task is in Vygotsky's "zone of proximal development." If the task is relevant to the reading instruction the child is receiving, practice with the teacher and other students who perform the task readily is in order. This too is sound diagnostic teaching. But to assume that because a child failed an item (or a series of items) like Figure 12.1, she does not distinguish between sounds, and to launch into a series of lessons where the child distinguishes between the sound of such things as a fire alarm and running water is a waste of time and energy, and that is bad teaching.

Don't assume that because a child does not respond correctly to an item (or items) that she does not have the skill or knowledge that the item (or test) is designed to measure. To base educational decisions on test results, the teacher should observe the child making responses to the test items and determine the reason for failure.

Responding to Performance—Not to Test Names.   When the teacher observes children responding to test items, the teacher's attention is focused on the test items with which the child has trouble. This avoids a common mistake: teachers sometimes assume that if they know the name of a test on which a child performed poorly, they know precisely what tasks the child failed to perform. The task in Figure 3.9 (Chapter 3) is referred to as a test of visual discrimination on one standardized test and a test of letter names on another. The task in Figure 3.5 (Chapter 3) is referred to as a test of auditory discrimination on one test and a test of phonemes on another.

What kind of lesson do you think would be in order if you were told that a child failed a test of "auditory reception"? Think about it for a minute.

The test of "auditory reception" on the Illinois Test of Psycholinguistic Abilities (Kirk et al., 1968) consists of 50 questions of the following form: "Do trees talk?" or "Do children play?" Do you think the lessons you had in store for the child would have helped with whatever problem caused the poor test results?

Don't assume from the name of a test that you know what the test measures. If educational decisions are to be based on test results, the teacher must look at the test items and decide for herself or himself what the significance of success or failure on those items is. (See Activity 12.D.)

ACTIVITY 12.D WHAT'S IN A NAME?

The following are names of subtests on the Stanford Diagnostic Reading Test.

Reading Comprehension	Beginning and Ending Sounds
Vocabulary	Blending
Auditory Discrimination	Sound Discrimination
Syllabication	Rate of Reading

1. Imagine you have a fourth grade student who earned a very low score on one of these tests. Be naive for a moment and plan a reading program for the child to help him or her to overcome this difficulty.

2. Obtain a copy of the test and see what it is exactly that the child failed to do. Is the program you had prepared appropriate or would you change it, having actually seen the items the child failed to answer correctly?

3. Would it help to see which items the child failed?

4. Would it help to observe the child taking the test or go over the items with the child on a one to one basis?

5. Repeat this process for each of the subtests.

The Relevance of Individual Tasks to Instruction

It is too often assumed that because some skill or knowledge is included on a diagnostic test, it is necessary to instill the skill or knowledge in a child before continuing with reading instruction. Although some reading programs appear to be based on this assumption, it is rarely stated explicitly. The assumption is often indefensible.

If Ellen, the student discussed earlier, is not immediately able to discriminate between the sounds /s/ and /z/ in words such as *hose* and *lace,* how much time and energy do you want to spend teaching her to understand what you are trying to get her to do— and then doing it? Can some problem in her performance in real reading situations be traced to her failure to perform this task? If not, failure on the example item on a diagnostic reading test is irrelevant.

Don't assume that because a skill or knowledge is included on a diagnostic test mastery of that skill is necessary before reading instruction continues. If educational decisions are going to be based on test results, the teacher should reflect upon the connection between the skill or knowledge measured by the test and the instruction which he or she plans. If the connection is not clear, the student's performance on the test may be irrelevant.

SUMMARY

Tests should be administered to gain specific information. Questions of how groups of students are performing as compared to others of the same age or in the same grade are most often asked by school administrators and policymakers. These questions tend to be answered exclusively through standardized norm-referenced tests.

Published standardized tests of reading achievement are the product of years of test-making technology. They are standardized in the sense that the directions and conditions under which they are taken by the students and graded by the administrators are uniform from setting to setting. These tests are norm referenced. They are administered to large numbers of students who represent a carefully described population called the normative group.

Through statistical procedures, scores earned by students taking the test are converted to scores that indicate the relative standing of the child as compared to the normative group. Grade-equivalent scores, age-equivalent scores, and percentiles are all derived scores of this kind. Most standardized tests are survey tests. The score they yield is a global estimate of a person's reading achievement—or a survey of one's skills. They are often designed to be administered in groups.

Two qualities that all tests must possess are validity and reliability. If a test has validity, it measures what it is designed to measure. Some methods of establishing validity are face validity, content validity, concurrent validity, and predictive validity. If a test is reliable, it measures some skill or knowledge that is relatively stable; it yields approximately the same measure from one testing session to the next (test-retest reliability); one set of items on the test yields about the same measure as another set of items (split-half reliability); one form of the test yields the same measure as another form of the test (alternate-form reliability); and one person scoring the test will arrive at the same score as another (interrater reliability). Since the procedures used to establish validity and reliability are beyond the technical skills of many teachers, in choosing tests it is best to be guided by reviews published by experts.

Assessment that is done as part of instruction or that is carried out to determine teaching strategies is called diagnostic or formative evaluation. Standardized individual diagnostic tests are one type of formative or diagnostic evaluation. Although these tend to be norm-referenced tests, norm referencing is not very useful for formative evaluation. Parts (subtests) of these tests are often used to get information on particular reading skills. At such times the norms cannot be legitimately referred to. It is sometimes useful for teachers to administer standardized individual diagnostic tests to observe the student engaging in a wide variety of reading tasks. This experience may help the teacher to become aware of the behaviors that are relevant to making instructional decisions.

Standardized group diagnostic tests are also available. These tests contain sections on various subskills. Performance on such tests might suggest areas of weakness, but student scores on such tests are not sufficient for planning instruction. The teacher cannot be sure that incorrect responses reflect lack of knowledge or skill; without examining test items, the teacher cannot be sure what the students failed to do correctly, and all areas tested are not necessarily relevant to the students' reading tasks.

Examining group diagnostic tests carefully, going over items individually with students and observing their responses, and reflecting on the connection between the skills tested and the child's normal reading tasks are ways of using standardized group diagnostic tests to plan instruction.

FOR FURTHER READING

Farr, R., & Carey, R. F. (1986). *Reading: What can be measured?* (2nd ed.). Newark, DE: International Reading Association.

Flood, J., & Lapp, D. (1987). Types of writing in basal readers and assessment tests: An imperfect match. *The Reading Teacher, 40*(9), 880–883.

Pumfrey, P. D. (1985). *Reading: Tests and assessment techniques* (2nd ed.). Newark, DE: International Reading Association.

Schell, L. M. (1988). Dilemmas in assessing reading comprehension. *The Reading Teacher, 42*(1), 12–17.

Squire, J. R. (Guest Ed.) (1987). *The reading teacher: The state of reading assessment.* Newark, DE: International Reading Association.

Informal Assessment

Some of the most illustrious persons in the field of teaching reading in the past half-century (Edward L. Thorndike, 1934; Arthur Gates, 1936; Donald Durrell, 1937; and Emmett Betts, 1957) have experimented with, written about, and made recommendations about informal assessment, which Durrell (1940) called "the best basis for planning instruction" (p. 18). One result of this inquiry has come to be known as the *Informal Reading Inventory*.

INFORMAL READING INVENTORY

An Overview

In an Informal Reading Inventory, the student reads a passage like the one in Figure 13.1 orally and answers comprehension questions about it. Next the student reads a second passage (about the same length and about equally as difficult) silently and answers comprehension questions about that passage. Based on the student's performance the teacher (1) decides whether the passages are too easy, too difficult, or exactly right for instruction and (2) records observations that will be used in planning the student's instructional program.

    If the passages are determined to be too easy, the student repeats the process on two passages that are more difficult. The process continues until the student encounters passages that are too difficult. At that point the teacher *reads the passage to the child* and asks questions about the passage. Based on the child's performance, the teacher decides whether or not the child understands the passage when it is read to him or her. If the child does understand the passage, a more difficult passage is read. This process continues until the child encounters a passage that he or she does not understand when it is read to him or her. When this process is completed, the teacher, based on these observations, determines what are known as the *functional levels of reading* for the child.

An Informal Reading Inventory has two purposes. One purpose is to determine a child's independent level, instructional level, frustration level, and capacity level. The second purpose is to observe and record what may be causing the difficulties and how the child attempts to overcome problems when they are encountered. When the teacher accomplishes these two purposes, he or she is ready to plan effective instruction.

Functional Levels of Reading

The Independent Level.   The independent reading level is the level at which the child can read the material with virtually no oral reading errors and with nearly perfect comprehension.

The Instructional Level.   The instructional reading level is the level at which the child is challenged by the material; he or she makes some oral reading errors and has less than perfect comprehension. However, with the aid of a teacher, the child should be able to cope satisfactorily with the material, and his or her reading skills should improve since they are being challenged.

The Frustration Level.   The frustration level is the level at which the child encounters numerous difficulties in oral reading and where his or her comprehension falls off to nearly zero. The child simply cannot read the material—with or without help.

The Capacity Level.   The highest level of material that the child understands when the passage is *read to him or her* is known as the *capacity level*. The four levels of reading ability are shown from a student's point of view and from a teacher's point of view in Box 13.1. (See Activity 13.A.)

Defining the Level of the Chosen Passage

It is customary for persons writing about the Informal Reading Inventory to stipulate that this procedure can be based on various kinds of instructional materials. However, this procedure is so intimately related to the use of basal readers, both historically and in current practice, that it is presumed that materials come from basal readers unless it is otherwise stated. Therefore, when a teacher says that a child's instructional level is third grade and his or her frustration level is fifth grade, the teacher is referring to the child's performance on passages taken from a third grade reader and a fifth grade reader from some basal reading series—usually the basal reading series used for reading instruction in the child's classroom.

The Young Newsboy

Almost everyone knew big Bill,

who worked on the morning newspaper.

"We like the way he writes," many people

would say. "A news story by Big Bill is

always the best in the Garden City News."

Almost no one knew Little Bill.

He wanted to follow in his father's footsteps.

Little Bill wanted to write for the paper,

too, when he grew up.

First, Little Bill wanted

to be a newsboy for the Garden City News.

For a long time Big Bill had told him,

"You are still too young."

201

Figure 13.1. A typical passage for use in an informal reading inventory. (*Source: Down Singing River*, Emmett Betts and Carolyn Welsh. Betts Basic Readers, 2nd ed. [D.C. Heath, 1958].)

At last Big Bill said, "I guess
you are old enough to carry papers.
I was a newsboy, too, when I was young.
In the morning I'll be glad to show you
how to be one. Get up early."

Next morning Little Bill dressed
very early. Big Bill was the one to oversleep.

Still, daylight had not come
when they both left for the office.
On the way they met the milkman.
Little Bill wanted to call, "Hello."

His father said, "Above all,
a newsboy must not make any noise.
He must not let the neighbors
say he woke them up too early."

BOX 13.1 FUNCTIONAL LEVELS OF READING FROM A TEACHER'S POINT OF VIEW AND FROM A CHILD'S POINT OF VIEW

From a Child's Point of View

Independent level

I can read by myself without help and can understand what I read; I can pronounce almost every word. I feel comfortable and enjoy reading. I read for fun and to find out things. I can give reports on what I have read.

Instructional level

I understand what I am taught from the readers and other books and can get honors in the tests. I can pronounce 95 out of 100 words. I don't fidget, read with my lips, or point as I read, but I feel at ease.

Frustration level

I don't understand half of what I read and I feel worried and unhappy. Sometimes I can't stand still as I read, and I'd like to point with my fingers and read with my lips. Often I can't pay attention. I should not read on this step often, for my reading will not improve.

Capacity level

I understand what is being read to me but I would be unable to read the story myself. I can listen to radio stories and other programs and lessons, understand them, and enjoy them. I can give oral reports on what I have heard.

From a Teacher's Point of View

Independent level

This is the level of supplementary and independent reading. Child should be able to read the book at home or school without aid. The material should cause no difficulty and have high interest value.

Instructional level

This is the teaching level. The reading material must be challenging and not too difficult.

Frustration level

This level is to be avoided. It is the lowest level of readability at which a child is unable to understand. The material is too difficult and frustrates the pupil.

Capacity level

This is the hearing level—the highest level of readability at which a child is able to understand when listening to someone read or talk. Pupil must understand the selection and be able to express himself accurately. No verbalism. Adequate background of experience.

Adapted from Betts, 1957, p. 448.

Creating an Informal Reading Inventory

Choosing Representative Passages.   Two passages are chosen from each level—one for oral reading and one for silent reading. When basal readers are carefully constructed, passages become progressively more difficult from the beginning to the end of each book. To find representative passages, it makes sense to select passages from near the middle of the book. It is advisable to choose two passages from the same selection since comparisons will be made between the student's oral reading and silent reading performance. If passages are taken from the same selection for the two trials, there is less chance that differences in the topic of the passages or in the author's style are responsible for differences in students' performances.

> *Definitions: "passage" and "selection."* The meanings of the words *passage* and *selection* can easily be confused. In this book, the word selection refers to whole stories,

ACTIVITY 13.A RELATING FUNCTIONAL READING LEVELS TO THE ZONE OF PROXIMAL DEVELOPMENT AND THE INTERACTIONAL PERSPECTIVE

1. Explain the functional levels of reading in terms of Vygotsky's zone of proximal development (Chapter 2, pages 39–40).

2. Discuss the similarities between the teaching strategies that are implied by the concept of functional levels of reading and following concepts derived from the interactional perspective

Leading from behind or scaffolding (discussed throughout Chapter 2)

Generalizations about parent-child interactions that facilitate development: intentionality, proximal development, collaboration, internalization, and continuous development (Chapter 2, page 37).

poems, or essays that appear in basal readers or literature anthologies. A passage refers to a portion of connected text taken from a book. It is usually longer than a sentence, but does not include a whole selection.

Passages should be typical of the reading levels they represent, and the student's performance should be typical of his or her usual performance. Therefore, passages that have peculiar features such as foreign words like *très bien* or unusual names like *Quiqueg* would be ruled out; passages that could not be understood without knowledge of some little-known fact such as that Theodore Roosevelt was sworn into the office of the President in Buffalo, New York, would also be ruled out.

Length of Passages. The length of the passages chosen for an Individual Reading Inventory should reflect both the characteristics of the texts at various levels and the kind of reading tasks that children in various grades are accustomed to. An entire selection in a primer may be fewer than 50 words in length, and during a typical reading lesson children are asked to read very short portions at one time. However, for an Individual Reading Inventory, one wants to observe as much reading performance as possible, so the minimum length of passages chosen at the preprimer and primer levels is 25 words. The minimum at first grade is 50 words.

Beyond primary grades, selections in basal readers become much longer, and students are asked to read several pages at a time in normal reading assignments. At third grade level and above, 100 words is considered a bare minimum for an Informal Reading Inventory. At this point, the time needed to administer the test becomes a limiting factor. Passages as long as 200 words would probably not be chosen at any level because of time considerations. (See Activity 13.B.)

Writing Comprehension Questions. About ten comprehension questions are written to accompany each passage chosen for an Informal Reading Inventory. Since passages through the second grade level tend to be very short, fewer comprehension questions (5 to 8) are written to accompany these passages.

Teachers are advised to ask only a few literal, factual questions about the passage (one-third such questions are sometimes recommended). The remaining questions should call for such skills as recalling sequences, stating main ideas, and perceiving cause and

ACTIVITY 13.B CHOOSE PASSAGES FOR AN INFORMAL READING INVENTORY

Obtain texts for several levels of a basal reading series—perhaps the third, sixth, and eighth grade levels.

1. Divide the class into two or more groups. Each group will choose two passages from each level of the basal reader using the criteria discussed in this section to select passages for an Informal Reading Inventory.

2. Each group will share the passages they chose and discuss the criteria they used with the rest of the class.

—Were any passages examined and rejected? For what reasons?

3. Groups will critique each other's choices.

—Do any of the passages chosen seem to violate the criteria considered?

4. Repeat the process until all the passages chosen by every group meet the approval of the entire class.

---

effect and should reflect higher levels of comprehension such as interpretation and application of knowledge gained through reading the passage. (See Activity 13.C.)

Each question is labeled in terms of the skill and/or level of comprehension it is designed to test. (See Figure 13.2, for example.)

Preparing Materials

Student's Copy. During the procedure, the student reads from the books where the passages appear. This permits the teacher to observe a child very closely and carefully while the child is reading from the materials normally used in instruction. The size of page and type and the artwork and graphics are all present and unchanged.

Teacher's Copy. After passages are selected they are typed (or photocopied) onto a sheet. Questions, identifying information, and other information that will be useful in

ACTIVITY 13.C WRITING COMPREHENSION QUESTIONS FOR AN INFORMAL READING INVENTORY

Work in the groups established in Activity 13.B.

1. Write the appropriate number of comprehension questions for the passages chosen by your group in Activity 13.B. Refer to the skills by level of comprehension framework in Chapter 10 in creating your questions.
2. Share your questions and the criteria used in creating them with the class.
   a. Were there any questions suggested and rejected?
   b. For what reason?
3. The class will critique the questions written by each group.
   a. Do they conform to the criteria suggested in this section?
   b. Do they conform to the skills by level of comprehension framework? That is, does everyone agree that questions labeled *factual* are factual questions, that questions labeled *inference* are inference questions, and so on?
4. Repeat the critique process, rewriting questions where necessary, until the questions for every passage meet the approval of the class.

recording observations and interpreting the results are typed onto the same page. This permits the examiner to write on his or her copy of the inventory as the procedure unfolds. Figure 13.2 is a typical teacher's copy of one level of an Informal Reading Inventory. (See Activity 13.D.)

ACTIVITY 13.D PREPARING A TEACHER'S COPY OF PASSAGES FOR AN INFORMAL READING INVENTORY

Work in the groups established in Activity 13.B.
Prepare a teacher's copy of the passages chosen in Activity 13.B and the comprehension questions written in Activity 13.C. Use Figure 13.2 as a model, but include only the passage and comprehension questions at this point.

Administering an Informal Reading Inventory

Where to Begin.   One wants to begin an Informal Reading Inventory at a level where the child will encounter no problems; however, since this is an individualized procedure, the amount of time expended becomes a crucial issue. Starting every child at the preprimer levels will undoubtedly waste much valuable time. Teachers are advised to begin an Informal Reading Inventory with materials at least two years below a child's grade-equivalent score on a standardized test.

Evaluating the oral reading of the first passage chosen will reveal any gross miscalculations. At this stage, as at every stage in this procedure, good judgment on the part of the teacher is indispensable.

The child is presented with the book containing the first oral reading passage. After the child has found the passage (usually marked with a bookmark), he or she is told to read the passage aloud and to read it carefully because questions will be asked about the passage.

Recording Oral Reading Performance.   As the child reads, the examiner records the child's performance. Two kinds of notations are made: errors in oral reading (that is, inaccurate renderings of the text as it is printed) and errors in responses to comprehension questions. The former includes such inaccuracies as omitted words, inserted words, substituted words, transposed words, and mispronounced words. If a child stays on a word for as long as five seconds without attempting to pronounce it, the examiner supplies the word and records that the word was supplied. Notations for recording these categories of oral reading inaccuracy are found in Box 13.2. There is a 1986 revised edition of the *Gray Oral Reading Test* (GORT-R, published by Pro-Ed, Austin, Texas). I refer here to the 1967 edition of the test because its directions are better suited to my purposes.

Kenneth Goodman (1967, 1969) and Kenneth and Yetta Goodman (1977) have made valuable observations about the causes of oral reading inaccuracy and the insights such inaccuracies may give researchers into reading-language processes (see Chapter 9). Goodman referred to oral reading inaccuracies as "miscues" rather than as "errors," and for a time it seemed the term *miscue* would replace *error* in discussions of oral reading performance.

However, in an Informal Reading Inventory, inaccuracies are interpreted as evi-

Figure 13.2. Teacher's copy of a passage prepared for an informal reading
inventory.

SECOND GRADE READER LEVEL

Passage

The Young Newsboy

Almost everyone knew Big Bill, who worked on the morning newspaper. "We like the way he writes," many people would say. "A news story by Big Bill is always the best in the *Garden City News.*"

Almost no one knew Little Bill. He wanted to follow in his father's footsteps. Little Bill wanted to write for the paper, too, when he grew up.

First, Little Bill wanted to be a newsboy for the *Garden City News.* For a long time Big Bill had told him, "You are still too young."

At last Big Bill said, "I guess you are old enough to carry papers. I was a newsboy, too, when I was young. In the morning I'll be glad to show you how to be one. Get up early."

Next morning Little Bill dressed very early. Big Bill was the one to oversleep. Still, daylight had not come when they both left for the office. On the way they met the milkman. Little Bill wanted to call, "Hello."

His father said, "Above all, a newsboy must not make any noise. He must not let the neighbors say he woke them up too early."

From *Down Singing River*, Betts Basic Readers, American Book Company, 1958, pp. 201–202.

Comprehension Questions
1. Who is Big Bill? (factual)
2. What do people like about him? (factual)
3. Who is Little Bill? (inference)
4. The story says Little Bill wants to "follow in his father's footsteps." What does that mean? (interpretive)
5. What does this expression tell us about this story? Why did the author use it? (applicative)
6. In what way does Little Bill start to be like his father? (interpretive)
7. What time did Little Bill and Big Bill go out in the morning? Why? (inference)
8. Do you think Little Bill will change his mind about what he wants to be by the time he is grown up? Explain why you think so. (applicative)

Word recognition errors_____
% word recognition errors _____
Number of words = 193
% per error = .52%

Word recognition in oral reading
  4 errors = 98%
  10 errors = 95%
  20 errors = 90%
Comprehension questions incorrect _____
% comprehension questions incorrect _____
Number of comprehension questions = 8
% per incorrect answer = 12.5%
Comprehension score
  1 error = 88% (independent level)
  2 errors = 75% (instructional level)
  4 errors = 50% (frustration level)

From an unpublished informal reading inventory, Carol Kelly. State University of New York at Buffalo, 1983.

This passage could be used for silent reading or it could be read to the child for a measure of his reading capacity. In either case, the word recognition errors would be ignored.

dence of difficulty with reading the text—not as evidence of properly functioning reading-language processes. Therefore, the term *error* seems to express more clearly and directly what is being observed, and the term *error* is used in this discussion.

Oral Reading Comprehension.   After the child has finished reading the oral reading passage, the book is closed and the examiner reads the questions in order from his or her copy. Correct answers are recorded with a checkmark after the question. Incorrect or doubtful answers are written on the teacher's copy as these answers may be useful in determining the child's weaknesses in comprehension. (See Activity 13.E.)

BOX 13.2 SYMBOLS USED TO RECORD ORAL READING ERRORS.

1. *Omission of a word or group of words.* Circle the omitted word or group of words. Example:
     They fly passengers, freight, and mail from one city to another.
2. *Insertion of a word or group of words.* Place an insert mark and write the word(s) above the point at which they were added. Example:
         clear
     The/\sky was bright blue.
3. *Substitution of one meaningful word or several for others.* Example:
         sat on
     A boy had a wagon.
4. *Inverting or changing word order.* Example:
     He ran rapidly there.
5. *Mispronunciation.* Such an error is marked by drawing a straight line under the entire word and writing the pupil's pronunciation phonetically.
                 fratific
     Example: traffic
6. *Aid.* When the pupil hesitates for *five seconds* without making any audible effort to pronounce the word, or *ten seconds* if he appears to be trying to pronounce it, the examiner pronounces the word. The error is marked by an underlined bracket.
         Example: [geologists]

Adapted from the *Gray Oral Reading Test, Manual of Directions for Administering, Scoring, and Interpretation* (W. S. Gray. Pro-Ed, 1967).

ACTIVITY 13.E RECORDING ERRORS IN ORAL
READING AND
RESPONSES TO COMPREHENSION QUESTIONS

Divide the class into groups of at least three persons each. Designate one person in each group as the "reader." Designate the remaining two (or more) persons the "recorders."

Each group will select a passage for this activity, perhaps Figure 13.2 or perhaps a passage prepared in Activity 13.D.

1. After studying Box 13.2, Symbols Used to Record Oral Reading Errors, the reader will prepare to read the passage, planning a variety of oral reading errors and marking his or her copy of the passage showing the errors planned.

2. The reader will prepare to answer the comprehension questions for the passage, introducing incorrect answers and, perhaps, doubtfully correct answers.

3. While the reader is preparing, recorders will study Box 13.2, Symbols Used to Record Oral Reading Errors, suggesting ways these errors might appear in reading this passage. Individuals might read sentences from the passage, introducing oral reading errors and letting others identify them.

4. The reader will read the passage orally for the recorders with errors as prepared in step 1. Recorders will record errors on their copies of the passage.

5. One recorder will read the comprehension questions and the reader will answer them as planned in step 2. Recorders will evaluate the answers and mark their copies as suggested in this section.

6. Recorders will compare their marked copies with each other and with the reader's prepared copy.

—How much agreement is there in recording oral reading errors?
—How much agreement is there in evaluating answers to comprehension questions?

7. Arrive at group consensus on the number of oral reading errors and the number of correct responses in answering comprehension questions. Record this information and save it for Activity 13.G.

8. Repeat this process, identifying a new reader.

ACTIVITY 13.F RECORDING FLAWS IN QUALITY OF ORAL READING

Divide the class into groups of at least three persons each. Designate one person in each group as the "reader." Designate the remaining two (or more) persons the "recorders."

Each group will select a passage for this activity, perhaps Figure 13.2 or perhaps a passage prepared in Activity 13.D.

1. After studying Box 13.3, Methods of Recording Flaws in Quality of Oral Reading, the reader will prepare to read the passage, planning a variety of flaws in quality of oral reading and marking his or her copy of the passage showing the planned flaws.

2. While the reader is preparing, recorders will study Box 13.3, Methods of Recording Flaws in Quality of Oral Reading, suggesting ways these flaws might appear in reading this passage. Individuals might read sentences from the passage, introducing flaws in quality of oral reading errors and letting others identify them.

3. The reader will read the passage orally for the recorders with flaws in quality as prepared in step 1. Recorders will record flaws in quality on their copies of the passage.

4. Recorders will compare their marked copies with each other and with the reader's prepared copy.

—How much agreement is there in recording flaws in quality of oral reading?

5. Arrive at group consensus on step 4.
6. Repeat this process, identifying a new reader.

BOX 13.3 METHODS OF RECORDING FLAWS IN QUALITY OF ORAL READING THAT ARE NOT COUNTED AS ORAL READING ERRORS IN DETERMINING FUNCTIONAL LEVELS

Symbols, explanations, and examples of flaws in quality of oral reading

1. *Repetition.* Wavy line under the word(s). Example:
   The boy ran away.
2. *Ignoring punctuation.* Punctuation mark is *X'd* out. Example:
   Wendy looked at the boys and girls. She looked at the toys, too.
3. *Lack of fluency.* Vertical lines where pauses occur. Example:
   Wendy | looked | at | the | boys and girls.

A checklist approach to recording flaws in the quality of oral reading

A checklist approach to recording flaws in the quality of oral reading
OBSERVATIONS

(Check statement and circle each part)

_____ Word-by-word reading
_____ Poor phrasing
_____ Lack of expression
_____ Monotonous tone
_____ Pitch too high or low; voice too loud, too soft, or strained
_____ Poor enunciation
_____ Disregard of punctuation
_____ Overuse of phonics
_____ Little or no method of word analysis
_____ Unawareness of errors
_____ Head movement
_____ Finger pointing
_____ Loss of place

From *Examiner's Record Booklet for the Gray Oral Reading Test* (W. S. Gray. Pro-Ed, 1963).

Recording Flaws in the Quality of Oral Reading.   A second kind of notation made during oral reading is designed to record flaws in the quality of the oral reading. Repeating words, ignoring punctuation marks, word-by-word (rather than fluent) reading, and pointing with a finger, for example, are observed and recorded. Such observations are useful in planning a child's program but are not taken into consideration in establishing functional levels of reading for the child. Notations for recording observations about the quality of the oral reading performance are found in Box 13.3. There is a 1986 version of the Record Booklet for the *Gray Oral Reading Test Revised* (published by Pro-Ed, Austin, Texas). I refer here to the 1963 edition of the Record Booklet because its directions are better suited to my purposes. (See Activity 13.F.)

Silent Reading.   The child is directed to read the passage chosen for silent reading. The examiner observes the child during silent reading and takes note of such habits as lip movement, finger pointing, and looking back and rereading. Such observations may be useful in planning the child's program.

Silent Reading Comprehension.   After the child has finished reading the silent reading passage, he or she closes the book and the comprehension questions for the passage are asked, answered, and recorded in the same manner as the oral reading comprehension questions were handled.

Oral Rereading.   After the silent reading comprehension questions have been asked and answered, the child may be asked to open the book once again to the silent reading passage, to find the answer to an additional question, and to read orally that portion of the text that answers the question. The examiner notes the child's performance in re-reading a portion of the passage that he or she has just read silently. The examiner also observes the child's behavior in looking for particular information. Such observations may be useful in planning the child's reading program. This is an optional phase of the inventory. The child's performance is not considered in establishing his or her functional levels of reading.

Interpreting an Informal Reading Inventory

Determining Functional Levels.   Two criteria are considered in determining a student's functional levels: the word recognition score in oral reading and the comprehension scores.

Word Recognition Errors in Oral Reading. The word recognition score in oral reading is determined by the number of reading inaccuracies (see Box 13.2) per hundred words in the test passage. Since passages are rarely exactly 100 words, the percentage per error is calculated based on the number of words in the passage:

$$\frac{1}{\text{Number of words in the passage}} \times 100 = \% \text{ per error}$$

The crucial percentages in determining the functional levels are 98 percent, 95 percent, and 90 percent. Therefore, the number of oral reading errors that result in these crucial percentages are sometimes calculated and recorded on the teacher's copy of the oral reading passage as in Figure 13.2.

Comprehension Score. The comprehension score is determined by the number of comprehension questions answered correctly and expressed as a percentage. The crucial percentages for comprehension in determining the functional levels are 90 percent, 75 percent, and 50 percent. Since the number of questions varies as a function of the length of the passage, the number of correct answers that result in these crucial percentages are sometimes calculated and recorded on the teacher's copy of the oral reading *and* silent reading passages as in Figure 13.2. (See Activity 13.G.)

Box 13.4 shows the criteria that are widely accepted in determining functional levels of reading. Unfortunately, an individual student's performance rarely fits these criteria precisely, and examiners have to rely on other observations to estimate the child's functional levels.

For example, an examiner estimated the functional levels of a fourth grade child whose scores are reported in Box 13.5 to be

ACTIVITY 13.G CONVERTING ORAL READING ERRORS
AND COMPREHENSION QUESTION SCORES
TO PERCENTAGES

Work in the groups established in Activity 13.B.

1. Using the same passages as those used in Activity 13.E, calculate the number of oral reading errors that would result in the crucial percentages—98 percent, 95 percent, and 90 percent.

2. Calculate the number of comprehension questions answered incorrectly that would result in the crucial percentages—90 percent, 75 percent, and 50 percent.

3. Using Figure 13.2 as a model, enter this information on the teacher's copies of the passages developed in Activity 13.D.

4. Using the figures arrived at in step 7 of Activity 13.E, determine the "percentage of word recognition errors" and "percentage of comprehension questions incorrect" for at least one reader in your group.

BOX 13.4 CRITERIA FOR DETERMINING FUNCTIONAL LEVELS
OF READING.

Functional Reading Level	Percent Word Recognition in Oral Reading	Percent Comprehension Questions Answered Correctly
Independent level	98%	90%
Instructional level	95	75
Frustration level	90	50
Capacity level		75

Independent level, grade 2
Instructional level, grade 3
Frustration level, grade 4

Although the word recognition score at third grade is below the instructional level, the comprehension scores at the third grade level are at the instructional level. The examiner took the seriousness of the word recognition errors at the third grade level into account and determined that the third grade passage would be appropriate for instruction.

BOX 13.5 INFORMAL READING INVENTORY SCORES
FOR A FOURTH GRADE PUPIL.

Grade Level of Passage	Percent Word Recognition in Oral Reading	Percent Oral Reading Comprehension	Percent Silent Reading Comprehension
2	99%	90%	90%
3	90	80	80
4	90	70	60

Noting Difficulties Observed During Oral Reading and Silent Reading.   The second and perhaps more important purpose of the Informal Reading Inventory is to discover and classify possible causes of reading difficulties. Betts (1957) suggests a "detailed form" (pp. 472–474) to be used by inexperienced examiners to record observations that will presumably determine the strategies that will be used in teaching the child to read. Box 13.6 presents a list of behaviors to be noted during oral reading and silent reading that follows Betts's list very closely. (See Activity 13.H.)

ACTIVITY 13.H GAINING SENSITIVITY TO BEHAVIORS TO BE NOTED DURING AN INFORMAL READING INVENTORY

> Divide the class into at least three groups.
>
> Assign each group one of the major categories of "difficulties" in Box 13.6: (1) "Difficulties Observed During Oral Reading," (2) "Difficulties Observed During Silent Reading," and (3) "Difficulties Observed Throughout the Procedure."
>
> 1. Each group plans a skit with a teacher administering an Informal Reading Inventory to a student. Materials developed in Activities 13.C, 13.D, and 13.E, or Figure 13.2 may be used.
>
> In each skit the "student" is to act out three or four difficulties from those assigned to the group.
>
> 2. Skits are presented to the class. Spectators jot down behaviors they believe they are observing.
>
> 3. Spectators compare notes with each other and with members of the group that prepared the skit.
>
> —. How much agreement is there in recording the "difficulties" observed?
>
> 4. Arrive at group consensus on step 3.
>
> 5. Repeat this process with the remaining groups.

Strengths of an Informal Reading Inventory

The chief advantages of the Informal Reading Inventory derive from the fact that the child can be tested on materials that are used in instruction and that procedures are used that are typical of instruction. This direct linkage between testing and teaching enables the teacher to incorporate his or her observations directly into lessons for the individual. It enables the student to see the relevance of the testing experience to his or her learning experiences.

Published Informal Reading Inventories

Several such inventories are listed in Activity 13.I. The advantage of these inventories is that the authors and publishers have had the time and resources to make sure that the passages fairly and accurately represent the level of reading that they are supposed to represent and that the comprehension questions assess the skill and level of comprehension that they are supposed to assess. Such inventories also offer aids to examiners such as oral reading scoring guides and student record sheets to aid in recording and analyzing performance.

The problem of these inventories is that they lose one of the primary advantages of the Informal Reading Inventory: the passages on which the child is tested are not in the materials that will be used for instruction. Therefore, the direct linkage between the test and the placement of the child at his or her instructional level *in the materials used in instruction* is lost, as is direct linkage between the difficulties discovered during testing and the difficulties he or she will encounter in the materials used for instruction. (See Activities 13.I, 13.J, and 13.K.)

BOX 13.6 SUGGESTED LIST OF BEHAVIORS TO BE NOTED DURING ORAL READING AND SILENT READING IN AN INFORMAL READING INVENTORY.

Difficulties Observed During Oral Reading

Comprehension
Inability to state main idea
Inaccurate recall of details
Inaccurate recall of sequence of ideas
Faulty inferences

Rate
Reads slowly
Reads slowly and haltingly
Reads too fast

Voice Control
High pitch
Too loud
Too soft
Breathing irregular

Rhythm
Word-by-word reading
Unable to anticipate meaning
Ignores punctuation
Hesitates
Skips lines

Word Recognition
Meaningful substitutions
Meaningless substitutions
Repetitions
Insertions
Omissions
Reverses letters
Reverses words
Reverses word sequence
Overdependence on picture clues
Overdependence on final clues
Confusion of initial consonants
Confusion of final consonants

Difficulties Observed During Silent Reading

Comprehension
Inability to state main idea
Inaccurate recall of details
Inaccurate recall of sequence of ideas
Faulty inferences

Rate
Reads slowly
Reads too fast

Vocalization
Silent lip movement
Whispering
Low vocal utterance
Reads audibly

Finger Pointing

Head Movement

Tension Movements
Hands
Feet
Legs
Body

Posture
Book too close
Book too far
Book at an angle

Visual Inefficiency
Frowns
Squints
Blinks
Rubs eyes
Shades eyes
Covers one eye
Complains that print blurs
Complains that print doubles

Difficulties Observed Throughout the Procedure

General Reaction Time
Overly slow
Too fast (at expense of accuracy and correctness)

Emotional Reactions
Indifferent
Shy
Fearful
Aggressive
Sullen
Rebellious
Overconfident

Speech Characteristics
Stutters
Lisps
Immature articulation

From *Foundations of Reading Instruction,* Emmett Betts (D. C. Heath, 1957).

ACTIVITY 13.I EXAMINING PUBLISHED INFORMAL READING INVENTORIES

Obtain one of the following published Informal Reading Inventories:

Bader, L. A. (1983). *Bader reading and language inventory*. New York: Macmillan.

Brown, D. A. (1982). *Reading diagnosis and remediation*. Englewood Cliffs, NJ: Prentice-Hall, pp. 316–363.

Johns, J. L. (1978). *Basic reading inventory pre-primer—grade eight*. Dubuque, IA: Kendall/Hunt.

Johns, J. L. (1981). *Advanced reading inventory grade seven through college*. Dubuque, IA: William C. Brown.

Rinsky, L. A., & de Fossard, E. (1980). *The contemporary classroom reading inventory*. Dubuque, IA: Gorsuch Scarisbreck.

Silvaroli, N. (1976). *Classroom reading inventory* (3rd ed). Dubuque, IA: William C. Brown.

Sucher, F., & Allred, R. A. (1973). *Reading placement inventory*. Oklahoma City: The Economy Company.

Woods, M. L., & Moe, A. J. (1977). *Analytical reading inventory*. Columbus: Charles E. Merrill.

1. Evaluate these inventories in terms of the characteristics discussed in this chapter: appropriateness of the reading passages, quality of the comprehension questions, usefulness of the recording forms, and criteria for establishing functional levels.
a. If you can obtain multiple copies of one of the inventories, work in small groups and compare your observations with those of the other groups.
b. If you can obtain two or more different inventories, compare them in terms of these characteristics.
2. Compare the published inventories to the ones produced in Activities 13.B, 13.C, and 13.D.

ACTIVITY 13.J ADMINISTERING PUBLISHED INFORMAL READING INVENTORIES

1. Audiotape or videotape several children reading passages orally and answering the questions from a published reading inventory. As an alternative, audiotape or videotape a student "reader" as in Activity 13.E.
2. Follow the procedures in the test manual. Record, score, and interpret the oral reading performance of the children. Replay the tape as necessary to record the children's performances accurately.
3. Repeat this procedure until you are able to administer, score, and interpret the test *without* replaying the tape.

ACTIVITY 13.K EXPERIMENTING WITH INTERRATER RELIABILITY USING PUBLISHED INFORMAL READING INVENTORIES

1. Audiotape or videotape several children reading passages orally and answering the questions from a published reading inventory. As an alternative, audiotape or videotape a student "reader" as in Activity 13.E.
2. Follow the procedures in the test manual. Record, score, and interpret the oral reading performance of the children. Replay the tape as necessary to record the children's performances accurately.
3. Compare your assessment of oral reading errors, comprehension question performance, and assessment of difficulties with others (the class instructor or other students) who have carried out this procedure on the same recorded reading performance. You will no doubt discover many discrepancies at first. Some can be resolved through replaying the recording. Others may be resolved through discussion that will clear up misconceptions relating to terminology or concepts.
4. Repeat this procedure until you begin to get similar results as others observing the same performance.

ONGOING INFORMAL ASSESSMENT

Contemporary thinking stresses two characteristics that must be present in diagnostic assessment. The first is the "naturalness" of the tasks students are engaged in when assessment is done. Readance and Martin (1988) refer to this as "ecological validity." Second, assessment must lead to teaching strategies that are consistent with the assessment outcome.

In ongoing, informal assessment, teachers *observe* students engaged in regular reading activities in the classroom and attend to successes and failures. Next they *interpret* students' successes and failures—that is, they formulate hypotheses about the sources of successes and failures. Finally, they *execute teaching strategies* to capitalize on success and remedy failures.

Of course, the teacher's basic assumptions about reading and learning to read will affect ongoing, informal assessment at every stage. Because of their basic assumptions, Charlotte's and Matthew's students will engage in different activities and lessons to some extent, and what can be observed by the teacher depends to a large extent on the nature of the activity. But even when Charlotte and Matthew make the same observations, they are likely to interpret them differently, and having different interpretations, they are likely to adopt different teaching strategies.

In the remainder of this chapter, I will refer to many of the discussions presented earlier in the book and call attention to the fact that assessment is inherent in nearly all parent-child and teacher-student interactions where the adult is attempting to enhance the child's communicative or literate performance.

Early Childhood

The collaborative efforts at communication engaged in by parents and young children can be seen from a perspective of ongoing, informal assessment including observing, interpreting, and executing a teaching strategy. In Chapter 2 there are four parent-child dialogues under the headings "Observing Children Using Language." These dialogues are each followed by the discussions of what the child can do with language and the parent's role in the child's communication.

In every case the parents' behavior is determined by their assessment of the child's intentions and abilities. In each of these cases, the assessment is made during real-life attempts at communication, so there is no doubt about the ecological validity of the assessment procedure. Assessment (observing, interpreting, and executing a teaching strategy) is inherent in the concepts of scaffolding, leading from behind, and proximal development.

Primary Grades

In Chapter 3, the traditional concept of reading readiness based on tests of such things as visual discrimination was contrasted with the concept of emergent literacy, where teachers look for evidence of children's catching on to reading and writing, where they convey the concept of printed words to children through repeated oral reading and word pointing and engage in the language experience approach to teaching reading. If you review this discussion from an assessment perspective, you will see that the reading readiness model fails at every step. The observations are based on artificial and often irrelevant tasks—they lack ecological validity. The interpretations are based on a bottom-up, atomistic view of reading and learning to read as are the teaching strategies that follow from them.

The emergent literacy model can also be viewed from an assessment perspective. Encouraging early attempts to "write" and "read," and instilling concepts about words, print, and books are seen as a collaborative effort on the part of the teacher and student that require continuous assessment by the teacher. Here, however, observations are based on tasks that involve books and print in ways appropriate to the proximal development of the students. Interpretations are based on top-down, holistic assumptions, and teaching strategies follow from these assumptions.

Throughout Elementary School

In activities suggested in Chapters 5, 6, and 7, you were asked to role play a student encountering a word recognition problem and a teacher coming to the student's aid by teaching a generalization about phonics (Activity 5.D), syllabication (Activity 5.E), word structure (Activity 6.B), or the use of context (Activity 7.A). If these activities were successful, they should supply you with good examples of ongoing, informal assessments that have ecological validity and where the teaching strategy is consistent with the observation and interpretation.

Goodman's psycholinguistic model of reading, with its miscue analysis (discussed in Chapter 9), is a straightforward assessment procedure. The important contribution of this discussion is not the kind of observations that are made (noting oral reading "errors" is a very old technique), but the interpretations and teaching strategies that follow from them. Some miscues may indicate an overreliance on phonics, while others may indicate inattention to graphic information. Some miscues may indicate a breakdown of comprehension, while others are evidence that comprehension is good.

All the methods, lessons, and strategies for teaching comprehension and study skills discussed in Chapters 10 and 11 have an assessment component inherent in them. From listening to a child's suggestions for words in a cloze exercise, to observing a student "teacher" in a reciprocal teaching strategy, teachers are able to observe, interpret, and initiate teaching strategies, which is the essence of ongoing, informal evaluation. The more such assessment is made on natural reading tasks, and the more teachers' interpretation of observations and their resulting strategies are based on top-down, holistic assumptions, the closer such assessment meets the ideal of ongoing, informal assessment—that it have ecological validity.

SUMMARY

The Informal Reading Inventory is an assessment technique where the student is asked to read a series of passages of increasing difficulty orally and silently. Through observing the child's word recognition errors in oral reading and his or her performance on comprehension questions, the examiner determines the child's independent, instructional, and frustration levels of reading. Through performance on comprehension questions on passages read to the child, a capacity level is also determined. The "levels" are determined by the level of the basal reader from which the passages are chosen.

Creating an Informal Reading Inventory involves choosing passages at each level that are representative and that are of the appropriate length. Comprehension questions are written, and teacher's copies of the materials are prepared with the passages, questions, and scoring and evaluating aids.

Administering an Informal Reading Inventory involves recording oral reading performance and administering the oral reading comprehension test questions, the silent reading passage, and the silent reading comprehension questions. Through a combination of evaluating the errors in oral reading and the answers to the comprehension questions, the students' levels are determined, which is the stated purpose of the Informal Reading Inventory. However, the insights gained through recording children's oral reading performance, their answers to comprehension questions, and through observing other difficulties during oral and silent reading, should give the examiner leads on what to teach and what strategies to use in teaching. This may, in fact, be a more important reason to use Informal Reading Inventories.

Administering published reading inventories may help both in constructing and learning to administer an Informal Reading Inventory.

Informal diagnostic assessment occurs continuously in a classroom. I refer to this as ongoing, informal assessment. Teachers *observe* students engaged in reading tasks. They *interpret* their observations, and they *execute teaching strategies* based on their observations and interpretations. Ongoing, informal assessment possesses two highly desirable characteristics of diagnostic assessment. The observations are done while the students are engaged in normal reading tasks. This gives the assessment "ecological validity." And, second, teaching strategies grow out of the assessment.

Ongoing, informal assessment occurs not only in school, but it is evident in parents' interactions with very young children. Assessment is inherent in the concepts of scaffolding, leading from behind, and proximal development.

The reading readiness model of beginning reading was contrasted with the emergent literacy model in terms of ongoing assessment. The reading readiness model was criticized because tasks children engage in are so often irrelevant to "natural" reading. The emergent literacy model, however, continues with the collaborative teaching and learning that is evident in parent-child interactions. Collaborative teaching depends on ongoing, informal assessment.

I referred to discussions from Chapters 4 to 12 and pointed out that here too teachers engage in ongoing, informal assessment in discovering and addressing students' problems with word recognition, comprehension, and study skills.

FOR FURTHER READING

Cardarelli, A. F. (1988). The influence of reinspection on students' IRI results. *The Reading Teacher, 41*(7), 664–667.

Duffelmeyer, F. A., & Duffelmeyer, B. B. (1987). Main idea questions on Informal Reading Inventories. *The Reading Teacher, 41*(2), 162–169.

Duffelmeyer, F. A., & Duffelmeyer, B. B. (1989). Are IRI passages suitable for assessing main idea comprehension? *The Reading Teacher, 42*(6), 358–363.

Glazer, S. M., Searfoss, L. W., & Gentile, L. M. (Eds.). (1988). *Reexamining reading diagnosis: New trends and procedures*. Newark, DE: International Reading Association.

Harris, L. A., & Lalik, R. M. (1987). Teacher's use of informal reading inventories: An example of school constraints. *The Reading Teacher, 40*(7), 624–631.

Henk, W. A. (1987). Reading assessments of the future: Toward precision diagnosis. *The Reading Teacher, 40*(9), 860–873.

Johns, J. L., Garton, S., Schoenfelder, P., & Skriba, P. (Compilers). (1977). *Assessing reading behavior: Informal reading inventories*. Newark, DE: International Reading Association.

Johnson, M. S., Kress, R. A., & Pikulski, J. J. (1987). *Informal reading inventories*. Newark, DE: International Reading Association.

Johnston, P. (1987). Teachers as evaluation experts. *The Reading Teacher, 40*(8), 744–748.

Johnston, P. H. (1983). *Reading comprehension assessment: A cognitive basis*. Newark, DE: International Reading Association.

Paratore, J. R., & Indrisano, R. (1987). Intervention assessment of reading comprehension. *The Reading Teacher, 40*(8), 778–783.

Pikulski, J. J., & Shanahan, T. (Eds.). (1982). *Approaches to the informal evaluation of reading*. Newark, DE: International Reading Association.

Valencia, S., & Pearson, P. D. (1987). Reading assessment: Time for a change. *The Reading Teacher, 40*(8), 726–733.

Wittrock, M. C. (1987). Process oriented measures of comprehension. *The Reading Teacher, 40*(8), 734–737.

CHAPTER 14

Individual Differences: Factors That Influence Learning to Read

No two individuals are exactly alike. In the discussion of reading readiness in Chapter 3, it was pointed out that individuals differ in many ways and that some of the characteristics on which people differ may be relevant to their success in learning to read while others may not be. The color of a person's eyes has no bearing on his or her potential to learn to read. The quality of his or her eyesight may have.

Many characteristics of individuals have been investigated for possible relationships with success in learning to read. These characteristics have been classified in many different ways in books written for specialists in teaching reading and language to severely delayed students. For example, Brown (1982) reviews psychological, neurological, physiological, and sociological factors related to reading difficulties. Harris and Sipay (1985) treat cognition factors, physical and physiological factors, and cultural factors. Bloom and Lahey (1978) identify "clinical syndromes": hearing impairment, childhood aphasia, mental retardation, and emotional disturbances (schizophrenia, psychosis, and autism) and what they term "specific abilities" such as visual and auditory memory.

Several of these characteristics will be discussed in this chapter, but no attempt will be made to present an exhaustive review of the literature. The discussions of those characteristics that are presented will be guided by the following objectives: (1) to familiarize classroom teachers with characteristics that affect learning to read so that they can make intelligent referrals to the appropriate specialist and make intelligent judgments about whether their referrals are appropriately acted upon, and (2) to familiarize readers with some controversies that surround the diagnosis and classification of these characteristics and the educational consequences of these diagnoses and classifications so that they can discuss these matters intelligently with parents and other professionals.

INTELLIGENCE

Measuring Intelligence

Intelligence is the capacity for reasoning and understanding and similar forms of mental activity. There is no doubt that people vary in this capacity, but *measuring* this capacity is an enterprise that is fraught with questions, doubts, and pitfalls.

History of IQ Testing. In this section a brief history of the measurement of intelligence (IQ testing) will be presented to arrive at an understanding of what an IQ test score means and what it is believed to measure.

Throughout history there have been references to the fact that some people are quicker to learn than others. The words *smart, quick, clever, brilliant, witty, keen,* and *bright,* on the one hand, and the words *slow, dull, dense,* and *stupid,* on the other, attest to the fact that judgments of the capacity for intelligence are commonplace among even the least sophisticated people.

Binet's Rationale for IQ Testing. Around the turn of the century, the French government became interested in setting up special schools for individuals who would not benefit from ordinary public schooling. Government officials were reluctant to ask teachers to identify slow learners or retarded children because they were afraid teachers would unconsciously (or perhaps consciously) identify troublesome children as children in need of special schools and fail to identify truly slow children who were cooperative. Instead they turned to Alfred Binet (1857–1911), a psychologist who had been studying individual differences and mental ability, to devise a test that would identify children who would not be likely to profit from regular schooling.

Binet experimented with test items ranging from simple tasks such as pointing to one's own head, ear, and nose to complex tasks such as figuring out what time it would be if the large and small hands of a clock placed at five minutes to three were reversed—and then explaining why it would be impossible to reverse them precisely.

Experimenting with different questions and different-aged children, Binet created test items that could be answered by most 11-year-old children but not by most 9-year-old children, test items that could be answered by most 9-year-old children but not by most 7-year-old children, and so on. His first test consisted of several items that one would expect children to answer at age 3, age 4, age 5, and so on through age 13. The questions were put in order from easy to difficult.

The Concept of Mental Age. By asking questions calibrated according to Binet's method, one can determine where a child ceases to be able to answer. One can then speak of a child's "mental age" as the age associated with the most difficult questions the child was successful in answering. One could speak of a child as having a mental age of 7, for example, if he or she answered questions that 7-year-olds typically could answer, but failed to answer questions 8-, 9-, or 10-year-olds could typically answer.

It would not matter whether the child was actually 5 or 15. His or her mental age would be determined from the highest level of questions that were answered correctly. Binet's test and the mental age that could be derived from it gave school authorities what they felt was a better guide for identifying children who needed special schooling than teachers' opinions on this matter.

Terman's Concept of "Intelligence Quotient." By 1916 Binet's test had been translated into English and revised by Louis Terman (1877–1956) so that it could be used with an American population. Terman published the test under the title Stanford-Binet. Terman extended two of Binet's ideas. First, he devised his test so that each item was assigned a certain number of months' credit. By multiplying the number of items successfully answered by the number of months assigned to each item, a child's mental age could be reported in terms of years and months.

Second, knowing a child's mental age gives one no sense of whether he or she is a fast or slow learner unless one knows the child's actual age. Making judgments about a child's learning facility from his or her mental age always *implied* a comparison of the individual's mental age and the actual age. Terman made this comparison explicit by expressing the relationship between mental age and chronological age (actual age) as a ratio or quotient. He referred to this as the intelligence quotient or IQ.

$$\frac{\text{Mental age}}{\text{Chronological age}} \times 100 = \text{Intelligence quotient}$$

A child who is 10 and has a mental age score of 10 is assigned an intelligence quotient of 100 because

$$\frac{10}{10} \times 100 = 100$$

A child who is 10 and has a mental age of 12 is assigned an intelligence quotient of 120 because

$$\frac{12}{10} \times 100 = 120$$

A child who is 10 and has a mental age of 8 is assigned an intelligence quotient of 80 because

$$\frac{8}{10} \times 100 = 80$$

A More Current Concept of Intelligence Quotient. As a result of advances in statistical sciences and study of ''normal distribution'' of characteristics in a population, some test scores are converted to IQ scores through a different arithmetic, but the rationale behind IQ scores remains the same. An individual's performance in answering questions on a test is compared with the performance of large numbers of others who are very nearly his or her own age. If an individual's score equals the average score for others the same age, the IQ is determined to be 100. If the score is below the average score for others the same age, the IQ is determined to be below 100. If the score is above the average score for others the same age, the IQ is determined to be over 100. Just how much over or under 100 an individual's IQ score is determined to be depends on how much higher (or lower) the score was compared to the average score for others the same age.

An Interesting Sidelight: The Whole/Part Controversy. Just as it is debated whether reading readiness, word recognition, and comprehension are better thought of as general, global affairs or whether they are better thought of as consisting of many separate parts that come together to make up the whole, there are two views of what is measured by an intelligence test.

One view is that intelligence tests measure a general factor and that in performing any intellectual task, a person calls on this general factor (or ''G'') plus knowledge or skill peculiar to the task. Therefore, people good at some things will tend to be good at most things simply because part of their performance on all tasks relies on their general intelligence. Charles Spearman (1863–1945), an English psychologist and a contemporary of Binet is the best known proponent of this global view of intelligence.

A second view is that intelligence is composed of separate and independent factors such as ''spatial ability,'' ''numerical ability,'' ''verbal meaning,'' and ''inductive reasoning.'' In this view, a person could have ample capacity for knowledge and skill dealing with spatial ability and limited capacity for inductive reasoning (for example). This view of the nature of intelligence is known as the *primary mental abilities* theory of intelligence. The best known proponent of this point of view is the American psychologist L. L. Thurstone (1887–1955).

Definition of ''Normal'' Intelligence Test Score.   Because tests are never perfect and because people's test performance is never perfect, one cannot assume that if a person's IQ score is over 100, he or she is a ''fast learner,'' or if the IQ score is under 100, he or she is a ''slow learner.'' Most experts consider IQ scores between 84 and 116 to be ''normal.'' About 70 percent of the population falls into this range. About 15 percent falls above this range and 15 percent falls below it.

Two Interpretations of IQ Test Scores.   IQ test scores indicate the extent of knowledge and skill relevant to school success that an individual has acquired at a given point in time. There are two ways to interpret the fact that children who are the same age have acquired differing amounts of knowledge and skill that are relevant to school success.

The ''Potential'' Interpretation. One interpretation is that the children differ in potential to learn. The assumption is that all children have roughly the same experiences, but that some of the children learn a great deal from these experiences because they are good learners—have a great potential for learning—while others learn little from these experiences because they are poor learners—have less potential for learning.

The "Rate of Learning" Interpretation. If a child has acquired more knowledge and skill that is relevant to school success than the average child the same age, then one assumes that his or her rate of learning has been faster than that of the average child. Conversely, if a child has acquired less knowledge and skill that is relevant to school success than the average child the same age, then one assumes that his or her rate of learning has been slower than the average child.

IQ test scores yield an estimate of the rate of learning of past achievement. It is presumed that a measure of rate of past learning is a good predictor of rate of learning in the near future. Therefore, to the extent that one can trust IQ scores, one can expect children with low IQ scores to learn less in the same amount of time than children with high IQ scores, or for children with low IQ scores to take more time to learn the same amount as children with high IQ scores.

The Use of IQ Test Scores in Planning Teaching Strategies

Carroll's Model of School Learning. Carroll (1963) proposed that school learning depends on five elements: (1) aptitude, (2) ability to understand the instruction, (3) perseverance, (4) opportunity, and (5) quality of instruction. Carroll defined three of these five variables in terms of time.

1. *Aptitude:* the amount of time needed to learn the task under optimal instructional conditions
2. *Ability to understand instruction:* the quality indicated by IQ test scores.
3. *Perseverance:* the amount of time the learner is willing to engage actively in learning
4. *Opportunity:* time allowed for learning
5. *Quality of instruction.*

Carroll argues that, by increasing the amount of time devoted to learning, three factors are enhanced—aptitude, perseverance, and opportunity—and that ability to understand instructions can be compensated for by quality of instruction.

Carroll's Model of School Learning takes that quality believed to be measured by IQ tests into account, but it is referred to in an effort to promote successful learning and teaching rather than as a method of explaining failure or classifying students.

Mastery Learning. Bloom (1971) developed the concept of mastery learning. For skills that are sequential and limited in number, such as instant recognition of graded lists of sight words (Harris & Jacobson, 1972, or Fry, 1972, for example), Bloom proposed that there should be no relationship between aptitude and mastery if all students are given enough time to learn.

Bloom suggests that in a mastery learning situation children who need extra help generally require only 10–15 percent more time to master the material. He suggests having children in triplets or pairs working on specific tasks—usually related to errors made on tests (Alper, 1982).

Individual tutoring is also suggested as a way of eradicating differences in achievement. Ellison, Harris, and Barber (1968) reported that two 15-minute periods per day of tutoring, first grade students improved the reading achievement of all the students—but it was most beneficial to slow learners, thereby closing the gap between children with high and low aptitude as measured by an IQ test.

Bloom also found that tutoring eradicates the relationship between aptitude and achievement. Bloom's tutors were not experienced teachers. He attributes their effectiveness to the one-to-one relationship where instruction is tailored to the student and where the tutor apprehends the pupil's misunderstandings immediately (Alper, 1982).

It is important to notice the qualifications Bloom places on the content of a mastery learning curriculum; the items of content of a mastery learning curriculum must be sequential and limited in number. It is important to notice too that the citations referring to mastery learning experiments deal with primary reading instruction. Beginning reading instruction frequently deals with outer aspects of reading, that is, skills that are sequential and limited in number such as basic sight word lists, the consonant letter-sound relationships, clues to vowel sounds, and so on. One would expect, then, that much of the beginning reading curriculum would be conducive to mastery learning techniques.

However, there are inner aspects of reading as well—reading as a thought-getting process, reading as reasoning. These aspects of reading do not lend themselves readily to sequencing, although some hierarchical schemes for comprehension have been proposed. Furthermore, these aspects of reading are not limited in number. The skill and the knowledge necessary to master the inner aspects of reading are open-ended, and therefore they do not conform to the assumptions about the content of a mastery learning curriculum. Lack of facility on these kinds of tasks does not appear to be remedied by simply increasing time in instruction. The quality of instruction and the child's involvement in the enterprise are of paramount importance.

The Use of IQ Test Scores to Label Students

Throughout this chapter the term *IQ score* has been used rather than *IQ,* and reference has been made to a person's *IQ score* rather than to his or her *IQ.* This may be considered a slightly unusual use of the word *score,* since a *score* (or *raw score*) usually refers to the number of items a person answered correctly on a test. However, to refer to a number derived from a test as an *intelligence quotient* or *IQ* seduces many people (even people who know better) into thinking that this number represents the "amount of intelligence" of the test taker in some straightforward and infallible way. This is a fallacious and dangerous assumption. Using the term *IQ score* is intended as a constant reminder that this number is ultimately derived from a test score; it is not some mystical quantity.

IQ Scores May Change.   There are dangers inherent in interpreting IQ test scores as indicators of general brightness. In the first place such interpretation implies more faith in the infallibility of the tests than is warranted by the facts. The same person may achieve different scores on IQ tests administered at different times in his or her life. It is for this reason that schools are often reluctant to report IQ scores to parents or students, and it is why attempts are sometimes made to ban IQ testing altogether (Green, 1975).

IQ Tests Do Not Attempt to Measure All Kinds of Intelligent Behavior.   A second reason why it is not legitimate to interpret IQ test scores as indicators of general brightness is that IQ tests, by design, do not attempt to measure all kinds of intelligent behavior. IQ tests are devised and used to predict achievement in school. Questions are invented and tried out for IQ tests with that purpose in mind. If test makers discover that students who are successful in school tend to answer a particular item correctly and students who are unsuccessful in school tend to answer that particular item incorrectly, the item is kept in the test. If research shows that this is not true of an item, the item is removed from the test.

There are many kinds of very useful knowledge that have no apparent relevance to success in school. For a 10-year-old raised in Aspen, Colorado, to be able to step outside, listen to the crunch of the snow under his boot, and tell a tourist what kind of wax to put on his skis for that day is certainly useful knowledge, and it demonstrates a kind of intelligence. For a 12-year-old to test a batch of boiling fudge by dropping samples into cold water and to know precisely when to remove the fudge from the heat is certainly useful knowledge, and it demonstrates a kind of intelligence. But since these kinds of skills and knowledge, and numerous other kinds of skills and knowledge, have no apparent relevance to school success, there is no attempt to measure them on IQ tests.

The Use of IQ Test Scores to Excuse Reading Failure

Rosenthal and Jacobsen (1968) popularized a concept called "the self-fulfilling prophecy." They reported that when children were identified as having high intelligence, they were treated differently by teachers and achieved higher test scores than similar students who were not identified as having high intelligence. This study is often cited by critics of IQ testing who believe that the self-fulfilling prophecy works *against* students who score low on IQ tests. The danger is that if teachers are led to expect students to be dull and incapable, they expect less of the students, and the students may put forth less effort.

The Use of IQ Test Scores for Evaluating Student Progress

However, IQ scores are useful to the reading teacher for evaluation of student progress. As an evaluator, a teacher may reasonably ask the question "Does this child's reading progress reflect his or her potential?" To answer this question an assessment of the child's reading performance and an estimate of the child's learning potential (such as an IQ score) are necessary. The use of the IQ score as an estimate of potential has two legitimate applications. One has to do with students who are exceptionally slow learners; the other has to do with children who appear to have the potential to be exceptionally fast learners.

The original aim of the French government in 1904, to identify children who would not profit from usual classroom instruction, is still a valid aim and use of IQ tests. When teachers' observations or an IQ test administered in a classroom reveals a child who is suspected of being a very slow learner, the child is usually referred to a psychologist who administers one or more individual IQ tests to determine whether the child qualifies for special placement. Very slow learners require more individual attention than it is possible to give in a regular classroom.

On the other hand, a child whose progress is average or slow is sometimes discovered to have a remarkably high IQ test score. Such discoveries may suggest that the child's performance may not be helped by additional time for learning, but that perhaps motivation or methods are at fault; special placement for such students is also sometimes indicated. This too is a legitimate use of IQ testing.

VISUAL ACUITY: THE TEACHER'S ROLE

Visual defects can seriously affect reading achievement; however, specialists in severe reading problems agree that visual defects are not a major cause of reading failure (Brown, 1982; Stauffer et al., 1978, for example). The reason why vision is not a major cause of reading failure may be that most schools conduct routine screening procedures to detect vision defects, and the most common visual defects can be corrected with eye glasses. However, some schools do not conduct screening procedures, or the procedures may be inadequate; therefore, the classroom teacher may detect symptoms of visual defects that are not discovered elsewhere.

Since problems of visual acuity are in the province of professional vision specialists, the classroom teacher appears to have only two responsibilities in dealing with suspected problems:

1. To recognize symptoms of visual defects.
2. To refer students with suspected visual defects to appropriate school personnel for testing and/or referral to a professional vision specialist.

However, sometimes "referral to appropriate school personnel" means to recommend that the child be given a visual screening test, and (as it has already been stated) such tests may not be adequate. Therefore, the classroom teacher should have some knowledge of the visual conditions that are associated with reading problems and some knowledge of the kinds of examinations necessary to detect these conditions. With this knowledge the teacher can make an informed judgment as to whether his or her referrals are adequately acted upon.

Symptoms of Vision Problems

Fry (1977) and Stauffer et al. (1978) suggest that the following may be symptoms of vision problems:
1. Unusual appearance of the eyes
    a. Redness
    b. Tearing

    c. Bloodshot appearance
    d. Crustlike accumulation near the eye
2. Unusual habits
    a. Rapid blinking
    b. Twitching
    c. Facial contortions
    d. Holding a book unusually close
    e. Holding a book unusually far
    f. Avoiding tasks requiring near-point vision
    g. Having to get closer to chart or chalkboard
    h. Squinting
    i. Closing one eye
    j. Rubbing eyes
3. Complaints by the student
    a. Dizziness, fatigue, pain, or nausea after reading
    b. Distortion of what is seen

Referrals and Follow-up

In the past many schools relied on the Snellen Chart for visual screening. Subjects are placed 20 feet from the chart that contains rows of letters of decreasing size. The subject is asked to read the rows, and his or her performance is compared with that of "normal" persons. A rating of 20/20 means the person is normal—he or she can see at 20 feet what a normal person can see at 20 feet.

The Snellen Chart is inadequate for identifying many vision defects that may cause reading problems. It is ironic that, in fact, the Snellen Chart is most effective in detecting nearsightedness, and nearsightedness, unless it is extreme, is not a source of reading difficulty. Moderately nearsighted people have no difficulty in focusing on printed materials at normal range. (Nearsighted children may have trouble focusing on the chalkboard or charts from a distance, however, and therefore, there is an educational reason to have this condition corrected if it is discovered.)

If a teacher detects symptoms of a vision problem, he or she should refer the child to the appropriate school personnel (usually the school nurse) and inquire whether the child has been tested for visual acuity in each eye at near point and far point and for binocular coordination at near point and far point. This kind of examination can be done by a nurse or a reading clinician, but it requires an expensive device. Two such devices in wide use are the Keystone Vision Screening Test and the Ortho-rater. When adequate screening reveals a suspected vision defect, parents are requested to have a professional visual examination.

AUDITORY ACUITY: THE TEACHER'S ROLE

There is a distinct probability that children who suffer from hearing loss will experience difficulty in learning to read. Some writers (Bond, Tinker, & Wasson, 1979) estimate that as many as 5 to 10 percent of our population has a hearing handicap.

Like problems in visual acuity, problems in hearing acuity are in the province of professional hearing specialists. It is the responsibility of the classroom teacher to recognize symptoms of hearing loss and to refer students with suspected hearing loss to the appropriate school personnel for testing and/or referral to professional hearing specialists.

Symptoms of Hearing Loss

The following may be symptoms of hearing loss:
1. Unusual appearances of the ear
    a. Inflammation
    b. Discharge
2. Unusual habits
    a. Inattention
    b. Frequent requests to have speech repeated
    c. Poor articulation; omitting or distorting sounds, particularly /s/, /z/, /ch/, /sh/, and /th/
    d. Turning one ear toward speaker
3. Complaints by student
    a. Ringing in the ear
    b. Dizziness
    c. Inability to hear

Brown (1982) reports that children who experience hearing loss are often thought to be dull. He suggests that such children do not respond normally to things going on around them, and when others do not realize they cannot hear, they attribute the lack of response to dull-wittedness. Brown further observes that children who experience hearing loss are often thought to be remarkably good-natured. He suggests that, as a defense against being scolded for inattention, they smile and pretend to hear. This defense may give others the impression that the children are exceptionally serene.

Hearing Loss and Difficulty in Learning to Read

Results of a hearing test are reported on two dimensions: frequency (or pitch) and intensity (loudness). Frequency is measured in cycles per second and intensity is measured in decibels. A device called an audiometer is used to check a child's ability to hear tones at "normal" intensity. If a child fails to hear a tone, the intensity is increased to the point where he or she can hear it. The amount the intensity must be increased is recorded as a "decibel loss." A child with normal hearing is reported to have zero decibel loss.

The speech range of the human voice is between 100 and 4,000 cycles per second, and therefore this range is of particular interest to reading teachers. Children who experience significant loss in the frequency range of the human voice are likely to experience speech and reading difficulty. Losses among hearing impaired children often occur in the high-frequency range of the human voice, which prevents them from hearing consonant sounds. This accounts for the poor articulation of children with severe hearing loss.

It is frequently recommended that a phonics approach to learning to read be avoided in favor of a whole word approach in teaching reading to children with hearing loss, but there is no experimental evidence to support that advice.

Referrals and Follow-up

Children suspected of experiencing hearing loss should be referred to the appropriate school personnel for testing on an audiometer. Children who are found to have hearing loss of 15 to 20 decibels in the frequency range of the human voice should be referred to a hearing specialist for further evaluation.

Children with significant hearing loss present unique teaching-learning problems and are, therefore, often placed in special education classes or are tutored in speech and reading by specialists. Such specialists ought to consult with and advise classroom teachers on ways to compensate for children's handicaps when part of a child's time is spent in regular classrooms.

NEUROLOGICAL AND EMOTIONAL FACTORS

Symptoms of Neurological Impairment

Some symptoms that may indicate neurological difficulties are

1. Extreme difficulty in paying attention.
2. Frequent distraction by unobtrusive stimuli.
3. Problems of gross and fine motor coordination.
4. Confusion in perception of stimuli.
5. Inconsistent response to stimuli.
6. Hyperactivity.

Symptoms of Emotional Disturbances

Some symptoms that suggest emotional disturbances are

1. Gross and sustained impairment of emotional relationships.
2. Apparent unawareness of personal identity.
3. Preoccupation with a few objects.
4. Extreme reaction to any change in routine or environment.
5. Excessive, diminished, or unpredictable responses to sensory stimulus.
6. Illogical anxiety.
7. Unaccounted for dysfunction in body movements.
8. Retardation of mental functioning.
9. Loss of, lack of, late development of speech (Creak et al., 1961).

Referrals and Follow-up

When teachers suspect that a child is suffering from neurological or emotional impairment, referral should be made to the school psychologist. Psychologists are usually trained and qualified to administer individual intelligence tests and tests of perception.

Individual evaluation by a psychologist can be used to determine whether a neurological or psychiatric evaluation by an M.D. is indicated.

The Difference Between Classifying Children and Getting Advice on How to Teach Them.   The purpose of such evaluation is to give the teacher or education specialist guidance on how teaching strategies should be altered to compensate for or to circumvent the neurological or emotional difficulties that appear to be interfering with learning. Unfortunately such evaluations often result in classifying the child in terms of a clinical syndrome (mentally retarded, autistic, aphasic, neurologically impaired, and so on) and nothing more. Such classifications tell the teacher practically nothing about how to teach the child to read.

There is reason to believe that children classified in different categories have similar educational needs, and the same child may be classified in different categories by different clinicians. Bortner and Birch (1969) observed that children classified as emotionally disturbed and children who were classified as brain damaged showed very similar patterns of intellectual organization. These authors question the educational value of the two separate categories.

Another study (Rosenthal, Eisenson, & Luckau, 1972) showed that the medical, psychological, and language evaluations were remarkably similar for children classified as hearing impaired, aphasic, and experiencing a maturational lag. Kessler (1966) observed that "The same child may receive four or five different diagnoses, as successive clinics diagnose the case in terms of their special area of interest and experience" (p. 260).

The point is that a teacher who is prompted to refer a child for examination for suspected neurological or emotional impairment should not be satisfied if he or she is given only a label with which to classify the child. The teacher should ask the specialist (neurologist, psychiatrist, and so on) *how* the child's impairment interferes with learning to read and obtain suggestions as to how the child should be taught in a way that will best circumvent or overcome the child's impairment.

The Difference Between Referring Children for Diagnosis and Making a Diagnosis.   Making medical diagnoses and giving advice based on such diagnoses is unwise and unethical (and probably illegal) for a person who is not a medical doctor or a licensed member of a medically allied profession. Teachers who suspect that a child has a condition whose diagnosis and treatment are in the province of a specialist should refer the child to the appropriate school personnel (nurse, psychologist, and so on). The teacher should describe the child's appearance, behavior, or complaints that led the teacher to suspect a problem. Teachers should *not* suggest (particularly to parents) that a child may have a severe hearing loss or brain damage or any other ailment that the teacher is not certified and licensed to diagnose.

SUMMARY

IQ tests were developed by Alfred Binet for the purpose of identifying children who would not profit from ordinary public schooling. Binet devised questions that could be answered by most 13-year-olds, but not by most 12-year-olds; questions that could be answered by most 12-year-olds, but not by most 11-year-olds; and so on. He then administered these items to children and took note of the most difficult items the subject was capable of answering. He referred to the age group associated with these items as the child's mental age. Terman introduced the idea of comparing people's mental age with their chronological age. He referred to this comparison (mental age divided by chronological age) as an intelligence quotient.

There are two theories about the nature of intelligence. Spearman is associated with the notion that intelligence is general quality, a global affair. Thurston is associated with the idea that intelligence is a collection of primary mental abilities and that an individual can possess one to a high degree and others to a lesser degree.

IQ tests are designed so that individuals who are successful in school will be successful on the tests. Items are tried out, and if successful students answer them correctly and unsuccessful students answer them incorrectly, they are used in the test. If this condition is not met, they are not used on the test. As a result, IQ tests are designed to measure knowledge and skills that are relevant to school success.

There are two interpretations of what success on an IQ test means. The "potential" interpretation is that people who do better than their age mates have a better learning facility. The "rate of learning" interpretation is that people who do better than their age mates learn more quickly than others.

Carroll's Model of School Learning suggests that increasing the time devoted to instruction and improving the quality of instruction can compensate for difficulty in understanding instruction (which is the quality Carroll believes is reflected in IQ test scores).

Bloom argued that skills that are sequential and limited in number could be mastered by all students if they are given enough time to learn. However, much of reading performance, such as comprehension or application of knowledge, cannot be easily sequenced or enumerated, and so increased time alone will not bring all students to the same level of performance. Attention to student involvement with instruction and the quality of instruction become crucial as curriculum goals become less atomistic and more global.

Although there is no question that IQ test scores frequently identify very able students and those who are not so able, the scores themselves should be treated very carefully. Individuals may earn different scores on different tests or at different times. Second, IQ tests are not designed to measure knowledge and skills that are not related to school success. A person may possess knowledge and skills that are very valuable in many life situations and still earn a low score on an IQ test.

A frequently cited danger of the use of IQ test scores is that they are sometimes used to explain failure rather than to plan teaching strategies. Deciding from IQ scores who will be able to learn to read is very likely to promote self-fulfilling prophecies.

IQ test scores play an important part in the decision to remove a child from a normal classroom and place him or her in a class for special students. The child's performance on an IQ test administered by a qualified psychologist is a valuable and necessary source of information in making this very serious decision. IQ test scores may also be instrumental in discovering gifted students whose talents have gone unnoticed.

Defects of visual acuity can affect reading achievement. Although most schools conduct routine visual screening, this screening is sometimes inadequate. A teacher may suspect that a child is experiencing visual acuity problems because of the appearance of the child's eyes or because of unusual habits or complaints from the child. In such cases the teacher should refer the child to the school nurse or appropriate professional and follow up on the referral. An adequate examination involves tests for acuity and binocular coordination at near point and far point.

Defects of auditory acuity can affect reading achievement. Symptoms of hearing loss involve the unusual appearance of the child's ears, unusual habits, and complaints from the child. Hearing loss frequently causes a child to be unable to distinguish between consonant sounds. Teachers should refer children whom they suspect of suffering from hearing loss to the appropriate school personnel and follow up on the referral. An adequate examination involves testing on an audiometer. Children whose tests reveal a 15- to 20-decibel loss in the frequency range of the human voice should be further evaluated by a hearing specialist.

Neurological impairment and emotional disturbances may affect reading achievement. Children who exhibit symptoms that may be indicative of neurological impairment or emotional disturbance should be referred to a psychologist, who may, in turn, refer the child to a medical doctor. In following up such a referral, the teacher should be aware that classifying a child as autistic or mentally retarded or brain injured (to name a few classifications) is not the goal of the referral. The purpose of the referral is to discover *how* the child's condition interferes with learning so that teaching strategies can be devised that will circumvent the child's difficulties.

CHAPTER 15

Organization for Instruction and Reading Programs

One of the greatest challenges that a beginning teacher faces is classroom management. One of the greatest complications of classroom management is the practice of having different children doing different things at the same time. This practice has a particularly long tradition in teaching reading.

If a principal walked into a room and found the entire class engaged in the same activity—listening to the teacher, doing the same written assignment, engaging in a discussion, and so on—he or she would probably not find that remarkable unless it were a reading lesson. Then the principal might ask why the children were not working individually or in groups and whether most of the instruction was not done with individuals or in groups. Of course, the teacher might have a perfectly good reason why the children were working together as an entire class. The point is that the tradition of children working in groups during reading lessons is so well established that one expects to find it. Why reading is taught in groups is the topic of the next section.

REASONS FOR GROUPING FOR INSTRUCTION

Some Activities Require Small Groups

Large groups are undesirable for some reading learning activities. Whereas the teacher might read to the class and each child is engaged in listening, in some activities a child is engaged only while he or she is performing. The teacher may, for example, have individual children read orally so he or she can evaluate the children's use of context for word recognition or their pronunciation or phrasing or expression. One likes to think that the other children are profiting by "following" the oral reading in their own books, but only one person is involved in the primary purpose of the lesson; that is the person doing the oral reading. It makes sense then to do oral reading in groups of one (ideally) or in small groups so that the children engaged are fully involved as much of the time as possible.

But if the nature of the lessons were the only factor calling for grouping, children could be assigned to groups arbitrarily. One could take any six children for an activity calling for a small group. The only concern would be that every child be included in *some* group covering the activity in question. That is not the case. Other factors must be considered.

Small Groups Are Formed on the Basis of Students' Characteristics

Achievement Levels.   Whatever the approach to reading instruction, teachers will find differences in how much individuals have learned almost as soon as instruction begins. Teachers who use the phonics- or skills-emphasis approach (described in Chapter 3) will discover that on the third or fourth day some children know the names of the letters taught thus far and recognize words that begin with the sound they were taught to associate with the letters. Other children know the names of the letters but do not recognize words that begin with the sound they were taught to associate with the letters.

Still other children do not know the names of the letters that have been taught. And, of course, some children will know some letter names (but not all) and will recognize some words that begin with the sounds they were taught to associate with the letters (but not all).

Teachers who use the language experience approach (described in Chapter 3) will soon have children with dozens of words in their ''word banks'' and will have begun to work on phonic relationships. At the same time there will be children in the class who have few or no words in their word banks.

By the middle grades, it is not unusual to find children who compare with seventh graders and children who compare with third graders on standardized tests of reading achievement in the same classroom. Some of the instruction and materials designed to challenge the children with the highest reading achievement scores will be too difficult for many children in the class, and some of the reading instruction and materials designed to develop the reading skills of the children with the very lowest achievement scores will be of little value to many of the children in the class. Thus, differences in levels of achievement give rise to grouping for instruction in reading in the typical classroom.

Skill Deficits.   At early stages most members of a class may be progressing satisfactorily with a given program, but the teacher will notice that not all individuals have mastered all the skills presented. Children who demonstrate roughly the same level of achievement differ from each other in terms of individual skills. One or two children may not know the names of all the letters. Others may not recognize the recommended sight words for their level. Another child may not use context to aid in word recognition. Two or three children may have particular problems with oral reading; a few may rely too heavily on phonics; others may fail to grasp main ideas.

Children who demonstrate the same general achievement level are often divided into groups for instruction in specific skills that are lacking or underdeveloped considering the children's general level of ability.

Interests.   An important component of effective instruction is to enlist the students' desire to learn. One way to enlist a child's desire to learn to read is by incorporating reading instruction into activities in which children are already interested. A short time ago one might have thought that girls could be motivated to learn to read through reading recipes and romance novels, that boys could be interested in learning to read through reading automobile repair manuals and Westerns, and that inner-city black children would be inspired to learn to read through reading the works of Langston Hughes and Richard Wright.

Fortunately, such stereotyping is no longer fashionable, but the principle behind these assumptions is still valid. If students see learning to read as something that will satisfy an immediate need, they are apt to learn to read. As a result, individual reading in the school or classroom library is encouraged, and groups are formed around common interests such as sports, hobbies, or careers. Therefore, individual interests give rise to forming groups for reading instruction. Groups formed around interest are very common in whole language classrooms.

USING BASAL READERS

The most widely used strategy for teaching reading in this country is to use a basal reading program (with or without supplementary materials and techniques) and to employ a three-group plan. Box 15.1 represents one week of such a plan for a first grade class. Box 15.2 represents one week of such a plan for a fifth grade class. Through commenting on these plans and suggesting ways in which they could be elaborated upon, many of the common practices of grouping and the reasons for these practices will be presented in this section.

Grade-Level Achievement

These plans are based on the assumptions that different achievement levels exist in classrooms and that by grouping children by achievement levels, one minimizes the risk that children will be asked to perform tasks that are too difficult for them, and therefore impossible, or too easy for them, and therefore a waste of time and effort.

In the first grade plan (Box 15.1), the groups were presumably formed as the children move at differing rates through the preprimers (usually three or four books), the primer, and finally grade 1 levels. In the fifth grade plans (Box 15.2), one presumes that the children in the groups are capable of mastering the reading tasks included at different levels of the basal reading series. In most classrooms this would mean that the middle group was using the grade-level reader designed for the grade, while the low group was using a lower-level reader and the high group was using a higher-level reader.

For example, in a fifth grade, one might find the low, middle, and high groups, using third, fifth, and sixth grade readers. However, it is not unusual to find that the high group is using the grade-level reader designed for the grade while the middle group is using a lower level and the lower group is using an even lower level. In such a fifth

BOX 15.1 THREE-GROUP PLAN FOR SECOND HALF OF FIRST GRADE.

Preprimer Group	Primer Group	First Reader Group
9:10–9:40 Work independently on teacher-made letter and word discrimination practice.	*Teacher conducts* lesson preparing for new story. Follows suggestions in teacher's guide for basal reader.	Silent reading of materials selected by pupils.
9:40–10:10 *Teacher conducts* lesson preparing for a new story. Follows suggestions in teacher's guide for basal reader.	Nonreading activity (Work independently on additional facts.)	Nonreading activity (Work independently on additional facts.)
10:10–10:40 Cut pictures from magazines for an initial consonant sound word file.	Work independently on duplicated worksheets: using letter-sound associations and context clues to recognize words.	*Teacher directs* lesson to check comprehension of last story. Selected oral reading.
10:40–11:10	Recess	
11:10–11:40	*Teacher directs* the whole class in developing an experience story about the school bake sale. Students practice reading the experience story.	

BOX 15.2 THREE-GROUP PLAN FOR FIFTH GRADE.

Red Book Group	Blue Book Group	Green Book Group
9:55– *Teacher conducts* 10:15 discussion and oral reading of story read on previous day.	Silent reading of story introduced on previous day.	Silent reading and written comprehension check of materials from supplementary program (self-corrected).
10:15– Workbook exercises 10:35 related to story.	*Teacher conducts* discussion and oral reading of story.	Plan dramatization of story with group chairperson or teacher aide.
10:35– Independent reading period.		
10:55 *Teacher conducts* individual conferences and works with a group of students who have a common oral reading problem.		

grade classroom, the three groups might be using second, third, and fifth grade readers. Depending on the diversity of achievement levels of the groups, any graduated sequence of grade-level readers is possible.

The Desirable Number of Groups

Classes are most often divided into three groups for reading instruction. Three is more of a practical number than an ideal number.

Fewer than Three Groups.   Beginning teachers are often advised to start with two groups: one wants to gain experience in teaching groups while being responsible for the entire class from the start, but attempting to maintain more than two groups at the start may be too ambitious.

One plan is to divide the class into children who can perform satisfactorily with on-grade materials and those who cannot. Materials are chosen at the average achievement level for the low group and at on-grade achievement levels for the high group. Soon the teacher can begin to plan individual or small group activities for the least able children in the low group and for the most able in the high group. These groups can meet during periods when the whole class is engaged in an activity where they can work independently of the teacher, such as in the whole class activity from 10:35 to 10:55 in Box 15.2.

As soon as the class is functioning well in two groups and the children have learned to work together in groups and to work independently without the teacher's guidance, a third group can be formed for the least able or most able students.

More than Three Groups.   At the center of a busy, productive classroom there must be a competent, stable, and steadfast presence: a teacher who enables children to learn and function securely in a setting where there is considerable activity and opportunity for distraction. Schemes that are beyond the teacher's competence to manage threaten the teacher's ability to assure the students of security. It is for this reason that permanent groups numbering more than three are the exception. This tension between the practical limitation on the number of groups the teacher can manage and the desirability of forming many groups for many reasons leads to the next observation about the plans in

Boxes 15.1 and 15.2. Namely, permanent groups and special-purpose groups exist simultaneously.

Temporary Groups Formed Around Needs

While membership in a permanent group should afford each child consistent instruction that is challenging but not too difficult, there are numerous reasons to form special-purpose groups that will last for a short duration. In a fifth grade, for example, one may discover three children in the low group who do not recognize the Dolch Basic Sight Vocabulary. These three children might be paired with three other children for practice in recognizing basic sight words on flash cards.

Additionally, two children from the middle group and one child from the high group may have similar oral reading problems; for example, they may read very rapidly and substitute words that are spelled like words in the text but do not make sense in the text. This group of three might meet with the teacher or with an aide to practice oral reading for meaning, reading with expression, and becoming aware of the role of context in word recognition. As soon as the child accomplishes the goal for which such a group is created, he or she is no longer a part of that group. As soon as all the children in the group have accomplished the goal of the group, the group no longer exists.

Temporary Groups Formed Around Interests

Children with different levels of achievement and different skill strengths can comprise groups based on common interest. Children interested in a common topic might find books written at levels each child can read and come together to discuss their books or write reports on their topics. For example, as a result of a social studies unit, some children in the class might become interested in finding out what it must have been like to be a child in colonial America. Children with varying levels of reading achievement might read from biographies of people who lived in colonial America and construct a list of differences under the headings: clothing, food, education, work, and so on.

Movement Between Groups

A point that is not obvious from Boxes 15.1 and 15.2 but that is fundamental to the assumption on which grouping for reading instruction is based is that teachers should always be alert for indications that a student should be moved from one group to another.

Initially, groups are formed on the best information available such as test scores or the teacher's evaluation of one or two oral reading performances. A child's performance from day to day in reading lessons sometimes indicates that he or she has been placed in a group that is too challenging or not challenging enough. Long-term observation of a child in learning situations is a more valid measure of achievement than are test scores or other assessment procedures, and teachers should not hesitate to move students from group to group as a result of such observations. A student's pace of achievement may pick up or slacken as well. This too can be the cause of a change in group assignment.

Naming Groups

Because of the time-honored practice of forming groups around basal reader levels, publishers of basal readers do not spell out the grade levels on textbooks or accompanying materials. This is done to avoid embarrassing children who are assigned to a reading level below their grade. Although even the youngest students know almost immediately which groups are doing the most advanced and least advanced work, there is no reason for them to know the precise level of material each group is using.

This leads to the question of what one should name the groups. Calling them "high, middle, and low" or "ones, twos, and threes" or "A's, B's, and C's" to reflect their actual order is a constant and unnecessary reminder of their rank order. Reversing the order (calling the lowest group "highs" or "ones" or "A's") does not deceive anyone. Calling them by the color of their book or the name of their book, however, clearly identifies the groups in a neutral and matter-of-fact way.

Whole-Class Reading Lessons

There are two reasons why whole-class reading lessons should occur regularly. One reason for regular whole-class reading lessons is that one does not want to lose sight of the value of a learning community. Separating children who know more from children who know less and separating children who lack a skill from children who have that skill prevents children from learning from each other.

The second reason why whole-class activities occur regularly is that some activities will benefit everyone in the class, and there is nothing about the activity that makes a large group inefficient. In a seventh grade class, for example, a teacher may conduct a lesson on Latin roots and their meanings with the entire class. Students might read and discuss a weekly current events magazine as an entire class in fifth grade. A first grade teacher may conduct a lesson on telling when word pairs begin with the same or different sounds with the entire class. A teacher may read passages from books to the entire class in preparation for selecting books for individual reading. When such activities will benefit everyone in a classroom, there is nothing to be gained by repeating the activity two or three times in small groups.

Children Work Independently.   One of the most striking facts revealed by Boxes 15.1 and 15.2 is that when teachers group children for reading instruction, children are expected to work independently of the teacher more times than they are engaged in a lesson conducted by the teacher. This kind of independent activity takes two forms: children work together as a group on some project or lesson, or they work individually at silent reading, work sheets, work book pages, and so on. Both kinds of activities take a great deal of planning on the part of the teacher and a great deal of understanding and cooperation on the part of the students.

The Approach Is Eclectic.   Traditional three-group plans shown in Boxes 15.1 and 15.2 are typically used with basal readers. It has been pointed out earlier in this book that most widely used basal reading series are eclectic—that is, they draw on both the empiricist tradition and rationalist traditions. Therefore, within the traditional three-group plan where a basal reader is the core of the program, one is not surprised to find a teacher doing an experience story (a holistic, top-down approach) and working on letter recognition using flash cards (an atomistic, bottom-up approach) on the same day.

Teachers who adopt such an approach do not feel compelled to draw phonics lessons out of children's individual successes with experience stories as they would if they adhered dogmatically to a top-down philosophy. On the other hand, teachers do not feel obligated to avoid words having letter-sound correspondences that have not been mastered in isolation as they would if they adhered dogmatically to a bottom-up philosophy.

Teachers using eclectic approaches view the teaching activities associated with top-down and bottom-up traditions as complementary rather than as contradictory. They see the experience story and the phonics lesson as two ways of entering into the process of learning to read. As teachers move toward whole language, they never abandon attention to skills when they appear to need attention. However, they are less and less apt to teach a skill without first observing a particular child in trouble because she or he is lacking in the skill.

Organizational plans that emphasize individual instruction tend to rely on rigidly rationalist, top-down assumptions *or* on rigidly empiricist bottom-up assumptions. As a result individualized reading programs fall into two easily identified categories: (1) Programs based on the rationalist assumption that learning to read is a holistic process where learners will acquire different skills in different order in essentially a top-down fashion, and (2) programs based on the empiricist assumption that learning to read is an atomistic process where students will learn approximately the same skills in the same order (but at different rates of speed) in essentially a bottom-up fashion.

An individualized instruction program based on rationalist assumptions and programs based on empiricist assumptions are discussed in the following sections.

INDIVIDUALIZED READING INSTRUCTION BASED ON HOLISTIC, TOP-DOWN ASSUMPTIONS

The Individualized Reading Program

The Individualized Reading Program as articulated by Veatch (1978, originally published in 1966) incorporates the rationalist language experience approach (described in Chapter 3) into a wider program. Soon after children have begun to learn to read what they themselves have written (or have taken part in writing), they are encouraged to investigate books and to choose books to read. The teacher meets with children individually to see what kind of progress they have made and where they are encountering difficulties.

The teacher then plans and carries out instruction. If more than one child is having the same problems, the instruction is carried out in groups. Some groups meet regularly with the teacher for direct instruction. Other groups work independently. The nature of what needs to be learned determines whether the children receive direct instruction or work independently. An occasional time for "sharing" enables children to come together as a whole class. A six-step plan for an Individualized Reading Program is shown in Box 15.3.

BOX 15.3 A SIX-STEP PLAN FOR AN INDIVIDUALIZED READING PROGRAM.

I. Selecting
Child chooses materials on two criteria
A. He likes it,
    and
B. He can read it.

II. Planning—child decides
A. To read the book for himself. When finished he goes back to step I,
    or
B. To prepare this book for an individual conference with the teacher.

III. Independent work
A. Reads.
B. Proceeds with preparation for individual conference such as
    1. Intensive study to retell story to teacher.
    2. Develop a report to share with class.
    3. Polish a skill from another curriculum area, such as writing a composition based on the story.

IV. Individual conference: an intensive, individual session on a one-to-one basis with the teacher. Teacher keeps detailed records of each conference. Instruction is based on these records.

V. Organization of groups. Based on observations made in individual conferences, teacher forms groups.
A. Groups for instructional purposes are based on specific clear-cut needs that require continuing direct instruction from the teacher.
B. Groups for independent work are based on specific clear-cut needs that do not require continuing direct instruction from the teacher.

VI. Sharing follow-up and evaluation
1. Children tell about the book they read—preferably during time allotted in addition to the regular reading period.
2. Children complete work book pages and similar materials chosen by the teacher to meet the needs of individuals and groups.
3. During individual conferences, children receive immediate evaluation of their progress. Reports to parents of student progress are based on records kept by the teacher.

As each child completes the six-step plan, he returns to step I to begin the cycle anew.

From *Reading in the Elementary School*, 3rd ed., Jeannette Veatch (John Wiley, 1978). Reprinted by permission of the author.

Assumptions Underlying the Individualized Reading Program.   Veatch (1978) argues the merits of this program in terms of how well the program provides for 20 assumptions she makes about learning to read (Box 15.4). These assumptions reflect "the profoundly revolutionary character of the instructional program" (p. 5). Box 15.3 shows the basic procedure one might follow in implementing an Individualized Reading Program.

The assumptions upon which this Individualized Reading Program relies are rationalist assumptions:

—Reading is viewed as a holistic enterprise.
—The teacher makes instruction decisions for each child based on the child's performance in working with whole stories.
—One presumes that the child will find a book he or she can understand in a general way.
—Problem areas or separate skills where instruction is needed are discovered within the framework of the child's total understanding.

BOX 15.4 TWENTY ASSUMPTIONS UNDERLYING THE INDIVIDUAL READING PROGRAM.

1. Reading must be taught as part of all of the other language arts.
2. Spelling is as important in learning to read as it is in learning to write.
3. Reading and spelling are but two sides of the same coin.
4. Children learn to read better and faster when they are free to pace their own growth, seeking help when necessary.
5. The act of reading must center on the child, with the materials used of secondary importance.
6. Children's own language is a valuable source material for reading instruction.
7. Individual differences are met by teaching individuals one by one.
8. Classroom efficiency is enhanced when groups are organized upon an identified need, problem, difficulty, or interest.
9. There is no established rank order of reading materials.
10. There is a series of progressions or developmental stages that can be recognized and provided for with a variety of materials.
11. Reading growth results when a pupil commits himself to a piece of material.
12. As reading is a personal act, the choice of material is an expression of self.
13. The human factor of personal commitment of the pupil will enhance reading growth when matched by the ability of the teacher to change and adapt procedures on the spot.
14. Not all skills need be taught to every child, nor in identical sequence to more than one child.
15. Progress may be steadily cumulative, but it may also be apparent in great leaps and bounds.
16. Skills are gained during the act of reading and not before it.
17. There is no clearly established sequence of skills for all children.
18. There is no single piece of material that meets the needs of every pupil in any given class.
19. While silent reading is central, oral reading is placed in a prominent position with a purpose.
20. The love of books and reading is encouraged when loved books are read.

From *Reading in the Elementary School*, 3rd ed., Jeannette Veatch (John Wiley, 1978). Reprinted by permission of the author.

—The order in which the child will learn skills is not thought to be predetermined.
—One expects the child to play an active part in discovering how to read and in identifying his or her own problem areas. (See Activities 15.A and 15.B.)

The Individualized Reading Program Presents Five Exceptional Demands

1. Because one does not expect to teach all skills to every child, nor does one expect to teach skills in the same order to every child, the teacher must possess extraordinary diagnostic skill and knowledge of the reading and learning process to determine what the child knows and what he or she needs to learn and how to teach what he or she needs to learn.
2. Because each child is working on his or her own project and individual conferences are at the heart of the program, classroom management becomes a central issue. Students must know how to work on their own and they must work independently enough so the teacher can engage in conferences without interruption.
3. Because each child is working individually and at the same time children are

ACTIVITY 15.A COMPARING THE INDIVIDUALIZED READING PROGRAM WITH THE INTERACTIONAL PERSPECTIVE OF LANGUAGE LEARNING

Compare Veatch's 20 assumptions underlying her Individualized Reading Program (Box 15.4) with

A. Generalizations about parent-child interactions that facilitate language development in Chapter 2: intentionality, proximal development, collaboration, internalization, and continuous development.
B. Conclusions drawn from the literature on emergent literacy (Chapter 3, page 76).

ACTIVITY 15.B COMPARING THE INDIVIDUALIZED READING PROGRAM WITH THE WHOLE LANGUAGE APPROACH

Review the following whole language teaching methods. Compare these discussions to Veatch's six-step plan for an Individualized Reading Program (Box 15.3).

1. Matthew Nicholson's teaching method (Chapter 1)
2. Marla McCurdy and Irene Silo-Miller teaching "The Writing Process" (Chapter 11)

grouped for instruction, extensive and accurate records must be kept on each child.

4. Because it is expected that the teachers will frequently have read the book the child has read, successful teachers must be familiar with dozens and dozens of books.
5. Because the method is based on a child's ability to do a great deal of reading from a great number of books, a large classroom library is necessary. (See Activity 15.C.)

ACTIVITY 15.C WEIGHING THE DIFFICULTIES

Compare these five exceptional demands of the Individualized Reading Program with the points raised in Chapter 2 "Why Whole Language?"

Do the reasons for the whole language approach given in Chapter 2 apply as well to the Individualized Reading Program?

Individualized Reading Program "Packages." Publishers of educational materials have produced packages of books and materials that help to solve some of the problems posed by using the Individual Reading Program. See Figure 15.1. One can purchase sets of approximately 50 to 100 books with additional materials designed to make the programs manageable. These materials may include summaries of books, vocabulary lists, comprehension checks, outlines for structuring individualized conferences, suggestions for forming skills instruction groups, suggestions for individual and group projects based on interests related to individual books, and forms for keeping records of students' progress and needs. Books in these packages are usually similar in level of difficulty. (See Activity 15.D.)

Figure 15.1. The Random House reading program.

ACTIVITY 15.D EXAMINING A "PACKAGED" PROGRAM

I. Examine one (or both) of the following programs:

Barrett, F. L., Holdaway, D., & Lynch, P. (1989). *Book center*. Richmond Hill, ONT: Scholastic-TAB Publications.

Cochran, E., Coleman, D., Cortright, A., Forman, D., & Reid, E. (1970). *Random House reading program*. New York: Random House.

  A. Compare them to the six-step plan (Box 15.3) and the 20 assumptions (Box 15.4) presented by Veatch (1966).

  B. Discuss ways in which these packages might alleviate the five problems inherent in an Individualized Reading Program cited in the last section.

II. Notice that as these packages become more structured and detailed, the "open-ended" flavor of this approach gives way to more controlled and predetermined choices of both reading materials and in the conduct of conferences.

  A. Discuss which of Veatch's 20 assumptions (Box 15.4) might possibly be violated by highly structured and detailed packages.

  B. How might the quality of conferences described in Chapter 11 by compromised by these packages?

  C. How might teachers use these packages in such a way as to maintain the spirit of the Individualized Reading Program and the whole language approach and reap the benefits of the aids offered in these packages as well?

Middle School Reading Workshops

Nancie Atwell (1987) advocates a reading program for the upper grades, or middle school, that shares many of the assumptions of Veatch's Individualized Reading Program. The Reading Workshop is based on the assumption that students need three "basics" in order to continue growing as readers: time, ownership, and response.

Time. Reading Workshops begin with a 10- to 15-minute "mini-lesson" followed by 30–60 minutes of sustained silent reading. Sustained silent reading means that each student reads his or her own book without interruption in an atmosphere conducive to silent reading. For the first 10–15 minutes of sustained silent reading, the teacher circulates, supervises, solves problems, and sees that everyone is on task. For the remaining 20 to 40 minutes, the teacher reads a book of his or her own silently along with the students. These regular periods of sustained silent reading give the students one of the basics—*time*.

Ownership. Students choose their own reading material from the library (classroom, school, or public), bookstores, or from home. The individual teacher may set limits. For example, a child who brings *Lady Chatterley's Lover* might be told to read that book at home if he or she wants to read it at all. But within a very broad range, the children are given genuine choice, which is the second basic—*ownership* over their reading material.

Response. Each student has a spiral-bound notebook called a "dialog journal" or "literature log." Students are required to write in their journals one letter a week to the teacher or to another student. These letters express the students' response to the literature they are reading. They tell why the students chose a particular book and what they liked or did not like and why. The person addressed responds to these letters in the student's journal, and the journals are returned. Dialog journals or literature logs provide the third basic—*response*.

Through the Reading Workshop, students read a great deal and learn from their experiences, from each other, and from their teacher. Through reading and responding to the students' literature logs, the teacher learns where students need guidance and exposure to new ideas. Mini-lessons that are taught at the beginning of each workshop session grow out of what the teacher learns from students' literature logs. Topics for mini-lessons range from how to choose a book to why authors sometimes use pseudonyms.

Rules are established for choosing books and stating exactly what behaviors are expected of students during reading workshops and what behaviors will not be tolerated. One-third of the student's grade is based on how well students observe these rules. Minimum requirements are set for entries into the literature logs, and the teacher's responses in the logs continually guide and evaluate the students' efforts in writing useful responses to the selections they read. Mini-lessons are often used to guide students to making more useful responses to their reading. One-third of students' grades are based on their literature logs. One week in each term the teacher has individual conferences with students to set goals and to evaluate progress on previously set goals.

One-third of students' grades are based on evaluation of progress toward goals that are set and evaluated during conferences.

Comparing Individualized Reading Program and Reading Workshop Approaches

Atwell's Reading Workshop and Veatch's Individualized Reading Program appear to share many assumptions about teaching and learning reading, but there are dissimilarities as well.

The Individualized Reading Program pays more attention to word recognition and comprehension skills than does the Reading Workshop. There are probably two reasons for this. The Individualized Reading Program was introduced at a time when bottom-up, skills-emphasis approaches were very widely accepted, and the program is addressed to younger children who presumably need instruction in word recognition and comprehension skills.

The Reading Workshop, on the other hand, was introduced at a time when top-down, holistic approaches are very widely accepted. Atwell has been much bolder in her assertion that teaching atomistic word recognition and comprehension skills is of limited value, if not counterproductive. Second, her program is addressed to readers beyond the intermediate grades who have presumably acquired such skills.

INDIVIDUALIZED METHODS BASED ON ATOMISTIC, BOTTOM-UP ASSUMPTIONS

Throughout this book I have been comparing the teaching strategies of Matthew and Mary, on the one hand, to the teaching strategies of Charlotte and Donald, on the other. I have argued that the whole language approach presents exceptional demands upon the teacher but that it is more consistent with what we know about parent-child interactions that facilitate language development, the concept of emergent literacy, and the good effect of giving learners control over their learning. I have argued that Matthew and Mary are on the right track. They are well grounded in the use of the eclectic basal reader and are working toward the whole language approach. I have implied, by contrast, that I do not subscribe to the methods of Charlotte and Donald—both bottom-up, skills-emphasis teachers—because their methods are inconsistent with what we know about parent-child interactions that facilitate language developments, the concept of emergent literacy, and the good effect of giving learners control over their learning.

People who accept this reasoning will find individualized programs based on atomistic, bottom-up assumptions even more objectionable than the teaching strategies attributed to Charlotte and Donald. I feel, however, that it is important to describe them here so that teachers will have an accurate understanding of the programs and materials they will find in the schools.

Linear Programmed Instruction

Figure 15.2 shows a page from *Programmed Reading* (Buchanan & Sullivan Associates, 1989), which is a reading series based on principles of programmed instruction. Programmed instruction is based on the premise that learning can be divided into small

Figure 15.2. A page from a program based on principles of linear programmed instruction.
(*Source: Programmed Reading,* Book 6 [Phoenix Learning Resources, 1989].)

units and organized into a sequence so that when students learn the sequence, they will have learned the whole concept or skill. Typically, each bit of instruction is presented in a frame. The frame presents instruction and a question (or questions). In a paper-and-pencil program, the answers are available to the students. The students read the instructions, answer the question(s), and check their answer(s). When answers are wrong, students presumably reflect on why their answer was wrong and why the correct answer was right and proceed to the next frame. Because the learner proceeds from frame to frame in a fixed order, such programs are called *linear programs*.

Although linear programmed instruction such as *Programmed Reading* clearly qualifies as reading instruction that is engaged in by individuals independently of the teacher, there is some question as to whether it qualifies as individualized reading instruction. Although children with varying degrees of achievement may start at different points in such a program and some children will proceed from frame to frame faster than others, there is no provision made for tailoring the skills, methods, and materials to fit the needs and interests of individual children. All children receive the same instruction in the same order, though not necessarily at the same time.

Branching Programmed Instruction

Computers make it possible to add another dimension to programmed instruction. Rather than moving relentlessly from frame to frame, the computer makes it possible to present the "next" frame if the child answers the question(s) correctly for a given frame or to present an alternative frame if the child answers the question(s) incorrectly. See Box 15.5 for an example of part of a programmed lesson designed to review the recognition and meaning of prefixes. This is an example of a branching program.

Branching Makes Individualization Possible. The capability for branching presents enormous possibilities for programming instruction. A pretest can be presented and frames can be selected and sequenced on the basis of wrong answers on the pretest. A wrong answer on any frame can call up remedial lessons. A series of correct responses on the remedial lessons can return the learner to the original flow of frames.

The Motivation Factor. At a recent convention where electronic aids to classroom instruction were on display, a salesperson described the computer as "an electronic workbook." Although that remark was meant to be a selling point, perhaps it should be taken as a warning.

Conceptualizing and implementing branching instructional programs for the computer calls for a great deal of ingenuity. The program designer must construct pretests to uncover problems, design series of frames to teach whatever is necessary to overcome the problems, and design alternate frames to be presented when wrong answers are given. While programming the computer—complete with graphics in full color—is fascinating work, sitting at a terminal typing in short answers to questions that can be only right or wrong may be far less interesting. As the novelty of video games and home computers wears off, what appears to be a highly motivating activity may become far less motivating.

Beginning in the middle grades, it may be useful to share the work of analyzing

BOX 15.5 AN EXAMPLE OF A COMPUTERIZED BRANCHING PROGRAM DESIGNED TO REVIEW THE RECOGNITION AND MEANINGS OF COMMON PREFIXES

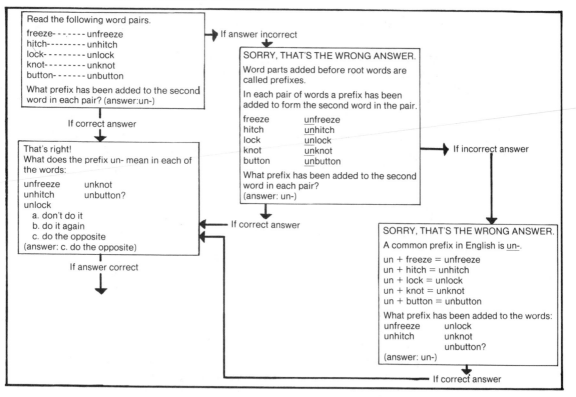

the reading process into steps and constructing lessons and mastery tests related to these steps with students. Students ought to be brought into the instruction designs and programming as early as possible in their learning careers. They will not only share in the fun; they may learn more.

Because computers have been introduced into a large number of classrooms only recently, one can only speculate as to whether they will result in more rapid learning and higher levels of accomplishment. This will undoubtedly be a tremendously active area of research and development for some time.

Skills Management Systems

Skills management systems are based on the following four premises:

1. That it is useful to think of the reading curriculum as a series of skills.
2. That the skills can be divided into small sequential steps.
3. That through testing, one can determine which steps a child has mastered and which steps are beyond his or her present achievement level.

4. That through careful management of instruction, no child will be asked to work on skill steps that she has mastered or that are beyond her present achievement level.

Skills management systems are constructed in the following way.

1. Reading experts analyze the reading process into elements or cognitive skill categories such as word recognition, vocabulary, comprehension, and study skills.
2. These elements are divided and subdivided until skills are identified that represent small sequential steps.
3. These steps are translated into behavioral objectives—objectives stated in a way that specifies the student behavior that signifies mastery of the skill.
4. Tests are devised that will determine whether the child has mastered the skill.
5. Materials are found or created that teach each skill.
6. Methods of keeping records are devised, forms for keeping records are produced, a management system is created.
7. Lists of objectives, tests of objectives, materials for teaching objectives (or references to places where such materials can be found), record forms, and a manual describing how the whole system is to be operated are published.

The most widely recognized skills management system is the Wisconsin Design for Reading Skill Development (Otto & Askov, 1973). This program consists of six "program elements" (see step 1 earlier): word attack, comprehension, study skills, self-directed reading, interpreter reading, and creative reading. Box 15.6 shows a portion of the skills (there are approximately 300 skills in all six elements) in the word attack element. Figure 15.3 shows a criterion-referenced test for recognizing root words. Figure 15.4 shows the teacher's resource file for teaching the variant sounds associated with the letters *c, s,* and *g.* The teacher is presumed to have access to a well-supplied materials center where he or she can find the lessons listed on the resource file to use with students who fail criterion-referenced tests on skills.

Through administering tests and keeping records, the teacher can determine which skill each child has mastered and which skill each child needs to work on. Groups can be formed and materials selected to teach each skill.

The typical instruction cycle for a skills management system is depicted in Figure 15.5. The groups formed in a skills management system are similar to the temporary groups formed on the basis of skills deficits in the more traditional grouping exemplified in Boxes 15.1 and 15.2. A child may be included in one group for a word attack lesson, another group for a comprehension lesson, and a third for an interpretive reading lesson.

Exceptional Demands Inherent in Skills Management Systems

Setting Learning Objectives.   While skills management systems enumerate and order skills to some extent, there are sometimes numerous skills at the same level in a skill element. For example, on the Wisconsin Design Word Attack Profile Card (Box 15.6)

BOX 15.6 FOUR LEVELS OF WORD ATTACK SKILLS IN THE WISCONSIN DESIGN FOR READING SKILL DEVELOPMENT

Level A:

Rhyming words
Rhyming phrases
Shapes
Letters, numbers
Words, phrases
Colors
Initial consonants
  All A skills

Level B:

Sight vocabulary
Left-right sequence
Beginning consonants
Ending consonants
Consonant blends
Rhyming elements
Short vowels
Consonant digraphs
Compound words
Contractions
Base words
Plurals
Possessives
  All B skills

Level C:

Sight vocabulary
Consonant variants
Consonant blends
Long vowels
Vowel $a + r, a + l, a + w$
Diphthongs
Long and short oo
Middle vowel
Two vowels separated
Two vowels together
Final vowel
Consonant digraphs
Base words
Plurals
Homonyms
Synonyms, antonyms
Independent application
Multiple meanings
  All C skills

Level D:

Sight vocabulary
Consonant blends
Silent letters
Syllabication
Accent
Unaccented schwa
Possessives
  All D skills

From *The Wisconsin Tests of Reading Skill Development*, K. Kamm (Learning Multi-Systems, Inc., 1972).

there are 18 word attack skills included in level C. It is not suggested that skill 1 must be mastered before skill 2, or even that children master all of level A before level B.

Record Keeping.   In skills management systems, record keeping becomes one of the teacher's greatest concerns. Teachers must administer and score tests, assign materials, and keep track of a wealth of materials. All this demands keeping records. The demand for excessive record keeping is often cited as a nearly insurmountable problem in using this approach. Carner (1973) reports that "Some teachers who initially embraced the systems approach later were inclined to feel trapped by it. The amount of testing, observational note taking and general bookkeeping has, in some cases, approached the point of absurdity."

Figure 15.3. Criterion-referenced test for recognizing root words from the Wisconsin design for reading skill development. (*Source: The Wisconsin Tests of Reading Skill Development*, K. Kamm [Learning Multi-Systems, Inc., 1972].)

1. fished   Ⓐ fi *shed*
   Ⓑ *fish* ed
   Ⓒ f *ish* ed

2. jumps   Ⓐ jum *ps*
   Ⓑ *jump* s
   Ⓒ *jum* ps

3. running   Ⓐ *ru* nning
   Ⓑ run *ning*
   Ⓒ *run* ning

4. that's   Ⓐ *that* 's
   Ⓑ t *hat* 's
   Ⓒ th *at* 's

5. going   Ⓐ *go* ing
   Ⓑ *goin* g
   Ⓒ go *ing*

6. washer   Ⓐ *was* her
   Ⓑ was *her*
   Ⓒ *wash* er

Schmidt (1982) reported on a large school system where a skills management approach was employed where there was a test for each of 525 skills taught in grades kindergarten through 8. He estimated that a teacher with a class of 30 or 35 students might administer grade and record scores for between 2,000 and 3,000 tests in a single year. The teachers' union in this district negotiated a reduction in the number of reading skills (and therefore in the record keeping related to these skills) to 273—one-half the original number. Schmidt commented drolly that "There was no more than a flicker of scientific interest in the fact that the number of 'essential' reading skills could be reduced by half through the collective bargaining process" (p. 39).

Assumptions Underlying Programmed Instruction and Skills Management Systems

Programmed instruction and skills management systems are based on the bottom-up, empiricist tradition. This tradition focuses on the outer aspects of reading (letter names, phonics, word recognition); it emphasizes parts (phonics, word structure, separation of comprehension skills); it assumes that mastery of parts leads to the complicated activity known as reading; it focuses on a predetermined sequence of steps; it presumes the reader is relatively passive.

Linear programmed instruction takes this presumption to an extreme. There is no

Word Attack—Level C
◼◼◼◼ Skill 2: Consonants and Their Variant Sounds ◼◼◼◼
Objective

Given words containing variant sounds of *c*, *s*, and *g* (e.g., *cake-city*, *sit-trees*, *go-giant*), the child indicates whether the underlined letters in given pairs of words have the same or different sounds.

Printed Materials

Allyn and Bacon, *Arrivals and Departures*, teacher's ed. (1968), pp. 60-61, 174; 192, 330.

Allyn and Bacon, *Believe and Make-Believe*, teacher's ed. (1968), p. 59.

Allyn and Bacon, *Fields and Fences*, teacher's ed. (1968), p. 298.

Allyn and Bacon, *Finding the Way*, teacher's ed. (1968), pp. 100, 102-103, 234.

Allyn and Bacon, *Letters and Syllables*, teacher's ed. (1971), pp. 31-36, T12.

Allyn and Bacon, *Magic Windows*, teacher's ed. (1968), pp. 119, 270, 281.

Allyn and Bacon, *Open Gates*, teacher's ed. (1969), pp. 116, 138-139.

Allyn and Bacon, *Our School*, teacher's ed. (1968), p. 129.

Allyn and Bacon, *Story Caravan*, teacher's ed. (1968), pp. 80, 149.

Allyn and Bacon, *Syllables and Words*, teacher's ed. (1971), pp. T7, T9, 12, 85-88.

Allyn and Bacon, *Town and Country*, teacher's ed. (1968), pp. 52-54, 175-176, 236, 271, 282.

American Book, *And So You Go! Be On the Go! Can You?*, Workbook, teacher's ed. (1968), pp. 35, 71-72.

American Book, *Can You?*, teacher's ed. (1968), p. 52a.

American Book, *Days and Ways*, teacher's ed. (1968), pp. 27a, 27b, 36a, 48b, 71a, 87a, 143a, 151a, 176, 181, 188.

American Book, *Days and Ways*, Workbook, teacher's ed. (1968), pp. 9, 19, 37, 44.

American Book, *Each and All*, teacher's ed. (1968), pp. 62a, 62b, 174, 220.

American Book, *Far and Away*, teacher's ed. (1968), pp. 57a, 57b, 73, 213, 222, 229.

American Book, *Far and Away*, Workbook, teacher's ed. (1968), p. 74.

American Book, *Gold and Silver*, teacher's ed. (1968), pp. 112, 133, 157.

American Book, *Gold and Silver*, Workbook, teacher's ed. (1968), p. 68.

American Book, *High and Wide*, teacher's ed. (1968), pp. 50, 67, 164, 164b, 235.

American Book, *Ideas and Images*, teacher's ed. (1968), pp. 172, 268.

American Book, *Kings and Things*, teacher's ed. (1971), p. 25.

American Book, *Launchings and Landings*, teacher's ed. (1968), p. 71b.

American Book, *Pattern Resources: Phonics Kit A* (1970), nos. 31, 65, 66.

American Book, *Pattern Resources: Phonics Kit C* (1970), nos. 177, 179, 183, 185.

American Education Publications, *Phonics and Word Power, Program 1: Book B* (1965), pp. 19-20.

American Education Publications, *Phonics and Word Power, Program 2: Book C* (1964), p. 6.

American Education Publications, *Phonics and Word Power, Program 3: Book A* (1964), pp. 6, 7.

American Education Publications, *Reading Success Series, Scores 1-6*, teacher's guide (1969), pp. 23, 24.

Benefic, *Reading Laboratory* (1966), Kit 405, card 6.

Continental Press, *Adventures in Wordland E* (1960), pp. 26-27.

Continental Press, *Phonics and Word-Analysis Skills, Grade 3, Part 1* (1968), p. 14.

Continental Press, *Phonics and Word-Analysis Skills, Grade 4, Part 1* (1968), p. 2.

Continental Press, *Phonics and Word-Analysis Skills, Grade 4, Part 2* (1968), p. 2.

Continental Press, *Phonics and Word-Analysis Skills, Grade 5, Part 2* (1969), p. 6.

Economy, *Keys to Independence in Reading*, Grade 4, teacher's manual (1964), pp. 49, 121.

Economy, *Phonetic Keys to Reading*, Grade 1, teacher's manual (1967), pp. 50-51, 70, 109.

Economy, *Phonetic Keys to Reading*, Grade 2, teacher's manual (1967), pp. 24-25, 27-28, 29, 66-72, 75, 130-133.

Economy, *Phonetic Keys to Reading*, Grade 3, teacher's manual (1967), pp. 67, 69, 105-106, 119.

Ginn, *All Sorts of Things*, teacher's ed. (1969), pp. 62, 64, 75, 77, 81-82, 186, 209, 210-211, 226, 314-315, 324.

Figure 15.4. Part of the teacher's resource file for word attack level C from the Wisconsin design for reading skill development. (*Source: The Wisconsin Tests of Reading Skill Development*, K. Kamm [Learning Multi-Systems, Inc., 1972].)

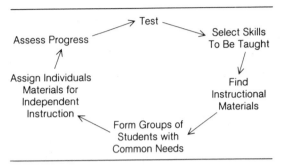

Figure 15.5. Typical instruction cycle for a skills management system.

variation in the order in which skills are presented or the method and materials used to present the skills. Branching programmed instruction permits flexibility, but the presumption that reading instruction can be conceived of as separate skills that can be specified and put in a hierarchical sequence is still central to branching programmed instruction.

Skills management systems rely heavily on the presumption that reading and instruction should be conceived of as separate skills that can be learned in small steps, but there is more flexibility in ordering the skills and in the materials and methods employed in teaching the skills. Once a teacher decides what skill to teach, there are dozens of sources of materials and methods suggested in the teacher's resource file, and there is no strong suggestion that any one skill at a given level must be taught before another. In fact, a lack of criteria for ordering skills instruction and for selecting instructional materials is sometimes cited as a weakness of skills management systems. (See Activity 15.E.)

ACTIVITY 15.E FINDING BIRDS OF A FEATHER AND HORSES OF A DIFFERENT COLOR

BIRDS OF A FEATHER

Compare programmed learning and skills management systems to the idea of reading readiness.

HORSES OF A DIFFERENT COLOR

Contrast the assumptions underlying programmed learning and skills management systems to the generalizations about parent-child interactions that facilitate language development (Chapter 2) and definitions of the whole language approach (Chapter 2).

ORGANIZATIONAL PROBLEMS

Teachers may encounter a variety of difficulties simply because they assume that classroom procedures for using instructional materials are self-evident, when indeed they are not. For example, a teacher who decides to use the *Random House Reading Program* may look the program over, put the materials out, and start the class using them with instructions such as: "Everyone choose a book and answer the questions on the survey card and the vocabulary card." Such a procedure will almost surely result in chaos.

The Teacher's Guide for the *Random House Reading Program* suggests that the program be introduced in several lessons over several days. Lessons include (1) introducing the program, (2) learning about book cards, and (3) learning how to check one's own answers and keep records. Several days later when some children are ready for a book conference, another lesson is suggested to teach the children how to use the skills exercises that are included in the program.

The lesson for learning about book cards takes up seven pages of the Teacher's Guide. It includes directions on how to use the answer sheet, descriptions of each of the five cards, directions on when to answer the questions on the cards, where to put one's answers, what the purpose of each card is, and how or when to sign up for a conference. How to correct answers and record scores are not taken up until the next lesson.

This kind of detail is typical of lessons for the use of basal reading programs, "packaged" individualized reading programs, programmed instruction, and skills-management systems. Such lessons are necessary for the orderly and efficient management of a classroom—but, in fact, even further instruction is necessary.

In each classroom local rules must be established. Children must learn how to conduct themselves when they are included in a group receiving direct instruction from the teacher. They must learn how to conduct themselves when they are assigned to work independently or when they are members of a group working independently of the teacher. Children must know what they are supposed to do, where to find materials they will need, what to do with their work when they have finished, whether or not to correct their own work, to whom to go for help, and what to do when they are finished. A variety of problems arise when teachers do not realize how much a student has to understand to make any plan work.

Problems Arising When Students Do Not Know What to Do

Time on Task Is Diminished.   Berliner (1981) describes the "learning student" as one who "works on an academic task that is designed to result in increased knowledge or skills" (p. 218). Presuming that the teacher has planned tasks designed to increase knowledge and skills for all the children, those children who do not know what to do or how to do it are not learning students. They are students whose time is being wasted.

Tranquility of the Classroom May Be Diminished.   Children who do not know what they are supposed to be doing are likely to engage in behavior that is aimless or disruptive—more often because they are bored than because of malicious intent.

The Teacher's Attention Is Diverted from the Groups or Individuals Who Are Entitled to the Teacher's Attention.   The benefit of teacher-led small groups and individual instruction is that children are given access to the most scarce commodity in the classroom, the teacher's undivided attention. If the teacher is interrupted by children asking for directions or by disruptive behavior in the classroom, the whole reason for small group instruction and individual conferences is defeated.

In observing classrooms, Harvey (1980) found that in low-achieving classrooms the teachers who were teaching small groups were frequently interrupted by students who were supposed to be working independently. In the high-achieving classrooms she observed, teachers working with small groups were rarely interrupted by students not in the group; students working independently understood what they were supposed to be doing, and they understood that the teacher would not tolerate interruption.

The Danger of "Busy Work"

A well-known and often-lamented hazard of grouping for instruction is that children who are working independently are sometimes given activities designed to keep them busy rather than activities designed to teach them or give them practice in some newly acquired skill.

One reason this happens is that teachers are attempting to satisfy demands that sometimes come into conflict. They want to choose the best activity to teach the children what they need to learn next, but, if a teacher works with groups, some activities must be ones that can be done independently. And sometimes a compromise must be struck between what is the best activity and what can be done without the guidance of the teacher. There are two ways to help ensure that the compromise will result in activities that will teach what the children need to learn next.

Using Teacher's Aides and Student Chairpersons.   One is to use a student or teacher's aide as a stand-in for the teacher in a group working independently. This will permit a wider choice of activities for groups working independently. Notice that in Box 15.2 in the second time slot the high group is scheduled to plan a dramatization of a story with a student chairperson or teacher's aide.

However, one should not entertain the notion that groups of students will work together productively because the teacher tells them to or appoints a chairman. Galton and Simon (1980) suggest that both social and intellectual skills are necessary for groups to work independently of the teacher.

> Of primary importance is the children's capacity to challenge each other's contributions, to raise questions and also to reason. These are intellectual skills which can be learned, but of course, they will (or may) not be learned unless teachers regard them as important. Then, for the maintenance of self-sustaining groups, the tasks set need to be structured so as to demand co-operative working, and relevant resources must be provided (Worthington, 1974). Finally, there are certain social skills, for instance a degree of tolerance of each other's idiosyncrasies, a willingness to listen to each other and a certain level of responsible behavior in the absence of an adult; in short, the skills needed to work co-operatively with others on a common task. Such skills, and they are complex, need to be learned, and so taught. (p. 207)

Choosing Materials and Activities from a Coherent Program.   The second way to ensure that independent work is not busy work is to follow suggestions for independent activities from coherent, sequential programs rather than to sample helter-skelter from spirit-duplicated worksheets, workbook pages, and boxes of reading activities. Basal readers and coherent, sequential supplemental reading programs often suggest whole-class activities, small group activities, and activities to be done independently. If these activities are sometimes uninspired, they are at least usually consistent with both the long-term and short-term aims of the reading program. Students working at the appropriate achievement level of such a program are likely to find the suggested independent activities relevant to their small group and whole group lessons and challenging as well.

Using a whole language approach helps to dispell the notion that subjects are taught in rigidly controlled time slots. While the teacher and some children are engaged in reading conferences or lessons, the remaining children might be reading silently, writing, doing spelling, or even participating in speaking and listening activities.

The Quality of Teacher-Student Interaction

British primary schools have had a longer tradition of individualization of instruction, and the nearly exclusive use of individualized instruction is much more frequently found in British primary schools than in schools in the United States. An important factor in the trend toward individualization of instruction in Great Britain was the Plowden Report (1967), which recommended that primary school children should be involved in more discovery learning (or what the British refer to as inquiry-based learning) and that the proportion of higher-order cognitive statements and questions on the part of teachers should be increased. The Plowden Report stated that these objectives could best be accomplished by an increase in individualization of instruction and in students working together and learning from each other in small groups.

However, a study of 58 classrooms in 19 schools over a five-year period (1975–1980) (Galton & Simon, 1980) cast doubt both on the question of whether the recommendations of the Plowden Report have been implemented and on the assumptions of the Plowden Report. Two observations regarding the entire sample of classrooms were that "Grouping appears to be an organizational or managerial device, rather than a technique for promoting inquiry-based learning using collaborative methods. There was, in fact, little co-operative group work in evidence in our sample" (p. 34), and

> the teacher-pupil interaction process does not appear to have a cognitive content; our data indicate that it is largely managerial or instructional in content, having the function of keeping things moving and assisting individual pupils with the completion of their tasks. Paradoxically, there are more questions and statements of a higher cognitive order by the teacher in the whole class situation than in the individualized or group situation. (p. 34)

Whole-class and group instruction is *direct* instruction. Ideally every child is involved with the teacher, although no child receives the benefit of all the teacher's exclusive attention. Teachers addressing whole classes or groups may spend more of their time concerned with cognitive, subject-oriented matters such as letter-sound correspondences or word meanings or comprehension.

Last, whole-class instruction and small group instruction focuses on characteristics that children have in common rather than on characteristics that differentiate them from one another. Individual instruction forecloses on the opportunity of students to learn from one another and detracts from a sense of community.

There are advantages that are unique to both individualized instruction and small group instruction. When teachers engage in either kind of instruction, they ought to consider not only the advantages they are getting, but the benefits of whole-class instruction that they are foregoing and attempt to balance the two.

Advice to the Beginning Teacher

In classrooms one practically never finds a single pattern of organization that does not incorporate some features of other patterns of organization. The basic three-group approach as represented in Boxes 15.1 and 15.2 is, by design, capable of incorporating each of the organizational patterns and methods discussed in this chapter. Teachers might assign programmed materials to an individual or a group formed to work on a common skill deficit. Groups formed on achievement levels might be given mastery tests from a skills management system and assigned individual work or to skills-deficit instruction groups on the basis of such tests. And an Individualized Reading Program or Writing Workshop may be employed one or two days a week—or as the mainstay of the program.

Although the basic three-group plan shown in Boxes 15.1 and 15.2 requires a great deal of knowledge on the part of the teacher and taxes the beginning teacher's managerial and organizational skills, the flexibility and eclectic nature of the plan permit beginning teachers to start with an organization that is realistic, but that gives them experience in whole-class, small group, and individual instruction. As they gain knowledge and experience, they can work toward an Individualized Reading Program or a whole language approach.

To get the best out of small group instruction and individualized instruction, the students need to learn a great deal about the mechanics of the program, what they are supposed to be learning, how they are supposed to learn it, and what their responsibilities are to themselves, their small group, and the entire class. In describing teaching styles, Galton and Simon (1980) single out one teacher whom they obviously admire: "As pupils acquired the desired learning habits, the original formal structure was deliberately relaxed, with the pupils taking increased responsibility for planning their own work on an individualized basis" (p. 38). When teachers are new, one might apply the principle observed here to both teacher and students: as the pupils acquire the desired learning habits and as the teacher acquires more knowledge of the reading process and the learning process and acquires the necessary organizational and managerial skills, the original formal structure is deliberately relaxed, with pupils taking an increasing responsibility in consultation with the teacher for their own learning on an individualized basis.

This does not mean, however, that structure is abandoned. Hansen, a strong advocate of the whole language approach, refers to *structure, order,* and *routine* repeatedly in *When Writers Read* (1987).

> Reading/writing classrooms are tightly structured. They must be. The classroom is full of decision makers, many of whom may be inexperienced and need guidelines. To complicate matters, many of us are new at this kind of teaching and don't know how to organize ourselves. We feel certain about only one thing: The classroom must be orderly. (p. 49)
>
> It bothers me when teachers say that basal-centered classrooms are more structured than those based on response [the whole language approach described in Chapter 11].

On the contrary, if children spend a lot of time reading and sharing books they have chosen, the classroom must be highly organized or it will be a mess. The structure is tight but in a different way than the basal classroom. In a response-based philosophy the teacher not only sets up the routine, she teaches the children to use it. This is probably what I found most difficult to understand and what many teachers find difficult to learn. Initially, when a few children meet to share their books, or a common book or story, the teacher establishes a structure. Every teacher's format will be different, but each teacher decides on a routine and initially adheres to it like Super Glue. If the system calls for children to read aloud a part that "works," then they practice this format until they can do it without the teacher. (p. 125)

SCHOOLWIDE ARRANGEMENTS TO NARROW INDIVIDUAL DIFFERENCES IN READING CLASSES

Classroom Assignment Strategies

Children with Special Needs.   Some children are not placed in regular classrooms or are removed from regular classrooms because they have needs that the classroom teacher is not trained to meet or because the regular classroom is not thought to be the best place to meet their needs. Children who score exceptionally low on achievement tests in reading or children who are observed by teachers exhibiting extraordinary difficulty in learning are sometimes placed in special classrooms or are often removed from regular classrooms for reading instruction. There are also comparatively rare cases of children who have been diagnosed as schizophrenic or autistic or who are blind or profoundly deaf. Such children are often assigned to special classrooms with teachers prepared to meet their needs, or they may be assigned to special reading teachers when they are members of regular classrooms.

Homogeneous Classrooms.   In larger schools, where there is more than one classroom for each grade, students are sometimes assigned to classrooms on the basis of scores on standardized reading tests. For example, if there are 60 third graders, they may be ranked from high to low on the basis of standardized reading test scores and the 20 children with the highest scores are assigned to one classroom, the next 20 to a second classroom, and the next 20 to a third classroom.

Homogeneous Reading Classes.   A variation on homogeneous classroom assignment is to have an entire school have reading during the same time period and to have children leave their regular classroom and report to a reading classroom for reading instruction. This permits one to group by achievement scores across grade level as well as within a grade. For example, in a school that has kindergarten through grade 6 with approximately 30 children per grade, the 90 children in grades 1, 2, and 3 are ranked from high to low on the basis of a standardized reading test and the 30 children with the highest scores are assigned to one classroom, the next 30 to a second classroom, and the next 30 to a third classroom. The same procedure is followed in assigning students to reading classes in grades 4, 5, and 6.

Advantages of Narrowing the Range of Achievement in Reading Classes

Narrowing the range of achievement within reading classes through schoolwide arrangements may permit more whole-class instruction and may require fewer groups within classrooms based on achievement. Each classroom may still have a range of achievement scores, but it may be necessary to use only two levels of a program rather than three. Or using three levels may more truly accommodate the range of levels than when these efforts are not made. When there is a reduced demand for grouping to accommodate different levels of achievement, teachers can devote their energy and organizational skills to grouping for activities that demand small groups for efficiency and to grouping children on the basis of needs and interests.

Problems Arising from Schoolwide Arrangements to Narrow Individual Differences in Reading Classes

Flexibility.   One of the great dangers of all grouping is that children may not be moved from group to group based on performance and need as readily as one would hope. The processes that impede easy movement from group to group within a classroom are exaggerated when the school administration must be involved in the transfer.

The Myth of Homogeneity.   Children with the same score on an achievement test may have very different strengths and weaknesses in areas measured by the achievement tests. Children who have the same number of correct responses on a test have not necessarily responded correctly to the same items. Furthermore, there is no reason to believe that children with the same scores on an achievement test are at all similar in areas not measured by the test. Where students are groups by achievement, teachers sometimes adopt the false notion that the children are the same in every way, and efforts at grouping on needs and interest are diminished rather than increased.

Tracking.   Segregating high achievers from low achievers may have some very undesirable effects. Being placed in low-achievement groups has been shown to have a negative effect on children's self-esteem (Esposito, 1973). Furthermore, identifying children as slow learners and then segregating them from other students may contribute to a self-fulfilling prophecy. This problem is made worse by the fact that school failure is related to economic status. It has been suggested that grouping by achievement segregates economically disadvantaged children and contributes to segregation within society based on income (McDermott, 1977).

Obscuring the Responsibility for Reading Instruction.   Several of the schoolwide plans to group children by ability involve removing a child from his or her regular classroom for reading instruction. Therefore, for most of the day the children are in a classroom with a teacher who is not their reading teacher. This encourages the teacher who has the major responsibility for the children to feel that he or she is not responsible for their reading performance.

This may be a particularly bad situation when low achievers are removed from their classrooms to work with remedial reading teachers alone or in groups of two to five. The child's classroom teacher may feel he or she is not responsible for the child's reading performance, but at the same time, the remedial reading teacher may see as many as 60 students during a week and feel that he or she is supplying *extra* instruction and that the classroom teacher bears the primary responsibility for each child's reading performance. This difficulty was cited as one of several reasons why federal programs to improve the education of inner-city school children met with limited success (Levine, 1982).

SUMMARY

There are two reasons why grouping is a common practice in teaching reading. One reason is that some of the lessons that are necessary or desirable in teaching reading cannot be conducted efficiently with groups as large as the whole class. When the teacher works with fewer children than the whole class, a group has emerged, and the teacher faces the responsibility for not only teaching the children in the group, but for seeing to it that the remaining children are profitably occupied.

A second reason for forming groups in reading instruction is that students differ in many respects; appropriate objectives, methods, and materials for some students may be inappropriate for others. Groups are also formed to comprise students of varying achievement levels, but who have a common interest in a topic.

Boxes 15.1 and 15.2 are examples of the most widely used organizational plans for teaching reading. Permanent groups are based primarily on general achievement levels; however, temporary groups are formed on the basis of skills deficits and special interests. When such plans are successful, movement between groups is easily accomplished, and temporary groups are easily established and dissolved. Whole-class activities and independent activities are regularly occurring features of this plan.

Usually, a basal reading series provides the mainstay of the program for the three-group plan. Such programs are usually eclectic; that is, lessons are suggested that are associated with both the top-down approach and the bottom-up approach.

Individualized instruction is used to some extent in the basic three-group classroom organization; however, some organizational plans are based primarily on individual instruction. In the Individualized Reading Program, students choose books that interest them. In conferences with the teacher, their skills are assessed, and they are assigned to groups for instruction and are assigned individual work. The whole class comes together regularly for sharing. The Individualized Reading Program is based on rationalist, top-down notions of how one learns to read. It is wholly consistent with the interactional perspective of language acquisition and the whole language approach to teaching reading and writing.

This approach demands extraordinary skills in diagnosis of difficulties, lesson planning, and classroom management. An extensive classroom library is necessary, and the teacher must be familiar with dozens of books.

Several "packaged" Individual Reading Programs exist that represent a compromise between a completely open-ended program and the more structured methods typical of classrooms where basal reading programs are the mainstay of the program.

The Reading Workshop is another approach based on top-down, holistic assumptions. The three "basics" of the approach are time, ownership, and response. Minilessons and sustained silent reading give the students time with reading; self-selection of reading materials gives them ownership; and dialog journals give them the opportunity to respond to what they read and to have other students and the teacher respond to them.

Programmed instruction is a form of individualized instruction based on the empiricist, bottom-up notion of dealing with specified skills in a specified order. In linear programmed instruction, the student progresses from frame to frame, answering questions, correcting his or her answers, and presumably learning one fact or skill after another that add up to proficient reading. This may be categorized more accurately as independent instruction rather than individualized instruction because every child covers every step. In branching programmed instruction, each child does not cover every frame. On the basis of answers to test questions and success in answering questions in the frames as they are presented, the student progresses to frames deemed appropriate to him or her as an individual. Computerized branching programmed instruction will no doubt receive a great deal of attention in the near future.

In skills management systems the reading process is divided into elements that are in turn divided into skills and subskills that are categorized by order of difficulty. Tests are devised to determine whether a student has mastered each skill at each level. Through administering these tests, learning objectives are determined for the individual. Students are brought into groups for instruction based on common learning objectives. Lessons are planned for groups using a resource file. This approach demands extraordinary skill in classroom management. It requires a prodigious amount of test administration, correcting, and record keeping.

All attempts to individualize or to group for instruction result in a situation where individual students must work without the immediate supervision and guidance of the teacher. This means that a great deal of attention must be given to establishing orderly, efficient, and effective classroom procedures and teaching students to operate within them. Failure to do this leads to disorder and an inefficient learning environment.

While teachers are working with small groups or individuals, students outside the teacher's immediate supervision must be kept occupied. Unfortunately, this often leads to assigning tasks (often in the form of spirit-duplicated sheets or workbook pages) forthe purpose of keeping students busy rather than to accomplish any clearly thought-out learning objective. The use of teacher's aides or student leaders gives teachers a wider choice of activities to assign to students working independently. However, teacher's aides and students must be trained to work in groups. Choosing materials for individuals and groups working independently of the teacher from a coherent program reduces the danger that children will be assigned tasks whose primary objective is to keep them busy.

While it is frequently presumed that individual instruction results in a higher quality of teacher-student interaction, this is not necessarily the case. Teacher-student interaction in some programs of individual instruction programs tends to center on what page the children should "do" next and where they should put their answer sheets. Teachers sometimes engage in more questions and statements of a higher order when addressing the whole class than when addressing either individuals or small groups.

It is often presumed that working in small groups permits children to learn from each other in ways that are not possible in large groups. However, small groups are often treated no differently from large groups, and students are offered no opportunities for learning that are notably different from those offered in large groups. Students need to be taught how to generate learning objectives and pursue them cooperatively in small groups.

Because of the demands of programs that emphasize individual instruction, it is probably advisable for a beginning teacher to gain experience in using a basal reader and a three-group approach and to work toward a whole language approach utilizing ideas suggested by the Individualized Reading Program or the Reading Workshop as he or she gains skill and experience. But it is important that teachers understand the principles of whole language and the assumptions that underlie them from the start. A whole language classroom demands a great deal of structure, and students must be taught a great deal about how it works, what is expected of them, what they must do, and what they must not do.

Schoolwide arrangements designed to narrow the range of differences within reading classes include (1) setting up special classes for students who have extremely low learning aptitudes or severe physical difficulties such as deafness or blindness, (2) assigning children to classrooms on the basis of reading scores, or (3) grouping children across grade levels by reading achievement scores during a special time slot designated for reading instruction. The obvious advantage of such schemes is that when there is a narrower range of achievement in a class, the teacher stands a better chance of being able to cater to individual needs.

Negative aspects of school-wide grouping by achievement levels include (1) the increased difficulty of changing a child's group assignment, (2) the inclination of some teachers to feel there is *less* necessity to attend to individual needs when a classroom is "homogeneously" grouped, (3) segregation of high achievers from low achievers, and (4) the perception of many classroom teachers that if a child is taught reading by another teacher, the child's reading performance is not the classroom teacher's responsibility.

FOR FURTHER READING

Clary, L. M., & Smith, S. J. (1986). Selecting basal reading series: The need for a validated process. *The Reading Teacher, 39*(5), 390–394.

Cullinan, B. E. (Ed.). (1987). *Children's literature in the reading program.* Newark, DE: International Reading Association.

Harp, B. (1988). When the Principal asks: "When you do whole language instruction, how will you keep track of reading and writing skills?" *The Reading Teacher, 42*(2), 160–161.

Templeton, S. (1986). Literacy, readiness, and basals. *The Reading Teacher, 39*(5), 403–409.

References

Allen, R. V. (1976). *Language experiences in communication*. Boston: Houghton Mifflin.

Alper, M. (1982). All our children can learn. *The University of Chicago Magazine*, 2–9 and 30.

Anderson, R. C., & Biddle, W. B. (1975). On asking people questions about what they are reading. In G. Bower (Ed.), *Psychology of learning and motivation*, Volume 9. New York: Academic Press.

Anderson, R. C. & Freebody, P. (1981). Vocabulary knowledge. In J. T. Guthrie (Ed.), *Comprehension and Teaching: Research reviews*. Newark, DE: International Reading Association.

Anderson, R. C., Reynolds, R. E., Schallert, D. L., & Goetz, E. T. (1977). Frameworks for comprehending discourse. *American Educational Research Journal, 14*, 367–381.

Ankney, P., & McClurg, P. (1981). Testing Manzo's guided reading procedure. *The Reading Teacher, 34*(6), 681–685.

Applebee, A. N., & Langer, J. A. (1984) Instructional scaffolding: Reading and writing as natural language activities. In J. M. Jenson (Ed.), *Composing and comprehending*. Urbana, IL: National Conference on Research in English.

Ashton-Warner, S. (1986a). *Spinster*. New York: Simon & Schuster.

Ashton-Warner, S. (1986b). *Teacher*. New York: Simon & Schuster.

Ashton-Warner, S. (1972). *Spearpoint: Teacher in America*. New York: Alfred A. Knopf.

Atwell, N. (1987). *In the middle: Writing, reading, and learning with adolescents*. Portsmouth, NH: Heinemann.

Bailey, M. H. (1966–67). The utility of phonic generalizations in grades one through six. *The Reading Teacher, 20*, 413–418.

Baker, L., & Brown, A. L. (1980). *Metacognitive skills and reading* (Technical Report No. 188). Urbana, IL: Center for the Study of Reading.

Bartlett, F. C. (1932). *Remembering*. Cambridge: Cambridge University Press.

Beck, I. L., McKeown, M. G., McCaslin, E. S., & Burkes, A. M. (1979). *Instructional dimensions that may affect reading comprehension: Examples from two commercial reading programs*. Pittsburgh: Learning Research and Development Center, University of Pittsburgh (ERIC Document No. ED197322).

Berger, N. (1975). *An investigation of linguistic competence and organizational processes in good and poor readers*. Unpublished doctoral dissertation, University of Pittsburgh.

Berliner, D. C. (1981). Academic learning time and reading achievement. In J. T. Guthrie (Ed.), *Comprehension and teaching: Research reviews*, pp. 203–226. Newark, DE: International Reading Association.

Bernstein, B. (1971). *Class, codes, and control: Theoretical studies towards a sociology of language*, Volume 1. London: Routledge & Kegan Paul.

Bernstein, B. (1973). *Class, codes, and control: Theoretical studies towards a sociology of language*, Volume 2. London: Routledge & Kegan Paul.

Bernstein, B. (1975). *Class, codes, and control: Theoretical studies towards a sociology of language*, Volume 3. London: Routledge & Kegan Paul.

Betts, E. A. (1957). *Foundations of reading instruction*. New York: American Book.

Bloom, B. S. (1971). Mastery learning and its implications for curriculum development. In E. W. Eisner (Ed.), *Confronting curriculum reform*. Boston: Little, Brown.

Bloom, B. S., Engelhart, M. D., Furst, E. J., Hill, W. H., & Krathwohl, D. R. (1956). *Taxonomy of educational objectives. The classification of educational goals. Handbook I: Cognitive domain*. New York: David McKay.

Bloom, B., Hastings, S., & Madaus, G. (1971). *Handbook of formative and summative evaluation of student learning.* New York: McGraw-Hill.

Bloom, L., & Lahey, M. (1978). *Language development and language disorders.* New York: John Wiley.

Bloomfield, L., & Barnhart, C. (1961). *Let's read: A linguistic approach.* Detroit: Wayne State University Press.

Blumenthal, A. L. (1980). *Language and psychology: Historical aspects of psycholinguistics.* New York: John Wiley.

Bond, G. L., Tinker, M. A., & Wasson, B. B. (1979). *Reading difficulties: Their diagnosis and correction.* Englewood Cliffs, NJ: Prentice-Hall.

Bormuth, J. R., Manning, J., Carr, J., & Pearson, D. (1970). Children's comprehension of between- and within-sentence syntactic structures. *Journal of Educational Psychology, 61,* 349–357.

Bortner, M. & Birch, H. G. (1969). Patterns of intellectual ability in emotionally disturbed and brain-damaged children. *Journal of Special Education, 3,* 351–369.

Bortnick, R., & Lopardo, G. S. (1973). An instructional application of the cloze procedure. *Journal of Reading,* 296–300.

Brainerd, C. J. (1978). *Piaget's theory of intelligence.* Englewood Cliffs, NJ: Prentice Hall.

Brand, M. (1969). Wine on the desert. In S. Dunning, E. Katterjohn, & O. S. Niles (Eds.), *Thrust,* pp. 332–340. Glenview, IL: Scott, Foresman.

Bransford, J. D., & Franks, J. J. (1971). The abstraction of linguistic ideas. *Cognitive Psychology, 2,* 331–350.

Bransford, J. D., & Johnson, M. K. (1973). Considerations of some problems of comprehension. In W. G. Chase (Ed.), *Visual information processing,* pp. 383–438. New York: Academic Press.

Brown, A. L., & Day, J. D. (1983). Macrorules for summarizing texts: The development of expertise. *Journal of Verbal Learning and Verbal Behavior, 22,* 1–14.

Brown, C. S., & Lytle, S. L. (1988). Merging assessment and instruction: Protocols in the classroom. In S. M. Glazer, L. W. Searfoss, & L. M. Gentile (Eds.), *Reexamining reading diagnosis.* Newark, DE: International Reading Association.

Brown, D. A. (1982). *Reading diagnosis and remediation.* Englewood Cliffs, NJ: Prentice Hall.

Brown, R. (1973). *A first language: The early stages.* Cambridge, MA: Harvard University Press.

Buchanan, C. D., & Sullivan Associates. (1989). *Programmed reading: Book 6* (3rd ed.). St. Louis: Phoenix Learning Resources.

Burmeiser, L. E. (1968). Vowel pairs. *The Reading Teacher, 21,* 445–452.

Buros, O. K. (Ed.). (1978). *The eighth mental measurements yearbook,* Volumes I–II. Highland Park, NJ: Gryphon Press.

Carner, R. L. (1973). Reading forum. *Reading News, 2.*

Carroll, J. B. (1963). A model of school learning. *Teachers College Record, 64,* 723–733.

Carroll, J. B., Davies, P., & Richman, B. (1971). *The American heritage word frequency book.* Boston: Houghton Mifflin.

Cazden, C. B., Cordeiro, P., & Giacobbe, M. E. (1985). Spontaneous and scientific concepts: Young children's learning of punctuation. In G. Wells & J. Nicholls (Eds.), *Language learning: An interactional perspective,* pp. 107–124. Philadelphia: The Falmer Press.

Chall, J. S. (1967). *Learning to read: The great debate.* New York: McGraw-Hill.

Chapman, C. A. (1971). A test of a hierarchical theory of reading comprehension. Unpublished doctoral dissertation, University of Chicago.

Cherry, C. (1957). *On human communication: A review, a survey, a criticism.* Cambridge, MA: MIT Press.

Chomsky, C. S. (1969). *The acquisition of syntax in children from 5 to 10.* Cambridge, MA: MIT Press.

Chomsky, N. (1957). *Syntactic structures.* The Hague: Mouton.

Chomsky, N. (1959). *Review of verbal behavior,* by B. F. Skinner. *Language, 35,* 26–58.

Chomsky, N. (1970). Phonology and reading. In H. Levin & J. P. Williams (Eds.), *Basic studies in reading.* New York: Basic Books.

Clay, M. M. (1972). *Reading: The patterning of complex behavior.* London: Heinemann.

Clay, M. M. (1979). *The early detection of reading difficulties: A diagnostic survey with recovery procedures* (2nd ed.). Lexington, MA: Ginn.

Clymer, T. (1963). The utility of phonic generalizations in the primary grades. *The Reading Teacher, 16,* 252–258.

Clymer, T. (1968). What is "reading"? Some current concepts. In H. M. Robinson (Ed.), *Innovation and change in reading instruction. Sixty-seventh yearbook of the National Society for the Study of Education, Part II,* pp. 7–29. Chicago: University of Chicago Press.

Clymer, T. (1976a). *Teacher's guide for reading 720, level 3.* Lexington, MA: Ginn.

Clymer, T. (senior author). (1976b). *Teacher's guide for reading 720, level 4.* Lexington, MA: Ginn.

Clymer T. (senior author). (1976c). *Teacher's guide for reading 720, level 7.* Lexington, MA: Ginn.

Cole, M., & Scribner, S. (1974). *Culture and thought.* New York: John Wiley.

Collins, A., & Quillian, M. (1969). Retrieval time from semantic memory. *Journal of Verbal Learning and Verbal Behavior, 8,* 240–247.

Creak, M., and committee. (1961). Schizophrenic syndrome in childhood. *Cerebral Palsy Bulletin, 3,* 501–504.

Davis, F. B. (1944). Fundamental factors of comprehension in reading. *Psychometrika, 9,* 185–197.

Davis, F. B. (1946). A brief comment on Thurston's note on a reanalysis of Davis' reading tests. *Psychometrika, 11,* 249–255.

Davis, F. B. (1968). Research in comprehension in reading. *Reading Research Quarterly, 3,* 499–545.

Davis, F. B. (1972). Psychometric research on comprehension in reading. *Reading Research Quarterly, 7,* 628–678.

Dewey, J. (1933). *How we think.* Boston: D. C. Heath.

Diederich, P. B. (1974). *Measuring growth in English.* Urbana, IL: National Council of Teachers of English.

Dolch, E. W. (1936). A basic sight vocabulary. *Elementary School Journal, 36,* 456–460, and *37,* 268–272.

Duckworth, E. (1967). Piaget rediscovered. In E. Victor & M. S. Lerner (Eds.), *Readings in science education for the elementary schools,* pp. 317–319. New York: Macmillan.

Dunning, S., Katterjohn, E., & Niles, O. S. (1969). *Thrust.* Glenview, IL: Scott, Foresman.

Durkin, D. (1966). *Children who read early.* New York: Teachers College Press, Columbia University.

Durkin, D. (1976). *Strategies for identifying words: A workbook for teachers and those preparing to teach.* Boston: Allyn & Bacon.

Durkin, D. (1979). What classroom observations reveal about reading instruction. *Reading Research Quarterly, 14,* 481–533.

Durkin, D. (1987). *Teaching young children to read* (4th ed.). Boston: Newton.

Durr, W. K. (senior author). (1976a). *The Houghton Mifflin reading series: Level G.* Boston: Houghton Mifflin.

Durr, W. K. (senior author). (1976b). *The Houghton Mifflin reading series: Level J.* Boston: Houghton Mifflin.

Durrell, D. (1937). Individual differences and their implications with respect to instruction in reading. In *Teaching of reading a second report, the 36th yearbook of the National Society for the Study of Education,* pp. 325–356. Bloomington, IL: Public School Publication.

Durrell, D. (1940). *Improvement of basic reading abilities.* Yonkers-on-Hudson, NY: World Book.

Durrell, D. & Catterson, J. (1980). *Durrell analysis of reading difficulty.* New York: Harcourt Brace Jovanovich.

Dykstra, R. (1968). Summary of the second-grade phase of the cooperative research program in primary reading instruction. *Reading Research Quarterly, 4,* 49–70.

Ehri, L. C. (1975). Word consciousness in readers and prereaders. *Journal of Educational Psychology, 67,* 204–212.

Ehri, L. C. (1976). Word learning in beginning readers: Effects of form class and defining contexts. *Journal of Educational Psychology, 68,* 832–842.

Eimas, P. D., Siqueland, E. R., Jusczyk, P., & Vigorito, J. (1971). Speech perception in infants. *Science, 171,* 303–306.

Ellison, D. G., Harris, P., & Barber, L. (1968). A field test of programmed and directed tutoring. *Reading Research Quarterly,* 307–368.

Emans, R. (1967). The usefulness of phonic generalizations above the primary grades. *The Reading Teacher, 20,* 419–425.

Esposito, D. (1973). Homogeneous and heterogeneous ability grouping: Principal findings and implications for evaluating and designing more effective educational environments. *Review of Educational Research, 43,* 163–179.

Farr, R., & Roser, N. (1979). *Teaching a child to read.* New York: Harcourt Brace Jovanovich.

Farr, R., Fay, L., & Negley, H. (1978). *Then and now: Reading achievement in Indiana (1944–45 and 1976).* Bloomington: School of Education, Indiana University.

Fitzgerald, J. (1983). Helping readers gain self-control over reading comprehension. *The Reading Teacher, 37*(3), 249–253.

Flesch, R. (1979, November). Why Johnny still can't read. *Family Circle Magazine.*

Flexner, S. B., & Hauck, L. C. (Eds.). (1987). *The Random House dictionary of the English language* (2nd ed.). New York: Random House.

Flood, J., & Lapp, D. (1987). Reading and writing relations: Assumptions and directions. In J. R. Squire (Ed.), *The dynamics of language learning.* Urbana, IL: ERIC Clearinghouse on Reading and Communication Skills.

Frase, L. T. (1977). Purpose in reading. In J. T. Guthrie (Ed.), *Cognition, curriculum and comprehension,* pp. 42–64. Newark, DE: International Reading Association.

Fry, E. B. (1967). *Comparison of three methods of reading instruction (ITA, DMS, TO): Results at the end of third grade* (Final Report, Project No. 3050). New Brunswick, NJ: Rutgers, The State University.

Fry, E. B. (1972). *Reading instruction for classroom and clinic.* New York: McGraw-Hill.

Galton, M., & Simon, B. (1980). Effective teaching in the primary classroom. In M. Galton & B. Simon (Eds.), *Progress and performance in the primary classroom,* pp. 179–212. London: Routledge & Kegan Paul.

Garnica, O. K. (1977). Some prosodic and paralinguistic features of speech to young children. In C. Snow & C. Ferguson (Eds.), *Talking to children,* pp. 63–68. London: Cambridge University Press.

Gates, A. I. (1936). *Improvement of reading.* New York: Macmillan.

Goodman, K. S. (1967). Reading: A psycholinguistic guessing game. *Journal of the Reading Specialist, 6,* 126–135.

Goodman, K. S. (1969). Analysis of reading miscues: Applied psycholinguistics. *Reading Research Quarterly, 5,* 9–30.

Goodman, K., & Goodman, Y. (1977). Learning about psycholinguistic processes by analyzing oral reading. *Harvard Educational Review, 47,* 317–333.

Goodman, K., & Goodman, Y. (1984). Reading and writing relationships: Pragmatic functions. In J. M. Jenson (Ed.), *Composing and comprehending,* pp. 155–164. Urbana, IL: National Conference on Research in English.

Gordon, N. (1984). *Classroom experiences: The writing process in action.* Portsmouth, NH: Heinemann.

Graves, D. (1983). *Writing: Teachers & children at work.* Exeter, NH: Heinemann.

Graves, D., & Hansen, J. (1984). The author's chair. In J. M. Jenson (Ed.), *Composing and comprehending,* pp. 69–76. Urbana, IL: National Conference on Research in English.

Gray, W. S. (1960). *On their own in reading* (rev. ed.). Chicago: Scott, Foresman.

Green, R. (1975, October). Tips on educational testing: What teachers and parents should know. *Phi Delta Kappan,* 89–92.

Greenberg, M. D., McAndrew, D., & Meterski, M. (1975). *Getting it together: A sentence combining workbook* (edited by C. Cooper and adapted by T. Callaghan and M. Sullivan). Mimeographed. Department of Instruction, State University of New York at Buffalo.

Greenlinger-Harless, C. S. (1987). A new cross-referenced index to U.S. reading series, grades K–8. *The Reading Teacher, 41*(3), 293–303.

Guralnik, D. B. (Ed.). (1986). *Webster's new world dictionary of the American language* (2nd college ed.). Englewood Cliffs, NJ: Prentice Hall.

Hall, M. A. (1981). *Teaching reading as a language experience* (3rd ed.). Columbus, OH: Charles E. Merrill.

Hall, R. A. (1950). *Leave your language alone!* Ithaca, NY: Linguistica.

Halliday, M. A. K. (1975). *Learning how to mean.* New York: Elsevier.

Hanna, P., Hanna, J., Hodge, R., & Rudolph, L. (1966). *Grapheme phoneme correspondence as cues to spelling improvement.* Washington, DC: U.S. Government Printing Office, USOE.

Hansen, J. (1987). *When writers read.* Portsmouth, NH: Heinemann.

Hare, V. C., & Borchardt, K. M. (1984). Direct instruction of summarization skills. *Reading Research Quarterly, 20*(1), 62–78.

Harris, A. J. (1940). *How to increase reading ability.* New York: Longman.

Harris, A. J., & Jacobson, M. D. (1972). *Basic elementary reading vocabularies.* New York: Macmillan.

Harris, A. J., Morrison, C., Serwer, B. L., & Gold, L. (1968). *A continuation of the CRAFT project: Comparing reading approaches with disadvantaged urban negro children in primary grades* (Final Report, U.S.O.E. Project No. 5-0570-12-1). New York: Selected Academic Readings.

Harris, A. J., & Sipay, E. R. (1985). *How to increase reading ability* (8th ed.). New York: Longman.

Harste, J. C., Woodward, V. A., & Burke, C. L. (1984). *Language stories and literacy lessons.* Portsmouth, NH: Heinemann.

Hartman, T. (1977). *The relationship among the ability to classify retrieval time from semantic memory and reading ability of elementary school children.* Unpublished doctoral dissertation, Memphis State University.

Harvey, M. R. (1980). Public school treatment of low-income children: Education for passivity. *Urban Education, 15,* 279–323.

Hayes, R. B., & Wuest, R. C. (1967). *Factors affecting learning to read* (Final Report, Project No. 6-1752). Harrisburg, PA: State Education Dept.

Heimlich, J. E., & Pittelman, S. D. (1986). *Semantic mapping: Classroom approaches.* Newark, DE: International Reading Association.

Hennings, D. S. (1984). A writing approach to reading comprehension—Schema theory in action. In J. M. Jenson (Ed.), *Composing and comprehending,* pp. 191–200. Urbana, IL: National Conference on Research in English.

Holden, M. H., & MacGinitie, W. (1972). Children's conceptions of word boundaries in speech and print. *Journal of Educational Psychology, 63,* 551–557.

Holt, J. (1967). *How children learn.* New York: Pitman.

Huey, E. B. (1908). *The psychology and pedagogy of reading.* New York: Macmillan. Reprinted, Cambridge, MA: MIT Press, 1968.

Huttenlocher, J. (1964). Children's language: Word-phrase relationship. *Science, 143,* 264–265.

Johnson, D. D. (1971). A basic vocabulary for beginning reading. *Elementary School Journal, 72,* 29–34.

Johnson, D. D., & Pearson, P. D. (1978). *Teaching reading vocabulary.* New York: Holt, Rinehart and Winston.

Johnston, P. H. (1983). *Reading comprehension assessment: A cognitive approach.* Newark, DE: International Reading Association.

Jongsma, E. (1971). *The cloze procedure as a teaching technique.* Newark, DE: International Reading Association.

Kant, I. (1963). *Critique of pure reason* (N. Kemp Smith, trans.). London: Macmillan. (Original work published 1781.)

Kantor, R. N. (1978). Anomaly inconsiderateness, and linguistic competence. In D. Gulstad (Ed.), *Papers from the 1977 Mid-Atlantic linguistics conference.* Columbia: University of Missouri.

Keats, E. J. (1966). *Jennie's hat.* New York: Harper & Row.

Kessler, J. (1966). *Psychopathology in childhood.* Englewood Cliffs, NJ: Prentice Hall.

Kintsch, W., & Van Dijk, T. A. (1978). Toward a model of discourse comprehension and production. *Psychological Review, 85,* 363–394.

Kirk, S. A., McCarthy, J. P., & Kirk, W. D. (1968). *The Illinois test of psycholinguistic abilities* (rev. ed.). Urbana, IL: University of Illinois Press.

Kucer, S. B. (1987). The cognitive base of reading and writing. In J. R. Squire (Ed.), *The dynamics of language learning,* pp. 27–51. Urbana, IL: ERIC Clearinghouse on Reading and Communication Skills.

Kucera, H., & Francis, W. N. (1967). *Computational analysis of present-day American English.* Providence, RI: Brown University Press.

Labov, W. (1970). The reading of the -ed suffix. In H. Levin & J. P. Williams (Eds.), *Basic studies in reading,* pp. 222–245. New York: Basic Books.

Lee, D. M., & Rubin, J. B. (1979). *Children and language.* Belmont, CA: Wadsworth.

Lennon, R. T. (1962). What can be measured? *The Reading Teacher,* 326–337.

Levine, D. U. (1982, April). Successful approaches for improving academic achievement in inner-city elementary schools. *Phi Delta Kappan,* 523–526.

Luria, A. R. (1976). *Cognitive development: Its cultural and social foundations.* Cambridge, MA: Harvard University Press.

MacGinitie, W. (1969). Evaluating readiness for learning to read: A critical review and evaluation of research. *Reading Research Quarterly, 4,* 396–410.

Mandler, J. M., & Johnson, N. S. (1977). Remembrances of things passed: Story structure and recall. *Cognitive Psychology, 9,* 111–151.

Mandler, J. M. (1978). A code in the node: The use of a story schema in retrieval. *Discourse Processes, 1,* 14–35.

Manzo, A. (1975). Guided reading procedure. *Journal of Reading, 18,* 287–291.

Matthews, M. M. (1966). *Teaching to read.* Chicago: University of Chicago Press.

McCurdy, M. (1984). Writing on their own: Kindergarten and first grade. In N. Gordon (Ed.), *Classroom experiences: The writing process in action.* Portsmouth, NH: Heinemann.

McDermott, R. P. (1977). The ethnography of speaking and reading. In R. W. Shuy (Ed.), *Linguistic theory: What can it say about reading.* Newark, DE: International Reading Association.

McDonald, A. S. (1965). Research for the classroom: Rate and flexibility. *Journal of Reading, 8*, 187–191.

Meichenbaum, D. (1977). *Cognitive behavior modification*. New York: Plenum Press.

Meichenbaum, D. (1980). Teaching thinking: A cognitive behavioral perspective. Mimeographed. Waterloo, ONT: University of Waterloo.

Miller, G. A. (1951). *Language and communication*. New York: McGraw-Hill.

Moe, A. J., Hopkins, C. J., & Rush, R. T. (1982). *The vocabulary of first-grade children*. Springfield, IL: Charles C. Thomas.

Morris, D., & Henderson, E. H. (1981). Assessing the beginning reader's "concept of word." *Reading World*, 279–285.

Murphy, H. (1957). The spontaneous speaking vocabulary of children in primary grades. *Journal of Education, 140*, 3–106.

Otto, W., & Askov, E. (1973). *The Wisconsin design for reading skill development*. Madison, WI: Learning Multi-Systems.

Palincsar, A. (1984). The quest for meaning from expository text: A teacher-guided journey. In G. Duffy, L. Roehler, & J. Mason (Eds.), *Comprehension instruction: Perspectives and suggestions*, pp. 261–264.

Palincsar, A. S., & Brown, A. L. (1986). Interactive teaching to promote independent learning from text. *The Reading Teacher, 39*(8), 771–777.

Pearson, P. D., & Camperell, K. (1981). Comprehension of text structures. In J. T. Guthrie (Ed.), *Comprehension and teaching: Research reviews*, pp. 27–54. Newark, DE: International Reading Association.

Pikulski, J. J. (1978). Approaches to evaluating reading. In R. G. Stauffer, J. C. Abrams, & J. J. Pikulski (Eds.), *Diagnosis, correction, and prevention of reading disabilities*, pp. 53–103. New York: Harper & Row.

Plowden Report. (1967). *Children and their primary schools* (Report of the Central Advisory Council for Education in England). London: HMSO.

Rankin, E. F. (1970). How flexibly do we read. *Journal of Reading Behavior, 3*, 34–38.

Raphael, T. E. (1982). Question-answering strategies for children. *The Reading Teacher, 36*(2), 186–190.

Raphael, T. E., & Wonnacott, C. A. (1985). Heightening fourth-grade students' sensitivity to sources of information for answering comprehension questions. *Reading Research Quarterly, 20*(3), 282–296.

Readance, J. & Martin, M. (1988). Comprehension assessment: Alternatives to standardized tests. In S. Glazer, L. Searfoss, & L. Gentile (Eds.), *Examining reading diagnosis: New trends and procedures*. Newark, DE: International Reading Association.

Robinson, F. P. (1970). *Effective reading*. New York: Harper & Row.

Rosenthal, R., & Jacobson, L. (1968, April). Teacher expectations for the disadvantaged. *Scientific American*, 19–23.

Rosenthal, W., Eisenson, J., & Luckau, J. A. (1972). A statistical test of the validity of diagnostic categories used in childhood language disorders. Implications for assessment procedures. In *Papers and reports in child language development*, Volume 4, pp. 121–143. Palo Alto, CA: Stanford University Press.

Ruddell, R. B. (1968). *A longitudinal study of four programs of reading instruction varying in emphasis on grapheme-phoneme correspondences and language structure on reading achievement in grades two and three* (Final Report, Projects Nos. 3099 and 78085). Berkeley: University of California.

Ruddell, R. (1974). *Reading language instruction*. Englewood Cliffs, NJ: Prentice Hall.

Ruddell, R. B. (1978). Developing comprehension abilities: Implications from research for an instructional framework. In S. J. Samuels (Ed.), *What research has to say about reading instruction*, pp. 109–120. Newark, DE: International Reading Association.

Salvia, J., & Ysseldyke, J. E. (1985). *Assessment in special and remedial education* (3rd ed.). Boston: Houghton Mifflin.

Samuels, S. J., & Dahl, P. R. (1975). Establishing appropriate purpose for reading and its effect on flexibility of reading rate. *Journal of Educational Psychology, 67,* 38–43.

Schatzman, L., & Strauss, A. (1955). Social class and modes of communication. *American Journal of Sociology, 60,* 329–339.

Schmidt, G. N. (1982, November). Chicago mastery reading: A case against a skills-based reading curriculum. *Learning,* 37–40.

Schneyer, J. W., & Cowen, S. (1968). *Comparison of a basal reader approach and a linguistic approach in a second and third grade reading instruction* (Final Report, Project No. 5-0601). Philadelphia: University of Pennsylvania.

Shores, H. J., & Husband, K. L. (1950). Are fast readers the best readers? *Elementary English, 27,* 52–57.

Silo-Miller, I. (1984). Expanding ideas: Fourth grade. In N. Gordon (Ed.), *Classroom experiences: The writing process in action.* Portsmouth, NH: Heinemann.

Skinner, B. F. (1957). *Verbal behavior.* New York: Appleton.

Slaughter, J. P. (1983). Big books for little kids: Another fad or a new approach for teaching beginning reading. *The Reading Teacher, 36*(8), 758–763.

Sloan, G. (1979). The subversive effects of an oral culture on student writing. *College Composition and Communication, 30,* 156–160.

Snow, C. E. (1977). The development of conversation between mothers and babies. *Journal of Child Language, 4,* 1–22.

Spearritt, D. (1972). Identification of subskills of reading comprehension by maximum likelihood factor analysis. *Reading Research Quarterly, 8,* 92–111.

Squire, J. R. (1984). Composing and comprehending: Two sides of the same basic process. In J. M. Jenson (Ed.), *Composing and comprehending.* Urbana, IL: National Conference on Research in English.

Stauffer, R. G. (1967). *The first grade reading studies: Findings of individual investigations.* Newark DE: International Reading Association.

Stauffer, R. G. (1980). *The language experience approach to the teaching of reading* (rev. ed.). New York: Harper & Row.

Stauffer, R. G., Abrams, J. C., & Pikulski, J. J. (1978). *Diagnosis, correction and prevention of reading disabilities.* New York: Harper & Row.

Stauffer, R. G., & Hammond, W. D. (1969). The effectiveness of language arts and basic reader approaches to first grade reading instruction—extended into third grade. *Reading Research Quarterly, 4,* 468–499.

Stein, N. L., & Glenn, C. G. (1977). *The role of structural variation in children's recall of simple stories.* Paper presented at the meeting of the Society for Research in Child Development, New Orleans.

Stotsky, S. (1984). Research on reading/writing relationships: A synthesis and suggested directions. In J. M. Jenson (Ed.), *Composing and comprehending.* Urbana, IL: National Conference on Research in English.

Strong, W. (1986). *Creative approaches to sentence combining.* Urbana, IL: National Council of Teachers of English.

Stubbs, M. (1980). *Language and literacy.* London: Routledge & Kegan Paul.

Taylor, S. E., et al. (1979). *EDL core vocabularies in reading, mathematics, science, and social studies.* New York: EDL/McGraw-Hill.

Teale, W. H., & Sulzby, E. (1987). Introduction: Emergent literacy as a perspective for examining how young children become writers and readers. In W. H. Teale & E. Sulzby (Eds.), *Emergent literacy.* Norwood, NJ: Ablex.

Temple, C., & Gillet, J. W. (1989). *Language arts: Learning processes and teaching practices* (2nd ed.). Boston: Little, Brown.

Terman, L. M. (1918). Vocabulary test as a measure of intelligence. *Journal of Educational Psychology, 9,* 452–466.

Thorndike, E. L. (1921). *The teacher's word book.* New York: Bureau of Publications, Teachers College, Columbia University.

Thorndike, E. L. (1934). Improving the ability to read. *Teachers College Record, 36,* 123–144.

Thorndike, E. L. (1971). Reading as reasoning: A study of mistakes in paragraph meaning. *Reading Research Quarterly,* Volume 6, pp. 425–434. (Reprinted from *Journal of Educational Psychology,* 1917, *8,* 323–332.)

Thorndike, E. L., & Lorge, I. (1944). *The teacher's word book of 30,000 words.* New York: Teachers College Press, Columbia University.

Thorndike, R. L. (1973). *Reading comprehension education in fifteen countries.* New York: John Wiley.

Thurston, L. L. (1946). Note on a reanalysis of Davis' Reading Tests. *Psychometrika, 11,* 185–188.

Tiedt, S. W., & Tiedt, I. M. (1978). *Language arts activities for the classroom.* Boston: Allyn & Bacon.

Tierney, R. J. & Pearson, P. D. (1984). Toward a composing model of reading. In J. M. Jenson (Ed.), *Composing and comprehending,* pp. 33–46. Urbana, IL: National Conference on Research in English.

Trevarthen, C. (1979). Communication and cooperation in early infancy: A description of primary intersubjectivity. In M. Bullowa (Ed.), *Before speech, the beginning of interpersonal communication.* London: Cambridge University Press.

Troyat, H. (1967). *Tolstoy.* Garden City, NY: Doubleday.

Tuinman, J. J., & Brady, M. E. (1974). How does vocabulary account for variance on reading comprehension tests? A preliminary instructional analysis. In P. Nacke (Ed.), *Interaction: Research and practice for college-adult reading,* pp. 176–184. Clemson, SC: National Reading Conference.

Veatch, J. (1978). *Reading in the elementary school* (2nd ed.). New York: John Wiley.

Veatch, J., Sawicki, F., Elliot, G., Flake, E., & Blakey, J. (1979). *Key words to reading.* Columbus, OH: Charles E. Merrill.

Vilscek, E. C., & Cleland, D. L. (1968). *Two approaches to reading instruction* (Final Report, Project No. 9195). Pittsburgh: University of Pittsburgh.

Vygotsky, L. S. (1978). *Mind in society.* Cambridge, MA: Harvard University Press.

Vygotsky, L. S. (1986). *Thought and language.* (A. Kozulin, ed. and trans.) Cambridge, MA: MIT Press. (Original book published 1962.)

Weikart, D. P. (1973). *Development of effective preschool programs: A report on the results of the High/Scope Ypsilanti preschool projects.* Paper presented at the High/Scope Educational Research Foundation Conference, Ann Arbor, MI.

Wells, C. G. (1981). *Learning through interaction.* Cambridge: Cambridge University Press.

Wells, G. (1986). *The meaning makers.* Portsmouth, NH: Heinemann.

Whaley, J. F. (1981). Readers' expectations for story structure. *Reading Research Quarterly, 17,* 90–114.

Wimmer, H. (1979, March). *Children's comprehension and recall of hierarchically structured stories.* Paper presented at the meeting of the Society for Research in Child Development, San Francisco.

Worthington, F. (1974). *A theoretical and empirical study of small group work in schools.* Unpublished doctoral thesis, University of Leicester, England.

Index